DEATH ATTITUDES AND THE OLDER ADULT

Theories, Concepts, and Applications

Edited by

Adrian Tomer, Ph.D.
Department of Psychology
Shippensburg University
Shippensburg, Pennsylvania

USA   Publishing Office: BRUNNER-ROUTLEDGE
A member of the Taylor & Francis Group
325 Chestnut Street
Philadelphia, PA 19106
Tel: (215) 625-8900
Fax: (215) 625-2940

Distribution Center: BRUNNER-ROUTLEDGE
A member of the Taylor & Francis Group
7625 Empire Drive
Florence, KY 41042
Tel: 1 (800) 634-7064
Fax: 1 (800) 248-4724

UK   BRUNNER-ROUTLEDGE
A member of the Taylor & Francis Group
27 Church Road
Hove
E. Sussex, BN3 2FA
Tel · +44 (0) 1273 207411
Fax: +44 (0) 1273 205612

DEATH ATTITUDES AND THE OLDER ADULT: Theories, Concepts, and Applications

1 2 3 4 5 6 7 8 9 0

Printed by Edwards Brothers, Ann Arbor, MI, 2000.
Cover design by Claire C. O'Neill.

A CIP catalog record for this book is available from the British Library.
∞ The paper in this publication meets the requirements of the ANSI Standard Z39.48-1984 (Permanence of Paper).

Library of Congress Cataloging-in-Publication Data
Death attitudes and the older adult : theories, concepts, and applications / edited by Adrian Tomer.
    p. cm. — (Series in death, dying, and bereavement)
    Includes bibliographical references and index.
    ISBN 0-87630-988-0 (alk. paper) — ISBN 0-87630-989-9 (alk. paper)
    1. Aged—Psychology. 2. Death—Psychological aspects. I. Tomer, Adrian.
II. Series

BF724.85.D43 D43 2000
155.9'37'0846—dc21

00-37859

ISBN 0-87630-988-0 (case)
ISBN 0-87630-989-9 (paper)
ISSN 1091-5427

CONTENTS

SERIES FOREWORD

The conjunction of death and late adulthood is marked by irony. On the one hand, mortality statistics demonstrate the obvious: that older adults are the segment of the population most likely to die, at least in developed countries, and are the age cohort most likely to experience the multiple losses of spouses, friends, and family through bereavement. Less obviously, they are also the group with the greatest statistical probability of suicide, both as a desperate bid for surcease from depression and loneliness, and as a potentially rational response to the pain and debilitation of terminal illness. On the other hand, many factors have conspired to produce a relative silence in the professional literature on these topics, as attention is diverted to the problems of other populations (e.g., youth suicide), and the medical/technical issues that surround end-of-life care. As a consequence, elemental human dimensions of the encounter with death in late life are rarely considered.

This book redresses this ironic imbalance. In recruiting seventeen substantial chapters by prominent authorities in the field, Adrian Tomer has covered the gamut of thanatological issues of relevance to older adults, and has done so with remarkable depth and breadth. Between the covers of this book the readers will find theoretically sophisticated models and discussions of attitudes held by elders for whom death becomes salient, as well as thorough summaries and evaluations of empirical research on their anxieties about death and dying. Likewise, topics such as suicide and more subtle forms of self-destructiveness among older adults are dealt with in clinically sensitive detail, as are the complexities of end-of life decision-making in the ethically complex circumstances that surround terminal care. These highly personal emotions, attitudes, and decisions are placed in relevant institutional and cultural contexts, as various authors consider the attitudes of medical staff who function as caregivers to those with life-threatening illness, as well as societal and ethnic factors that shape individual actions. Counterbalancing this emphasis on the particular problems of older adults is a focus on their special resources, defined in terms of coping skills, spirituality, and meaningful connection to their culture. The result is a well-rounded, empirically informed, and thoughtful source book for all of those who are concerned with psychological, ethical, and clinical aspects of confronting death at the end of life.

My hope as Editor of the Taylor & Francis *Series on Death, Dying, and Bereavement* is that the efforts of Tomer and his collaborators will spark a new level of interest in the sometimes daunting, but always fascinating, study of death attitudes and the older adult. The multifaceted contributions to this task that comprise the present volume offer an invaluable beginning.

Robert A. Neimeyer, Ph.D.
Series Editor
January, 2000

FOREWORD

Death, in the western world, has become the domain of the old. Yet fear of death, death anxiety, and attitudes about death are with us throughout life. Anticipated events of aging, flavored by the cultural experience, are also part of the thought process. These phenomena shape the behavior of the individual and the family. Additionally, these phenomena change as we age, increasing the complexity of human behavior. Individuals in second adulthood often begin to think about the number of years remaining and the inevitability of death. This produces changes in behavior, employment of new defenses, and frequently a refocusing of life activities.

This assembly of scholarly works brings theory, perspective, and empirical findings together to explore meaningfully issues of the fear of death, death anxiety, and attitudes about death in the cultural context of western society. The writings range from the individual's reaction to death and attitude about death to ethical considerations and attitudes toward older adults in the culture. Scholars and practitioners alike who seek to understand and explain the effects of death will find this unique collection challenging, informative and timely.

The majority of older adults report they want to extend life for as long as possible. At the same time, older adults report low levels of death anxiety as compared to the young. These low levels are associated with religiosity, ego-integrity, a strong sense of meaningfulness, and higher education. High levels of death anxiety for older adults are associated with frequent thoughts of death, psychological problems, being institutionalized, and low levels of education. Older adults who experience death anxiety think more frequently about death, but they also have other fears. Interestingly, suicide, often related to anxiety and depression, is more prevalent for older adults, especially white males. Fear of being victimized by crime is high despite the statistics to the contrary. Many older adults also fear the loss of independence. Thus, one contributor thoughtfully remarks, " . . . perhaps there is a more elaborate structure to death anxiety for older adults."

Comparison of the public reaction to the deaths of Mother Theresa (87 years old) and Princess Diana (36 years old) that occurred at relatively the same time (offered by one of the chapters), illustrates public attitudes about death at a young age versus death at old age. For the most part, people are expected to die at old age, having had time to complete tasks and leave a legacy. Death in the 20th century incorporates many interpretations: death as inevitable, death as punishment, death as deliverance from misery or illness, death as the beginning of a new life, and death that is untimely. Attitudes about death vary greatly with age. An empirical study presented in these pages provides specifics on the differences and some of the similarities among young and old. For example, the young group was higher in fearing painful death, uncertainty after death, loss of control, long slow death, and fear of cancer. No differences between older adults and young were reported for thoughts of a coffin, fear of an operation, or concerns about life after death. Among young and old alike, death of others (especially relatives, friends, and public figures) typically brings thoughts and anxieties about one's own death.

For the gerontologist, whose sphere of study is the aging process beginning with birth, the attention in this work to issues of death across the life span and differences by age, gender, race, and profession are most relevant. Much of the information challenges existing gerontological theories, which seldom incorporate death-related issues of the individual and society. For example, considering Disengagement Theory and the information presented in several of the chapters, it becomes difficult to accept how disengagement of a dying individual would benefit either society or the individual. Similarly, Exchange Theory that postulates an unequal exchange between an aging individual and society struggles to recognize what is available to society by engagement with the process of dying. The popular book and movie "Tuesdays with Morrie" illustrate gifts to society. Conversely, Symbolic Interaction Theory holds that both the individual and society are able to create new alternatives and is consistent with many of the contributions in this collection. The lifespan-developmental perspective, independent or combined with theory, is most constructive in understanding death-related attitudes of all ages.

Further, there are contributions to theory building, such as the presentation and testing of a Comprehensive Model of Death and Anxiety, and an enlightened perspective on successful aging. The Terror Management perspective incorporates Psychoanalytic Theory and expands the notion that knowledge of inevitable death is an underlying source of other fears. Successful aging certainly occurs in different degrees, and is not limited to, as suggested by some scholars, physical health, psychological functioning, and an active life style. Successful aging also can be achieved existentially and spiritually—one author in this work suggests that successful aging is 80% attitude.

Successful aging can incorporate preparation for death beyond funeral arrangements, financial planning, and a close-to-death humane experience, such as that offered by Hospice. There is evidence in society that successful death planning and successful death are a concern for future cohorts of older adults. Universities are increasingly offering continuing education on spiritual death, virtuous death, and personally preparing for death. Consider also "The Tibetan Book of Living and Dying," which portrays death as a transition has sold 50,000 copies a year since 1993. Tomer's collection on death attitudes, which explores successful aging, spirituality, and different views of death by older adults, young adults, and professionals, is most consistent with contemporary interests.

Hospice care, which revolutionized treatment of the dying individual, focuses on the time just prior to death. The Hospice movement began when Dr. Cicely Saunders opened St. Christopher's Hospital in London to enable dying individuals to have a humane and peaceful death with family and friends. It is a philosophy of care that acknowledges death as a natural part of life. These services, which are comprehensive, from pain control to family counseling, are generally available only six months prior to predicted death. Several authors of this collection find evidence in contemporary society that suggests Hospice needs to be expanded to include incurable diagnosis and prolongative treatment. Expanded mental health treatment at earlier stages for the individuals and the family is also necessary. In addition to issues of loneliness, the experience of losses and dependency counseling should focus on past accomplishments, connecting with the continuity of life and spirituality to gain a sense of life's meaning. Counseling need not wait for a terminal diagnosis.

This volume furnishes information and evidence that contribute to the literature of many disciplines and professions. It divulges important and useful findings, raises awareness of critical factual and ethical issues, and offers challenges to existing theory and practice related to issues of death and dying. Surely, those who partake of these readings will be stimulated to alter beliefs, modify practice, or engage in further systematic inquiry. Hopefully, as one author concluded, "The 21st century may be expected to moderate the ritual avoidance of the dying and the death."

Jeffrey A. Giordano, Ph.D.
Department of Gerontology
University of South Florida

PREFACE

Being unable to cure death, wretchedness and ignorance, men have decided, in order to be happy, not to think about such things

–Pascal (Pensées, 1670/1966, p. 66)

The motivation for editing this book on death attitudes and the older adult is anchored in dissatisfaction. As probably anybody who teaches or conducts research in the field of aging can testify, death and death attitudes are not yet well integrated in the gerontological literature. As an illustration to this point we can consider the concept of successful aging, a concept that plays an important role in the general orientation to the study of aging today. Successful aging was introduced by Rowe and Kahn in their classical 1987 article and elaborated recently in a later article (Rowe & Kahn, 1997). The successfully aging person is described as having a low probability of disease, functioning cognitively and physically at a high level, and being actively engaged in life. Assuming further that this is a 85-year-old adult, it follows, paradoxically, that he or (more frequently) she is likely to face death in the next ten years, perhaps much sooner than this. We should expect this person's attitudes toward personal death and toward death in general to "color" or to inform in some way his or her "successful aging." The model of successful aging, with its emphasis on "engagement with life," cannot easily accommodate personal death (cf. Tornstam, 1992).

Other models are still "waiting" to be extended in a direction that will encompass death and death attitudes. An example taken from life-span developmental psychology is the model of selective optimization with compensation developed by Baltes and colleagues over the last decade or so (e.g., Baltes, 1997). Selection, optimization, and compensation are universal developmental processes but in older age two of the processes, selection and compensation, become more important. The reason for this is increased losses and the reduction of resources that characterize old age. The increased limitations make the need to select (e.g., to focus on a few important goals), and the need to compensate (e.g., to find alternative means to attain a goal) only more imperative. Our personal anticipated death is not a loss but rather an **anticipated** loss. Moreover, this anticipated death may cast its shadow over our present achievements. The question is whether an "anticipated death" still may have some of the effects of occurring losses—whether it can be expected to result, for example, in further selection and perhaps in enhanced efforts of optimization.

In the same vein, we can consider the elaborated model of regulation or control across adulthood developed by Heckhausen and Schultz (1993), in part by extending Baltes' model of selective optimization with compensation. Their model includes concepts such as compensatory, secondary control (e.g., disengagement) that may be used to prevent self-esteem declines. Can this model be applied to explain how older adults might successfully deal with "the challenge of death"? Can we successfully disengage from life?

There were several recent attempts to develop models that will "accommodate death." One is Tornstam's theory of gerotranscendence (e.g., Tornstam, 1999) that postulates a fundamental shift in perspective with increased age in the direction of a sense of unity with the universe. Another important model is Carstensen's socioemotional selectivity theory (e.g., Carstensen, Isaacowitz, & Charles, 1999) according to which there is a shift in time perspective with age: Older people reformulate life goals and become more present-oriented. These are timely theoretical developments that are still in need of further development.

The relationship between the two disciplines gerontology, and thanatology, an uneasy relationship so far, should be based, at the conceptual level, on the realization that our life informs our death and vice-versa. The fact that the way we lived our life is a powerful determinant of our facing-the-death style in later life is, of course, the essence of the Eriksonian view of the eighth psychosocial stage of life, the one characterized by the conflict between ego integrity and despair. A recent attempt to construct a comprehensive model (Tomer & Eliason, 1996; see also Chapter 1 in this volume) places death anxiety (as the "dependent variable") at the "end" of a complex and intertwined structural model containing variables such as beliefs about the self or beliefs about the world.

Our death also informs our life. The famous "search for meaning" imperative can be plausibly construed as a reaction to the realization of personal death. An influential theory today, the terror management theory, following Becker (1973), argues in fact that the aspiration for immortality is the foundation of a significant part of human motivation. In particular, the theory is relevant to the way members of a cultural system relate to this systems' standards of values and to people who either embody or who dissent with the system (e.g., Greenberg, Solomon, & Pyszczynski, 1997; see also Chapter 3 in this volume). In fact, the desire for immortality may be one of the foundations for cultural systems designed to achieve particular functional goals.

From a more general perspective, the anticipated death makes the issue of the construction or realization of meaning (or meaningfulness) more acute. Several authors—Wong, Reker, Tornstam, among others—have addressed in their writings this difficult issue, suggesting the existence of some form of transcendence and/or increase in the importance of religion and spirituality in older age (e.g., Reker & Wong, 1988; Tornstam, 1994; Wong, 1998).

While acknowledging the meaning-giving character of death, it is also important to realize that death is a meaning-depriver: It tends to deprive one not only of "future meaning" but also, retroactively so to speak, of whatever meaning his or her existence may be felt to possess in the present. Even the "well-lived life" or the "self-actualized life" has its share of inconsistencies, pure chance, and incongruities, and may seem under a honest examination to be pretty incomprehensible. It is indeed doubtful that complete meaningfulness can be achieved and it is arguable that the precarious and contingent situation of Homo-sapiens does not realistically allow more than some degree of realization of "partial meaningfulness." The present research on constructions of life narratives by older adults has portrayed both achievements of coherence (e.g., Ruth & Kenyon, 1995) and limitations thereof (Ruth & Öberg, 1992).

It is interesting to speculate on how developments in the field of health, population developments, and medical and other forms of technology will affect death attitudes in the next millennium. There is good evidence for what is called the "rectangularization of the survival curve," the change in the survival curve that parallels the decreased mortality throughout the life-span and the shrinking of the interval of time (say between age 85 and 90) during which most people will die (e.g., Nusselder & Mackenbach, 1996). The knowledge of the approximate age of death may make the process of "facing death" more difficult. Much less agreement exists regarding a possible rectangularization of the "morbidity curve," the possible shrinking of the period of disability that typically precedes death. The image of a person living "successfully" for ninety years and dying abruptly is appealing. Gradual losses in later life, however, perform the useful function of allowing one to adapt gradually to the idea of personal death. Shrinking of the period of disability may have, therefore, the effect of making more difficult the process of coming to grips with one's own mortality. Perhaps, from this point of view, we can hope that the period of "gentle decline" that characterizes the second half of life will be maintained in the future.

The challenge of "integration" of life and death themes will continue, probably, throughout the next century. The present volume, by bringing together concepts of death and aging, should be seen mainly as an effort toward integration.

The book is divided into four parts. The first part focuses on theories, models, and concepts that attempt to fill, at least in part, the conceptual vacuum that exists in this area. The second part presents empirical findings on death attitudes and death anxiety in connection to age. Trends and correlates of death anxiety and death attitudes, as well, as possible causal connections are discussed in this part which also provides a general discussion of the concept of a death attitude. The third part is dedicated to applied issues. This part deals with end-of-life decisions including older-adult suicide, nursing personnel attitudes toward death, aging and assisted suicide, and hospice care. Ethnicity, as an important variable that may affect death attitudes and end-of-life decisions, is also examined in this part.

Finally, the fourth part of the book is dedicated to the issues of counseling of the older adult and to the future of death attitudes and aging in the 21st century.

☐ References

Baltes, P. B. (1997). On the incomplete architecture of human Ontogeny. *American Psychologist,* 52, 366–380.

Becker, E. (1973). *The denial of death.* New York: Free Press.

Carstensen, L. L., Isaacowitz, D. M, & Charles, S. T. (1999). Taking time seriously: A theory of socioemotional selectivity. *American Psychologist, 54*(3), 165–181.

Greenberg, J., Solomon, S., & Pyszczynski T. (1997). Terror management theory of self-esteem and cultural worldviews: Empirical assessments and conceptual refinements. In M. E. P. Zanna (Ed.), *Advances in experimental social psychology* (Vol. 29) (pp. 61–139). New York: Academic Press.

Heckhausen, J., & Schultz, R. (1993). Optimization by selection and compensation: Balancing primary and secondary control in life-span development. *International Journal of Behavioral Development, 16,* 287–303.

Nusselder, W. J., & Mackenbach, J. P. (1996). Rectangularization of the survival curve in the Netherlands, 1950–1992. *The Gerontologist, 36,* 773–782.

Pascal, B. (1966). Pensées (A. J. Krailsheimer, Trans.). London: Penguin Books. (Original work published 1670)

Reker, G. T., & Wong, P. T. (1988). Aging as an individual process: Toward a theory of personal meaning. In J. E. Birren & V. L. Bengtson (Eds.), *Emergent theories of aging* (pp. 214–246), New York: Springer.

Rowe, J. W,, & Kahn, R. L. (1987). Human aging: Usual and successful. *Science, 237,* 143–149.

Rowe, J. W., & Kahn, R. L. (1997). Successful aging. *The Gerontologist, 37,* 433–430.

Ruth, J.-E, & Kenyon, G. (1995). Biography in adult development and aging. In J. E. Birren, G. Kenyon, J.-E. Ruth, J. J. F. Schroots, & T. Svensson (Eds.), *Aging and biography: Explorations in adult development* (pp. 1–20). New York: Springer.

Ruth, J.-E, & Öberg, P. (1992). Expressions of aggression in the life stories of aged women. In K. Björkqvist & P. Niemelä (Eds.), *Of mice and women: Aspects of female aggression* (pp. 133–146). San Diego, CA: Academic Press.

Tomer, A., & Eliason, G. (1996). Toward a comprehensive model of death anxiety. *Death Studies, 20,* 343–365.

Tornstam, L. (1992). The quo vadis of gerontology: On the gerontological research paradigm. *The Gerontologist, 32,* 318–326.

Tornstam, L. (1994). Gerotranscendence: A theoretical and empirical exploration. In L. E. Thomas & S. A. Eisenhandler (Eds.), *Aging and the religious dimension* (pp. 203–225). Westport, CT: Greenwood.

Tornstam, L. (1999). Late-life transcendence: A new developmental perspective on aging. In L. E. Thomas & S. A. Eisenhandler (Eds.), *Religion, belief, and spirituality in late life* (pp. 178–202). New York: Springer.

Wong, P. T. P. (1998). Spirituality, meaning, and successful aging. In P. T. P. Wong & P. S. Fry (Eds.), *The human quest for meaning* (pp. 359–394). Mahwah, NJ: Lawrence Erlbaum.

ACKNOWLEDGMENTS

I wish to thank the contributors of this book. Their willingness to share their findings and ideas, as I found by interacting with them, reflects their conviction that a book on death attitudes and aging is long needed.

Furthermore, I would like to express my deep gratitude to Robert Neimeyer. Without his active support and encouragement the book would not have left the incipient stage of a tentative idea.

ABOUT THE CONTRIBUTORS

Sara Carmel, Ph.D., M.Ph., is a medical sociologist with a degree in public health. She is currently the Head of the Department of Sociology of Health and the Director of two M.A. programs—Gerontology and Sociology of Health—in the Faculty of Health Sciences, The Ben Gurion University of the Negev, Beer Sheva. Her major research interest today is in issues related to artificial prolongation of life, with a focus on the public's point of view versus health care providers' preferences and practices. She is currently writing a book entitled *The Artificial Prolongation of Life* (under a contract with Brunner/Mazel Publishers), which will be based on studies in Israel, Japan, Russia, the United States, and the Netherlands.

Victor G. Cicirelli, Ph.D., is Professor of Developmental and Aging Psychology in the Department of Psychological Sciences at Purdue University in West Lafayette, Indiana. He holds doctoral degrees from the University of Michigan and Michigan State University, and is a fellow of both the American Psychological Association and the Gerontological Society of America. His recent research interests include end-of-life decision making.

Stephen R. Connor, Ph.D., has worked continuously in the hospice movement since 1975. In addition to being a hospice executive, he is a licensed clinical psychologist and researcher. Dr. Connor has published a number of articles, reviews, and book chapters on issues related to the hospice movement and care of dying patients and their families. His first book, *Hospice: Practice, Pitfalls, and Promise* was published by Taylor & Francis in 1998. He is currently Vice President for Research and Professional Development at the National Hospice Organization in Arlington, Virginia.

Stephen DePaola, Ph.D., is a Social Psychologist and Associate Professor of Psychology at Georgia Southwestern State University. Dr. DePaola studies death anxiety in medical personnel and its relationship to job satisfaction, job stress, and coping. In addition, Dr. DePaola is examining death anxiety in the elderly using traditional self-report methods along with text-based measures.

Grafton Eliason, M.Div., is Adjunct Faculty and Scholar in Residence at Duquesne University. He is a Nationally Certified Counselor and an Ordained Presbyterian Minister.

Robert W. Firestone, Ph.D., is affiliated with the Glendon Association in Santa Barbara, California. He completed his doctoral dissertation, *A Concept of the Schizophrenic Process*, in 1957 and received his doctorate in clinical psychology from the University of Denver that same year. From 1957 to 1979, he was engaged in the private practice of psychotherapy as a clinical psychologist working with a wide range of patients, amplifying his original ideas on schizophrenia, and applying these concepts to a comprehensive theory of neurosis. In 1979, he joined the Glendon Association, which has made possible a longitudinal study that provided supporting data for his theory and an understanding of the fantasy bond in normal couples. Dr. Firestone's major works include: *The Fantasy Bond; Voice Therapy; Compassionate Child-Rearing* and *Combating Destructive Thought Processes.* His studies of negative thought processes and their associated affects have led to the development of an innovative therapeutic methodology, which was described in *Suicide and the Inner Voice.* Recently he has developed the Firestone Assessment of Destructive Thoughts (FAST), a scale that assesses suicide potential. Dr. Firestone serves as a consultant to several large corporations.

Barry V. Fortner, Ph.D., completed his doctoral training in clinical psychology at the University of Memphis in 1999. He is currently an assistant professor of psychology at Rush University and Rush-Presbyterian-St.Luke's Medical Center where he is an active teacher, clinician, and researcher. He has conducted research and published articles and book chapters related to death anxiety, grief therapy and counseling, suicide counseling, psychotherapeutic interventions for cancer patients, pain management, and psychotherapy process and outcome.

Jeff Greenberg, Ph.D., is professor of psychology at the University of Arizona. Since receiving his Ph.D. from the University of Kansas, he has conducted research with Sheldon Solomon and Tom Pyszczynski, on self-esteem, defensiveness, depression, prejudice, and unconscious processes; and, collaborated on the development of terror management theory.

Rachel L. Hawkins, B.A., graduated with a degree in Psychology at Georgia Southwestern State University and is currently employed by the Department of Family and Child Services in Albany, Georgia.

Robert Kastenbaum, Ph.D., is a clinician, researcher, educator, and dramatist with a special interest in lifespan development, aging, and death-related issues. His books include *Death, Society and Human Experience, The Psychology of Death,* and *Dorian, Graying: Is Youth the Only thing Worth Having?* He has written the libretto for the operas *Dorian, Closing Time and American Gothic.* Robert Kastenbaum is now Professor Emeritus at Arizona State University.

Shannon McCoy, M.A., was formerly a Masters-level student of Tom Pyszczynski's at the University of Colorado at Colorado Springs, and is currently working on her doctorate at the University of California at Santa Barbara. Her research interests include self-esteem, defensiveness, prejudice, and discrimination.

Robert A. Neimeyer, Ph.D., is Professor in the Department of Psychology, University of Memphis, where he also maintains an active clinical practice. Since completing his doctorate at the University of Nebraska, he has conducted extensive research on the topics of death attitudes and suicide intervention. He has published 17 books, including *Lessons of Loss: A Guide to Coping; The Death Anxiety Handbook: Research, Instrumentation and Application;* and *Dying: Facing the Facts* (with Hannelore Wass), and is editor of *Treatment of Sui-*

cidal People (with Antoon Leenaars and Terry Maltsberger). The author of over 200 articles and book chapters, he is currently helping advance a more adequate theory of grieving as a process of meaning reconstructions. Dr. Neimeyer is the Editor of the respected international journal, *Death Studies* and served as President of the Association for Death Education and Counseling.

Nancy J. Osgood, Ph.D., is Professor of Gerontology and Sociology at Virginia Commonwealth University/Medical College of Virginia in Richmond, Virginia. Dr. Osgood has taught at VCU/MCV for the past 19 years. She received her Ph.D. in Sociology and Certificate in Gerontology from Syracuse University in Syracuse, New York, in 1979. Dr. Osgood is a former member of the National Committee on Vital and Health Statistics (NCVHS) and currently a Fellow of the Gerontological Society of America (GSA) and Secretary of the Board of Directors of the American Association of Suicidology (AAS). Her major areas of interest and research include: elderly suicide; geriatric alcoholism; recreation, leisure, and aging; creative arts and aging; and pet therapy for older adults. Dr. Osgood has published numerous articles and book chapters, and authored or co-authored 10 books, four of which are on the topic of elderly suicide.

F. C. Powell, Ph.D., is a Professor at the Department of Gerontology, University of Nebraska at Omaha. He developed (with Professor James A. Thorson) the Revised Death Anxiety Scale (RDAS). With Professor Thorson he used the RDAS in more than a dozen studies of death anxiety in younger and older adults. Professor Powell is a member of the Gerontological Society of America and of the American Statistical Association.

Michael J. Prewett, Ph.D., is an Associate Professor of Psychology and chair of the Department of Psychology at Georgia Southwestern State University. In addition to his work in death anxiety, he is currently conducting research on optimism and retention in college students.

Tom Pyszczynski, Ph.D., is professor of psychology at the University of Colorado at Colorado Springs. Since receiving his Ph.D. from the University of Kansas, he has conducted research with Sheldon Solomon and Jeff Greenberg on self-esteem, defensiveness, depression, prejudice, and unconscious processes; and, collaborated on the development of terror management theory.

Bruce Rybarczyk, Ph.D., is an Assistant Professor and licensed clinical psychologist at Rush-Presbyterian-St. Luke's Medical Center. He specializes in the intersecting areas of geropsychology, medical psychology, and rehabilitation psychology. The main theme in his work has been developing age-specific approaches to facilitating the adjustment of older adults to chronic illness. Collaborative efforts with colleagues have led to numerous articles, book chapters and a 1997 book entitled *Listening to Life Stories: A New Approach to Stress Intervention in Health Care*. Dr. Rybarczyk was the 1998 recipient of the James Garrett Early Career Award in rehabilitation psychology (Division 22).

James Smith, B.A., graduated with a degree in Psychology at Shippensburg University where he is pursuing now a second degree.

Sheldon Solomon, Ph.D., is professor of psychology at the Skidmore College and Brooklyn College. Since receiving his Ph.D. from the University of Kansas, he has conducted research with Jeff Greenberg and Tom Pyszczynski on self-esteem, defensiveness, depression, prejudice, and unconscious processes; and, collaborated on the development of terror management theory.

James A. Thorson, Ed.D., is Professor and Chairman, Department of Gerontology, University of Nebraska at Omaha. He developed (with Professor F.C. Powell) the Revised Death Anxiety Scale (RDAS). With Professor Powell he used the RDAS in over a dozen studies of death anxiety in younger and older adults. Professor Thorson is a Fellow of the Gerontological Society of America and a recipient of University Award for Distinguished Research, 1991. He is on the editorial board of *Death Studies*.

Adrian Tomer, Ph.D., is Associate Professor at the Department of Psychology at Shippensburg University, Pennsylvania, where he teaches psychology of aging and developmental psychology. Since completing his doctoral training at the University of Florida in 1989 and his post-doctorate on a MacArthur Foundation grant at Penn State University in 1991, he has engaged in research on the topics of death and dying and cognitive changes with age. He is the author of numerous articles, chapters, and reports on these and other related topics. His other interests are methodological, in particular Structural Equation Modeling.

Paul T. Wong, Ph.D., is Professor of Psychology and Director of the Graduate Program in Counseling Psychology at Trinity Western University, Langley, British Columbia, Canada. After receiving his Ph.D. from the University of Toronto, he taught at the University of Texas in Austin, York University, Trent University, and the University of Toronto. He has been promoting the role of personal meaning in aging and health. His latest edited book is *The Human Quest for Meaning: A Handbook of Psychological Research and Clinical Application*, published by Lawrence Erlbaum Associates, 1998.

Hanna Ziederman, R.N., M.A., is a Clinical Nursing Teacher and a Teacher in Nursing Ethics at the Recanati School for Community Health Professions, the Faculty of Health Sciences, at Ben Gurion-University of the Negev, Israel. She is currently in charge of the important course on clinical supervision and, in addition, she teaches the topic of the dying patient. She served for a number of years as Head Nurse in Kibbutz Beit Kama, a settlement in South Israel that is the home of about 200 adults and children.

THEORIES
AND CONCEPTS

1
CHAPTER

Adrian Tomer
Grafton Eliason

Attitudes about Life and Death: Toward a Comprehensive Model of Death Anxiety[1]

A review of the literature on death anxiety (e.g., Neimeyer & Van Brunt, 1995; Tomer, 1992) reveals the need for the formulation of a comprehensive, operational, and testable model that will relate death anxiety to possible determinants. Such a model can serve several purposes. From an empirical point of view, a comprehensive model has the potential of explaining some of the inconsistent or paradoxical findings regarding death anxiety. A simple example will clarify this: It is plausible to expect a direct, simple relationship between death salience and death anxiety, so that people who are "closer to death" will evidence higher anxiety. Empirical findings have found, however, no clear or strong relationship between age and death anxiety (e.g., Kastenbaum, 1992). In fact, some evidence shows *less* death fear in older adults (e.g., Neimeyer & Van Brunt, 1995; Neimeyer, Moore, & Bagley, 1988; Wong, Reker, & Gesser, 1994) than in middle age or young adults. Some of the evidence suggests a linear decrease of death anxiety with age starting in adolescence (e.g., Neimeyer et al., 1988; Thorson & Powell, 1994), while other evidence suggests more of a curvilinear relationship, with death anxiety peaking in middle age (Gesser, Wong, & Reker, 1987). In both cases, there is nothing such as a systematic increase in death anxiety from young to old age. Similarly, relationships between death anxiety and health status seem to be complex, resisting the generalization that more severe illness is always associated with increased death

[1]This chapter represents an update of the article: "Toward a Comprehensive Model of Death Anxiety" by A. Tomer & G. Eliason (1996). In *Death Studies, 20*, 343–365.
We want to thank Lori Nelson from the Department of Psychology at Shippensburg University for her comments on a prior version of this chapter. We thank also the reviewers of *Death Studies* for their very helpful comments.

anxiety (e.g., Neimeyer & Van Brunt, 1995). Thus, the results on age and health status suggest that both variables (and therefore death salience) are related to death anxiety in a rather roundabout way that should be specified by a comprehensive model.

The ability of a comprehensive model to solve paradoxes and to reconcile contradictions can extend to the compatibility of theoretical approaches. Indeed various components of the model may be consistent with one or multiple theories. As a result, a comprehensive model may indicate where various theories converge and where they supplement one another (Neimeyer, 1994a; Tomer, 1992). Empirical confirmation of the model will serve as a partial corroboration of these theories and will emphasize the need for integration.

☐ Feasibility of a Comprehensive Model

Is the construction of a comprehensive model a feasible task? The reader will not be surprised by our positive answer to this question. First, there is already a large amount of empirical data. Although contradictory, or inconsistent to some extent, the results allow some broad generalizations (e.g., the existence of a relationship between death anxiety and self-actualization; for example, see Neimeyer, 1994b, for a short review). Second, there are a few models that, although not comprehensive nor fully corroborated by evidence, can serve as building blocks and points of departure. Such is, for example, Wood and Robinson's (1982) "additive model" according to which actualization (e.g., discrepancy between self and ideal self) and integration (inverse of self–death discrepancy) act together to affect death anxiety. Other, more general, theoretical approaches can also inform a comprehensive model (see Tomer, 1992 for a review). Finally, there are intuitions and general observations upon which we can build. Such is Neimeyer's (1994a) perceptive remark about life as a process of identity construction having as components "both reflection on the past and anticipation of the future" (p. 265).

We conclude that a comprehensive model is not only needed but is also feasible. Certainly, at this point, such a model will be tentative and in need of confirmation, and possibly modification, in the light of additional empirical data.

It is important to provide a "working definition" of death anxiety before proceeding to the task of formulating the model. The concept of death anxiety as used here is that of a negative emotional reaction provoked by the anticipation of a state in which the self does not exist. We exclude, therefore, related aspects such as fear of dying or fear related to the death or dying of others. While the term "anxiety" also has its problems (cf. Neimeyer, 1995), we use it in this paper in a general sense that encompasses, for example, fear. We start with providing a succinct presentation of the model followed by a justification of its components. We use for this purpose existent findings as well as theoretical underpinnings. The last sections of the chapter deal with developmental and practical implications of the model and methodological considerations.

☐ The Death Anxiety Model

According to the proposed model (presented schematically in Figure 1), there are three direct determinants of death anxiety: past-related regret, future-related regret, and meaningfulness of death. The first two determinants refer to types of regret induced by the contemplation of one's death. Past-related regret refers to the perception of not having fulfilled basic aspirations. Future-related regret refers to the perceived inability to fulfill basic goals in the future. The third determinant, meaningfulness of death, refers to the individual's conceptualization of death as positive or negative, as making sense or being senseless, etc. According to the model, a person will experience high death anxiety when he or she feels much past- and future-related regret or perceives death as meaningless.

The three determinants of death anxiety are related to the extent to which the individual contemplates or ponders his or her mortality, making death salient. Death salience can be connected to these three determinants (and therefore to death anxiety) in three ways:

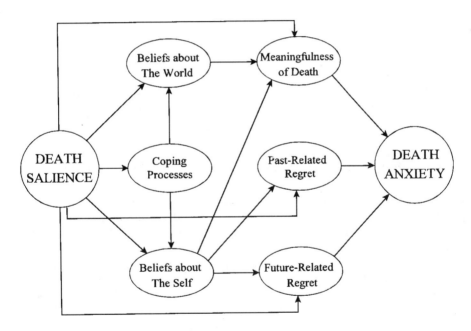

FIGURE 1. A Model of Death Anxiety. Death anxiety is determined by meaningfulness of death and two types of regret. These three determinants are affected by death salience directly or indirectly. The indirect paths from death salience are through two types of beliefs: beliefs about the world and beliefs about oneself. Death salience can also activate coping processes including: life review, life planning, identification with one's culture, and self-transcendence. The coping mechanisms will affect the two types of beliefs, and through them, the three determinants of death anxiety.

1. by directly activating feelings of regret and thoughts concerning the meaningfulness (or meaninglessness) of death;
2. by affecting the determinants by modifying one's beliefs about the self and/or the world; and finally;
3. by activating a variety of "coping mechanisms" including life review, life planning, identification with one's culture, self-transcending processes and, perhaps, other processes. These processes will then have an impact on one's beliefs about self and/or the world and, in this way, on the three immediate determinants of death anxiety.

These three patterns of influence will combine to determine the overall effect of death salience on death anxiety.

To explain how the model works, let us assume that, due to life circumstances (e.g., illness or death in the family), there is an increase in death salience. A direct effect will usually imply an increase in death anxiety with activation of the two types of regret and thoughts of the meaninglessness of death. Death salience can also affect self-concept and lower self-esteem with a further increase in death anxiety. On the other hand, an increased sense of vulnerability can intensify processes such as life review, life planning, self-transcending processes, and processes of identification with one's culture. A positive result of these processes will be a positive change in self-concept, an improved self-esteem, and a change in worldview that may lower regret and make death more meaningful. The net result (increase, decrease, or lack of change in death anxiety) will depend on how effective the protective processes were in counteracting the other effects produced by increased death salience.

Past-related Regret, Future-related Regret, and Self-actualization

Past-related regret can be defined in relation to life goals that the individual, in a given cultural context, believes should have been (but were not) attained in the past. The prospect or possibility of death activates past-related regret. The individual feels guilty for not having accomplished what he or she (and perhaps others as well) expected to accomplish. These feelings of guilt and remorse contribute to an increased death anxiety.

On the other hand, a being that projects himself or herself toward the future via tasks, goals, and projects (e.g., Sartre, 1943/1966), is a being that cannot avoid fearing death as an event that will negate these projections. From this perspective, we can expect that the more important these projects are to one's self-definition or to one's personal identity, the more death will be associated with anxiety. On the contrary, a person who has no great expectations for the future will feel low future-related regret in the face of a potential or expected death. Future-related regret is therefore an emotional response to the realization that the future necessary for the completion of these goals may no longer be available. The ensuing frustration and disappointment are expressed as increased death anxiety.

The two concepts of regret, regret about actions or inactions in the past, and future-related or anticipated regret, have been used particularly in the last decade (cf. Landman, 1993) to examine people's perceptions about their past or (in the case of anticipated regret) their decision making processes, which are, of course, future-oriented. For example, there is a debate regarding the importance of feelings of regret and their focusing more on actions taken or on inactions that should have been prevented (e.g., Gilovich & Medvec, 1995). There is evidence indeed that, in the long run, people regret more inactions than actions and that this type of regret may elicit despair (Gilovich, Medvec, & Kahneman, 1998).

Research regarding anticipated (or future-oriented) regret has tried to document the importance of this type of regret in making decisions that we might regret later. An incentive to this type of research was the regret theory, particularly in the form proposed by Bell (1982, 1985) and by Loomes and Sugden (1982, 1987). The gist of the theory is that people try to anticipate regret and that this anticipated regret is taken into account in the process of maximization of expected utility in relation to possible courses of action. In recent years, empirical research has documented the importance of anticipated regret in decision making (e.g., whether to engage or not in sexual behavior, see Richard, deVries, and van-der-Plight, 1998) or in life planning. Thus, Stewart and Vandewater (1999) presented longitudinal data in a recent publication showing that regret about early adult life choices motivates goal setting in mid-life women. Well-being was found to be lower in women who were both regretful and did not make life changes.

It is important to point out that our use of future-related regret is broad: We consider regret not only in relation to possible courses of action but in relation to possible futures that may or may not be "up to us," including the possibility of "no future" (death). Such a notion of regret is consistent with Landman's (1993, p. 36) definition which includes among "regretted matters" "uncontrollable and accidental" events.

The relationship between regret and death anxiety may be made plausible by an examination of the literature on death anxiety and self-actualization as well as by a discussion of relevant theories. There is substantial evidence supporting an inverse relationship between actualization and death anxiety (e.g., Neimeyer, 1994b; Neimeyer & Van Brunt, 1995). For example, Neimeyer and Chapman (1980) found less actualized subjects in a heterogenous sample of adults to score higher on Templer's (1970) DAS as well as on several scales of the Collett-Lester (1969) instrument. Subsequent studies (e.g., Neimeyer, 1985; Robinson & Wood, 1983; Wood & Robinson, 1982) further refined these results pointing to the importance of another variable—how death is conceived vis-a-vis the self.

The theoretical explanation of this inverse relationship is somewhat uncertain. Thus, Neimeyer and Chapman (1980) proposed an existential hypothesis based on Sartre's ontology and description of death. The relationship is also consistent with self-actualization theories (e.g., Maslow, 1968; Rogers, 1959). Self-actualization should bring about an openness to experience that may include death (Rogers, 1980). It can also be argued that a highly-realized person has less to lose than a less-realized person: He or she has already achieved much and has, perhaps, less left to achieve (a point quite consistent with Neimeyer and Chapman's interpretation of Sartre). In this way, self-actualization draws our attention to both past and future. In terms of the present model, a self-actualized person has little past-related and future-related regret.

Death acceptance is traditionally considered an attribute of wisdom. The wise person, in the eighth stage of Erikson's psychosocial theory (Erikson, 1963), feels that he or she has lived a meaningful life (consistent with the concept of self-actualization) and accepts death. The unwise person feels that he or she has wasted his or her life. Given the proximity of death, no further plans for the future are either existent or feasible for the unwise. We can formulate Erikson's view by saying that past-related regret expresses itself as despair and fear of death (see also Landman 1993, p. 121). Moreover, the wise person in the Eriksonian model is not only a person at peace with his or her life but also a person without many important projects left to achieve, and therefore a person with little future-related regret.

In conformity with the Eriksonian position on past and future-related regret Orwoll (1989) found that a group of old adults identified by their peers as wise scored higher than a control group on integrity (reflecting lack of regret). Also, Ryff and Heincke (1983), found elderly individuals to report less regret than middle-aged or young individuals when they are asked to describe themselves in the present, past, and future. In another study, Ryff (1991) measuring six dimensions of well-being (two of which are particularly relevant to regret: self-acceptance and purpose in life) found in general increased convergence between the various selves— the present, past, ideal, and future. The increased closeness in old age of past and present self on the self-acceptance dimension can be interpreted as lesser regret with increased age. Lower scores on the purpose in life dimension can be interpreted as a lowering of expectations and an adjustment in goal setting that serves the purpose of minimizing future-related regret. The decrease in purposeful life in older individuals was also reported by Ryff and Keyes (1995).

Occasionally, a different position according to which actualization and individuation are the source of an increased death anxiety has been presented (e.g., Becker, 1973; Firestone, 1994). Unfulfillment does not produce death anxiety, but rather, "an ontological guilt about a life not fully lived" (Firestone, 1994, p. 237). There is not much in terms of research evidence (as opposed to clinical experience, etc.) to support this position. Still, there is something to be said for the conceptual distinction between "ontological guilt" (in our terminology: past-related regret) and death anxiety. However, it is important to realize that past-related regret (or guilt) may be particularly poignant *because* of the realization of finitude. For an immortal being, an unrealized past will not constitute a serious problem. Past-related regret is therefore a regret "in the face of death," and will be expressed as intensified death anxiety.

We still have to reckon with the argument that states of intensified death anxiety can occasionally follow fulfilling or happy experiences (Firestone, 1994). Certainly, a fulfilling experience may have the effect of changing a person's basic goals or projects for the future. A person may increase his or her future expectations and by doing this may increase the amount of future-related regret and, with it, death anxiety. Therefore, analyzing self-actualization into two types of regret has the advantage of accounting for the research evidence, as well as for the clinical experience mentioned by Firestone.

It is instructive to relate the two types of regret to the Threat Index that was extensively used by Neimeyer and colleagues (e.g., Neimeyer, Dingemans, & Epting, 1977). The Index, that was designed and frequently used to measure self-death discrepancy (or death threat), can also be used to provide a measure of actualization based on a self-ideal discrepancy. Small or no discrepancy between the self and the ideal self may indicate that the individual has achieved his or her main goals and therefore there is not much past-related regret. Because there are no main goals left, there is also not much future-related regret. A large discrepancy, on the other hand, may correspond to the existence of increased past-related regret, the existence of increased future-related regret, or both. We can therefore see the existence of a connection between beliefs related to the self and the two types of regret.

Death Meaningfulness

The way death is conceptualized vis-à-vis the self and in relation to the self's future can be expected to affect the amount of anxiety related to anticipation of death. Perception of death as meaningful may reduce the level of death anxiety. Death perceived as absurd and meaningless may, on the other hand, result in elevated death anxiety. Some evidence of such a relationship was provided by Holcomb, Neimeyer, & Moore (1993). Participants who tended to describe death as purposeless, "bad" and negative, involving suffering, unintelligible, etc., in personal narratives on their meanings of death, were more likely to indicate on Hoelter's (1979) Multidimensional Fear of Death Scale that they feared death.

Wong, Reker, and Gesser (1994) conceptualized death acceptance to include three components: neutral acceptance, approach acceptance (related to belief in afterlife), and escape acceptance (death as an alternative to a miserable life). Their Death Attitude Profile–Revised (DAP-R) measures these three components, as well as death avoidance and fear of death. The researchers found that young adults who showed high approach acceptance displayed less fear of death. Consistent with this, belief in an afterlife was found to be negatively related to death anxiety by Rigdon and Epting (1985). However, Krieger, Epting, and Leitner (1974) found no relationship between death anxiety measured on the Threat Index and belief in an afterlife, while a complex relationship is suggested by Thorson and Powell (e.g., 1994).

It is important to realize that belief in an afterlife, or immortality, is only one way to think about death as meaningful. Alternative ways may be related to a process of de-individuation in which the self tends to transcend its boundaries, reuniting with the universe (e.g., Dickstein, 1977; Kohlberg & Ryncarz, 1990). This idea is congruent with the assumption of a universal consciousness beyond the individual (cf. Goswami, 1993). From such a perspective, death is a reabsorption into cosmic unity.

Another way in which death can be meaningful is as an escape from a miserable life. Indeed, Wong et al. (1994) found a negative correlation between "escape acceptance" and fear of death.

Meaningfulness of death is determined by one's beliefs about the world and about self. In order to clarify this point, we can use Antonovsky's sense of coherence model (e.g., Antonovsky, 1979; 1987; see also Korotkov, 1998 for a succinct but comprehensive presentation of the model) as an example. The model postulates the existence of three components: comprehensibility, manageability, and meaningfulness. The first component refers to the perception of the world as structured, predictable, and explicable. The other two components are self related, dealing with an individual's perception of self as resourceful and able to find meaning in life's demands. All three components may affect the way death is being perceived (see Tomer, 1992).

Religiosity, in particular intrinsic religiosity (Allport, 1950; see also Batson & Ventis, 1982, for a distinction between different types of religious orientation), as well as spirituality (Fehring, Miller, & Shaw, 1997) may influence directly the perception of death (for example by involving a belief in an after-life) or may have an effect on this perception by affecting the extent to which life is perceived as meaningful. Negative correlations between intrinsic religiosity and death anxiety (e.g., Rasmussen & Johnson, 1994; Thorson & Powell, 1990) are consistent with such a position (see also Wong et al., 1994, Wong, 1998).

Similarly, a strong belief in a just world (Lerner, 1970) may make one more likely to believe that death is meaningful. Meaningfulness of death, therefore, should be treated as a multidimensional construct (cf. Florian & Kravetz, 1983), presumably related in complex ways to one's philosophy, religion, and life circumstances. Our model depicts meaningfulness of death as a variable that affects death anxiety and is related to one's beliefs about the self and the world.

☐ Beliefs about the Self and Death Anxiety

Self-concepts

Our discussion about regret and self-actualization made clear the connection between self concepts and death anxiety. In particular, we have seen that a large discrepancy between the actual and the ideal self was found to be related to higher death anxiety. It may be instructive to consider the self discrepancy theory (e.g., Higgins, 1987), although this theory has not yet been applied to the area of death anxiety (cf. Tomer, 1992). According to this theory, a discrepancy between an actual and an ideal self-state is conducive to "dejection-related emotions." In addition, a discrepancy between the actual self-state and the ought self-state (the latter includes a representation of duties, responsibilities, etc., that someone—the individual or another person—believes the individual should possess) is conducive to fear, threat, etc. More recent elaborations (Higgins, Vookles, & Tykocinski, 1992) include an extension of the theory to other self-beliefs related to the "future self" and to the "can self." For example, a discrepancy between the actual self and the ideal self is more likely to be associated with distress if the ideal self is congruent with the future self. This is analogous to a situation in which the person has important goals to realize in the future. These are goals that may be compromised by a "premature" death (future-related regret). A more precise specification of the relationship between self-beliefs and death anxiety should await further developments of the self-discrepancy theory. From the perspective of the model described here, self-beliefs and discrepancies between self-beliefs (cf. Moretti & Higgins, 1990) affect the level of past-related and future-related regret, as well as the level of the individual's self-esteem. They can also affect the perception of death as meaningful or not.

Self-esteem

The relationship between self-esteem and death-related anxiety was demonstrated experimentally by Greenberg, Solomon et al. (1992) in a series of three studies. In one of these studies, the researchers manipulated self-esteem by providing feedback to subjects concerning their personality. Subjects who received positive feedback showed less anxiety in response to a "death video." Further evidence was provided in subsequent studies by Greenberg et al. (1993), which demonstrated that subjects high in self-esteem have less need to deny that they might be vulnerable to a short life expectancy. These results are consistent with other studies indicating a positive correlation between low self-esteem (or a low sense of purpose in life) and death anxiety (e.g., Amenta & Weiner, 1981; Davis, Bremer, Anderson, & Tramill, 1983).

In our model, self-esteem is included in "beliefs about the self" and is related to death anxiety mainly by affecting the two types of regret.

☐ Coping Processes

Life Review

The concepts of life review and reminiscence (Butler, 1963; Romaniuk, 1981) and the concept of biography construction (Marshall, 1980) were introduced in reference to important developmental processes that take place as the individual examines his or her past. More specifically, they can be viewed as mechanisms of coping with death anxiety. Life review was considered by Butler (1963, 1974) to be particularly important in old age (or with the terminally ill) when it is "prompted by the realization of approaching dissolution and death" (Butler, 1963, p. 66). Life reviewing can foster the integration of past conflicts and therefore is especially relevant to a person who has experienced most of the life cycle and is acutely aware of his or her time and place in the "seasons of life." For this reason, it was also proposed as a mechanism to attain ego integrity in the eighth Eriksonian stage (Erikson, 1963). Butler also acknowledges that life review may occur in response to other life crises and different ages. Consistent with this recognition, Merriam (1993), in her study of 100, 80, and 60 year-olds, found that there were no significant differences among the three age groups in the percentage of subjects who have reviewed or were reviewing their lives. Other studies have found that life review is not limited to old age and that it is used throughout the life span (Cameron, 1972; Giambra, 1977; Lieberman & Tobin, 1983; Lowenthal, Thurnher, & Chiriboga, 1975; Merriam & Cross, 1982). It can be argued, however, that life review might fulfill different functions at different stages of the life span. Support for this position can be found in Webster (1993), who built and validated a reminiscence functions scale with a seven-factor solution. One of the factors was death preparation. The results indicated a monotonic increase in the use of reminiscence for death preparation with age. However, it is interesting to point out that even in the teens, twenties, and thirties, some individuals used reminiscence for this purpose.

Life review is not a panacea to a wasted life and may in fact increase the amount of regret one feels rather than decrease it. It may produce guilt and depression (Butler, 1963). As a result, the relationship between life review and death anxiety is complex.

Some experimental findings have shown that individuals who participated in a life review workshop showed decreased death denial (Georgemiller & Maloney, 1982) and correlational studies have also obtained other positive results such as improved ego integrity (Taft & Nehrke, 1990), life satisfaction (e.g., Merriam & Cross, 1982), lower depression (e.g., McMahon & Rhudick, 1967), or stress reduction (e.g., Lewis, 1971). On the other hand, older people may be satisfied with life without engaging in life review (e.g., Merriam, 1993). Also, the type of life review one engages in makes a difference. Thus, Wong and Watt (1991) found in a sample of older men and women that successful aging is associated with integrative reminiscence (similar to life review) and with instrumental reminiscence (subjective perception of competence and continuity). However, engaging in obsessive reminiscence (evidenced in feelings of guilt and bitterness over one's past) was found to be related negatively to successful aging. It is worth pointing out that the authors did not measure death anxiety in this study. Successful aging was based on an interview that considered subject's coping capabilities, physical well-being, mental well-being and adjustment.

In conclusion, the literature supports the roles of life review and reminiscence as an individual's responses to increased death salience. This corresponds to the arrow leading from death salience to coping processes in our model. The outcomes of reminiscence may be positive or negative and they may be mediated by variables such as well-being or self-esteem, rather than being direct effects on death anxiety (cf. Wong & Watt, 1991). This process is represented in our model by allowing life review to either improve or diminish one's beliefs about oneself (e.g., self-esteem, self-concept, and life satisfaction) and, as a result, to either increase or decrease the amount of past-related regret. We also consider plausible an effect of life review on one's beliefs about the world (e.g., religion, culture, etc.). A discussion about the connection between processes and belief systems is included in the section dealing with identification processes.

Life Planning

While life review considers the past, life planning considers the future. Both processes are particularly salient during periods of transition. According to Levinson (1978), the task of a developmental transition is, among other things, "to review and evaluate the past; to decide which aspects of the past to keep and which to reject; and to consider one's wishes and possibilities for the future" (p. 51). Consideration and redefinition of one's main life goals are particularly important in times of increased death salience. This point was emphasized by Taylor (1983) in her theory of cognitive adaptation to threatening events. A person faced with a potentially fatal illness will have recourse to search for meaning that includes a reordering of priorities.

There are several types of restructuring of basic goals. "Selective optimization with compensation" is a term introduced by Baltes and colleagues (e.g., Baltes, 1987; Baltes, Dittmann-Kohli, & Dixon, 1984) to account for the way older people deal with reduced biological, mental and social resources (*time*, as a resource, can also be added to this list). One process included in selective optimization is the process of increased focusing on a number of goals or domains of particular importance in which the individual has particular strengths or from which one derives particular satisfaction, or both.

A somewhat different type of redefinition is obtained by adopting more realistic goals, renouncing goals that are impossible to obtain, and/or changing criteria of success and failure. Levinson (1978), in his description of the mid-life transition, wrote perceptively of the need to make one's aspirations more realistic, thus reducing "the tyranny of the dream" (p. 248). These changes come together with a more acute sense of one's mortality and a process of disillusionment that includes giving up the chimera of immortality. External success is not so important. Failure, or what the society may consider failure, is no longer viewed as a catastrophe (p. 249). Brantstadter, Wentura, and Greve (1993) have addressed the following puzzling question: How are older people able to maintain their self-esteem intact in the face of frequent losses? They posed a process of accommodation allowing the older adult to disengage from unrealizable goals and/or to lower aspirations. Using accommodation (as well as assimilation), older adults are able to maintain the same distance between their actual self and their desired self across the life span (Brandstadter et al., 1993).

In our model, life-planning processes are considered, together with life-review processes, to affect self-esteem and self-concept. Reformulation of life goals can help to close the gap between the self and the ideal self, thus lowering the intensity of past-related and future-related regret. By changing unrealistic goals, the individual may be able to reduce the amount of future-related regret that the prospect of a not-too-distant death may produce. By adapting one's main goals, one may also moderate the amount of (past-related) regret resulting from not having lived up to some ideal standards.

Identification with One's Culture

According to terror management theory (e.g., Greenberg, Pyszczynski, & Solomon, 1986; Solomon, Greenberg, & Pyszczynski, 1991; Greenberg, Solomon, & Pyszczynski, 1997) the individual is protected from his or her awareness of mortality and the associated anxiety by the cultural worldview and its values. This, according to the theory, is accomplished through the effects cultural worldviews have on one's self-esteem. Self-esteem protection and/or enhancement are the result of identifying with one's culture and living up to its standards of values. Self-esteem shields individuals from anxiety, in particular from the anxiety that comes with an awareness of one's mortality. Thus, culture acts as an anxiety buffer for the "complying" individual (Greenberg, Simon, Pyszczynski, Solomon, & Chatel, 1992).

Numerous studies (Lori Nelson reports 25 studies; see Nelson, 2000) have indicated that reminding subjects of their own mortality increases their inclination to respond favorably to people who bolster their worldviews and to respond negatively to other people who are different from them (e.g., Arndt, Greenberg, Pyszczynski, & Solomon, 1997; Greenberg et al., 1990; Rosenblatt, Greenberg, Solomon, Pyszczynski, T. & Lyon, D., 1989). A recent study by Florian and Mikulincer (1998) generalized this effect to children as young as 11. These results are also in line with older findings obtained by Osarchuk and Tatz (1973); the researchers found that exposing individuals who believe in afterlife to death-related stimuli increased their faith in an afterlife.

In our model, processes of identification with one's culture are included as one type of coping mechanism that may be induced by death salience and may protect the individual from increased death anxiety. This is accomplished via their effects on self-esteem and self-concept as well as on one's view of the world.

Self-transcending Processes

The issue of transcendence is often discussed in thanatology for reasons that are not difficult to surmise. If death is the annihilation of the self, the only way for a self to accept death is through transcendence. The existence of a stage of a selfless self was postulated by Dickstein (1977). The life-review and life-planning processes discussed before may perform a self-transcending, liberating function. Other processes that promote self transcendence are the generative and self-detachment processes.

Generative Processes

Recent findings by McAdams, de St. Aubin, and Logan (1993) showed age differences in four categories of generativity: generative concerns (about welfare of future generations), generative strivings, generative actions, and generative narration (past memories). Middle-aged and older adults displayed an increase in generativity. These results support Erikson's theory that postulates a stage of generativity versus stagnation in middle age. However, contra Erikson, older people were found to be as high in generativity as middle-aged people. Generativity processes can be viewed, therefore, at least in part, as a response to increased death salience and as a way to deal with the issue of personal death throughout the life-span.

Self-detachment or Loss of Self-consciousness

Self-detachment, or loss of self-consciousness, was described by Csikszentmihalyi (e.g., 1990, 1993) as part of the flow experience. Its essence is the disappearance of the self from the consciousness of a person that is all focused on something else. As such, this loss of self-consciousness can lead to self-transcendence, to the feeling of a close connection with an Other and to a sense of unity with the world (Csikszentmihalyi, 1990, p. 64). A similar concept of self-transcendence as an aspect of wisdom, typically developing in older age, was described by Erikson (1982).

Gerotranscendence

Tornstam (1992, 1994) formulated his theory of gerotranscendence taking as point of departure theories and concepts elaborated by Erikson (1963), Jung (1930), Gutmann (1976) and others. The essence of his theory is the assumption that living into old age is associated with a shift of perspective toward the cosmic dimension as an integral part of a developmental process. The empirical examination of the concept of transcendence in several Danish and Swedish samples (Tornstam 1994, 1997a) generated consistently (as a main factor) a dimension of cosmic transcendence characterized by feelings of connection with the universe. Moreover, cosmic transcendence was found to be higher in older adults (Tornstam, 1997a, 1997b) and in adults who experienced more crises. Surprisingly, however, Tornstam (1997a) did not find that cosmic gerotranscendence correlates with fear of death.

Generativity as well as self-detachment experiences and cosmic gero-transcendence are likely to transform one's self-concept and one's worldview by making the self a part of a encompassing entity (cosmos) and by imbuing the world with meaning and, perhaps, consciousness.

☐ Developmental and Practical Implications

A developmental perspective should focus on changes in death salience throughout different developmental periods. A general increase of death salience with increased age magnifies the importance of the coping mechanisms. These mechanisms may decrease the discrepancy between self-concepts (e.g., between the ideal self and the actual self), may enhance self-esteem, and may provide a meaningful view of the world.

Life review and reminiscing may play a more important function with heightened death salience, and life planning will be adjusted accordingly. The evidence reviewed in this article is consistent with these predictions. We can also expect self-transcending processes and identification with cultural values to be of greater importance as the individual proceeds through stages of life toward old age and death. There is much room, of course, for interindividual differences in preferred coping style.

The level of past- and future-related regret is likely to vary among individuals, depending on circumstances and period of life. Past-related regret is likely to be relatively low in young adolescence, but will tend to increase, particularly during periods of major decisions in late adolescence and adulthood. Consistent with the latter, Sterling and Van Horn (1989) found that adolescents in the moratorium status (when they are typically uncertain about their life decisions) scored higher in death anxiety. Future-related regret is likely to be particularly great in youth and in middle age when the future has taken the form of well-formulated goals. In youth and middle age, we are likely to find a relatively negative view of death that, together with regret and the existence of high death salience, is conducive to pronounced death anxiety. Some empirical results are consistent with this prediction. Successful aging should be accompanied by reduced past and future-related regret and by a positive view of death. This is consistent with empirical findings (e.g., Gesser et al., 1987; Thorson & Powell, 1994; Wong et al., 1994). On the other hand, relatively high death salience in old age may cause interindividual variability in death anxiety to be particularly large.

The comprehensive model presented here may have practical benefits. The model enables us to bridge the gap between theory and practice, providing the basis for multimodal applications directed to the clinician, counselor, or nurse. Our attitudes toward death may be affected by our experiences of grief and loss (death salience). Inversely, death attitudes can influence the way we cope with grief and loss (Neimeyer, 1994a). Psychotherapists in this field will be better equipped to deal with these issues if they have an understanding of the multiple factors affecting death attitudes. Coping processes such as the ones described here can be used with different degrees of success. Therapists can teach their clients how to use life review, life planning, or self-transcending processes more effectively.

The present model encourages researchers, as well as psychotherapists, to explore the issue of personal meanings of death (frequently addressed from a qualitative, ideographic perspective) in connection to the issue of death anxiety (typically measured using a quantitative, nomothetic approach, (e.g., Neimeyer, 1994b).

Finally, death education programs accompanied by components for evaluation (e.g., Durlak, 1994) should be based on a comprehensive model. These programs can have as a main goal, modification of death attitudes in the general population or training of health professionals in dealing with issues of death anxiety.

☐ Methodological Observations

The model of death anxiety presented here can be used as a basis for empirical research. The most promising avenue to this goal is, in our view, the use of Structural Equation Modeling (SEM). This powerful approach allows the researcher to move easily from a conceptual model to a structural equation model that can be estimated and tested (cf. Bollen, 1989). Several observations are pertinent in this context. Variables such as death anxiety, types of regret, meaningfulness of death, etc., are likely to be represented in a structural equation model as latent or theoretical variables. These latent variables should be measured (indirectly) using multiple indicators. For example, death anxiety may be measured using several death anxiety scales. The relationships assumed here will be modeled as linear relationships between the latent variables in the SEM. Death anxiety will function as a dependent (or exogenous) variable, and types of regret, meaningfulness of death, etc., will be endogenous variables. Indicators for the latent variables will be measured in a sample of individuals, and their relationships (typically expressed as covariances) will serve for purposes of estimation and evaluation of the fit between model and data. Revisions and/or refinements of the model, followed by further reevaluation on the basis of new data (e.g., Raykov, Tomer, & Nesselroade, 1991), are then possible.

The model can also be modified to accommodate reciprocal paths. For example, increases in death anxiety may activate the coping processes and will be represented in the model by a path leading from death anxiety back to the coping processes. In this case, coping mechanisms will be affected by both death salience and death anxiety. In addition, one might consider possible interactions between past- and future related-regret. Carefully designed models with reciprocal paths ("non-recursive" models), can also be estimated and tested using the advanced programs for structural equation models such as LISREL and EQS (e.g., Bentler, 1989; Jöreskog & Sörbom, 1988).

In conclusion, a structural equation modeling approach will allow one not only to test and estimate the conceptual model presented here, but will also provide a way toward further improvements of this conceptual model.

Points to Remember

Recent theoretical and empirical advances have made possible the development of a comprehensive, albeit tentative, model of death anxiety and death attitudes. Such a model would establish a structured base from which to work and grow, provide an opportunity for further and more systematic empirical research, and allow for the development of application programs. Empirical research based on the model will enable further modifications and refinements. Eventually, we can hope, this process will not only increase our ability to help those in need, but will make possible a deeper understanding of death anxiety and how it relates to our lives as humans.

☐ References

Allport, G. (1950). *The individual and his religion*. New York: Macmillan.

Amenta, M. M., & Weiner, A. W. (1981). Death anxiety and purpose in life in hospice workers. *Psychological Reports, 49*, 920.

Antonovsky, A. (1979). *Health, stress, and coping*. San Francisco: Jossey-Bass.

Antonovsky, A. (1987). *Unraveling the mystery of health*. San Francisco: Jossey-Bass.

Arndt, J., Greenberg, J., Pysczynski, T., & Sdomon, S. (1997). Subliminal exposure to death-related stimuli increases defense of the cultural worldview. *Psychological Science, 8*, 379–385.

Baltes, P. B. (1987). Theoretical propositions of life-span developmental psychology: On the dynamics between growth and decline. *Developmental Psychology, 23*, 611–626.

Baltes, P. B., Dittmann-Kohli, F., & Dixon, R. A. (1984). New perspectives on the development of intelligence in adulthood: Toward a dual-process conception and a model of selective optimization with compensation. In P. B. Baltes & O. G. Brim, Jr. (Eds), *Life-span development and behavior* (Vol. 6, pp. 33–76). New York: Academic Press.

Batson, C. D., & Ventis, W. L. (1982). *The religious experience*. New York: Oxford University Press.

Becker, E. (1973). *The denial of death*. New York: Free Press.

Bell, D. E. (1982). Regret in decision making under uncertainty. *Operations Research, 30*, 961–981.

Bell, D. E. (1985). Disappointment in decision making under uncertainty. *Operations Research, 33*, 1–27.

Bentler, P. M. (1989). *EQS: A structural equations program manual*. Los Angeles: BMDP Statistical Software Inc.

Bollen, K. A. (1989). *Structural equation with latent variables*. New York: John Wiley & Sons.

Brandstadter, J., Wentura, D., & Greve, W. (1993). Adaptive resources of the aging self: Outlines of an emergent perspective. *International Journal of Behavioral Development, 16*, 323–350.

Butler, R. N. (1963). The life review: An interpretation of reminiscence in the aged. *Psychiatry, 26*, 65–76.

Butler, R. N. (1974). Successful aging and the role of the life review. *American Geriatric Society, 22*, 529–535.

Cameron, P. (1972). The generation gap: Time orientation. *The Gerontologist, 12*, Part 1, 117–119.

Collett, L. J., & Lester, D. (1969). The year of death and the year of dying. *Journal of Psychology, 72*, 179–181.

Csikszentmihalyi, M. (1990). *Flow: The psychology of optimal experience*. New York: Harper & Row.

Csikszentmihalyi, M. (1993). *The evolving self*. New York: Harper Collins Publishers.

Davis, S. F., Bremer, S. A., Anderson, B. J., & Tramill, J. L. (1983). The interrelationship of ego strength, self-esteem, death anxiety and gender in undergraduate college students. *Journal of General Psychology, 108*, 55–59.

Dickstein, E. (1977). Self and self esteem: Theoretical foundations and their implications for research. *Human Development, 20*, 129–140.

Durlak, J. A. (1994). Changing death through death education. In R. A. Neimeyer (Ed.), *Death anxiety handbook: Research, instrumentation, and application* (pp. 243–260). Washington, DC: Taylor & Francis.

Erikson, E. (1963). *Childhood and society* (2nd ed.). New York: W. W. Norton.

Erikson, E. H. (1982). *The life cycle completed*. New York: W. W. Norton.

Fehring, R. J., Miller, J. F., & Shaw, C. (1997). Spiritual well-being, religiosity, hope, depression, and other mood states in elderly people coping with cancer. *Oncology nursing forum, 24*(4), 663–671.

Firestone, R. W. (1994). In R. A. Neimeyer (Ed.), *Death anxiety handbook: Research, instrumentation and application* (pp. 217–241). Washington, DC: Taylor & Francis.

Florian, V., & Kravetz, S. (1983). Fear of personal death: Attribution, structure and relation to religious belief. *Journal of Personality and Social Psychology, 44,* 600–607.

Florian, V., & Mikulincer, M. (1998). Terror management theory in childhood: Does death conceptualization moderate the effects of mortality salience on acceptance of similar and different others? *Personality and Social Psychology Bulletin, 24,* 1104–1112.

Georgemiller, R., & Maloney, H. N. (1984). Group life review and denial of death. *Clinical Gerontologist, 2*(4), 37–49.

Gesser, G., Wong, P. T. P., & Reker, G. T. (1987). Death attitudes across the life-span: The development and validation of the Death Attitude Profile (DAP). *Omega, 18,* 109–124.

Giambra, L. M. (1977). Daydreaming about the past: The time setting of spontaneous thought intrusions. *The Gerontologist, 17,* 35–38.

Gilovich, T., & Medvec, V. H. (1995). The experience of regret: What, when, and why. *Psychological Review, 102*(2), 379–395.

Gilovich, T., Medvec, V. H., & Kahneman, D. (1998). Varieties of regret: A debate and partial resolution. *Psychological Review, 105*(3), 602–605.

Goswami, A. (1993). *The self-aware universe.* New York: G. P. Putnam's Sons.

Greenberg, J., Pyszczynski, T., Solomon, S. (1986). The causes and consequences of a need for self-esteem: A terror management theory. In R. F. Baumeister (Ed.), *Public self and private self* (pp. 189–212). New York: Springer-Verlag.

Greenberg, J., Pyszczynski, T., Solomon, S., Pinel, E., Simon, L., & Jordan, K. (1993). Effects of self-esteem on vulnerability-denying defensive distortions: Further evidence of an anxiety-buffering function of self-esteem. *Journal of Experimental Social Psychology, 29,* 229–251.

Greenberg, J., Pyszczynski, T., Solomon, S., Rosenblatt, A., Veeder, M., Kirkland, S., & Lyon, D. (1990). Evidence for terror management theory II: The effects of mortality salience on reactions to those who threaten or bolster the cultural worldview. *Journal of Personality and Social Psychology, 58,* 308–318.

Greenberg, J., Simon, L, Pyszczynski, T., Solomon, S., & Chatel D. (1992). Terror management and tolerance: Does mortality salience always intensify negative reactions to others who threaten one's worldview? *Journal of Personality and Social Psychology, 63,* 212–220.

Greenberg, J., Solomon, S. & Pyszczynki, T. (1997). Terror management theory of self-esteem and cultural worldviews: Empirical assessments and conceptual refinements: In M. Zanna (Ed.), *Advances in Experimental Social Psychology, Vol. 29* (pp. 61–139). New York: Academic Press.

Greenberg, J., Solomon, S., Pyszczynski, T., Rosenblatt, A., Burling, J., Lyon, D., Simon, L., & Pinel, E. (1992). Why do people need self-esteem? Converging evidence that self esteem serves an anxiety-buffering function. *Journal of Personality and Social Psychology, 63,* 913–922.

Gutmann, D. (1976). Alternative to disengagement: The old men of the Highland Druze. In J. F. Gubrium (Ed.), *Time, roles and self in old age* (pp. 88–108). New York: Human Sciences Press.

Higgins, E. T. (1987). Self-discrepancy: A theory relating self and affect. *Psychological Review, 94,* 319–340.

Higgins, E. T., Vookles, J., & Tyrocinski, O. (1992). Self and health: How "patterns" of self-beliefs predict types of emotional and physical problems. *Social Cognition, 10,* 125–150.

Hoelter, J. W. (1979). Multidimensional treatment of year of death. *Journal of Consulting and Clinical Psychology, 47,* 996–999.

Holcomb, L. E., Neimeyer, R. A., & Moore, M. K. (1993). Personal meanings of death: A content analysis of free-response narratives. *Death Studies, 17,* 299–318.

Jöreskog, K. G., & Sörbom, D. (1988). *LISREL7 : A guide to the program and its application.* Chicago: SPSS Inc.

Jung, C. G. (1982, 1930). Die Lebenswende, Lecture, *Ges. Werke: vol. 8*, Olten: Walter-Verlag.

Kastenbaum, R. (1992). *The psychology of death.* New York: Springer.

Kohlberg, L. W., & Ryncarz (1990). Beyond justice reasoning: Moral development and consideration of a seventh stage. In C. N. Alexander & E. J. Langer (Eds.), *Higher stages of human development* (pp. 191–207). New York: Oxford University Press.

Korotkov, D. (1998). The sense of coherence: Making sense out of chaos. In P. T. P. Wong & P. S. Fry (Eds.), *The human quest for meaning* (pp. 51–70). Mahwah, NJ: Lawrence Erlbaum.

Krieger, S. R., Epting, F. R., & Leitner, L. M. (1974). Personal constructs, threat, and attitudes toward death. *Omega, 5,* 299–310.

Landman, J. (1993). *Regret.* New York: Oxford University Press.

Lerner, M. J. (1970). The desire for justice and reactions to victims. In J. MacCauley & L. Berkowitz (Eds.), *Altruism and helping behavior* (pp. 205–229). New York: Academic Press.

Levinson, D. (1978). *The seasons of a man's life.* New York: Balantine.

Lewis, C. N. (1971). Reminiscing and self-concept in old age. *Journal of Gerontology, 26,* 240–243.

Lieberman, M. A., & Tobin, S. S. (1983). *The experience of old age.* New York: Basic Books.

Loomes, G., & Sugden, R. (1982). Regret theory: An alternative theory of rational choice under uncertainty. *Economic Journal, 92,* 805–824.

Loomes, G., & Sugden, R. (1987). Some implications of a more general form of regret theory: *Journal of Economic Theory, 41,* 270–287.

Lowenthal, M. F., Thurnher, M., & Chiriboga, D. (1975). *Four stages of life.* San Francisco: Jossey-Bass.

Marshall, V. W. (1980). *Last chapters: A sociology of aging and dying.* Monterey, CA: Brooks/Cole.

Maslow, A. H. (1968). *Toward a psychology of being* (2nd ed.). New York: Van Nostrand Reinhold.

McAdams, D. P., de St. Aubin, E., & Logan, R. L. (1993). Generativity among young, midlife and older adults. *Psychology and Aging, 8,* 221–230.

McMahon, A. W., & Rhudick, P. J. (1967). Reminiscing in the aged: An adaptational response. *Psychodynamic studies on aging: Creativity, reminiscing and dying.* New York: International Universities Press.

Merriam, S. B. (1993). Butler's life review: How universal is it? *International Journal of Aging and Human Development, 37*(3), 163–175.

Merriam, S. & Cross, L. (1982). Adulthood and reminiscence: A descriptive study. *Educational Gerontology, 8,* 275–290.

Moretti, M. M, & Higgins, E. T. (1990). Relating self-discrepancy to self-esteem: The contribution of discrepancy beyond actual-self ratings. *Journal of experimental social Psychology, 26,* 108–123.

Neimeyer, R. A. (1985). Actualization, integration and fear of death: A test of the additive model. *Death Studies, 9,* 235–250.

Neimeyer, R. A. (1994a). Death attitudes in adult life: A closing coda. In R. A. Neimeyer (Ed.), *Death anxiety handbook: Research, instrumentation, and application* (pp. 263–277). Washington, DC: Taylor & Francis.

Neimeyer, R. A. (1994b). The threat index and related methods. In R. A. Neimeyer (Ed.), *Death anxiety handbook: Research, instrumentation, and application* (pp. 61–101). Washington, DC: Taylor & Francis.

Neimeyer, R. A., & Chapman, K. M. (1980). Self/ideal discrepancy and fear of death: Testing an existential hypothesis. *Omega, 11,* 233–240.

Neimeyer, R. A., Dingemans, P., & Epting, F. R. (1977). Convergent validity, situational stability, and meaningfulness of the Threat Index. *Omega, 8,* 251–265.

Neimeyer, R. A., Moore, M. K., & Bagley, K. (1988). A preliminary factor structure for the Threat Index. *Death Studies, 12,* 217–225.

Neimeyer, R. A., & Van Brunt, D. (1995). Death anxiety. In H. Wass & R. A. Neimeyer (Eds.), *Dying: Facing the facts* (3rd ed., pp. 49–88). Washington, DC: Hemisphere.

Nelson, L. J. (2000). Alternative theoretical accounts for the effects of mortality salience: Need for ingroup protection or terror management? Paper submitted for publication.

Orwoll, L. (1989). *Wisdom in later adulthood: Personality and life history correlates.* Doctoral Dissertation, Boston University.

Osarchuk, M., & Tatz, S. J. (1973). Effect of induced fear of death on belief in afterlife. *Journal of Personality and Social Psychology, 27,* 256-260.

Rasmussen, C. H., & Johnson, M. E. (1994). Spirituality and religiosity: Relative relationships to death anxiety. *Omega, 29*(4), 313–318.

Raykov, T., Tomer, a., & Nesselroade, J. R. (1991). Reporting structural equation modeling results in *Psychology and aging*: Some proposed guidelines. *Psychology and Aging, 6,* 499–503.

Richard, R., de-Vries, N. K., & van-der-Plight, J. (1998). Anticipated regret and precautionary sexual behavior. *Journal of Applied Social Psychology, 28*(15), 1411–1428.

Rigdon, M. A., & Epting, F. R. (1985). Reduction in death threat as a basis for optimal functioning. *Death Studies, 9,* 427–448.

Robinson, P. J., & Wood, K. (1983). The Threat Index: An additive approach. *Omega, 14,* 139–144.

Rogers, C. R. (1959). A theory of therapy, personality, and interpersonal relationships, as developed in the client-centered framework. In S. Koch (Ed.), *Psychology: A study of a science* (Vol. 3, pp. 184–256). New York: McGraw-Hill.

Rogers, C. R. (1980). *A way of being.* Boston: Houghton-Mifflin.

Romaniuk, M. (1981). Reminiscence and the second half of life. *Experimental Aging Research, 7,* 315–336.

Rosenblatt, A., Greenberg J., Solomon S., Pyszczynski T., & Lyon, D. (1989). Evidence for terror management theory: I. The effects of mortality salience on reactions to those who violate or uphold cultural values. *Journal of Personality and Social Psychology, 57,* 681–690.

Ryff, C. D. (1991). Possible selves in adulthood and old age: a tale of shifting horizons. *Psychology and Aging, 6,* 286–295.

Ryff, C. D., & Heinke, S. G. (1983). The subjective organization of personality in adulthood and aging. *Journal of Personality and Social Psychology, 44,* 807–816.

Ryff, C. D., & Keyes, C. L. M. (1995). The structure of psychological well-being revisited. *Journal of Personality and Social Psychology, 69*(4), 719–727.

Sartre, J. P. (1966). *Being and nothingness: An essay on phenomenological ontology* (H. Barnes, Trans.). New York: Citadel Press. (Original work published in 1943).

Solomon, S., Greenberg J., & Pyszczynski T. (1991). A terror management theory of social behavior: The psychological functions of self-esteem and cultural worldviews. In M. Zanna (Ed.), *Advances in Experimental Social Psychology, 24,* 93–159, Orlando, FL: Academic Press.

Sterling, C. M., & Van Horn, K. R. (1989). Identity and death anxiety. *Adolescence, 24,* 321–326.

Stewart, A. J., & Vandewater, E. A. (1999). "If I had it to do over again . . . ": Midlife review, midcourse corrections, and women's well-being in midlife. *Journal of Personality and Social Psychology, 76*(2), 270–283.

Taft, L. B., & Nehrke, M. F. (1990). Reminiscence, life review, and ego integrity in nursing home residents. *International Journal of Aging and Human Development, 30,* 189–196.

Taylor, S. E. (1983). Adjustment to threatening events. *American Psychologist, 38,* 1161–1173.

Templer, D. I. (1970). The construction and validation of a death anxiety scale. *Journal of General Psychology, 82,* 165–177.

Thorson, J. A., & Powell, F. C. (1990). Meanings of death and intrinsic religiosity. *Journal of Clinical Psychology, 46,* 379–391.

Thorson, J. A., & Powell, F. C. (1994). A revised death anxiety scale. In R. A. Neimeyer (Ed.), *Death anxiety handbook: Research, instrumentation, and application* (pp. 303–381). Washington, DC: Taylor & Francis.

Tomer, A. (1992). Attitudes toward death in adult life—theoretical perspectives. *Death Studies, 16,* 475–506.

Tornstam, L. (1992). The Quo Vadis of gerontology: On the Scientific paradigm of gerontology. *The Gerontologist, 32,* 318–326.

Tornstam, L. (1994).Gerotranscendence–a theoretical and empirical exploration. In L. E. Thomas & S. A. (Eds.), *Aging and the religious dimension* (pp. 203–225). Westport, CT: Greenwood Publishing Group.

Tornstam, L. (1997a). Gerotranscendence in a broad cross-sectional perspective. *Journal of Aging and Identity, 2,* 17–36.

Tornstam, L. (1997b). Life crises and gerotranscendence. *Journal of Aging and Identity, 2,* 117–131.

Webster, J. D. (1993). Construction and validation of the reminiscence scale. *The Journals of Gerontology: Psychological Sciences, 48,* P256–P262.

Wong, P. T. P. (1998). Spirituality, meaning and successful aging. In P. T. P. Wong & P. S. Fry (Eds.), *The human quest for meaning* (pp. 359-394). Mahwah, NJ: Lawrence Erlbaum.

Wong, P. T. P., & Watt, L. (1991). What types of reminiscence are associated with successful aging? *Psychology and Aging, 6,* 272–279.

Wong, P. T. P., Reker, G. T., & Gesser, T. (1994). Death Attitude Profile-Revised: A multidimensional measure of attitudes toward death. In R. A. Neimeyer (Ed.), *Death anxiety handbook: Research, instrumentation, and application* (pp. 121–148). Washington, DC: Taylor & Francis.

Wood, K., & Robinson, P. J. (1982). Actualization and fear of death: Retesting an existential hypothesis. *Essence, 5,* 235–243.

Paul T. P. Wong

Meaning of Life and Meaning of Death in Successful Aging

I can never forget the angry reaction from a number of seniors right after the keynote address on successful aging at a major gerontological society convention. The speaker was a prominent authority on the topic, yet his message was met with disapproval and even anger from a small group of seniors standing close to me. These protestors included three or four women, a clergyman, and a lanky, tall, white-haired man leaning on a cane. We were standing at the door because there were no empty seats left inside the lecture hall. One advantage of being outside was that people could freely express their opinions without embarrassing the speaker.

The tall, elderly gentleman with a cane was visibly angered at the proposition that successful agers were relatively free from disease and disability. "How about those on wheelchairs or using a walker! That would make *us* failures!" he said, shaking his head. Those with him were in total agreement with him. Their main complaint was that the speaker almost exclusively emphasized successful agers' physical health and physical activities with no mention of their spiritual and existential dimensions.

This incident caused me to rethink the meaning of successful aging: Have the experts on successful aging missed something important to the aging population? The same question resurfaced a few years later when I read Rowe and Kahn's (1995) report on the MacArthur Successful Aging Project. They defined successful aging as " . . . the ability to maintain three key behaviors or characteristics: (1) low risk of disease and disease-related disability, (2) high mental and physical functions and (3) active engagement with life" (p. 38). By active engagement, they meant such "happy activities" as *relating to others* and *continuing productive activities* (p. 45).

It is worth noting that happy activities are not necessarily productive as defined by Rowe and Kahn (1995): they "count as productive all activities, paid or unpaid, that create goods or services of values." (p. 47). They seem to imply that only activities contributing to the *gross national product* are considered productive. But how about spiritual and existential activities, such as prayer and meditation? How about activities of experiencing and appreciating nature? Are these activities productive?

In Rowe and Kahn's (1995) expanded definition of successful aging, there was also no reference to spirituality and existential wisdom as contributors to successful aging. This omission is not surprising, since none of the 16 researchers of the MacArthurs Foundation Research Network on Successful Aging have done authoritative research on the spiritual and existential aspects of aging.

☐ The Hidden Dimension of Successful Aging

During the past decade, I have consistently emphasized the importance of meeting the existential and spiritual needs of seniors (Wong, 1989, 1994, 1998; Wong & Watt, 1991). I have proposed that personal meaning is the hidden dimension of successful aging (Wong, 1989), because having a positive meaning and purpose in life will not only add years to one's life, but also add life to one's years. Without a clear sense of meaning and purpose in the face of physical decline, longevity may prove to be an unbearable burden. People need to develop a positive attitude towards life in order to maintain life satisfaction in the midst of losses and illness. I have presented a more detailed argument (Wong, 1989):

> When many of the major sources of meaning, such as work, social status, and activity are threatened or diminished, as in the case of advancing age, the question 'Why survive?' becomes urgent. One's health and life satisfaction importantly depends on whether this existential need is met. The main thesis of the present paper is that discovery/creation of meaning through inner and spiritual resources is a promising way of transcending personal losses and despair in old age. (p. 516)

No one would question the benefits of trying to prolong years of vitality and to compress the time of poor health to a minimum period (Fries & Crapo, 1981). The problem with this approach is that it "devalues" those who, for various reasons, cannot achieve this ideal. Furthermore, even the healthiest may succumb to chronic disabilities. Is life still worth living in these cases? In a nutshell, this is the question that was probably behind the grumbling of some the seniors at the gerontological meeting.

Cole (1984) has offered a similar critique of the Western culture, which values vitality and productivity and devalues the frail and sick. He has correctly pointed out that increase in longevity as a result of medical progress has been accompanied "by widespread spiritual malaise . . . and confusion over the meaning and purpose of life" (p. 329). The following quote points to the futility of emphasizing physical vitality without any reference to existential needs:

> While many do live through their old age with personal vigor and integrity, many more suffer from segregation, desolation, and loss of self in a culture that does not value the

end of life. Today's 'enlightened' view of aging, which encourages older people to remain healthy, active, independent, etc., has yet to confront this crucial issue and therefore harbours potentially pernicious effects. . . . Unless the attack on ageism is applied to address the existential challenges and tasks of physical decline and the end of life, we will perpetuate a profound failure of meaning. (p. 333)

In his bestselling book *Successful Aging: The Myths, Realities and Future of Aging in Canada,* Novak (1985) has made much the same point: "There is no secret, no magic formula. A good old age doesn't come about from some special talent or as a secret gift. It comes about when, given a basic income, reasonable health, good self-esteem and a little energy, a person sets out to discover a meaningful life for him- or herself" (p. 273). He then goes on to say that merely focusing on physical activities, such as playing golf or travelling, may have the unexpected negative effect of covering up "the void of old age and keep people from coming to grips with the challenge of living beyond middle age. Meaningless action can short-circuit the chance to discover a good age" (p. 297).

Thus, the challenge of successful aging is to discover positive meanings of life and death even when one's physical health is failing. We need to address the needs of the frail, the disabled, and the chronically ill; we should not view them as unsuccessful agers. We need to look deeper and discover what enables one to triumph over prolonged illness and disability. Yes, the secret to successful aging for the frail and the dying lies in discovering the transcendental meaning of life and death.

Numerous authorities on aging (e.g., Birren, 1964; Butler, 1963; Erikson, 1963) have concluded that the search for personal meaning and integrity becomes crucial for adaptation in old age. Schulz (1986) pointed out that personal meaning becomes a major source of life satisfaction and personal growth in old age. He maintained that existential acceptance may be more adaptive for the elderly than active striving for personal control.

The Ontario Project on Successful Aging

In our Ontario Project on Successful Aging (conducted in cooperation with Gary Reker and supported by a Strategic Reseach Grant from Canada's Social Sciences and Humanities Research Council), we defined successful aging in terms of mental and physical health and adjustment as rated by an interviewer as well as a panel of psychologists or psychiatrists, a geriatric nurse, and a gerontological recreational worker. The third criterion—adjustment—was based on the observation of how well they coped with stressful life situations. A number of the questions were designed to measure the respondent's general attitudes towards life and aging.

On the basis of these ratings, we were able to select successful agers and less successful agers from both the residential community and institutions for the elderly. We provided a comprehensive study of various psychosocial factors contributing to resilience and vitality in old age. These factors include variables emphasized by Rowe and Kane (1995), such as Healthy Lifestyles and Social Resources. In addition, we also measured Religiosity, Personal Meaning, Optimism, Commitment, and Coping. The *Successful* and *Less Successful* groups differed significantly in all of these measures. More importantly, regression analyses showed that Personal Meaning was the best predictor of happiness, perceived well-being, and the absence of psychopathology and depression. In short, these results suggest that successful aging is 80% attitude, and 20% everything else.

On the basis of open-ended interviews with participants in this project, Wong (1986) concluded that successful agers are more likely to report positive meanings of life and death as sources of happiness and life satisfaction. The following are a few examples:

> I want to be of value in whatever days left to me. I want to do it with dignity. . . . When I take my last breath, I want to be remembered not for any property or valuable things in a monetary sense, but for what I was capable of doing and what I have done for others.

This newly retired man was very active in various seniors' groups. He was trying to organize various seniors' organizations under one umbrella and apply for government funding. He expressed a strong desire to be "needed, wanted and loved." He wanted to work hard to benefit others. To him, successful aging was not so much being engaged as keeping active for a worthy cause. Successful aging involved serving others and leaving a good legacy.

> *I still have certain ambitions. I would like to do something for my country, for the Peterborough area, and for the Province. We started a while ago back a project called POP—Preserve Ontario Pickerel. We are great fishermen and we saw that the fishing was going down. So we started this project. We have now 20,000 signatures. We also believe that there is the urgent need for a beautiful art centre. We have started a drive for membership. Third, the Constitution we have. It is good, but there is a lot that should and could be done to it. It is not a people's constitution. So these are the kind of things I would be very glad to give the rest of my life to.*

At 73 years old, the above successful ager was still fully engaged with life. His happy activities not only consisted of golfing, travelling, and enjoying himself; he wanted to give all his energy and the rest of his life to projects that benefited humanity. His life goals of conservation and civil duties endowed his life with purpose and passion.

What happens when one becomes frail and institutionalized? What gives one a sense of meaning and purpose in a nursing home? One 92-year-old man derived real satisfaction from helping those who were worse off than he was. His eyes sparked and his voice quivered with excitement as he talked about the joy of helping others:

> *I help anyone. If I see a wheelchair waiting at the elevator or going around and they want a little help, even though I'm crippled myself, I can do without the walker as long as I can have the cane. If I see a wheelchair that wants help, I'll go and help that wheelchair every time.*

The common thread of these successful agers is that they have a zest for life and a clear sense of meaning and purpose. They consistently say "Yes" to life and all the trials of aging. For most of them, their happy activities can be considered purposeful and altruistic rather than leisurely or economically productive. They seem to derive energy and satisfaction from serving others and pursuing a meaningful goal that transcends self-interest.

Another common theme was that the successful agers had a positive attitude towards life. "Be cheerful and try to be as happy as you can," advised a 74-year-old senior. "Well, get out and smile and the world smiles. There is no use grouching about it," mused an 81-year-old lady.

The following quote was from a 73-year-old man who brimmed with zest for life. There was an eager anticipation for each day and each season. He had a profound appreciation for what life had to offer. This kind of positive attitude towards life does not allow much room for death anxiety. Here are his words:

> I look forward to tomorrow and all the days to come. You know, tomorrow is the first day of the rest of your life, so you just take what comes and enjoy it. I look forward to summer, I look forward to fall, I look forward to winter and I look forward to next spring when everything starts bursting out.

A 77-year-old mentioned the importance of being positive and grateful. He had this to say:

> Be thankful for what you have and get the most out of everyday. Keep a healthy, happy attitude. If you start thinking about tomorrow and tomorrow's illness, which is liable to creep up on you or anyone, then you're going to spoil today. Be thankful for what you have today.

Another successful ager summed it up this way:

> Your attitude is the biggest part. If you want to go around with a chip on your shoulder all the time, you're going to have health problems—you're going to think this is wrong with me or that is wrong with me. But, if you have the right attitude, and think, well, gee whiz, is this aging or what is it?

Successful agers also demonstrated a positive attitude towards death and dying. For most of this cohort, the positive meaning of death was often derived from their religious beliefs. Here is a quote from a 76-year old man:

> What I really look forward to is to see the culmination of all the experiences of life . . . is when the Lord comes and we go to be with Him. Then, we are out of this scene. I am not afraid to die, because I am ready. Life is sweet even at that. When it comes, I am satisfied that that is it. The Lord knows best, and I'll leave that up to him.

Another successful ager talked about how his Christian faith and his positive attitude helped him face present difficulties as well as the prospect of dying:

> If we have sufficient faith in God, who is always with us and we are in his hands, I don't think anyone has any need to fear the future. We need to come to grips with the fact that it's only a problem, if you allow it to be a problem. If you can accept the fact of our diminishing activities, whatever they might be, you would realize that there is still life ahead of you.

The untold story of successful aging is about positive attitudes towards life and death, about the spiritual and existential quest, and about personal growth in wisdom and spirituality. From this spiritual, existential perspective, successful aging is attainable for everyone with positive meanings, regardless of his or her physical condition.

In the remaining sections of this chapter, I will discuss (a) the relationship between one's meaning of life and one's meaning of death, and (b) the implications of death attitudes for successful aging.

☐ The Relationship between One's Meaning of Life and Meaning of Death

Life teaches us how to survive, while death teaches us how to live. Life is a taskmaster, while death is a master teacher. We cannot learn how to appreciate the preciousness of life without coming to grips with the reality of death. When people spend so much time in trivial and self-destructive activities, it is often because they have denied the reality of personal mortality. Firestone (1994) observes: "Much of people's destructiveness toward themselves and others can be attributed to the fact that people conspire with one another to create cultural imperatives and institutions that deny the fact of mortality" (p. 221). On the other hand, there are also those who are motivated to make something of their lives before death puts an end to their aspirations. Thus, how we react to personal death has considerable impact on how we live.

Tomer (1994) reviews several philosophical approaches towards death. Each of these philosophies has implications for the meaning of life. For example, Martin Heidegger's position is that since death is a threat of non-existence, it provides the precondition for fuller understanding of life, thereby freeing us from anxiety. For Sartre, death reduces one's being to nothingness; therefore, to reflect on death is to realize the meaninglessness of existence. However, Neimeyer and Chapman (1980) derive a more positive view of life from Sartre's notion of nothingness; they propose that death anxiety can be reduced through self-actualization. In other words, those who have realized their central life goals are less likely to experience death anxiety than are those who have not completed their life tasks.

Wong, Reker, and Gesser (1994) provide a broader conceptual framework for death attitudes, which include fear of death, death avoidance, approach acceptance, neutral acceptance, and escape acceptance. Fear of death can be considered the most powerful and universal death attitude; the other four attitudes may be considered as the various human attempts to cope with death anxiety.

There are many reasons for fear of death. Some of the common reasons are fear of the pain of dying, fear of separation, fear of the unknown, and fear of divine judgement. According to Goodman (1981), "The existential fear of death, the fear of not existing, is the hardest to conquer. Most defensive structures, such as the denial of reality, rationalization, insulation, erected to ward off religiously conditioned and separation-abandonment fears do not lend themselves readily as protective barriers against existential fear of death" (p. 5). Another type of existential fear is that death will come before one has lived a meaningful life. Butler (1963) even suggests that people are more afraid of a meaningless existence than of death.

The effects of fear of death are complex and pervasive. At one extreme, fear of death may lead to intentionally confronting death in extreme sports or on the battlefield—by staring death in the eye. Individuals may have the exhilarating feelings of being free from the iron grip of fear of death. At the other extreme, individuals may live very cautiously in a protected "bubble"—they are extremely safety conscious and don't want to try anything. Such extreme reactions clearly do not contribute to successful aging.

Even less extreme forms of death anxiety are unhealthy. Preoccupation with mortality and worries about death and dying will rob one of the joys of living. Indeed, we have found that fear of death as measured by the Death Attitude Profile–Revised (DAP-R) (Wong, Reker, & Gesser, 1994) was negatively correlated with psychological well being as well as positive meanings of life and death, and was positively correlated with depression. Positive meanings were measured by the semantic differential (SD) method with 7-point bipolar adjectives (e.g., meaningful–meaningless, satisfying–dissatisfying, pleasant–unpleasant, etc.). These bipolar scales were used to provide SD ratings for life and death.

Fear of death can lead to unconscious avoidance, which expresses itself in different ways: living in a drunken stupor, treating death as a taboo subject, refusing to even think about it, or living in the illusion of perpetual youth through cosmetic surgery. However, the most common manifestation of death avoidance is probably the pursuit of busy but trivial activities, as if life would go on forever.

At the heart of death avoidance is denial. Unfortunately, the psychological defenses of denial and avoidance eventually fail in the face of mounting evidence of aging and dying. That is why, sooner or later, people need to come to some form of death acceptance in order to overcome the fear of death.

We have identified three types of death acceptance: (a) neutral acceptance, (b) approach acceptance, and (c) escape acceptance (Gesser, Wong, & Reker, 1987; Wong et al., 1994). Escape acceptance is very different from the other two types of acceptance because it is based on problems of life rather than a fear of death. Even the prospect of hell after death seems more tolerable to some than the pain of earthly life. In other words, when one finds life unbearable, suicide seems a more attractive alternative.

There are many reasons why people say: "I see death as a relief from the burden of life." More often than not, their burden has to do with the crushing weight of meaninglessness rather than physical suffering. In such situations, suicide becomes a cry for meaning. In other situations, people contemplate suicide because they have a very low tolerance for suffering and do not know how to cope with it.

Neutral acceptance refers to coming to terms with the inevitable reality of personal mortality, no matter how uncomfortable one may feel. All living things must die. Death is just a natural cycle of life. One has to accept this fact at the cognitive level, and then gradually adjust to it as the affective level.

Neutral acceptance can have different effects on how one lives. Some may feel that since life is short, they should indulge in hedonistic behavior—"let's eat and be merry, because tomorrow we die." These individuals have accepted death only at the cognitive level, because deep down in their hearts they remain anxious about the finality of death and the termination of all that they hold dear.

A more positive type of neutral acceptance is related to self-actualization. Given the brevity of life, some people may want to make good use of their time and accomplish something worthwhile and significant. Both Kaufmann (1976) and Goodman (1981) have also proposed the idea of conquering the fear of death through self-actualization; being able to accomplish meaningful life goals leads to death acceptance. This idea has been eloquently expressed by Goodman (1981):

> "I don't think people are afraid of death. What they are afraid of is the incompleteness of their life," wrote Ted Rosenthal (1973), who at the age of thirty was told that he had acute leukemia and was going to die. This is one of the most positive statements made on the most fundamentally aversive human condition. It contains an implicit solution to the existential fear of death: completion of one's life, attainment of self-fulfillment. (p. 3)

Goodman (1981) provides numerous illustrations of the above thesis based on his conversations with eminent artists and scientists. For example, in response to Goodman's question: "Would you banish death if you could?," Dr. John Wheeler, a renowned physicist, gave the following answer:

> We have no stronger way to mark our commitment to a great cause than to die for it. So long as there is any such thing as death, human beings can be great. Nobody can take away one's possibility to die for a cause. So long as that measure of ultimate commitment is attainable, the world will be a *live* place to live in. Were death to be abolished, all that we call precious in the world would die. (p. 81, italics his)

Dr. Wheeler has raised an interesting point—the nobleness of human beings lies in their ability to find a cause that is worth dying for. This ultimate commitment constitutes the highest criterion of a meaningful existence. Death becomes a friend rather than an enemy when it brings a natural conclusion to a completed life task. Goodman (1981) explains the psychological process that transforms fear of death into death acceptance:

> To assert in the face of death, "I have fulfilled myself, I can die," certainly takes the sting out of that fateful final hour. But even more important, to know that one is doing all that one is equipped to do, to experience life as meaningful while one is still in the midst of it, may well take the sting of death and liberate us from the fear that inhibits most people to strive toward self-actualization in the first place. . . . There may be an optimal way in the lifelong process of approaching death: a way that would allow us to experience the human condition as meaningful rather than absurd; life as fulfilling and terminable rather than frustrating and incomplete; death as an ultimate goal, worth striving for, rather than lifelong threat to dash our hopes. (pp. 157–158)

The main weakness with Goodman's thesis, in my opinion, is that creative energy does not end with the completion of one task. In fact, creative people are constantly searching for new challenges, but life is too short to complete all the exciting projects available. I can't imagine that truly creative people would say: "I have completed my life task. Therefore, I'll spend the rest of my life on a rocking chair waiting to die." It is more likely that as long as health permits, creative people will continue to pursue projects. When it is time for them to depart, they have the satisfaction that they have done all they can given the years they have, even though much remains to be done.

Furthermore, I do not agree with Goodman that self-actualization represents an optimal way to approach death. Some have to die prematurely, not able to complete their life tasks, let alone fulfill all of their potential. There is also little hope beyond the grave if the significance of one's existence rests on one's performance.

Approach acceptance seems to be the most satisfying way to approach death, because it not only incorporates the completion of one's mission in life, but also extends to a rewarding afterlife. The sting of death is removed by faith in resurrection and eternal life. After presenting evidence on the resurrection of Jesus Christ, the apostle Paul declares:

> When the perishable has been clothed with the imperishable, and the mortal with immortality, then the saying that is written will come true: "Death has been swallowed up in victory. Where, O death, is your victory? Where, O death, is your sting?" (1 Cor. 15:54–55)

Many of our successful agers have expressed such faith. They looked forward to returning to their Heavenly Home, not on the merit of their own accomplishment, but on the basis of their faith in Christ. This type of approach acceptance is not only more attainable, but also more satisfying that self-actualization, provided that one believes in the after-life.

In her memoir of living and dying, Elisabeth Kübler-Ross (1997) epitomizes the triumphant spirit of a religiously-based death acceptance:

> When we have passed the tests we were sent to Earth to learn, we are allowed to graduate. We are allowed to shed our body, which imprisons our soul the way a cocoon encloses the future butterfly, and when the time is right we can let go of it. Then we will be free of pain, free of fears and free of worries . . . free as a beautiful butterfly returning home to God . . . which is a place where we are never alone, where we continue to grow and to sing and to dance, where we are with those we loved, and where we are surrounded with more love than we can ever imagine. (p. 284)

We have found that both neutral acceptance and approach acceptance are significantly correlated with positive meanings of life. However, approach acceptance was also positively correlated with positive meanings of death, providing evidence that approach acceptance is an optimal way to approach death.

☐ Implications for Successful Aging

We have seen that those who endorse both neutral and approach acceptance are likely to have a sense of mission and derive meaning from pursuing their life tasks.

Their commitment to meaningful living not only banishes the fear of death but also makes life worth living whatever their circumstances. That is why Elisabeth Kübler-Ross (1997) is able to declare: "Dying is nothing to fear. It is the most wonderful experience of your life. It all depends on how you have lived" (p. 286).

According to Frankl (1963, 1971), the prospect of death motivates individuals to assume responsibility and respond to the opportunities life has to offer. It also provides the challenges to transform the reality of death into new possibilities for meaning. Kovacs (1982) offer this useful insight on Frankl:

> An apparent obstacle or a limitation in life may become a source for new personal meaning and self-realization. Thus, for Frankl, death is not the end but rather the beginning of the birth of meaning in human living. (p. 202)

In his edited book *The Courage to Grow Old*, Berman (1989) provides numerous examples of individuals who have faced old age and death with courage because of their abiding sense of meaning and unfailing faith. Leland Stowe (1989), one of the contributors in Berman's volume, summarizes it well:

> If it doesn't take courage to grow old, what does it take? Faith in living, I believe, faith that its compensations will multiply with time. . . . It all adds up to this equation: Attitudes + Habits = Motivations; Motivations + Goals + Dreams = Character—all cindered into solid bricks for the passageway into growing old. (p. 303)

Indeed, attitude matters a great deal. It is attitude more than action that ultimately determines whether a person ages well and dies well. Many of the participants in the Ontario Project on Successful Aging have demonstrated this important truth over and over again. I believe that our existential and spiritual emphasis will bring hope to many seniors who are suffering from chronic illness or physical disability.

Fortunately, it is within almost everyone's reach to discover meaning and spirituality. Regardless of the extent of their physical limitations, people can always choose positive attitudes towards life. All that is required is a grateful heart, an open mind, and a searching soul. We have initiated the International Network on Personal Meaning (http://www.meaning.twu.ca) to facilitate people's existential and spiritual quests. Our Meaning of Life Forum is particularly relevant to those interested in meaning-oriented successful aging.

What happens when seniors are no longer able to do productive work? What happens when their health declines to the point that they require institutional care? Can they still achieve successful aging? The answer to these questions is a resounding "Yes." Elsewhere, I have discussed in detail how to promote meaning and spirituality in successful aging (Wong, 1989, 1998). I believe that society and individuals can work together to make aging and death more meaningful.

To follow up on the incident reported at the beginning of this chapter, I was able to engage in a discussion with this group of disgruntled seniors. Almost instantly, they caught on to my message and agreed wholeheartedly that the medical and gerontological establishment should pay more attention to the existential and spiritual needs of seniors.

Psychologists and researchers all need to pay more attention to existential and spiritual issues. Neugarten (1997) had this recommendation:

> Psychologists will probably gain enormously by focusing more attention upon the issues that are of major concern to the individual —what the person selects as important in his past and his present, what he hopes to do in the future, what he predicts will occur, what strategies he selects, and what meanings he attaches to time, life, and death. (pp. 639–640)

With respect to spiritual care, Cluff (1984) emphasized that "Spirituality must be accepted as a dimension of what it means to be human—to live and die, to suffer and rejoice, to succeed and to fail, to hope and despair" (p. 609). He suggested that when one is facing death,

> . . . what is important is not whether the individual finds peace in God or attains a satisfactory answer to the questions of life's meaning, although this may be desirable. What is important is whether the individual continues to question and seek out God, meaning, purpose, and value. (p. 610)

Points to Remember

1. Rowe and Kane's (1995) model of successful aging focuses on physical health, psychological functioning, and active lifestyle. Some seniors, especially those with physical disability, feel that this model devalues them and treats them as failures.
2. Wong's (1989, 1998) model of successful aging emphasizes the existential and spiritual needs of seniors. He proposes that successful aging is 80% attitude and 20% everything else; therefore, it is attainable even by those who are frail and chronically ill. Results from the Ontario Project on Successful Aging support Wong's existential model.
3. According to Wong's existential-spiritual model of aging, positive meanings of life and death provide the necessary motivation for pursuing a healthy life style as well as worthy life goals. Furthermore, the model allows for a high level of life satisfaction, even when physical health is failing.
4. Death anxiety and death avoidance can be replaced by neutral acceptance and approach acceptance. Individuals demonstrate the death attitude of neutral acceptance when they come to grips with the reality of their personal mortality and try to make the most of their lives. Individuals exhibit the death attitude of approach acceptance when they look forward to approaching a rewarding afterlife.
5. Approach acceptance promises to be the optimal approach to living well and dying well. Therefore, gerontological care and death education should take into account the spiritual and existential needs of seniors.

Thus, the quest for meaning and spirituality is an ongoing process, making the journey of life rewarding until the very end.

I am pleased that things are moving in the right direction. Both researchers and health care professionals are beginning to recognize the important role of meaning and spirituality (Wong & Fry, 1998). I hope this chapter will encourage more people to take seriously the existential approach to successful aging and death education.

☐ References

Berman, P. L. (1989). *The courage to grow old.* New York: Ballantine Books.

Birren, J. E. (1964). *The psychology of aging.* Englewood Cliffs, NJ: Prentice-Hall.

Birren, J. E., & Bengtson, V. L. (Eds.) (1988). *Emergent theories of aging.* New York: Springer.

Butler, R. N. (1963). Life review: An interpretation of reminiscence in the aged. *Psychiatry, 4,* 1–18.

Cluff, C. B. (1984). Pastoral enlightenment for seniors: Do they need it? Do they want it? *Journal of the American Geriatrics Society, 32*(8), 609–613.

Cole, T. R. (1984). Aging, meaning, and well-being: Musings of a cultural historian. *International Journal of Aging and Human Development, 19,* 329–336.

Erikson, E. H. (1963). *Childhood and society.* New York: W. W. Norton.

Firestone, R. W. (1994). Psychological defenses against death anxiety. In R. A. Neimeyer (Ed.), *Death anxiety handbook: Research, instrumentation, and application* (pp. 217–241). Washington, DC: Taylor & Francis.

Frankl, V. E. (1963). *Man's search for meaning: An introduction to logotherapy.* New York: Pocket Books.

Frankl, V. E. (1971). *The doctor and the soul* (2nd ed.). New York: Bantam Books.

Fries, J. S., & Crapo, L. M. (1981). *Vitality and aging.* New York: W. H. Freeman.

Gesser, G., Wong, P. T. P., & Reker, G. T. (1987). Death attitudes across the life-span: The development and validation of the Death Attitude Profile (DAP). *Omega, 18,* 109–124.

Goodman, L. M. (1981). *Death and the creative life: Conversations with eminent artists and scientists as they reflect on life and death.* New York: Springer.

Kaufmann, W. (1976). *Existentialism, religion and death.* New York: New American Library.

Kovacs, G. (1982). The philosophy of death Viktor E. Frankl. *Journal of Phenomenological Psychology, 13,* 197–209.

Kübler-Ross, E. (1997). *The wheel of life: A memoir of living and dying.* New York: Simon & Schuster.

Neimeyer, R. A., & Chapman, K. M. (1980). Self/ideal discrepancy and fear of death: Testing an existential hypothesis. *Omega, 11,* 233–240.

Neugarten, B. L. (1977). Personality and aging. In J. E. Birren & K. W. Schaie (Eds.), *Handbook of the psychology of aging* (pp. 626–649). New York: Van Nostrand Reinhold.

Novak, M. W. (1985). *Successful aging: The myths, realities and future of aging in Canada.* Markham, ON: Penguin Books Canada.

Reker, G. T., Peacock, E. J., & Wong, P. T. P. (1987). Meaning and purpose in life and well-being: A life-span perspective. *Journal of Gerontology, 42,* 44–49.

Rosenthal, T. (1973). *How could I not be among you?* New York: George Braziller.

Rowe, J. W., & Kahn, R. L. (1995). *Successful aging.* New York: Dell Publishing.

Schulz, R. (1986). Successful aging: Balancing primary and secondary control. *Adult Development and Aging News, 13,* 2–4.

Stowe, L. (1989). A reporter looks back. In P. L. Berman (Ed.), *The courage to grow old* (pp. 303–307). New York: Ballantine Books.

Tomer, A. (1994). Death anxiety in adult life—Theoretical perspectives. In R. A. Neimeyer (Ed.),

Death anxiety handbook: Research, instrumentation, and application (pp. 3–28). Washington, DC: Taylor & Francis.

Wong, P. T. P. (1986). *Personal meaning and happiness in the elderly.* Paper presented in a symposium at the Annual Convention of the Canadian Psychological Association, Toronto, ON.

Wong, P. T. P. (1989). Successful aging and personal meaning. *Canadian Psychology, 30,* 516–525.

Wong, P. T. P. (1995). The adaptive processes of reminiscence. In B. Haight & J. D. Webster (Eds.), *Reminiscence: Theory, research methods, and applications* (pp. 23–35). Washington, DC: Taylor & Francis.

Wong, P. T. P., & Fry, P. S. (1998). Introduction in P. T. P. Wong & P. Fry (Eds.), *The human quest for meaning: A handbook of psychological research and clinical applications* (pp. XVII–XXVI). Mahwah, NJ: Lawrence Erlbaum.

Wong, P. T. P., Reker, G. T., & Gesser, T. (1994). Death Attitude Profile–Revised: A multidimensional measure of attitudes toward death. In R. A. Neimeyer (Ed.), *Death anxiety handbook: Research, instrumentation, and application* (pp. 121–148). Washington, DC: Taylor & Francis.

Wong, P. T., & Stiller, C. (1999). Living with dignity and palliative care. In B. de Vries (Ed.), *End of life issues: Interdisciplinary and multidimensional perspectives* (pp. 77–94). New York: Springer.

Wong, P. T. P., & Watt, L. (1991). What types of reminiscence are associated with successful aging? *Psychology and Aging, 6,* 272–279.

3

CHAPTER

Shannon K. McCoy
Tom Pyszczynski
Sheldon Solomon
Jeff Greenberg

Transcending the Self:
A Terror Management Perspective
on Successful Aging

It is true that the statement 'All men are mortal' is paraded in textbooks of logic as an example of a general proposition; but no human being really grasps it, and our unconscious has as little use now as it ever had for the idea of its own mortality.

—Sigmund Freud (1919, p. 242)

. . . for the aging person death is no longer a general abstract fate, it is a personal event, an event that is near at hand.

—Simone de Beauvoir (1948; p. 440)

The first signs that we are getting older are usually small, minor things noticeable only to ourselves—but they are monumental in their portent. It might be a slight stiffness when getting up after sitting for a long while, or perhaps the hint of a wrinkle off the corner of the eye, an eye having increasing difficulty deciphering menus. These subtle changes seem to increase exponentially as the body begins the slow road to deterioration. How frightening to discover the increasing limitations of the physical body—that which ties us to life. Not only are our own bodies bearing constant witness to the inevitability of our demise, but our experience with death, through the deaths of those we have known and loved, increases. For the aged, death is no longer an abstract concept for the future, but a concrete crisis of the present. The cord is weakening and we can feel it . . . we can watch it.

What role does this nearness to death play in the psychology of the elderly individual? How do the elderly come to grips with the inescapable reality that their days are numbered? Terror management theory (Greenberg, Pyszczynski, & Solomon, 1986; Solomon, Greenberg, & Pyszczynski, 1991) posits that the knowledge of the inevitability of death is the underlying source from which all other fears are ultimately derived. From this perspective, the fear of death lies at the root of a diverse array of seemingly unrelated behaviors that all function to provide the anxiety-assuaging meaning and value which people need to face life in spite of their awareness of their inevitable fate. Unfortunately, the latter years of life are not a time when meaning and value are particularly easy to come by, at least for members of contemporary Western societies. How, then, do the elderly cope with the undeniable fact that, for them, death lies just around the corner?

The present chapter attempts to address this issue. The growing literature on the psychology of aging makes it clear that people vary widely in how, and how well, they cope with their later years. Whereas for some, their final decades truly are the "golden years," a time marked by clear signs of increased psychological well-being, others lapse into hopelessness and depression. This suggests that, at least in some cases, wisdom may indeed come with age. There may be lessons to be learned from the elderly from which even the young can benefit.

Our goal is to bring our general perspective as social psychologists, and our unique perspective as researchers of terror management theory, to the role of awareness of the inevitability of death in aging. While we are novices in the area of aging, as we are not developmental psychologists by training, it is our belief that important insights into the psychology of aging and the processes underlying terror management theory can be achieved via this preliminary synthesis of these two approaches. We will start by providing a brief overview of terror management theory and research. We will then discuss how the structure and content of contemporary Western cultures conspire to reduce the usefulness of the strategies for coping with the inevitability of death that sustain people through the early and middle years of life. Finally, we will use terror management theory to develop a model of the psychological adjustments that can lead to both successful and less successful aging.

Terror Management Theory

Terror management theory (TMT; Greenberg et al., 1986; Solomon et al., 1991), inspired by the work of the late cultural anthropologist Ernest Becker (1962, 1971, 1973), proposes that the human fear of death results from our uniquely human ability to self-reflect. We are able to conceive of ourselves in the past, present, and future, which inevitably thrusts upon us the knowledge of our own inescapable demise. This knowledge is terrifying because it exists simultaneously with the instinctual drive for continued survival that we share with all animals. This paradox, the knowledge of our own mortality coupled with a primal desire for continued life, creates the potential for paralyzing terror. The management of this terror becomes our lifelong vocation.

How might this paralyzing terror be managed? Clearly, we are skilled death-deniers, adept at certain defensive strategies that protect us from this terror. We do not, on the whole, dwell on the infinite variety of ways we could "buy the farm" or ruminate that at any moment it might be our time to "check out." In fact, we label those who do obsess on such morbid thoughts with various forms of psychopathology. However, given that we profoundly desire to survive, and realistically could "go" at any moment, isn't it a wonder that we don't spend more time obsessing about this rather unpleasant reality?

Terror management theory proposes that we use our shared systems of value and beliefs, our cultural worldviews, to imbue our random, chaotic world with order and meaning. These worldviews provide predictable systems of rewards and punishments that enable us to perceive the world as controllable, fair, and just. Cultural constructions (e.g., calendars, laws, religion, mores, values, and roles) contribute to our efforts to command and rule our universe. As such, we use the cultural worldview to instill order in the chaos: to give our world meaning and to define our place in that world.

The cultural worldview also provides the recipe for immortality. Some form of promise of symbolic or literal immortality is a universal feature of all cultural belief systems. By following the guidelines set forth by the worldview, we can be assured of remembrance in the history books, academic journals, or the Fortune 500. These concrete symbols of the self remind others, and remind ourselves, of our existence and life's worth. They provide us with a sense that the self will continue long after our physical body has withered and turned to dust. We are also often promised literal immortality by our worldviews. Success in meeting the standards of the worldview over a lifetime is rewarded with entrance and exaltation in heaven or reincarnation as a more enlightened being; failure in this regard results in damnation to the inferno, or perhaps reincarnation as a cockroach. The pervading theme in these cultural conceptions of reality is that there is a way to continue to *be*. This existence might be in an altered form, as in the Buddhist conception of becoming one with the universe, but it is existence nonetheless. For this reason we cling fiercely and defensively to our belief systems; they provide the formula for immortality, for continued being, both literal and symbolic.

These cultural worldviews contain the standards for good, appropriate, and valued behavior, the prerequisites for immortality. By successfully meeting these standards, by fulfilling our role in this socially orchestrated world, we feel of value and are able to derive self-esteem. It is this self-esteem that provides our primary barrier against the paralyzing fear of non-being. It is an interesting paradox: the valued "self" is created as a defense against the fear of death, yet it is the loss of this "self" that makes death especially terrifying. According to TMT, self-esteem, therefore, is an indirect result of the fear of death; without the knowledge of our own impending nonbeing we would not be driven to establish meaning in life and value in ourselves. Our views of the world, our value systems, and our successes in meeting the standards that follow from these values are essential defenses against the knowledge of our own mortality. It follows, then, that threats to these vital defenses, our worldview, or our valued place in it, would be especially threatening and would result in vigorous attempts to bolster or affirm our view of ourselves and the world.

Two Distinct Modes of Defense Against the Fear of Death

Terror management research has consistently shown that reminders of our mortality make us especially defensive of our cultural worldviews and our self-esteem (for a review, see Greenberg, Solomon, & Pyszczynski, 1997). This defensiveness may take the form of seeking support, consensus, and inclusion from others who share our beliefs, but it can also lead to derogating and aggressing against those whose beliefs differ. That death would exaggerate intergroup conflict, and may be ultimately responsible for it, seems like quite a theoretical leap. Wouldn't one defend against death anxiety in more "death-focused" ways?

The inevitability of death is certainly not a thought upon which people enjoy dwelling. Individuals who report high levels of death anxiety are more distressed and less satisfied with life than those who report lower levels of death anxiety (White & Handal, 1991). People defend against their knowledge of death in a variety of direct threat-focused ways, by suppressing death-related thoughts, overestimating the amount of time they have left, and underestimating their susceptibility to disease and disaster (for a review, see Pyszczynski, Greenberg, & Solomon, 1999). They also tend to distance themselves from those who are ill by describing themselves as not like "those people who get cancer" (Pyszczynski et al., 1995). These defenses are proximal; they occur when thoughts of death are in current focal consciousness and they have a direct and logical connection to the problem of death. However, defenses of this sort have clear limitations in that it is impossible to successfully deny the inevitability of death. Although good genes, proper nutrition, and a healthy lifestyle might buy us an additional decade or two of life, they do nothing to undermine the inescapable reality that death is inevitable. Just as we know our names regardless of whether we are currently thinking of them or not, we *know* that death is an inevitable fact of life, regardless of what thoughts we might be currently entertaining in focal consciousness.

The terror management defenses of finding meaning in the cultural worldview and value in ourselves function to assuage the potential for terror, which this knowledge creates. These are distal defenses, in the sense that they bear no direct semantic or logical connection to the problem of death. They help us cope with our unconscious knowledge of the inevitability of death by enabling us to view ourselves as valuable contributors to an eternal meaningful reality. By maintaining faith in our cultural worldviews and the valuable roles that we play within this context, we are able to keep thoughts of death safely outside of consciousness. Indeed, recent research has shown that defending one's cultural worldview reduces the accessibility of death-related thoughts. The pursuit of self-esteem and faith in our cultural worldviews increase as the accessibility of death-related thoughts increases (even if such thoughts have been made accessible without the individual's awareness using subliminal death primes; Arndt, Greenberg, Pyszczynski, & Solomon, 1997), and function to keep the accessibility of such thoughts as low as possible. Once such thoughts enter consciousness, these distal defenses are discontinued in favor of the more proximal defenses that attack the problem of death in a more head-on fashion.

Empirical Support for Terror Management Theory

To date, well over 80 separate experiments conducted in 5 countries have provided empirical support for TMT. This research has been focused on two major hypotheses and their corollaries.

The *anxiety-buffer hypothesis* states that, to the extent that a psychological structure provides protection against anxiety, then strengthening that structure should reduce one's proneness to exhibit anxiety and anxiety-related thoughts and behavior in response to reminders of what one is afraid of. Research has shown that high self-esteem, both dispositional and situationally induced, leads to lower levels of physiological arousal and self-reported anxiety while watching a death-related video or anticipating a painful electric shock (Greenberg, Solomon et al., 1992) and reduces cognitive distortions designed to deny one's vulnerability to an early death (Greenberg et al., 1993). High self-esteem has also been shown to eliminate the effects that reminders of one's mortality otherwise produce on the tendency to defend one's cultural worldview (Harmon-Jones et al., 1997). Other studies have shown that both boosts to self-esteem and defense of one's cultural worldview reduce the increase in the accessibility of death-related thoughts produced by priming thoughts of death (Arndt, Greenberg, Solomon, Pyszczynski, & Simon, 1997; Harmon-Jones et al., 1997).

The vast majority of terror management research has been focused on the mortality salience hypothesis, which states that, to the extent that a psychological structure provides protection against anxiety, then reminding people of the source of their anxiety should lead to increased need for that structure and increased tendencies to defend it against threats. These studies have operationalized reminders of death in a variety of ways, including open-ended questions about death, death anxiety scales, graphic videos of fatal auto accidents, proximity to a funeral home, and subliminally presented death-related words. They have consistently shown that mortality salience leads to more favorable evaluations of people and ideas that support one's worldview and more unfavorable evaluations of people and ideas that threaten one's worldview.

To cite just a few examples, mortality salience has been shown to lead to increased liking for those who praise their worldview and decreased liking for those who criticize it (e.g., Greenberg et al., 1990), increased liking for and behavioral approach toward ingroup members and decreased liking for and behavioral avoidance of outgroup members (e.g., Ochsman & Mathy, 1993), harsher punishments for moral transgressors and higher reward recommendations for those who uphold moral principles (e.g., Florian & Mikulincer, 1998a; Rosenblatt, Greenberg, Solomon, Pyszczynski, & Lyon, 1989), and increased aggression against attitudinally dissimilar others (McGregor et al., 1998). Research has also shown that mortality salience increases consensus estimates for important attitudes (Pyszczynski et al., 1996), optimal distinctiveness striving (Simon et al., 1997), and discomfort when treating a culturally valued object with disrespect (Greenberg, Porteus, Simon, Pyszczynski, & Solomon, 1995). More recent research has shown that mortality salience also increases self-esteem striving, in the form of increased risk-taking among those who value risk (Ben-Ari, Florian, & Mikulincer, 1999), increased identification with the physical body among those high in body self-esteem (Goldenberg, McCoy, Pyszczynski, Greenberg, & Solomon, 1999), and increased tolerance among those committed to this value (Greenberg, Simon, Pyszczynski, Solomon, & Chatel, 1992).

The effects of mortality salience appear to be specific to the problem of death. Parallel conditions in which subjects are induced to think about other aversive events, such as failing a test in an important class, giving a speech in front of a large audience, being socially ostracized, being paralyzed, or experiencing intense physical pain, do not produce parallel effects on worldview defense and self-esteem striving (e.g., Arndt, Greenberg, Solomon et al., 1997; Greenberg, Pyszczynski, Solomon, Simon, & Breus, 1994; Greenberg, Porteus et al., 1995; Schimel et al., 1999).

In sum, the evidence available to date provides strong and consistent evidence that people are protected against death-related concerns by maintaining faith in their cultural worldviews and a sense of personal value within the context of their worldviews. High levels of self-esteem and faith in one's cultural worldview have been shown to lead to lower levels of anxiety, anxiety-related behavior, and access to death-related thoughts. Reminders of one's mortality have been shown to lead to increased commitment to and defense of one's cultural worldview and increased self-esteem striving. Taken as a whole, the empirical evidence provides compelling support for the TMT view that people need self-esteem and faith in their cultural worldviews because of the protection against death-related concerns that these psychological structures provide.

Developmental Changes in the Cultural Anxiety Buffer

It would be naïve to presume that terror management processes are the same at every stage of life. Unfortunately, very little research has attempted to address the effect of development on terror management processes or on the terror itself. In fact, most studies to date have utilized the subject pool of convenience: undergraduates. Thus, the exploration of TMT processes has been focused primarily on the 18–24 age range. A few notable exceptions, in the lab and field, with broader age ranges have allowed us to comfortably conclude that these processes are not age specific and do in fact occur from childhood to old age. For example, the very first published terror management study demonstrated the effect of mortality salience on the amount of bond recommended for a woman accused of prostitution, in a sample of middle-aged municipal court judges (Rosenblatt et al., 1989, Study 1). In addition, the field experiments in which participants were interviewed either in front of or 100 meters away from a funeral home used participants ranging in age from 13 to 80 (Pyszczynski et al., 1996).

Nonetheless, we know that cognitive abilities change over the course of the life span (e.g., Piaget, 1952; Salthouse, 1998). It is also obvious that the proximity to death increases over the life span. It seems reasonable to suggest, then, that to the extent that TMT processes are influenced by underlying cognitive abilities and mortality salience, these processes might be differentially manifested across the life span.

A recent investigation of TMT processes in children illustrates the importance of sophisticated cognitive abilities in the use of the distal defenses (Florian & Mikulincer, 1998b). Ingroup preference and outgroup derogation in response to mortality salience was found in children as young as 11 years old. As in research with adult samples (Harmon-Jones, Greenberg, Solomon, & Simon, 1996), this effect was particularly strong among children with lower self-esteem. However, younger children (7-year-olds), did not respond with differential preference for an ingroup over an outgroup child. These children responded to mortality salience by rejecting the other child—regardless of ingroup or outgroup membership. Clearly both age groups were affected by thoughts of death; however only the older children, perhaps because of their cognitive maturity, sought refuge in the cultural worldview. (For an excellent developmental account of cultural worldview defense see Florian and Mikulincer, 1998b.)

That worldview defenses develop and change over the course of life is intriguing, and leads us to examine the form such processes might take in the aged; preliminary evidence indicates that age does indeed influence how people respond. McCoy, Solomon, Pyszczynski, and Greenberg (1999) had elderly participants ranging in age from 57–87 report their subjective life expectancy following a mortality salience or dental pain control induction. As neurotics have been shown to be a group especially defensive following reminders of death (Goldenberg, Pyszczynski, McCoy, Greenberg, & Solomon, 1999), our elderly participants also completed a scale measuring neuroticism before the manipulation of mortality salience. Based on Erikson's (e.g., 1985) notion that the very end of life is fundamentally different than other stages, we were inclined to expect differences in young-old and old-old participants. However we had no a priori expectations about the specific pattern of differences that might be obtained. Our general prediction was that in highly neurotic individuals, who tend to have weak anxiety-buffers, mortality salience should lead to especially high life expectancy estimates. This prediction was partially supported. Among younger participants (ages 57–72), those high in neuroticism exaggerated their subjective life expectancy following mortality salience, whereas those low in neuroticism actually exhibited decreased subjective life expectancy. However, the older (ages 73–87) participants reported significantly lower subjective life expectancies following mortality salience regardless of level of neuroticism. These findings suggest that, whereas the young-old high in neuroticism need to perceive that death is far in the future, the low neurotic young-elderly and the old-old in general may have achieved greater acceptance of death. Therefore, following mortality salience, they become particularly unlikely to perceive death as far off. Although extensive theoretical and empirical inquiry into the influence of mortality salience on aging and the aged has yet to be undertaken, these findings will hopefully serve as a first step in this direction.

What role does the nearness to death play in the ability to suppress thoughts of death, and death anxiety, by clinging to a worldview from which we derive self-esteem? Will these processes be affected by the salience of our own declining bodies and the deaths of our peers and loved ones? In terror management terms, what effect does this increased mortality salience have on the defensive processes that we use to cope with the inevitability of death?

The Plight of the Elderly: A Grim Picture?

The defensive buffers used in early and mid-life seem likely to become less effective in managing our fear of death as we grow older. Our cultural worldviews are effective because we believe them to be right and true and we believe that others do, or should, agree with this assessment. However, as we age, the correctness and consensual nature of our cultural worldviews are inevitably challenged. As Esposito (1987) put it, the elderly are " . . . a dying breed, the remainder of a dwindling cohort. They represent a specific period of history and a worldview that is dying with them" (p. 69). The world is constantly changing, and as new worldviews emerge, it may be difficult for the elderly to find protection and solace in a worldview that seems to be fading with them. Furthermore, many standards of value, easily achieved in youth, may now be beyond reach. The body may simply be too slow or too weak to successfully perform its previous role. Although the elderly do not decline in intellectual ability or memory as drastically as was once believed, explicit memory is compromised with age and reaction time is increased (Salthouse, 1998). These declines may make achieving past standards more difficult.

Inability to achieve these standards is but one facet of the diminution of the defensive structures that served one well earlier in life. The present youthful majority may no longer value the role for which the elderly person was lauded in their youth. This may be especially true for contemporary elderly who have witnessed a century of such rapid technological advancement that their roles may have become outdated even before they lost the ability to achieve them. Most observers seem to think that the pace of changes in science, technology, and cultural beliefs will only continue to accelerate in the years to come. In the past, the elderly could make use of the cultural worldview for its protective function up to the point of inability to achieve the standards for the role. This may hold true today for those elderly who reside in less technologically dependent parts of the world. Rural elderly have the advantage of a community that continues to value them because of their knowledge and close emotional attachments (Rowles, 1984). However it is becoming increasingly probable in this advancing technological age that many of the roles the elderly pursued earlier in life are on their way to obsolescence, making it increasingly difficult for the elderly to derive self-esteem from their cultural worldviews.

In this way, both sources of protection from the fear of nonbeing are compromised. How then is the elderly person to cope? The reality of one's own impending death is readily apparent; it is much less easily repressed or denied. Simultaneously, the changing times and a lack of ability to attain past standards have weakened the defenses, those that would repress and help us to deny death—the cultural worldview and self-esteem. The prognosis appears bleak; exposure to the " . . . Dread of ultimate nonbeing" seems certain (Erikson, 1985). A spiral into despair, neurosis, depression, and bitterness could all be predicted.

In experiments where these conditions—mortality salience and/or threats to self-esteem or the worldview—have been manipulated with relatively youthful participants, we have seen increases in defensiveness. This defensiveness has most often been linked to the cultural worldview, with threatened participants bolstering the worldview through derogation or aggression toward attitudinally dissimilar others. Does this imply that the elderly are likely to become increasingly defensive, bitter, and hostile as they grow older? This may indeed happen in some individuals. However, the difference for the elderly is that these threats are not an acute state easily dealt with through defensive fortification of the worldview or self-esteem. On the contrary, the elderly face a chronic state of mortality salience coupled with a possibly lessened capacity to use the cultural worldview or resultant self-esteem to maximally protect the self. However, one has only to look to studies of the psychological well being of the elderly to know that the true prognosis is far from the grim picture we have just painted.

The Psychological Resilience of Older Adults

Empirical support for increased psychological well-being among older adults is plentiful. The deterioration of the body and the increased exposure to the realities of death through the loss of loved ones does not appear to be linked to an increase in death anxiety. In fact, there is evidence that experience of death anxiety decreases over the course of the life span (Rasmussen & Brems, 1996). Older adults do not express more death anxiety than younger adults (Templer, Ruff, & Franks, 1971; Tate, 1982), and in some studies have been shown to exhibit lower death anxiety than younger adults (Devins, 1979; Cole, 1979). Thus the elderly do not appear to be living in a state of constant existential anxiety as one might expect from the age-associated increase in mortality salience.

Nor does chronically low self-esteem appear to be any more a problem for the elderly than for younger adults, as the grim picture painted above might predict. In fact, some studies suggest that the elderly may have higher self-esteem than the young (Dietz, 1996). For a group that might be expected to be spiraling into despair under the weight of increased mortality salience without the protective comfort of the cultural worldview, the elderly appear to be faring quite well. They report themselves as more content (Lawton, Kleban, & Dean, 1993) and as having better psychological well-being than the young (Blazer, Crowell, George, & Landerman, 1986). Despite the loss of significant correlates of life satisfaction, the elderly report no decline in life satisfaction (Diener & Suh, 1998), and have reported more satisfaction with present life than the young in some studies (Heckhausen, 1997). Clearly the elderly are not suffering from the combination of increased mortality salience and decreased effectiveness of the cultural worldview. How could this be?

One possibility is that, as with other abilities and skills, we simply get better at managing our death-related anxieties as we age. After all, the older one is, the more time one has had to perfect one's anxiety-buffering tactics. It is also possible, however, that the elderly have found alternative routes for self-esteem maintenance other than through the consensual worldview employed by younger adults. It may be that the elderly are not unaffected by the increase in mortality salience associated with aging, but rather, that this combination of increased mortality salience and decreased effectiveness of the typical modes of buffering anxiety leads to psychological transformations that leave the elderly *better* defended than they were in their youth. It is entirely conceivable that the elderly, in their accumulated wisdom, have found means of shielding themselves from terror that are more effective than the contingent sense of value provided by the worldview. Clearly this would be adaptive. If terror management processes follow a developmental track, what would the end goal of such a track be? The end of the line should be the station that provides the best possible defense against the fear of nonbeing.

☐ Transcending the Self

"The greatest limitation for man is the self."
—Carl Jung (1961, p. 325)

Stepping back from our current focus on aging and simply attempting to imagine a better, more effective defense against the terror of death returns us to the original paradox that gave rise to the human existential dilemma in the first place. Terror management theory posits that the fear of death results from the conflict between the desire for continued life and the simultaneous knowledge that we will inevitably die. For most of our lives, we struggle valiantly to deny this terrifying reality. Successful aging may require a different approach to this paradox.

Clearly the elderly have not found effective means of escaping the inevitability of death. In fact, this inevitability becomes only more apparent as we age. As denial becomes increasingly difficult due to advancing age, this may force us to try new ways of coming to grips with the problem. What of acceptance, then? Several theorists have argued that acceptance of the inevitable is a form of exerting control over the uncontrollable (Aldwin, 1994; Brandtstaedter & Greve, 1994; Thomae, 1992). Death is inevitable, yes, but one may be able to control one's psychological reaction to it. This form of control has been termed "secondary control" (Rothbaum, Weisz, & Snyder, 1982) and there is evidence that the elderly are particularly adept at exerting this form of control (Heckhausen & Schulz, 1993). Perhaps the elderly are able to discover new means of coping that are more effective than denial and that enable them to accept the reality of their own impending death. Indeed, if one were able to eliminate the desire for continued existence of the self, the inevitable reality of death would no longer be threatening. This suggests that a better defense against the terror associated with nonbeing is to eliminate the desire to be a "being" . . . to come closer to accepting the inevitability of death.

The central point of our analysis is that *the decreasing effectiveness of one's earlier means of coping, coupled with the increased salience of death that comes with advancing age, provide an impetus to psychological reorganization that ultimately functions to help the older adult cope with the nearness to death that is an inherent part of the later years of life.* The reduced effectiveness of one's old modes of coping leave the elderly individual little choice other than to either change or suffer the consequences of facing death with an anxiety-buffer that is rapidly losing its effectiveness. Of course not everyone makes this transition, and those who do, make it to varying degrees of effectiveness. Although research shows that the *average* elderly individual is no worse off and perhaps even better off than his or her younger counterparts, there is great variability in how and how well people cope with the problems of advancing age and proximity to death. Depression, anxiety, and despair, and the problems that go with them, such as alcoholism, destructive anger, and health problems, are widespread among the elderly population. Successful aging requires a transformation of self to make one better able to cope with the different realities with which one is faced in later years.

Accepting the inevitability of death requires a fairly radical transformation of the self. One way to accomplish this is to loosen the connections between the self and aspects of life; after all, the tragedy of death is the loss of life. The gradual physical changes that accompany aging may contribute significantly to this process. Although not inevitable, the tendency for eyesight, hearing, smell, taste, and physical abilities in general to deteriorate may gradually reduce one's attachment to these components of life, thereby facilitating the process of letting go of life and accepting death.

Another aid in this process may be the gradual letting go of the self, for in death, along with life, the self is presumably lost. Of course this would not often entail literally losing the self. As we have argued elsewhere (Pyszczynski, Greenberg, & Solomon, 1998; see also Becker, 1969), the self is the mechanism through which humans achieve some measure of self-determination and control over their own fate. Without a self, we would be unable to engage in coherent purposeful behavior. What needs to be accomplished is a freeing of the self from dependence on social consensus and the social conception of reality put forth by the mainstream consensual cultural worldview. This is no simple task to accomplish. However, the difficulties that many elderly people have maintaining a sense of meaning and self-worth within the context of the mainstream worldview provides an impetus for such disengagement and reinvestment.

☐ The Process of Reinventing the Self

Like all developmental changes, the transformation of self that is needed to facilitate successful aging occurs slowly over an extended period of time. As the individual experiences difficulties maintaining security from his or her previously established defenses, s/he alternates between increasingly vigorous attempts to maintain the old structures and tentative forays into new ways of viewing the world and oneself. Whereas the early stages of this transformation are probably dominated by attempts to cling to one's old defenses, the latter stages reflect the emergence of new modes of construing self and reality that are used, tentatively at first, and later with greater confidence, to cope with the problem of approaching mortality. This is undoubtedly a highly individualized process, which proceeds differently for different individuals. As we noted above, many people may persist in clinging to their longstanding defenses and exhibit little in the way of meaningful psychological change. In the following paragraphs, we outline some of the tactics the maturing adult is likely to employ, with no implication of a rigid or universal developmental sequence that applies to all. These tactics feed on each other, in the sense that successful deployment of one often paves the way for more effective use of others.

Defending One's Pre-existing Worldview

As suggested above, with advancing age, one's pre-existing conception of self and reality are likely to become less effective as buffers against anxiety, either because the aging individual is less able to meet the standards for the roles from which they had previously derived their value, or because, due to changing times, the cultural worldview they subscribe to is no longer the norm, and the role they fulfill is no longer valued. Most people are likely to initially respond to this threat with attempts to protect the existing anxiety buffer, perhaps by derogating the new order ("What's wrong with kids these days? Things were better back in my day") or striving harder then ever to demonstrate one's competence ("I'll show those young whippersnappers how to . . . "). We suspect that such behavior is especially prevalent among middle-aged and relatively young elderly individuals. These strategies might include various tactics for minimizing threats to the worldview, downward adjustment of the standards of the worldview to the realm of the attainable, and cognitive reframing of events to emphasize the positive aspects of one's competencies and situation.

Minimizing Threat to the Cultural Worldview

By minimizing exposure to alternative viewpoints the aging individual is able to protect his or her worldview from the threat of dissenting opinion. If contact is limited to familiar others, and, within those familiar others, to those who agree with one's worldview, the elderly individual may continue to utilize their pre-existing shield and avoid protracted assaults to his or her worldview. Consistent with this possibility is evidence that people, increasingly, narrow their social networks as they get older (Carstensen, 1992). One perspective on this limiting of social contact is that the elderly are simply less mobile, that they are unable to sustain relationships due to inability to visit or receive visits. However, more recent research suggests that there may be a more strategic and motivational impetus for this limiting of the social network.

Socio-emotional selectivity theory, as proposed by Carstensen (1992), posits that the elderly "prune" their social network to keep rewarding relationships and discard less rewarding ones. From this perspective, the elderly select relationship partners based on the potential of the relationship to maximize positive affect and minimize negative affect (Carstensen, Gross, & Fung, 1998). To the extent that such affective consequences of relationships with others often reflect how the others impinge on one's worldview and self-esteem, this implies that the aging individual may be selectively narrowing his or her social network so as to maximize contact with those who support their anxiety-buffering conceptions of self and world and to minimize contact with those who threaten these conceptions. Research shows that older adults place more importance on anticipated affect when selecting relationship partners, whereas the young place more importance on information availability and reward potential of future contact (Fredrickson & Carstensen, 1990). Research also shows that older adults, in contrast with the young, choose less confrontational responses to threat (Blanchard-Fields, Jahnke,

& Camp, 1995). This may be an active response calculated to reduce challenges to their worldview. It may be that the elderly are selecting their social relationships to maintain the validity of their worldview, simply choosing not to associate with those who disagree. When such contact does occur they avoid active confrontations.

This approach, pruning the social network, is a viable defense only to the extent that one no longer requires interaction with a wide range of other people. In the first half of life it is through our relationships with others that we are able to gather information needed to form and consolidate a self to protect us from terror. Without immersion in a large social network this process would be difficult. The older adult, on the other hand, is likely to have sufficient experience, both direct and through reflected appraisals from others, to have developed a reasonably confident conception of self and the world. Thus, as we age we are likely to require less and less information from others. For this reason, the elderly may be especially able to choose their social relationships not on the basis of the information they provide and their potential for future gain, but on the emotional support they offer in the present. Consequently, the use of this strategy of limiting one's social network and minimizing threat to the cultural worldview and self may be more viable for older adults than for younger ones.

Downward Adjustment of Standards

At all ages it is possible to adjust the standards of the cultural worldview to facilitate their attainment. Decreasing the discrepancy between our actual and ideal selves has been shown to be a desirable and effective goal in psychotherapy (Horney, 1950; Rogers, 1954). Rogers used a Q-sort technique to demonstrate that people not only think better of themselves after therapy; they also reduce their ideal standards to more humanly attainable aspirations. Horney denounced unrealistically high standards for the self ideal as the "tyranny of the should" in the "search for glory" and urged movement to more attainable but nevertheless laudable standards for the self. By changing the expectations for a given role and thus rendering them more attainable, the older adult may be able to continue to derive self-esteem despite dwindling abilities. For example, for a young person, fulfillment of the role of 'teacher' may mean long hours spent on one's feet and endless grading of papers. However for an elderly person this role may be fulfilled by one-on-one tutoring. What it means to be a good teacher has changed; no longer is success based on the achievements of a classroom of students, but rather on the achievement of a single student. The role has been adjusted to meet the present capacities of the individual, thus facilitating the experience of success in meeting the role expectations. This approach, resetting goals to the realm of the attainable (Brandstaedter & Greve, 1994), is a strategy well documented in the elderly (Brandstaedter & Rothermund, 1994). As age increases, the individual may strategically choose goals that are more age appropriate and reduce the importance of goals that are no longer feasible (Heckhausen, 1997; Schulz & Heckhausen, 1996). These adjustments in goals may result in less discrepancy between the ideal self and the actual self (Ryff, 1991). As we age, and increasingly utilize this strategy, the discrepancy between our actual and ideal self continues to diminish.

Recall that our sense of value results from our comparison of the self to the contingencies of the worldview. To the extent that we are able to adjust the standards and, thereby, preserve our ability to meet these standards, we may continue to derive self-esteem from our long-held worldview. The clear implication of a decreasing discrepancy between our selves and our standards is a gradual rise in self-esteem. Why not use this strategy in youth? In youth, objective standards of success have real consequence. They determine our rate of pay and societal acceptance: both required commodities in youth. As we age, due to retirement we may no longer be paid for our role; we also may have pruned our social networks such that we no longer have to prove ourselves to earn acceptance as we did in youth. This strategy, too, becomes more viable as we age.

Cognitive Reframing of Events

Other strategies available to the elderly person to maintain and protect self-esteem are less dependent on one's social position and are used by individuals of all ages. However there is some evidence that the elderly make more use of certain strategies. The elderly are particularly adept at "downward social comparison" (Festinger, 1954; Wills, 1987), a process through which they compare themselves to those who are worse off, thus making their own situation, the happy lucky one. An unfortunate side effect of this outlook is the coincident tendency to hold those less fortunate responsible for their plight and thus avoid guilt for one's lucky position. Nevertheless, this process of comparing to those who are worse off can effectively serve self-evaluation needs (Hegelson & Taylor, 1993), and when utilized in response to threat, downward comparison has been shown to increase self-esteem (Taylor & Lobel, 1989). The elderly are more likely than the young to believe that they are "better off" than others of the same age (Heckhausen & Brim, 1997; Rickabaugh & Tomlinson-Keasey, 1997). This type of reframing seems particularly effective in maintaining psychological well-being and self-esteem in the face of aging (Heidrich & Ryff, 1993; Kleinke & Miller, 1998; Robinson-Whelen & Kiecolt-Glaser, 1997). As long as the elderly individual believes they have it better than most, and that decline is inescapable, they can take comfort in their position of relative well-being.

A general tendency toward optimism is another defensive strategy commonly used by the elderly. The elderly report fewer negative emotional experiences (Gross, Carstensen, Pasupathi, & Tsai, 1997), are more likely to view situations from a positive angle (Heckhausen & Krueger, 1993), and are more likely to cognitively reinterpret an event to emphasize the positive aspects than the young (Diehl, Coyle, & Labouvie-Vief, 1996). As a general defensive strategy, this propensity to "see the glass as half full" in even the most dire of circumstances must be of great comfort to the aging individual. However, prerequisites to such cognitive reinterpretation are both the acceptance that the event itself is unchangeable and the choice to interpret the event in a positive light. In younger years, the individual may react to such negative events with more of a confrontational style and be less prone to accept and consequently reinterpret the event. Vigilance for negative events and active confrontation with those who might be threatening may be adaptive in youth because it increases one's ability to escape such threats when they occur or prevent them from happening altogether. Therefore, optimistic interpretations may be more commonly utilized by the elderly as a powerful and efficient strategy.

The strategies outlined above are just a few examples of the many ways the aging adult might struggle to maintain the protective function of self-esteem despite the age-related changes that he or she is experiencing. By minimizing exposure to dissenting opinions, redefining the standards for achieving the self-ideal, adjusting goals to the realm of the achievable, and reinterpreting events to emphasize their positive aspects, the elderly person is able to maintain, and perhaps increase self-esteem without relinquishing his/her hold on the cultural worldview. These strategies provide the foundation for further exploration of alternative defensive strategies against the fear of non-being. Armed with this protected self-esteem, the ability to accept and positively reinterpret inevitable events, and less reliance on the social world at large through trimmed social networks, the elderly individual may embark on the journey toward reconstructing the self.

Attaining Independence from Social Validation

A critical transition in this journey involves attaining increasing independence from the need for social validation of one's self and worldview. Much of the anxiety and heartache of everyday life results from our dependence on the validation (or lack thereof) that we receive from others for maintenance of our conceptions of self and reality. Although most young people like to think of themselves as independent and free from needs for validation and approval from others, it is not until the later years of life that something approximating this ideal is possible for most people. Whereas it is essential for young people, who are building their identities, struggling to fulfill social roles, and striving to generally "make it" in society, to rely on others for feedback about the appropriateness of their attitudes and behaviors, this may be less necessary for older adults who have already established who they are, fulfilled a successful niche in life, and who may, in fact, be gradually becoming less essential for the day-to-day operation of social institutions. The defensive responses, discussed above, of distancing from the current vision of social reality, becoming more selective in one's social contacts, and reframing one's experience may be the first step in this gradual reduction in dependence on the opinions of others. These defensive tactics may set the stage for a more independent mode of functioning that leaves one's anxiety-buffering psychological structures more secure and less susceptible to threat—and therefore less in need of defense.

Of course *complete* independence from social validation is probably not attainable for most people at any point in life, nor would it be particularly desirable or adaptive. Social opinion is a powerful motivating force that helps keep individuals in line with the requirements of orderly group living. Reliance on social consensus for validation of self and worldview should be thought of as operating on a continuum, with most people falling somewhere in the middle, and those who occupy either extreme as likely to suffer negative psychological and social consequences. We are simply suggesting that with advancing age, many adults reduce their dependence on others for such validation and move toward the independent end of the spectrum. This may be why some elderly individuals are seen as eccentric and idiosyncratic. Indeed, this reduced need for social consensus may help explain some behavior that might be labeled as senile. The point here is that although increasing independence from social validation can be a sign of successful adaptation to one's later years, taking this independence too far can be maladaptive and lead to social ostracism and perhaps institutionalization. Nonetheless, up to a point, decreased reliance on the opinions of others is likely to be associated with a more resilient buffer against anxiety, and consequently lessened defensiveness and better overall psychological functioning.

Increased Individualization of One's Worldview

TMT assumes that each individual creates his or her individualized version of the cultural worldview by integrating the multitude of experiences to which they have been exposed. Thus, at least in theory, our worldviews have the *potential* for constant change as we integrate new experiences with existing structures. Of course, a constantly changing conception of self and reality would hardly be adaptive in most circumstances (cf., Swann, 1987) and, consequently, such flexibility and openness is relatively rare. Because of the defensive anxiety-buffering functions that these structures serve, people are highly committed to them and struggle valiantly to defend them against threats. Indeed, the bulk of the terror management literature documents the many ways in which reminders of our mortality increase our efforts to defend our conceptions of self and world against information that might change them.

However, with advancing age and decreased reliance on social consensus for validation, it may be possible to increase this flexibility and openness, and create a more individualized idiosyncratic conception of self and the world. One such individualized conception may be one of religion. Intrinsic religiousness and spirituality have been shown to become both more important as we age, and to be protective against the anxiety associated with thoughts of death (Wong, 1989; see Tomer & Eliason, Chapter 9, in this volume).

Although in our younger years conformity to social norms and acceptance of the consensually shared group vision of reality may be adaptive, in that it helps us establish social relationships, fulfill social roles, and generally maximize our potential for social and occupational success, this may be less necessary as we age because these things are already established and society's need for our services may be lessened. The decreased reliance on others for validation of our worldviews further facilitates the individualized construction of our own unique vision of reality that is more responsive to experience and less vulnerable to threat.

Humanistic psychologists, such as Maslow (1968), Rogers (1954), and more recently, Deci and Ryan (1980), have argued that the more an individual actively processes and integrates external values, norms, or other sources of information, and thus transforms them into their own unique conceptions, the greater his or her sense of freedom, self-determination, and general psychological well-being.

From these perspectives, a sense of self-determination and freedom is required for optimal psychological functioning, and people will go to great lengths to restore this sense of freedom when it is threatened (cf., Brehm, 1966). The literature on reactance documents the many ways in which people rebel against threats to their freedom (for a review, see Brehm & Brehm, 1981) which provides further support for the view that a subjective sense of self-determination is a highly valued and psychologically useful commodity.

Self-Complexity, Integration, and the Life Review

Many developmental theorists have proposed that one of the tasks of aging is to undertake a "Life Review" wherein one evaluates the successes and failures of the past and attempts to integrate these experiences and derive a sense of meaning (Wong, 1989). From a terror management perspective, one would expect this increased meaning to provide added protection against anxiety. Consistent with this reasoning, research suggests that life review activity is indeed associated with lower death anxiety among the elderly (Fishman, 1992). In what specific ways might a review of one's past experiences protect the self from death anxiety?

The life review proposed by many theorists can be understood as an opportunity to increase self-knowledge and enhance self-understanding (Quackenbush & Barnett, 1995). This review entails a re-visiting of past selves, roles that were pursued in youth, increasing the complexity of the self and illustrating one's ability to derive self-esteem from a number of past roles. It may remind aging individuals that they have survived and prospered after many changes in the past, which may increase their hope that they can successfully adapt to the many changes with which aging faces them. It may also remind them of how truly varied people are, which should further reduce their dependence on social consensus for maintenance of their essential anxiety-buffering structures. Put simply, the life review may help one gain perspective on one's life and how it relates to other people and the world at large.

This self-understanding can be viewed as providing increased clarity and complexity of self-concept (Campbell, 1990; Linville, 1985), both of which have been shown to be associated with higher levels of psychological well-being. Clarity of self-concept is positively correlated with self-esteem (Campbell, Trapnell, Heine, Katz, Lavallee, & Lehman, 1996); a review of the past may provide the information necessary for constructing a more stable, well-defined self-concept. Cognitive complexity has been shown to lead to more stable and higher self-esteem and provide protection against depression (Linville, 1985, 1987; Pyszczynski & Greenberg, 1987). The complexity of self made apparent by the life review allows the elderly person to derive self-esteem from a number of possible selves, and, therefore, to compensate for a loss of esteem from one role by focusing on achievement in another (Cross & Markus, 1991; Kling & Ryff, 1997). Indeed, those elderly individuals with more complex self-representations have been found to have lower rates of depression than elderly with less complex self-representations (Labouvie-Vief, Chiodo, Goguen, & Diehl, 1995).

Self-efficacy

One of the most basic differences between the old and the young is that the elderly simply have had more experience with life—and their role in it—than the young. They have had more time to accumulate knowledge, successes, and a broader variety of experiences. Because they have a lifetime of self-related information to consult, their need for social consensus and specific group identities is lessened. The elderly can look back at the past as a "stockpile" of self-understanding (Gurin & Brim, 1984). The elderly have the unique ability to derive self-esteem from the *experienced* rather than the *experiencing*:

> It is true that the old have no opportunities, no possibilities for the future. But they have more than that. Instead of possibilities for the future, they have realities they have realized—and nothing and nobody can ever remove these assets from the past. (Frankl, 1959, p. 151)

In this regard the elderly are truly enviable. In addition to the self-esteem looking back on past accomplishments may offer, the true jewel in all this wealth of knowledge is the feeling of self-efficacy that awareness of such experiences provide. The elderly person who is able to pull a global sense of mastery and efficacy from the experiences of the past, rather than simply reveling in specific instances of heroism of the present, has a kind of freedom from the limitations of deriving self-esteem from specific prescriptions of the worldview. Research suggests that this kind of reminiscence is indeed associated with greater well-being in the elderly (Gurin & Brimm, 1984; Wong & Watt, 1991). To the extent that this reminiscence leads to feelings of mastery and self-efficacy, the elderly person no longer requires validation of the "self" and is able to let go of the contingent self-esteem of the cultural worldview.

In a world of growing loss, the elderly have at hand a valuable and comforting resource—their stockpile of self-understanding (Gurin & Brim, 1984). They are in a position to draw upon this resource and derive esteem from recollection of past success, to utilize their self-complexity to compensate for failures by recalling other roles, and most importantly, to derive a sense of mastery, competence, and self-efficacy. To the extent that reviewing one's life creates these valuable assets, one is able to detach that much more from reliance on the cultural worldview for derivation of self-esteem and protection from terror.

Broadening Social Identity: Generativity

To this point, we have depicted the process of transcending the self as involving primarily a lessened dependence on social consensus and a disengagement from the mainstream cultural worldview. This is only part of the picture, however, and without a vital addition, would likely leave the elderly person happy but largely useless to those around him. There is a paradox inherent in creating a more idiosyncratic individualized worldview. The more idiosyncratic one's worldview becomes, the more out of step with the rest of the world it becomes, and the more other existing conceptions inevitably contradict it. Thus far we have emphasized the positive aspects of such idiosyncratic conceptions and the reduction in potential for threat that results from decreased need for social validation. We have also noted, however, that, if taken too far, these changes can leave the elderly individual alone and alienated, without the vital sense of connection to ongoing human life necessary to provide the symbolic immortality needed for continued equanimity. How is this paradox resolved?

Erick Erikson (1985) proposed that the final development crisis that must be resolved is one of ego-integrity vs. despair, which is successfully resolved by acting on a desire to "give something" to future generations, to help the next generation better adapt to the realities of life. In Erikson's view, human development in later life entails "widening circles of identification" from family and peers, to the culture, and finally to the human community at large and a shift from "I am _____" to "I am what survives me." Alfred Adler's (1929) theorizing emphasized the importance of a similar construct, social interest, for optimal psychological functioning and well-being throughout the lifespan. Similarly, Otto Rank (e.g., Rank, 1932) posited that the fear of death produced by human consciousness engenders a simultaneous need to distinguish ourselves as individuals and to be securely embedded in a collective social order.

Robert Jay Lifton (1983) suggests that psychological well-being in old age requires a sense of self in the context of time and an acknowledgment of those that have come before us and those who will come ahead. Lifton proposed that there are a number of ways to attain a sense of death transcendence through generativity. Perhaps most pertinent to the elderly are the passing on into the future traces of one's self through children and grandchildren, spiritual beliefs in the soul or oneness with the universe, contributions to groups and causes, and one's teachings, guidance, and positive effects on others. Of course the life review can reinforce one's faith that one has made these types of contributions to the continuity of life.

More recently, McAdams suggests that we should adjust our autobiographical narrative or "stories we live by" to "generate" legacies of self concerned with "establishing and guiding the next generation" (McAdams, de St. Aubin, & Logan, 1993). Indeed, the value of caring for others as a pathway to self-transcendence and improved well-being is central to a wide range of religious and ideological systems, from Buddhism to Christianity to Marxism. By identifying with large groups that encompass a variety of more limited worldviews, the individual can create a broad overarching cultural worldview. If sufficiently broad, it would be near impossible to be exposed to threat in the form of opposing viewpoints.

The little empirical research available on this broadening of identity is generally consistent with the above arguments. Elderly individuals who focus more on others tend to have better psychological and physical well-being than those focused more narrowly on their own self-preservation (Lapierre, Bouffard, & Bastin, 1997). The elderly themselves indicate that goals describing a "mature well adjusted fulfilled person" involve having an orientation towards others and not the self (Ryff, 1989). Also, goals involving transcendence become more important with age

(Lapierre, Bouffard, & Bastin, 1993). The elderly have been shown to increase in perceptions of control and to show a decrease in depression following giving assistance to others (Krause, Herzog, & Baker, 1992). Generativity, operationalized as concern for others, has been shown to be positively correlated with well-being in the elderly (McAdams, de St. Aubin, & Logan, 1993). Thus, transforming one's concern for self into a broader concern for others appears to have positive mental health effects.

In younger years, this strategy is less viable of a defense, primarily due to the lack of experience and development of the self. Specific group memberships provide validation and information about the self, which is needed to form the self-concept. The paradox continues: to lose the self, one must first have created the self. Jung (1963; p. 343) comments on this task of losing the self:

> All collective identities such as membership in organizations, support of 'isms' and so on, interfere with the fulfillment of this task. Such collective identities are crutches for the lame, shields for the timid, beds for the lazy, nurseries for the irresponsible; but they are equally shelters for the poor and weak, a home port for the shipwrecked, the bosom of a family for orphans, a land of promise for disillusioned vagrants and weary pilgrims, a herd and a safe fold for lost sheep, and a mother providing nourishment and growth. It would therefore be wrong to regard this intermediary stage as a trap; for a long time to come it will represent the only possible form of existence for the individual.

As a consequence of the fear of death, the young seek protection from the worldview and group identities. These identities serve us well when death is a concept for the future. However, in the face of the increasing mortality salience of aging and the devaluing our cultural worldview has been subjected to, expanding our group identification and broadening our worldviews may be a more appropriate defense for the elderly.

☐ In Conclusion

The successful use of the strategies delineated above may have profound effects on the well-being of the aging individual. These strategies are part of a developmental process through which the individual is able to transform the self. This may begin through attempts to minimize threats to the cultural worldview, but as the nearness to death increases and the effectiveness of the existing anxiety-buffering system deteriorates, different strategies must be employed. There is evidence that the aging individual is particularly adept at downward social comparison, adjustment of goals to the range of the feasible, and reinterpretation of events to emphasize their positive aspects. These defenses help to maintain self-esteem within the context of the existing worldview and set the stage for a transition to a more autonomous mode of functioning. The elderly individual may simultaneously broaden their social identity to include others as more integral parts of self, thereby adding further stability to their anxiety buffering system. The life review offers its own assets, with the possibility of self-complexity, esteem for past achievements, and a stable sense of mastery and self-efficacy.

Does Self-transcendence Really Increase with Age?

Is this depiction of a transformed self a viable explanation for the relative wellbeing observed in the elderly? While mortality salience is increasing and the cultural worldview may be losing effectiveness, is there evidence that the elderly are more accepting of death and are utilizing these strategies for coping with the fear of nonbeing? The elderly have been shown to be lower in self-consciousness (Mueller, & Ross, 1984) and lower in self-monitoring (Reifman, Klein, & Murphy, 1989) than the young, indicating that perhaps the elderly are on the road to "loss of self." The elderly have also been shown to be less influenced by group references and rules while the young are more concerned with norms and convention (Labouvie-Vief, Hakim-Larson, DeVoe, & Schoeberlain, 1989). These group references and rules all function to maintain the integrity of the cultural worldview; perhaps less concern with these standards for behavior indicates some detachment of the self from the cultural worldview, a further step toward the loss of self.

While this evidence may support that the elderly are pursuing the ultimate goal of loss of self, it does not indicate how this is achieved. Clearly this would not be an overnight realization. One does not wake up and decide that the self no longer matters. We can't simply choose to be less self-aware or to detach our sense of

---

Points to Remember

The central point of our terror management analysis of aging is that the defenses typical of youth, those well documented by previous research, may decrease in effectiveness as we age. This developmental perspective suggests that the use of the cultural worldview to derive self-esteem is compromised through changing or unreachable standards as we move through the decades. This, coupled with the increasing proximity to our own death that necessarily comes with advancing age, creates a need for a more effective coping strategy. We have argued that it is through the weakening of the cultural worldview defenses that the door is opened for the elderly to pursue self-transcendence, perhaps the loftiest and most elusive of human goals. The coping mechanisms presented in this chapter suggest that the elderly may be pursuing this goal through a decreased focus on the self and the standards of the contemporary world view, and an increasing focus on their life accomplishments, connections with the continuity of life, and acceptance of the inevitability of their own mortality. It may be that only by facing death in this way can we free ourselves from terror:

" . . . *healthy children will not fear life if their elders have integrity enough not to fear death.*"

—Erik Erikson (1963, p. 269)

value from the contingencies of the worldview. The disengagement from the anchor may be a long process instigated by the dawning knowledge that we are being dragged down, that our worldview no longer offers the protection of the past. The first step in this process as indicated earlier would be to accept the inevitableness of death. The elderly may focus on the part of the conflict that they can control, not the inevitability of death, but rather their own desire for the continuation of the self.

We have presented these strategies as changes particular to aging. However, we by no means wish to imply that this process is as inevitable and ordered as we have delineated. Individuals will use the most efficient defensive strategy available. Just as the defenses of youth are achieved to varying degrees of success, so too will the defenses of aging be achieved to varying degrees. There will always be those among us who have never been able to successfully deal with thoughts of their own mortality, those whose defenses seem tenuous and unstable, and those who seem well-defended and content. Independence from social consensus, creation of a truly individualized worldview, and a broad concern for all of humankind are difficult to achieve. For this reason, this type of transformation is probably most often implemented in late life when other avenues for defense have lost their utility.

☐ References

Adler, A. (1929). *Problems of Neurosis.* New York: Harper Torchbooks.

Aldwin, C. M. (1994). *Stress, Coping, and Development: An Integrative Perspective.* New York: Guilford Press.

Arndt, J., Greenberg, J., Pyszczynski, T., & Solomon, S. (1997). Subliminal exposure to death-related stimuli increases defense of the cultural worldview. *Psychological Science, 8,* 379–385.

Arndt, J., Greenberg, J., Solomon, S., Pyszczynski, T., & Simon, L. (1997). Suppression, accessibility of death-related thoughts, and worldview defense: Exploring the psychodynamics of terror management. *Journal of Personality and Social Psychology, 73,* 5–18.

Becker, E. (1969). *The Birth and Death of Meaning: an Interdisciplinary Perspective on the Problem of Man.* New York: Free Press.

Becker, E. (1971). *The Birth and Death of Meaning: an Interdisciplinary Perspective on the Problem of Man* (2nd Ed.). New York: Free Press.

Becker, E. (1973). *The Denial of Death.* New York: Free Press.

Ben-Ari, O. T., Florian, V., & Mikulincer, M. (1999). The impact of mortality salience on reckless driving: A test of terror management mechanisms. *Journal of Personality & Social Psychology, 76,* 35–45.

Blanchard-Fields, F., Jahnke, H. C., & Camp, C. (1995). Age differences in problem-solving style: The role of emotional salience. *Psychology & Aging, 10,* 173–180.

Blazer, D., Crowell, B. A., George, L. K., & Landerman, R. (1986). Urban-rural differences in depressive disorders: Does age make a difference? In J. E. Barrett & R. M. Rose (Eds.), *Mental disorders in the community: Progress and challenge.* New York: Guilford Press.

Brandtstaedter, J., & Greve, W. (1994). The aging self: Stabilizing and protective processes. *Developmental Review, 14,* 52–80.

Brandtstaedter, J. & Rothermund, K. (1994). Self-percepts of control in middle and later adulthood: Buffering losses by rescaling goals. *Psychology & Aging, 9,* 265–273.

Brehm, J. W. (1966). *A Theory of Psychological Reactance.* New York: Academic Press.

Brehm, S. S., & Brehm, J. W. (1981). *Psychological reactance: A theory of freedom and control.* New York: Academic Press.

Brewer, M. (1991). The social self: On being the same and different at the same time. *Personality and Social Psychology Bulletin, 17,* 475–482.

Campbell, J. D. (1990). Self-esteem and clarity of the self-concept. *Journal of Personality & Social Psychology, 59,* 538–549.

Campbell, J. D., Trapnell, P. D., Heine, S. J., Katz, I. M., Lavallee, L. F., & Lehman, D. R. (1996). Self-concept clarity: Measurement, personality correlates, and cultural boundaries. *Journal of Personality & Social Psychology, 70,* 141–156.

Carstensen, L. L. (1992). Motivation for social contact across the lifespan: A theory of socioemotional selectivity. In J. E. Jacobs (Ed), *Nebraska Symposium on Motivation, 1992: Developmental Perspectives on Motivation.* Lincoln, NE: University of Nebraska Press.

Carstensen, L. L., Gross, J. J., & Fung, H. H. (1998). The social context of emotional experience. In K. Warner Schaie & M. Powell Lawton (Eds.), *Annual Review of Gerontology and Geriatrics, 17.* New York: Springer.

Cole, M. A. (1979). Sex and marital status differences in death anxiety. *Omega 9,* 139–147.

Cross, S., & Markus, H. (1991). Possible selves across the life span. *Human Development, 34,* 230–255.

de Beauvoir, S. (1948). *The Ethics of Ambiguity.* New York: The Citadel Press.

Deci, E. L., & Ryan, R. M. (1980). Self-determination theory: When mind mediates behavior. *Journal of Mind & Behavior, 1,* 33–43.

Devins, G. M. (1979). Death anxiety and voluntary passive euthanasia: Influences of proximity to death and experiences with death in important other persons. *Journal of Consulting & Clinical Psychology, 47,* 301–309.

Diehl, M., Coyle, N., & Labouvie-Vief, G. (1996). Age and sex differences in strategies of coping and defense across the life span. *Psychology & Aging, 11,* 127–139.

Diener, E., & Suh, M. E. (1998). Subjective well-being and age: An international analysis. In K. Warner Schaie & M. Powell Lawton (Eds.), *Annual Review of Gerontology and Geriatrics, 17.* New York: Springer.

Dietz, B. E. (1996). The relationship of aging to self-esteem: The relative effects of maturation and role accumulation. *International Journal of Aging and Human Development, 43,* 249–266.

Erikson, E. H. (1963). Childhood and society. New York: W. W. Norton.

Erikson, E. H. (1985). *The Life Cycle Completed: A Review.* New York: W. W. Norton.

Esposito, J. L. (1987). *The Obsolete Self: Philosophical Dimensions of Aging.* Berkeley, CA: University of California Press.

Festinger, L. (1954) A theory of social comparison processes. *Human Relations, 7,* 117–140.

Fishman, S. (1992). Relationships among older adult's life review, ego integrity and death anxiety. *International Psychogeriatrics, 4,* 267-277.

Florian, V. & Mikulincer, M. (1998a). Symbolic immortality and the management of the terror of death: The moderating role of attachment style. *Journal of Personality & Social Psychology, 74,* 725–734.

Florian, V., & Mikulincer, M. (1998b). Terror management in childhood: Does death conceptualization moderate the effects of mortality salience on acceptance of similar and different others? *Personality and Social Psychology Bulletin, 24,* 1104–1112.

Frankl, V. E. (1959). *Man's search for meaning: An introduction to logotherapy.* Boston: Beacon Press.

Fredrickson, B. L., & Carstensen, L. L. (1990). Choosing social partners: How old age and anticipated endings make people more selective. *Psychology and Aging, 5,* 335–347.

Freud, S. (1919/1955). The uncanny. In *The complete psychological works of Sigmund Freud, Volume 17* (pp. 219–256). London: Hogarth Press.

Goldenberg, J. L., McCoy, S. K., Pyszczynski, T., Greenberg, J., & Solomon, S. (1999) *The body* as a source of self-esteem: The effect of mortality salience on identification with one's body, interest in sex, and appearance monitoring. Manuscript under review. University of Colorado, Colorado Springs, CO.

Goldenberg, J. L., Pyszczynski, T., McCoy, S. K., Greenberg, J. & Solomon, S. (1999). Death, sex, love, and neuroticism: Why is sex such a problem? *Journal of Personality and Social Psychology, 77,* 1173–1187.

Greenberg, J., Porteus, J., Simon, L., Pyszczynski, T., & Solomon, S. (1995). Evidence of a terror management function of cultural icons: The effects of mortality salience on the inappropriate use of cherished cultural symbols. *Personality & Social Psychology Bulletin, 21,* 1221–1228.

Greenberg, J., Pyszczynski, T., & Solomon, S. (1986). The causes and consequences of the need for self-esteem: A terror management analysis. In R. F. Baumeister (Ed.), *Public self and private self* (pp. 189–212), New York: Springer-Verlag.

Greenberg, J., Pyszczynski, T., Solomon, S., Rosenblatt, A., Veeder, M., Kirkland, S., & Lyon, D. (1990). Evidence for terror management theory II: The effects of mortality salience on reactions to those who threaten or bolster the cultural worldview. *Journal of Personality & Social Psychology, 58,* 308–318.

Greenberg, J., Pyszczynski, T., Solomon, S., Pinel, E., Simon, L., & Jordan, K. (1993). Effects of self-esteem on vulnerability-denying defensive distortions: Further evidence of an anxiety-buffering function of self-esteem. *Journal of Experimental Social Psychology, 29,* 229–251.

Greenberg, J., Pyszczynski, T., Solomon, S., Simon, L., & Breus, M. (1994). Role of consciousness and accessibility of death-related thoughts in mortality salience effects. *Journal of Personality & Social Psychology, 67,* 627–637.

Greenberg, J., Simon, L., Harmon-Jones, E., Solomon, S., Pyszczynski, T., & Lyon, D. (1995). Testing alternative explanations for mortality salience effects: Terror management, value assessibility, or worrisome thoughts? *European Journal of Social Psychology, 25,* 417–433.

Greenberg, J., Simon, L., Pyszczynski, T., Solomon, S., & Chatel, D. (1992). Terror management and tolerance: Does mortality salience always intensify negative reactions to others who threaten one's worldview? *Journal of Personality & Social Psychology, 63,* 212–220

Greenberg, J., Solomon, S., & Pyszczynski, T. (1997). Terror management theory of self-esteem and cultural worldviews: Empirical assessments and conceptual refinements. In M. Zanna (Ed.), *Advances in experimental social psychology* (Vol. 29, pp. 61–141). San Diego: Academic Press.

Greenberg, J., Solomon, S., Pyszczynski, T., Rosenblatt, A., Burling, J., Lyon, D., & Simon, L. (1992). Why do people need self-esteem? Converging evidence that self-esteem serves an anxiety-buffering function. *Journal of Personality & Social Psychology, 63,* 913–922.

Gross, J. J., Carstensen, L. L., Pasupathi, M., & Tsai, J. (1997). Emotion and aging: Experience, expression, and control. *Psychology and Aging, 12,* 590–599.

Gurin, P., & Brim, O. G., Jr. (1984). Change in self in adulthood: The example of a sense of control. In P. B. Baltes & O. G. Brim, Jr. (Eds.), *Life-span development and behavior* (Vol. 16, pp. 282–334). Orlando, FL: Academic Press.

Harmon-Jones, E., Simon, L., Greenberg, J., Pyszczynski, T., Solomon, S., & McGregor, H. (1997). Terror management theory and self-esteem: Evidence that increased self-esteem reduced mortality salience effects. *Journal of Personality & Social Psychology, 72,* 24–36.

Harmon-Jones, E., Greenberg, J., Solomon, S., & Simon, L. (1996). The effects of mortality salience on intergroup bias between minimal groups. *European Journal of Social Psychology, 26,* 677–681.

Heckhausen, J. (1997). Developmental regulation across adulthood: Primary and secondary control of age-related challenges. *Developmental Psychology, 33,* 176–187.

Heckhausen, J., & Brim, O. G. (1997). Perceived problems for self and others: Self-protection by social downgrading throughout adulthood. *Psychology and Aging, 12,* 610-619.

Heckhausen, J., & Krueger, J. (1993). Developmental expectations for the self and most other people: Age grading in three functions of social comparison. *Developmental Psychology, 29,* 539–548.

Heckhausen, J., & Schulz, R. (1993). Optimisation by selection and compensation: Balancing primary and secondary control in life span development. *International Journal of Behavioral Development, 16,* 287–303.

Hegelson, V. S., & Taylor, S. E. (1993). Social comparisons and adjustment among cardiac patients. *Journal of Applied Social Psychology, 23,* 1171–1195.

Heidrich, S. M., & Ryff, C. D. (1993). The role of social comparisons processes in the psychological adaptation of elderly adults. *Journals of Gerontology, 48,* 127–136.

Horney, K. (1950). *Neurosis and human growth; the struggle toward self-realization.* New York: W. W. Norton.

Jung, C. G. (1963). *Memories, dreams, reflections.* New York: Random House.

Kleinke, C. L., & Miller , W. F. (1998). How comparing oneself favorably with others relates to well-being. *Journal of Social and Clinical Psychology, 17,* 107–123.

Kling, K. C., & Ryff, C. D. (1997). Adaptive changes in the self-concept during a life transition. *Personality and Social Psychology Bulletin, 23,* 981–990.

Krause, N. M., Herzog, A. R., & Baker, E. (1992). Providing support to others and well-being in later life. *Journals of Gerontology, 47,* 300–311.

Labouvie-Vief, G., Chiodo, L. M., Goguen, L. A., & Diehl, M. (1995). Representations of self across the life span. *Psychology & Aging, 10,* 404–415.

Labouvie-Vief, G., Hakim-Larson, J., DeVoe, M., & Schoeberlein, S. (1989). Emotions and self-regulation: A life span view. *Human Development, 32,* 279–299.

Lapierre, S., Bouffard, L., & Bastin, E. (1993). Motivational goal objects in later life. *International Journal of Aging and Human Development, 36,* 279–292.

Lapierre, S., Bouffard, L., & Bastin, E. (1997). Personal goals and subjective well being in later life. *International Journal of Aging and Human Development, 45,* 287–303.

Lawton, M. P., Kleban, M. H., & Dean, J. (1993). Affect and age: Cross-sectional comparisons of structure and prevalence. *Psychology and Aging, 8,* 165–175.

Lifton, R. J. (1983). *The broken connection: On death and the continuity of life.* New York: Basic Books.

Linville, P. W. (1985). Self-complexity and affective extremity: Don't put all your eggs in one cognitive basket. *Social Cognition, 3,* 94–120.

Linville, P. W. (1987). Self-complexity as a cognitive buffer against stress-related illness and depression. *Journal of Personality and Social Psychology, 52,* 663–676.

Maslow, A. H. (1968). *Toward A Psychology of Being.* Princeton, NJ: D. Van Nostrand.

McAdams, D. P., de St. Aubin, E., & Logan, R. L. (1993). Generativity among young, midlife, and older adults. *Psychology & Aging, 8,* 221–230.

McCoy, S., Solomon, S., Pyszczynski, T, & Greenberg, J. (1999). *The effects of mortality salience on subjective life expectancy in the elderly as a function of neuroticism.* Manuscript in preparation.

McGregor, H. A., Lieberman, J. D., Greenberg, J., Solomon, S., Arndt, J., Simon, L., & Pyszczynski, T. (1998). Terror management and aggression: Evidence that mortality salience motivates aggression against worldview-threatening others. *Journal of Personality & Social Psychology, 74,* 590–605.

Mueller, J. H., & Ross, M. J. (1984). Uniqueness of the self-concept across the life span. *Bulletin of the Psychonomic Society, 22,* 83–86.

Ochsmann, R., & Mathy, M. (1994). *Depreciating of and distancing from foreigners: Effects of mortality salience.* Unpublished manuscript, Universitat Mainz, Mainz, Germany.

Piaget, J. (1952). *The Origins of Intelligence in Children.* New York: International Universities Press.

Pyszczynski, T., & Greenberg, J. (1987). Self-regulatory perseveration and the depressive self-focusing style: A self-awareness theory of reactive depression. *Psychological Bulletin, 102,* 122–138.

Pyszczynski, T., Greenberg, J., & Solomon, S. (1999). A dual process model of defense against conscious and unconscious death-related thoughts: An extension of terror management theory. *Psychological Review, 106,* 835–845.

Pyszczynski, T., Greenberg, J., & Solomon, S. (1998). A terror management perspective on the psychology of control: Controlling the uncontrollable. In M. Kofta & G. Weary (Eds.), *Personal Control in Action: Cognitive and Motivational Mechanisms.* New York: Plenum Press.

Pyszczynski, T., Greenberg, J., Solomon, S., Cather, C., Gat, I., & Sideras, J. (1995). Defensive distancing from victims of serious illness: The role of delay. *Personality & Social Psychology Bulletin, 21,* 13–20.

Pyszczynski, T., Wicklund, R. A., Floresku, S., Gauch, G., Koch, H., Solomon, S., & Greenberg, J. (1996). Whistling in the dark: Exaggerated consensus estimates in response to incidental reminders of mortality. *Psychological Science, 7,* 332–336.

Quackenbush, S. W., & Barnett, M. A. (1995). Correlates of reminiscence activity among elderly individuals. *International Journal of Aging and Human Development, 41,* 169–181.

Rank, O. (1932). *Art and artist: Creative urge and personality development.* New York: Alfred A. Knopf.

Rasmussen, C. A., & Brems, C. (1996). The relationship of death anxiety to age and psychosocial maturity. *Journal of Psychology, 130,* 141–144.

Reifman, A., Klein, J. G., & Murphy, S. T. (1989). Self-monitoring and age. *Psychology and Aging, 4,* 245–246.

Rickabaugh, C. A. & Tomlinson-Keasey, C. (1997). Social and temporal comparisons in adjustment to aging. *Basic and Applied Social Psychology, 3,* 307–328.

Robinson-Whelen, S., & Kiecolt-Glaser, J. (1997). The importance of social versus temporal comparison appraisals among older adults. *Journal of Applied Social Psychology, 27,* 959–966.

Rogers, C. R. (1954). *Psychotherapy and personality change: Co-ordinated research studies in the client-centered approach.* Chicago: University of Chicago Press.

Rosenblatt, A., Greenberg, J., Solomon, S., Pyszczynski, T., & Lyon, D. (1989). Evidence for terror management theory: I. The effects of mortality salience on reactions to those who violate or uphold cultural values. *Journal of Personality & Social Psychology, 57,* 681–690

Rothbaum, F., Weisz, J. R., & Snyder, S. S. (1982). Changing the world and changing the self: A two-process model of perceived control. *Journal of Personality & Social Psychology, 42,* 5–37.

Rowles, G. D. (1984). Aging in rural environments. *Human Behavior & Environment: Advances in Theory & Research, 7,* 129–157.

Ryff, C. D. (1989). In the eye of the beholder: Views of psychological well-being among middle-aged and older adults. *Psychology & Aging, 4,* 195–210.

Ryff, C. D. (1991). Possible selves in adulthood and old age: A tale of shifting horizons. *Psychology & Aging, 6,* 286–295.

Salthouse, T. A. (1998). Independence of age-related influences on cognitive abilities across the life span. *Developmental Psychology, 34,* 851–864.

Schimel, J., Simon, L., Greenberg, J., Pyszczynski, T., Solomon, S., Waxmonsky, J., & Arndt, J. (1999). Stereotypes and terror management: Evidence that mortality salience enhances stereotypic thinking and preferences. *Journal of Personality and Social Psychology, 77,* 905–926.

Schulz, R., & Heckhausen, J. (1996). A life span model of successful aging. *American Psychologist, 51,* 702-714.

Simon, L., Greenberg, J., Arndt, J., Pyszczynski, T., Clement, R., & Solomon, S. (1997). Perceived consensus, uniqueness, and terror management: Compensatory responses to threats to inclusion and distinctiveness following mortality salience. *Personality & Social Psychology Bulletin, 23,* 1055–1065.

Solomon, S., Greenberg, J., & Pyszczynski, T. (1991). Terror management theory of social behavior: The psychological functions self-esteem and cultural worldviews. In M. Zanna (Ed.), *Advances in experimental social psychology* (Vol. 24, pp. 93–159). San Diego, CA: Academic Press.

Swann, W. B. (1987). Identity negotiation: Where two roads meet. *Journal of Personality and Social Psychology, 53,* 1038–1051.

Tate, L. A. (1982). Life satisfaction and death anxiety in aged women. International *Journal of Aging & Human Development, 15,* 299–306.

Taylor, S. E., & Lobel, M. (1989). Social comparison activity under threat: Downward evaluation and upward contacts. *Psychological Review, 96,* 569–575.

Templer, D. I., Ruff, C. F., & Franks, C. M. (1971). Death anxiety: Age, sex, and parental resemblance in diverse populations. *Developmental Psychology, 4,* 108.

Thomae, H. (1992). Contributions of longitudinal research to a cognitive theory of adjustment to aging. *European Journal of Personality, 6,* 157–175.

White, W., & Handal, P. J. (1991) The relationship between death anxiety and mental health/distress. *Omega, 22,* 13–24.

Wills, T. A. (1987). Downward comparison as a coping mechanism. In C. R. Snyder & C. E. Ford (Eds.), *Coping with Negative Life Events: Clinical and Social Psychological Perspectives.* New York: Plenum Press.

Wong, P. T. (1989). Personal meaning and successful aging. Canadian Psychology, 30, 516–525.

Wong, P. T., & Watt, L. M. (1991). What types of reminiscence are associated with successful aging? *Psychology & Aging, 6,* 272–279.

CHAPTER

Robert W. Firestone

Microsuicide and the Elderly: A Basic Defense Against Death Anxiety

The common denominator of all negative ways of dealing with anxiety is a shrinking of the area of awareness and of activity. . . . We are afraid to die, and therefore we are afraid to live, or as Tillich puts it, we avoid nonbeing by avoiding being. The avoidance of anxiety then means a kind of death in life.

—Joseph Rheingold (1967, pp. 204–205)

"Microsuicide" refers to those behaviors, communications, attitudes, or lifestyles that are threatening, limiting, or antithetical to an individual's physical health, emotional well-being, or personal goals. Examples of microsuicidal behavior include patterns of progressive self-denial, inwardness, withholding, dependency bonds, and physically harmful actions and lifestyles (Firestone & Seiden, 1987). These behaviors, as well as the destructive thought patterns and attitudes that mediate them, function as a basic defense, first against separation anxiety, and later against the fear of death.

Statistics show that suicide intent is high in prisoners awaiting execution on death row, necessitating strict preventive measures such as suicide watch. Thinking about this paradox leads to other conclusions about human self-destructiveness. The situation faced by a convicted killer is analogous to the circumstances faced by all human beings, especially the elderly (see R. Firestone & Seiden, 1987). Like the convict, people are conscious of an inescapable sentence of death as a function of life itself. The prisoner, faced with the knowledge of the exact hour of

Portions of this chapter have been excerpted from "Microsuicide and Suicidal Threats of Everyday Life," by R. W. Firestone and R. H. Seiden, 1987, *Psychotherapy, 24,* pp. 31–39. Copyright 1987 by Division of Psychotherapy (29) of the American Psychological Association. Adapted by permission.

execution, attempts suicide to take life and death into his or her own hands, while the "normal" individual commits "micro" suicide in an effort to accommodate to death anxiety. In both instances, suicide, actual or partial, is a desperate attempt to avoid feelings of dread, anxiety, and despair surrounding the existential awareness of separation and death. As individuals give up their lives through progressive self-denial and other microsuicidal behaviors, they are able to maintain a sense of omnipotence, as if they can retain some power over life and death. In withdrawing feeling or affect from personal pursuits and goal-directed activity, they reduce their vulnerability to hurt, rejection, or loss (R. Firestone, 1985).

My objectives in this chapter are to examine microsuicidal behaviors that are prevalent in our society and to analyze the underlying negative thought process or "voice" that controls or strongly influences them. Although destructive attitudes and thoughts are operant in individuals throughout the life-span, they become progressively more ascendant in people's thinking as they grow older.

In explaining how psychological defenses formed in relation to death anxiety shape people's behavior and lifestyle, several questions come to mind when considering the relationship between self-destructive behavior manifested by older people and their attitudes about death and dying. Why are microsuicidal behaviors, such as noncompliance with medical regimens (Szanto, Prigerson, Houck, Ehrenpreis, & Reynolds, 1997) and withdrawal from favored activities, interests, and friendships, so commonplace in this population?[1] Do these indicators of increased self-destructiveness reflect older people's views or perceptions of death? What are the basic negative assumptions about self, others, and events in life underlying these views? How do these dysfunctional beliefs develop and how are they maintained over the course of a person's life? Is the elevated rate of suicide among older people related to their heightened awareness of death?[2] Lastly, do the conventional attitudes toward the elderly (ageism) that permeate our society function to exacerbate their self-destructive thinking and behavior?

☐ The Demographics of Elderly Suicide

Older people (over 75) in the United States have the highest suicide rates compared to other age groups. In 1992, the suicide rate for people between the ages of 80 and 84 was 24.6 per 100,000 population. In 1990, white males, ages 80 to 84, had a rate of 68.4 per 100,000, more than five times that of the national suicide rate for all age groups (12.4 per 100,000) (Kachur, Potter, James, & Powell, 1995). The number of young people in this country who commit suicide is larger than the number of elderly; however, suicide among older people is higher in proportion to their numbers.

Suicides attempted by older people tend to be more lethal. This trend is evident in the ratio of attempted to completed suicides in the elderly, which is estimated to be approximately 4:1 or even lower. In comparison, the ratio of attempted to completed suicide in the general population is from 8:1 to 20:1, and in young people, the rate is as high as 300:1 (Stenback, 1980). Studies of the methods typically used in suicide and parasuicide have shown that older people use more lethal means when they try to kill themselves: "Those prone to suicide are more likely to be older men, more often unmarried, divorced or widowed, living alone and unemployed or retired. The lethality of the method used in their previous (para)suicidal acts (previous to suicide) is often higher" (Diekstra, 1996, p. 18). For this reason, McIntosh (1995) has cautioned physicians and mental health professionals that it is crucial to take seriously *any* threats of suicide made by older patients.

According to McIntosh and Hubbard (1988), suicide as a cause of death for the aged is under reported, since the elderly use methods that are not as obviously or instantaneously suicidal, but result in premature avoidable death. They also stressed an equally important variable: the omission of behaviors that "would sustain life and health, including neglecting routine medical examinations and prescribed medical treatment, ignoring or delaying needed medical aid, and refusing medications and/or nourishment" (p. 37).

☐ The Interrelatedness of Self-Destructive Behavior: Brief Review of the Literature

It has long been acknowledged that many self-harmful behaviors and lifestyles are not necessarily undertaken with the conscious aim of self-destruction. These behaviors have been referred to as indirect self-destructive behavior, partial suicide, embryonic suicide, parasuicide, and chronic suicide. While there are slight distinctions between these terms, they all describe lifestyles of gradual self-destruction.

Durkheim was one of the first to recognize an essential continuity of self-destructive behaviors. In *Suicide: A Study in Sociology*, Durkheim (1897/1951) declared:

> Suicides do not form, as might be thought, a wholly distinct group, an isolated class of monstrous phenomena, unrelated to other forms of conduct, but rather are related to them by a continuous series of intermediate cases. They are merely the exaggerated form of common practices. (p. 45)

Menninger (1938) used the term "partial suicide" to signify a variety of self-destructive lifestyles which amount to suicide on a continuing, attenuated basis. In the preface of his book, *Man Against Himself*, Menninger declared: "In the end each man kills himself in his own selected way, fast or slow, soon or late" (p. vii). He went on to enumerate the various methods some perversely clever people use to accomplish their self-defeating objectives, such as ascetic denial, repetitive accidents, alcohol addiction, unwise financial speculation, failure to follow medical advice, among others.

Suicidologist Edwin Shneidman (1966) proposed a similar conceptual scheme in the analysis of what he calls "inimical patterns of living." He defined these "unfriendly" behavioral responses as the "multitudinous ways in which an individual can reduce, truncate, demean, narrow, shorten, or destroy his own life" (p. 199). Such responses, he cautions, are not necessarily a "substitute suicide" but a range of behaviors in which completed suicide is but one, albeit the most extreme example.

In *The Many Faces of Suicide,* Farberow (1980) enumerated a wide range of specific self-destructive behaviors which:

> by their very familiarity and frequency of occurrence . . . must merge into the normal, acceptable end of the continuum of behavior. On the other hand, if they can be so self-destructive or self-injurious, they must merge into the pathological end of the continuum represented by overt suicidal activity. (p. 2)

In describing self-harm behaviors manifested by institutionalized older people, Nelson (1977) called attention to the fact that "indirect life-threatening behavior [ILTB] may injure, defeat, distress, and shorten life as much as direct self-destructive behavior. . . . The principal differences are that ILTB generally takes longer and is often not readily identifiable" (p. 69). Conwell (1994) stressed the fact that self-destructive acts are common among the elderly in nursing homes, "but that they are not ordinarily labeled 'suicidal'" (p. 154).

In this sense, we can say that all people have the potential for suicide; it is only the individual style and strength of the movement toward self-destruction that varies from one individual to the next. It also follows that this universal tendency toward self-destruction is not due to a death instinct, but represents instead a powerful defense against death anxiety. People do not want to die, yet they do want to protect themselves from agonizing feelings associated with the specter of death. Through the process of progressive self-denial, the terror of death is transformed into a fear of living or of becoming too attached to life. Individuals are self-destructive to varying degrees because they are aware that they must die. In a sense, they achieve an illusion of mastery over life and death by committing small suicides on a daily basis.

☐ The Psychodynamics of Microsuicide

A Developmental Perspective

Microsuicidal behaviors and the destructive thought processes that govern them can be understood in terms of their role as a basic defense. Defenses arise early in life in relation to separation anxiety, prior to the awareness of death. Early frustration and emotional deprivation lead to the formation of a fantasy bond—an imagined connection with the primary caretaker—that becomes the core defense. Later in the developmental sequence, the child's evolving knowledge of death crystallizes the defense system. This new awareness predisposes a general tendency in children to withdraw libido or genuine feeling for themselves and others in favor of defenses and self-parenting behaviors that shield them from the consciousness of being alone and exposed to death. At this crucial juncture, youngsters unwittingly make firm resolutions regarding their lives and future behavior, based on fear and a sense of helplessness and vulnerability to death.[3] These vows become a fundamental part of their defensive apparatus. Although these resolutions often exist on an unconscious level, nonetheless, they impel young people to embark on developmental pathways that lead them away from what otherwise would have been their true destiny.

Neglectful or emotionally impoverished parenting further complicates separation experiences and leads to even greater anxiety. The more rejected the child, the more he or she resists individuation and clings to the disturbing parental atmosphere. However, even if a child experienced little or no interpersonal stress, he or she would develop a defensive process in relation to the tragic aspects of the human condition: the painful realities of crime, economic stresses, war, sickness, aging, aloneness, and ultimately, death.[4]

Secondary defenses, which include predictions of rejection, the anticipation of negative outcomes, and cynical views of others that foster distrust, function to protect the core defense or fantasy bond. These views are maintained by a destructive thought process or internal "voice" that also supports defenses against death anxiety. Because all children form defenses against pain, no child, indeed no person, is completely free of these critical thoughts or voice attacks.

The Formation of the Self and Antiself Systems

Under circumstances of extreme tension and stress, children tend to depersonalize in an attempt to escape from painful emotions. In the process, they internalize or incorporate the negative attitudes and feelings that are directed toward them. These parental introjects or voices lead to an essential dualism within the personality. This "division of the mind" reflects a primary split between forces that represent the self and those that oppose or attempt to destroy the self. These tendencies can be conceptualized as the "self system" and the "antiself system." The two systems develop independently; both are dynamic and continually evolve and change over time (R. Firestone, 1997a). The self system is made up of the unique characteristics of the individual, the assimilation of parents' positive qualities and strivings, and ongoing effects of experience and education. The antiself system consists of the accumulation of internalized cynical or hostile thought processes or voices that represent the defensive aspect of the personality.[5]

The Concept of the Voice

The voice is an integrated system of negative thoughts and attitudes, antithetical to the self and cynical toward others, that is at the core of maladaptive behavior (R. Firestone, 1988). This partially conscious thought process represents the introjection of the parents' rejecting thoughts and attitudes, both covert and overt, toward the child. Because human beings defend themselves under conditions of stress, children incorporate into themselves the attitudes of their parents at their worst, that is, on those occasions when they (the parents) were critical, the most aggressive, and the most feared.[6] These negative parental introjects come to have a basic autonomy within the personality and may ultimately dominate the scene, as in a suicidal crisis. Hostile thought patterns or voices are distinguishable from hallucinated voices in the psychoses, although they have a similar character. In the case of the psychoses, hallucinated voices reflect a more drastic split within the personality.

In their everyday lives, most people are aware of self-critical thoughts or a running inner dialogue: "I'm going to make a fool of myself;" "I'm a failure;" "I just don't fit in;" "I'm different from other people." These negative cognitions are accompanied by varying degrees of angry affect. Even when these hostile attitudes have little or no basis in reality, they have a profoundly detrimental effect on an individual's behavior. They interrupt the ongoing pursuit of goals by creating painful feelings of self-consciousness and alienation in interpersonal relationships. However, when these self-critical thoughts are brought directly into consciousness through voice therapy procedures and articulated in the second person, as though another person were addressing them, (e.g., "*You're* going to make a fool of yourself"' "*You're* a failure," and so on), they can be effectively evaluated and countered. When the voice goes unchallenged, it influences people to maintain undesirable traits and behaviors that are opposed to their self-interest and well-being.

To summarize, the objective of the voice is to foster self-denial and ultimately the self-destruction of the individual. The voice is the mechanism that regulates and dictates a person's microsuicidal behavior. Hostile thought patterns and attitudes that make up the antiself system strongly influence the narrowing of life experiences and the relinquishing of one's unique identity. Suicide represents the ultimate renunciation of self (R. Firestone, 1997b).

The Continuum of Negative Thought Patterns

Microsuicidal behavior exists on a continuum ranging from asceticism or self-denial to accident proneness, substance abuse, and other self-defeating behaviors, culminating in self-mutilating acts and actual suicide. Similarly, thoughts antithetical to the self vary along a continuum of intensity from mild self-reproach to malicious self-accusations and suicidal thoughts (see Figure 1, Continuum of Negative Thought Patterns). The continuum depicts levels of increasing self-destructiveness. It delineates specific negative thoughts, attitudes, and beliefs typically reported by nonclinical individuals and a broad spectrum of clinical patients, including substance abusers, self-mutilators, suicide ideators, and suicide attempters.[7]

The progressive ascendancy of the voice process over rational thinking manifests itself strongly in older people. Behaviorally, there is an established pattern of giving up favorite activities, special interests, and gratifications in life that eventually reaches the point where individuals feel they have little or nothing left to live for. The increase in voice attacks and the resultant self-denial are operant in the trance state that Heckler (1994) identified as a fundamental part of any suicidal process.

Suicidologists Clark (1993), Maris (1981), and Shneidman (1985) have emphasized that "there are lifelong patterns that characterize the suicidal person" (McIntosh, 1995, p. 189). In considering the prevention of suicide in the elderly, McIntosh concluded: "If they [the suicidologists] are correct, then those who may be vulnerable to the problems in old age might be identified earlier in life and taught more effective coping methods" (p. 189). If we are to modify or change these "life-long" patterns, we must first be able to identify them and isolate the thought patterns that function to regulate them. With this goal in mind, I have delineated behavioral patterns that I refer to as the microsuicides of everyday life.

☐ Manifestations of Microsuicide in Older People[8]

Several basic divisions of microsuicidal behavior can be delineated. These actions, as well as the underlying thought patterns that control them, are not discrete, but they can be categorized for purposes of clarity and elucidation:

1. Increased involvement in an inward lifestyle.
2. Behaviors that adversely affect physical health.
3. The formation of restrictive fantasy bonds.
4. Withholding—renunciation of personal and vocational goals.
5. Progressive self-denial.

Increased Involvement in an Inward Lifestyle

A gradual withdrawal into isolation and fantasy, obsessional ruminations, unusual reserve and quietness, loss of feeling for oneself, withdrawal of affect, and a shirking of responsibilities are all microsuicidal behaviors indicating regression to an inward posture. The term "inwardness" can be defined as a retreat into oneself, resulting in various degrees of a depersonalized mind-state and a lifestyle characterized by reliance on painkilling habits and/or substances and a defensive, self-gratifying orientation toward life. It is necessary to distinguish the inward syndrome from self-reflection, introspection, time spent alone for creative work or planning, meditation, or other spiritual or intellectual pursuits. The inward posture represents a withdrawal from emotional exchanges with others in the interpersonal environment based on early attempts in childhood to avoid frustration and primal pain. As people approach old age, many tend to retreat from the give and take of offering love and accepting love.

Manifestations of the inward posture include: an unprecipitated breakup of a close relationship; continually changing relationships, jobs, or careers; frequent moves to new surroundings; a lack of concern with one's living circumstances; and an increase in the acting out of behavior that is degrading and demoralizing to the individual. These actions, in turn, give rise to increased feelings of self-condemnation and self-hatred. Guilt about acting-out behavior that is beneath one's standards contributes to a downward spiraling cycle of withdrawal and paranoid feelings toward others.

Thoughts that predict rejection are common in people who are inward. For example, they may tell themselves: "People won't want you as a friend once they really get to know you." Injunctions of the "voice" effectively persuade older men

CONTINUUM OF NEGATIVE THOUGHT PATTERNS

Levels of Increasing Suicidal Intention	Content of Voice Statements
Thoughts that lead to low self-esteem or inwardness (self-defeating thoughts):	
1. Self-depreciating thoughts of everyday life.	*You're incompetent, stupid. You're not very attractive. You're going to make a fool of yourself.*
2. Thoughts rationalizing self-denial; thoughts discouraging the person from engaging in pleasurable activities	*You're too young (old) and inexperienced to apply for this job. You're too shy to make any new friends, or Why go on this trip? It'll be such a hassle. You'll save money by staying home.*
3. Cynical attitudes toward others, leading to alienation and distancing	*Why go out with her (him)? She's cold, unreliable; she'll reject you. She wouldn't go out with you anyway. You can't trust men (women)*
4. Thoughts influencing isolation; rationalizations for time alone, but using time to become more negative toward oneself	*Just be by yourself. You're miserable company anyway; who'd want to be with you? Just stay in the background, out of view.*
5. Self-contempt; vicious self-abusive thoughts and accusations (accompanied by intense angry affect)	*You idiot! You bitch! You creep! You stupid shit! You don't deserve anything; you're worthless.*
Thoughts that support the cycle of addiction (addictions):	
6. Thoughts urging use of substances or food followed by self-criticisms (weakens inhibitions against self-destructive actions, while increasing guilt and self-recrimination following acting out)	*It's okay to do drugs, you'll be more relaxed. Go ahead and have a drink, you deserve it. (Later) You weak-willed jerk! You're nothing but a drugged-out drunken freak.*
Thoughts that lead to suicide (self-annihilating thoughts):	
7. Thoughts contributing to a sense of hopelessness, urging withdrawal or removal of oneself completely from the lives of people closest	*See how bad you make your family (friends) feel. They'd be better off without you. It's the only decent thing to do—just stay away and stop bothering them.*
8. Thoughts influencing a person to give up priorities and favored activities (points of identity)	*What's the use? Your work doesn't matter any more. Why bother even trying? Nothing matters anyway.*
9. Injunctions to inflict self-harm at an action level; intense rage against self	*Why don't you just drive across the center divider? Just shove your hand under that power saw!*
10. Thoughts planning details of suicide (calm, rational, often obsessive, indicating complete loss of feeling for the self)	*You have to get hold of some pills, then go to a hotel, etc.*
11. Injunctions to carry out suicide plans; thoughts baiting the person to commit suicide (extreme thought constriction)	*You've thought about this long enough. Just get it over with.* *It's the only way out!*

Any combination of the voice attacks listed above can lead to serious suicidal intent. Thoughts leading to isolation, ideation about removing oneself from people's lives, beliefs that one is a bad influence or has a destructive effect on others, voices urging one to give up special activities, vicious self-abusive thoughts accompanied by strong anger, voices urging self-injury and a suicide attempt are all indications of high suicide potential or risk.

FIGURE 1. Continuum of Negative Thought Patterns

and women to avoid the risks of forming new attachments: "Why bother making new friends at this age?"; "If you don't have anybody close to you by now, you never will"; "Nobody wants to be around older people, they're so uninteresting." In general, inwardness is the breeding ground for voice attacks.

As an older person retreats from seeking gratification in the external world, he or she becomes increasingly indifferent to life and finds it easier to give up social relationships he or she once found pleasurable and meaningful. Thoughts such as "Why bother going out to dinner with your friends? You'd feel better if you just stayed home tonight" or, "You really need more time alone to just relax and think" often disguise self-destructive motives in people who are seeking isolation from others. Extended periods of time away from social contact can be conducive to depressive reactions and progressive withdrawal, patterns that are detrimental to mental health in general, and especially in the case of older individuals.

Behaviors that Adversely Affect Physical Health

Accident proneness, working compulsively, and certain psychosomatic illnesses are obvious manifestations of self-destructive tendencies that have long been recognized (Nelson & Farberow, 1982). These types of tendencies and a myriad of addictive behaviors including drinking to excess, drug abuse, obesity, and eating disorders represent direct assaults against the individual's physical health and emotional well-being, leading to gradual deterioration. Painkillers and other substances that are habitually used for self-soothing purposes and as compensations for the lack of close personal interactions become more appealing to people as they get older.

The destructive thought process supporting addictive tendencies functions in a manner similar to other forms of microsuicide. Initially, the voice influences or seduces people into indulging the self-destructive behavior, then punishes them with self-recriminations for succumbing to the temptation, which in turn increases feelings of futility and demoralization, which increases the need for relief in the form of more painkillers. Seemingly positive suggestions that they give themselves rewards, for example, "Have a drink. It'll relax you," are followed by vicious self-accusations: "You have no will power. You're a hopeless drunk. You never live up to your resolutions."

Reactions to physical deterioration and poor health are also important factors affecting the mental health and vitality of older individuals. For example, physical handicaps and chronic physical pain can make death seem more appealing.[9] The depression and irritability that accompany ill health in older adults can be intensified or may be directly caused by negative cognitions: "You're always sick"; "You're always complaining about your aches and pains"; "Nobody wants to be around a sick person." Illness can also arouse morbid, obsessive thoughts about death, thereby increasing one's feelings of resignation and futility about life.

As people grow older, poor health and sickness tend to precipitate self-depreciating thoughts about their body integrity. Perceived bodily weaknesses and a deterioration in physical fitness become the target of self-depreciating thoughts. Those who suffer from chronic illness frequently attack themselves as malingerers or see themselves as burdens. In anticipating a routine checkup, even apparently healthy individuals are likely to torture themselves with such thoughts as: "The doctor is going to discover something really wrong with you this time. You probably have a terminal illness. Why go? It's better not to know."

The Formation of Restrictive Fantasy Bonds

A *fantasy bond*, similar to the original illusion of connection to the mother or care-taker, is manifested in an addictive attachment formed by many couples to defend against separation and death anxiety. It is addictive in that both partners are using each other primarily to relieve feelings of anxiety and insecurity. This misuse of the other leads to a deterioration of their original feelings. A progressive loss of identity and individuality is symptomatic of the mutual self-destructiveness inherent in a fantasy bond. In some cases, there is observable physical deterioration or illness directly attributable to the negative, disrespectful style of interacting that characterizes many marriages.

In a fantasy bond, both partners use the relationship to externalize their destructive thoughts. Through projective identification, both provoke the other into criticizing them in a manner similar to the way they criticize themselves. Each responds with depreciating comments that increasingly undermine the other's self-confidence. In many long-term "enduring" marriages, the habit of mutually mistreating one another becomes routine, yet if asked, most of these couples would say they still loved each other. The pattern of negative interactions manifested by these warring couples, combined with their exaggerated dependency on each other, contributes to further deterioration in the overall mood and sense of well-being of the individuals involved.[10] Further, members of the couple may come to share negative attitudes and cynical views of other people. In more serious cases, they develop distrustful attitudes about the world which sometimes approach delusional proportions and which reinforce their tendencies to isolate themselves.

The fantasy bond, as manifested in many marital relationships, can be considered to be a serious form of microsuicide. The more rejection or deprivation individuals experienced during the formative years, the more they seek security and a sense of wholeness through a fantasized connection with another person. These ties are so powerful in couple relationships that when they are broken, they are the most prominent cause of personal distress and potential suicide (Heckler, 1994; Richman, 1986). Because the fantasy bond offers members of the couple an illusion of safety, when one partner dies, the surviving partner feels lost and is more vulnerable to depression and complicated grief reactions that can precipitate a suicidal crisis.[11]

Withholding—A Renunciation of Personal and Vocational Goals

Withholding refers to a holding back of positive responses, talents, and capabilities as a form of microsuicide or retreat from life. Whenever an individual withholds behaviors or qualities that were once an important expression of his or her personal motivation, he or she is no longer goal-directed and becomes more oriented toward failure. Withholding or negativistic behavior can become habitual with a subsequent reduction in one's ability to function adequately in the real world. In a fantasy bond, patterns of withholding manifested by one partner can effectively change the other's positive feelings of love to those of hostility and anger. For example, many men and women hold back qualities that originally attracted their mates, such as their sense of humor, affection, attractiveness. They are able to manipulate their partner into taking care of them by regressing to more childish modes of relating and by withholding adult responses. Self-destructive behaviors that are commonplace in old age, such as neglect of one's health, often elicit or provoke negative parental reactions, worry, fear, or anger in the partner. This collusive pattern acts to cement the fantasy of being connected to another person and relieves the anxiety of being separate, alone, and vulnerable to death.

Paradoxically, significant achievement, unusual success, or personal fulfillment in a relationship often lead to anxiety states that precipitate withholding responses. In these cases, an individual gives up or holds back the very behavior which led to success, accomplishment, or fulfillment. Any unusual positive event or evidence that heightens a person's awareness of having value, of being separate and alone, of being a free agent, arouses separation and death anxiety and fosters withholding and other regressive behavior patterns (R. Firestone, 1990a).[12]

Progressive Self-Denial—Giving Up Interest in Life-Affirming Activities

As noted previously, beginning in early childhood, most people deny death on a personal level and gradually adapt to the fear of death by giving up, or seriously restricting, their lives. In our society, it is often considered a sign of "maturity" to withdraw from specific activities as one grows older. The tendency to give up interest in and excitement about life is built into an individual's defensive posture. Examples of this retreat from life can be found in every area of human endeavor: early retirement, a premature giving up of participation in sports and physical activities, a diminished interest in sex and reduction in sexual activity, a loss of contact with old friends, and a decline in social life. At the same time, people may develop sedentary or self-nourishing habits, and, as a result, become plagued with a sense of boredom.

Negative thoughts or voices are directly connected with patterns of self-denial. In human sexuality, the intrusion of negative cognitions and attitudes can have a debilitating effect on each partner's ability to achieve satisfaction in the most intimate part of his or her relationship (R. Firestone, 1990b). Men and women have "voices" criticizing their bodies and their sexual behavior, especially the sexual and genital regions, the way they move, and their own and their partner's level of excitement. As people grow older, they tend to have stronger attacks on their sexuality and use their age as a rationalization for denying themselves sexual pleasure and fulfillment: "People your age don't need that much sex"; "There are other, more important things in your life now"; "Sex is for young people, not for you"; "You're old and wrinkled, why would he want to make love to you?"; or "You can't keep an erection anymore. You won't be able to satisfy her."

Attitudes and thoughts that govern self-denial are prevalent in people of all ages; however, they are especially prominent among the elderly. For example, an older person who loves adventure and travel may justify his or her decision to stay home with such thoughts as: "It's so much easier to stay home. It's such a hassle to pack and get ready. The flights are so long and the accommodations will probably be uncomfortable, the weather too hot or cold, etc." Many people use rationalizations dictated by the voice to postpone vacations and recreation until they retire, only to find themselves plagued by ill health and serious monetary concerns when they have the freedom to travel.

Destructive thoughts or voices also provide older people with excuses for relinquishing interest in their favorite activities: "You're crazy to still play sports at your age. People will think you're just trying to act young" or "Whoever heard of falling in love at 65?" or "Why bother to plan building a new house at your age? By the time it's finished, you probably won't be around to enjoy it."

In general, people follow the dictates of their voices as they progress through the life cycle. Harmful patterns of behavior regulated by the destructive thought process that have gone unchallenged throughout life have had a profound effect on an individual's functioning by the time he or she reaches the middle years. As individuals follow the dictates of the voice and reduce their activity levels, they generally remain unaware that they are acting against their own best interests. People rarely question their loss of enthusiasm or excitement for the lively pursuits they enjoyed when they were younger. During the final stages in the developmental sequence, the defended individual is plagued by painful existential guilt about a life unfulfilled, a life not really lived. When people can no longer deny the emptiness of their lives, these feelings of existential guilt erupt into consciousness and often take the form of self-recriminations by the voice. The cycle of despair and hopelessness that follows can lead to various forms of microsuicide or indirect self-destructive behavior described by Farberow (1980).

Angry self-attacks and obsessive ruminations further deplete the energy of people who have denied their wants and desires for many years and for whom life no longer holds any interest or excitement: "Nothing matters anymore. Why bother to go on living?" As the voice predominates over rational thought processes, the individual becomes increasingly cut off from feeling and dissociated from him or herself. Under these conditions, microsuicidal behavior can be dangerous as one approaches the extreme end of the continuum. At this point, angry, vindictive voices often besiege the older person: "You've caused your family enough worries and problems. No one wants to have you around. You make people feel bad. If you were dead, they'd all be better off!" The voice, in effect, persuades the person that his or her absence would enhance the lives of family members and friends rather than diminish their lives and cause them grief. This shift in thinking transforms suicide from an "immoral" act (in the sense that at least six people are negatively impacted by a loved one's suicide) into a moral act in the mind of the person determined to destroy him or herself.

☐ Other Defenses Against Death Anxiety

Clinicians may find it difficult to identify defenses specifically related to death anxiety because defenses are often instituted before the patient becomes aware of the anxiety on a conscious level. In addition to the behavioral patterns described above, a number of basic defenses against death anxiety manifested by older individuals can be delineated:

Vanity—Specialness

Vanity may be defined as a fantasized positive image of the self that an individual uses to compensate for deep-seated feelings of inadequacy and inferiority. It represents remnants of the child's imagined invincibility, omnipotence, and invulnerability that live on in the psyche, available as a survival mechanism when the person becomes too conscious of the fallibility of his or her physical nature and the impermanence of life. In some sense, vanity expresses itself in the universal belief that death happens to someone else, never to oneself (R. Firestone, 1994). Soldiers going into battle are well-acquainted with the deep-seated belief that the bullet will not hit them—their comrades may fall to the left and right, yet their life is charmed. Throughout the life-span, people's efforts to deny death and the inevitable deterioration of physical strength and perceived attractiveness that occurs in the later years undermines the image of being special and therefore exempt from death. Studies have shown that suicide and suicide attempts among the elderly are often related to a crisis in which their vanity was threatened (Clark, 1993).[13]

Suicidologists report that the high suicide rate in elderly white males appears to be significantly correlated with their loss of status, role, power, and money. I suggest that this high rate is related to the fact that male vanity commonly centers around aspects of achievement, success, performance, and sexual potency. When a man experiences a declination in any of the above, there is an increase in depression and self-depreciating attitudes.

Religiosity

Religious dogma (as well as nationalism, capitalism, communism, and other isms) can function as a narcotic, a psychic painkiller, that fosters a deep dependency in people who are searching for comfort, security, and relief from ontological anxiety. For the most part, religious doctrine, including belief in an afterlife, reincarnation, or union with a universal consciousness (Toynbee, 1968) consists of consensually validated concepts of existential truth. Traditional religious beliefs of both Western and Eastern cultures reinforce people's tendencies to deny the body (Western) or transcend or devalue the self (Eastern). It is the author's view that transcendence over the body which must die, the postulation of a soul or spirit, and the union with a powerful being are the principal motivations behind people's allegiance to religious dogma based on serious distortions of the original teachings.

Voice attacks against one's sexuality are partly supported by religious dogma that misinterprets the concept of "original sin" to alienate people from their own bodies, sensations, and feelings.[14] Religion can act as a defense against death anxiety in offering hope of eternal life for the soul in exchange for renunciation of the body and bodily pleasure. Faced with the obvious awareness that the body would not live on after death, early man postulated the concept of a soul that would survive the death of the body, thereby opening up the possibility of eternal life. To preserve this possibility, many people are willing to renounce earthly desires, especially sexual desires.

However, religious beliefs and other socially constructed defenses never completely "work" as a solution to the problem of mortality[15]; if they did, there would be no need for controversy and no reason to go to war over differences in religion, race, or custom. On some level, people remain unconvinced (Berger & Luckman, 1967), and the fear of death still intrudes on their consciousness, particularly when they are confronted by others with alternative resolutions that challenge their own (R. Firestone, 1996). The tragedy is that people of all ages resist facing existential realities and try to deal with life as though it will last forever. In the process, they give up present-day experiences and vast areas of functioning.

☐ Societal Influences on Microsuicidal Behavior in Older Adults

Microsuicidal attitudes and behaviors, as well as self-destructive patterns and lifestyles, are indicative of a broader pattern in the larger society and are supported by its institutions and mores. To some extent all cultural patterns represent a form of adaptation to people's fear of death. Despite the fact that each family or group has its own unique lifestyle, there are generalized negative attitudes, behaviors, roles, and routines in society that most of us accept uncritically. These socially approved patterns of behavior and points of view reflect a compilation of individual defenses. In other words, "a society represents a pooling of the individual defense systems (of its members)" (Firestone & Catlett, 1989, p. 29).

Progressive self-denial is reinforced by social mores that define age-appropriate roles and behaviors in a severely restrictive manner. In spite of our professed beliefs in the value of staying vital and lively and remaining youthful, our concept of "maturity" often implies a gradual retreat from energetic activities as we grow older. Indeed, remaining involved and energetic often elicits disparaging remarks from one's friends, relatives, and children, comments that reinforce the voice: "Still playing baseball at your age? That's ridiculous!" Similarly, signs of romance in the elderly bring on derisive comments: "There's no fool like an old fool!"

In light of the above discussion, the prejudice against the elderly in contemporary society, deplorable as it may be, serves a function. Basically, defended individuals and family members do not want to be around those who remind them of their own mortality.[16] Richman (1993) noted the prevalence of social beliefs that perceive old age "purely as a time of decline, illness, sexual impotence, physical weakness, mental senility and approaching death" (p. 81). McIntosh (1995) stressed the effect of media's devaluation of old age, stating that "The old tend to be viewed as expendable, as having lived long enough and, perhaps, as having outlived their usefulness" (p. 190).

Thus, conventional attitudes regarding the last stages in adult development, old age, support a process of self-denial that appears to be almost universal, wherein people gradually ease themselves out of the mainstream of life. Although they maintain their physical life, they become emotionally deadened to life, to the point where the transition to death seems almost inconsequential.

☐ Conclusion

Throughout their lives, people treat themselves as objects in much the same way they were treated as children; this defensive process is maintained by a destructive thought process. Individuals' voice attacks become more ascendant as they get older and their defenses become fixated and unyielding. Moreover, men and women tend to externalize their voices in their intimate relationships and receive feedback from their partners that reinforces their own self-critical attitudes.

The methods people use to defend themselves against the dread of death and interpersonal stress are regulated by the voice process and become a basic part of their character structure. Microsuicidal behaviors and other defenses are increasingly relied upon as individuals attempt to cope with the social and psychological stressors of old age. As time passes, there is increased demoralization. Positive elements and resources that make up the ego or self system diminish as a result of years spent in a defended, inward lifestyle. Emotional suicide, the obliteration of the personality, can be the outcome, as people face the adversities of old age and the fact of their impending death.

An overall analysis of the destructive thought process indicates that the majority of the voice's injunctions and rationalizations are attempts to limit life by persuading the individual to gradually eliminate exciting and spontaneous pursuits. Physical life is thus maintained, yet psychological suicide is being committed on an everyday basis as people gradually narrow their world and trivialize their experiences. Their strivings are diminished, their hopes dimmed, and in a society that tends to dismiss older people as expendable, they find themselves feeling more isolated and abandoned, and their opinions and feelings largely ignored.

Finally, in studying the attitudes toward death held by older people as well as their potential for microsuicide and suicide, we must be sensitively aware of individual idiosyncracies of mood, i.e., meaninglessness, purposelessness, or emptiness. Suicidologists Fournier, Motto, Osgood, and Fitzpatrick (1991) described these attitudes as "essentially 'spirit-less' or without satisfaction" (p. 8).

It is important to note that all people utilize psychological defenses that cut into their experiences, but they submit differentially to problems of aging. Some rise to the challenge posed by existential threats and continue to strive and love life, while others tend to progressively give up. People essentially give meaning and

---

Points to Remember

1. Microsuicidal behaviors exist on a continuum ranging from self-denial to accident proneness, substance abuse, and other self-defeating behaviors, culminating in self-mutilating acts and actual suicide. They are influenced by destructive thought processes or internalized "voices" that also range along a continuum of intensity. These thought processes become more prominent in people's thinking as they grow older.
2. A wide variety of microsuicidal behaviors and thought processes are related to defenses against death anxiety.
3. Social institutions and mores support microsuicidal behaviors.
4. Microsuicidal actions in older people include increased involvement in an inward lifestyle, noncompliance with recommended medical practices, increased dependence and desperation toward one's partner (intensified fantasy bond), progressive self-denial, and gradual renunciation of important life goals.
5. Vanity (a sense of omnipotence and belief in one's invulnerability and specialness), religious dogma, and nationalistic attitudes (based on in-group feelings of specialness), are other defenses against death anxiety.
6. Recognizing and understanding how negative thought processes operate and how they influence microsuicidal behaviors can help clinicians plan appropriate interventions for older patients.

---

purpose to their lives through investing themselves emotionally in personal relationships, activities, interests, and causes that express their true identity. Sustained investment leads to a zest for life. The philosophy that "it is better to have loved and lost than never to have loved at all" offers a resolution to the dilemma faced not only by older people, but by every human being. The core decision throughout life is whether to restrict life and dull experience in an attempt to escape feelings of dread and anxiety regarding death's inevitability, or to live fully, with humility, meaningful activity, and compassion for oneself and others in spite of life's limitation in time.

☐ Endnotes

[1] Szanto et al. (1997), citing the work of Kastenbaum & Mishara (1971), Meerloo (1968), and Osgood (1991), reported that "In the elderly, indirect self-destructive behavior (such as medication noncompliance, intentional abstinence or restriction of foods or fluids, or fatal 'accidents') that leads to premature death, or 'hidden' suicide, is common" (p. 202).

See also Lewinsohn's (1985) discussion "The Relevance of the Behavioral Theory of Depression to the Phenomena of Aging," in "A Behavioral Approach to Depression," in which he suggests that because of decreased levels of activity and interests, the elderly person "like the depressed person, is on an extinction schedule," that is, "his behavior is no longer being reinforced by his environment" (p. 170).

[2] Rappaport, Fossler, Bross, and Gilden (1993) asserted that "Anxiety about death is . . . a basic human concern, which is clearly critical to persons of advancing age" (p. 370).

[3] Developmental research is necessary to study and integrate dynamics involved in resolutions formulated by children after they become aware of the personal nature of death. Longitudinal investigations on the ongoing effects of these resolutions would be valuable.

[4] It is important to note that a certain degree of alienation from oneself is inevitable in relation to death anxiety because direct contemplation of death's finality is too painful to face without defending or cutting off some amount of feeling for oneself.

[5] See Orbach's (1994) paper entitled "Dissociation, Physical Pain, and Suicide: A Hypothesis," in which he discusses this type of splitting.

> The split creates two distinct patterns of behavior, which represent different substructures of the self and lead to two drastically different modes of experiencing the world and the self. . . . One of the destructive consequences of such intrapsychic splits is the development of serious dissociation from the self and the body, which, in the long run, facilitates the decision to commit suicide. (p. 70)

[6] In situations where parents are punitive or abusive, the child ceases to identify with him or herself as the helpless victim and assumes the characteristics of the powerful, hurtful, or punishing parent. This maneuver of splitting from the self partially alleviates the child's terror. However, in the process, the child takes on not only the parent's animosity and aggression directed toward him or herself, but the guilt, the fear, and indeed, the total complex of the parent's defensive adaptation (R. Firestone, 1997a).

[7] The *Firestone Assessment of Self-Destructive Thoughts* (FAST) (R. Firestone & L. Firestone, 1996) assesses suicide intent and microsuicidal behaviors along a continuum. Items are made up of self-destructive thoughts gathered from subjects and patients. A subsequent factor analysis of scores obtained from 1,300 subjects in an empirical study investigating the reliability and validity of the scale yielded three composite factors—inwardness and low self-esteem, cycle of addictions, and self-annihilation—that were related to increasing intensity of angry affect associated with self-destructive thought patterns (L. Firestone, 1991).

[8] Portions of the descriptions of some of the microsuicidal behaviors, particularly those numbered 1, 2, and 4 below, have been excerpted from "Microsuicide and Suicidal Threats of Everyday Life," R. W. Firestone, and R. H. Seiden, 1987, *Psychotherapy, 24*, pp. 31–39. Copyright 1987 by Division of Psychotherapy (29) of the American Psychological Association. Adapted by permission.

[9] It must be stressed that suicidal thinking is not always due to underlying psychological conflict and emotional pain; sometimes the pain of physical ailments reach unbearable proportions. It would be difficult to deny the right to die to patients who suffer from intractable pain or who are tortured by a terminal illness. In my opinion, however, only in these extreme instances would physician-assisted suicide be valid. This statement applies in particular to cases of emotional stress and depressive states that are often transitional but have the illusion of permanence (R. Firestone, 1997b).

[10] In other cases, the fantasy bond may be maintained through the process of idealization. Partners may idealize, falsely praise, and build up each other to maintain a sense of security. Usually, one partner assumes the role of caretaker, while the other acts out the part of a dependent child needing care.

[11] It appears that death of their spouse or separation/divorce has more negative consequences for men than for women. In 1980–1992, suicide rates for persons age 65 were highest for divorced or widowed men (76.4 per 100,000 as compared with 8.0 per 100,000 for divorced or widowed women (U. S. Department of Health & Human Services, 1996).

Richman (1993) emphasized that social isolation *as a couple* can be equally as deadly as isolation in an individual. In his discussion of the dangers of symbiotic partnerships, he declared: "The problem in suicide is not only separation, but the wish to merge, to become one with the person who is lost or unavailable" (p. 106).

Becker (1964) focused on the difficulties that partners who are overly dependent on each other face in trying to maintain affirmation of their identity in the face of object loss:
We train people to "love, honor, and obey" only a few others. And when death or some other train of events leaves the haplessly loyal person in the lurch, the psychiatrist is apt to hold a microscope to his body chemistry, or measure his saliva. . . . In other words, in our culture we champion limited horizons—a limited range of objects—and call people "mentally ill" when they suffer its effects. (pp. 127–128)

[12] Several theorists subscribe to the view that death anxiety is a manifestation of unfulfilled strivings in life and is *"inversely proportional to life satisfaction"* (Yalom's italics) (Yalom, 1980, p. 207). However, my clinical experience tends to support the converse proposition: death anxiety is related to the degree of individuation, self-actualization, and satisfaction in one's life (R. Firestone, 1990a).

[13] In one study, Clark and Clark (1992) conducted psychological autopsies of 73 cases of suicide by men and women aged 65 and over occurring in Cook County during the first ten months of 1990. They found that only "14% of the suicide victims were terminally ill, . . . 23% had a severe chronic medical illness," yet "two-thirds of the sample had not been exposed to unusual kinds or degrees of acute life stress" (p. 235). Clark (1993) concluded that some of these older people who committed suicide "are fiercely proud and independent, and their sense of self is defined in large part by their productivity as a worker. . . . When the cumulative strain of denying the reality of ordinary life stressors of aging exceeds the individual's own tolerance threshold, a 'narcissistic crisis of aging' erupts" (p. 24). This crisis is manifested by angry denial, refusal of help, or negative and suicidal communications.

[14] See Pagels (1988) for a scholarly review of St. Augustine's misinterpretation of teachings originally meant to enhance the spiritual and human aspects of life.

[15] See Nelson's (1977) article reporting findings from a study of "Religiosity and Self-Destructive Crises in the Institutionalized Elderly." Patients who professed "no religious preference"engaged in slightly less ILTB than did patients who professed a loose affiliation with the Protestant faith but did not indicate the denomination to which they belonged.

[16] Richman (1993) noted that in the "suicidogenic" family, the individual who most often becomes suicidal is often the most open, "as though it is the messenger who must die" (p. 119). According to Richman, these family members typically associate old people with loss or death in their minds, making them "almost taboo to family members who are particularly fearful of separation and death" (p. 102). In considering the impact of social beliefs and mores on suicide in the elderly, one should also take into account social and economic conditions that may influence changes in suicide rates. For example, Richman (1993) noted that the suicide rate decreased with the onset of social security during the 1930s and fell even further with the inception of Medicare. He pointed out that during the 1980s, the elderly suicide rate increased and "appeared to be correlated with threats to such services as Social Security and Medicare and the gradual, though covert, rationing of health care" (p. 13).

☐ References

Becker, E. (1964). *Revolution in psychiatry*. New York: Free Press.

Berger, P. L. & Luckman, T. (1967). *The social construction of reality: A treatise on the sociology of knowledge*. Garden City, NY: Anchor.

Clark, D. C. (1993). Narcissistic crises of aging and suicidal despair. *Suicide and Life-Threatening Behavior, 23*, 21–26.

Clark, D. C., & Clark S. H. (1992). Psychological autopsy of elderly suicide. In D. Lester (Ed.), *Proceedings, Silver Anniversary Conference, American Association of Suicidology, Chicago, Illinois, April 1–4, 1992* (p. 235). Denver, CO: American Association of Suicidology.

Conwell, Y. (1994). Suicide and aging: Lessons from the nursing home. *Crisis, 15*, 153–154.

Diekstra, R. F. W. (1996). The epidemiology of suicide and parasuicide. *Archives of Suicide Research, 2*, 1–29.

Durkheim, E. (1951). *Suicide: A study in sociology* (J. A. Spaulding & G. Simpson, Trans.). New York: Free Press. (Original work published 1897)

Farberow, N. L. (1980). Introduction. In N. L. Farberow (Ed.), *The many faces of suicide: Indirect self-destructive behavior* (pp. 1–12). New York: McGraw-Hill.

Firestone, L. (1991). *The Firestone Voice Scale for Self-Destructive Behavior: Investigating the scale's validity and reliability* (Doctoral dissertation, California School of Professional Psychology, 1991). *Dissertation Abstracts International, 52,* 3338B.

Firestone, R. W. (1985). *The fantasy bond: Structure of psychological defenses.* New York: Human Sciences Press.

Firestone, R. W. (1988). *Voice therapy: A psychotherapeutic approach to self-destructive behavior.* New York: Human Sciences Press.

Firestone, R. W. (1990a). The bipolar causality of regression. *American Journal of Psychoanalysis, 50,* 121–135.

Firestone, R.W. (1990b). Voices during sex: Application of voice therapy to sexuality. *Journal of Sex & Marital Therapy, 16,* 258–274.

Firestone, R. W. (1994). Psychological defenses against death anxiety. In R. A. Neimeyer (Ed.), *Death anxiety handbook: Research, instrumentation, and application* (pp. 217–241). Washington, DC: Taylor & Francis.

Firestone, R.W. (1996). The origins of ethnic strife. *Mind & Human Interaction, 7,* 167–180.

Firestone, R. W. (1997a). *Combating destructive thought processes: Voice therapy and separation theory.* Thousand Oaks, CA: Sage Publications.

Firestone, R.W. (1997b). *Suicide and the inner voice: Risk assessment, treatment, and case management.* Thousand Oaks, CA: Sage Publications.

Firestone, R. W., & Catlett, J. (1989). *Psychological defenses in everyday life.* New York: Human Sciences Press.

Firestone, R. W., & Firestone, L. (1996). *Firestone Assessment of Self-Destructive Thoughts.* San Antonio, TX: Psychological Corporation.

Firestone, R. W., & Seiden, R. H. (1987). Microsuicide and suicidal threats of everyday life. *Psychotherapy, 24,* 31–39.

Fournier, R. R., Motto, J., Osgood, N., & Fitzpatrick, T. (1991). Rational suicide in later life. In D. Lester (Ed.), *Proceedings, 24th Annual Meeting, American Association of Suicidology, Boston, Massachusetts, April 17–21, 1991* (pp. 7–8). Denver, CO: American Association of Suicidology.

Heckler, R. A. (1994). *Waking up, alive: The descent, the suicide attempt, and the return to life.* New York: Ballantine.

Kachur, S. P., Potter, L. B., James, S. P, & Powell, K. E. (1995). *Suicide in the United States, 1980–1992* (Violence Surveillance Summary Series, No. 1). Atlanta, GA: National Center for Injury Prevention and Control, Centers for Disease Control.

Kastenbaum, R., & Mishara, B. L. (1971). Premature death and self-injurious behavior in old age. *Geriatrics, 26,* 71–81.

Lewinsohn, P. M. (1985). A behavioral approach to depression. In J. C. Coyne (Ed.), *Essential papers on depression* (pp. 150–180). New York: New York University Press.

Maris, R. W. (1981). *Pathways to suicide: A survey of self-destructive behaviors.* Baltimore: Johns Hopkins University Press.

McIntosh, J. L. (1995). Suicide prevention in the elderly (age 65–99). In M. M. Silverman & R. W. Maris (Eds.), *Suicide prevention: Toward the year 2000* (pp. 180–192). New York: Guilford.

McIntosh, J. L., & Hubbard, R. W. (1988). Indirect self-destructive behavior among the elderly: A review with case examples. *Journal of Gerontological Social Work, 13,* 37–48.

Meerloo, J. A. M. (1968). Hidden suicide. In H. L. P. Resnick (Ed.), *Suicidal behaviors: Diagnosis and management* (pp. 82–89). Boston: Little, Brown.

Menninger, K. (1938). *Man against himself.* New York: Harcourt, Brace & World.

Nelson, F. L. (1977). Religiosity and self-destructive crises in the institutionalized elderly. *Suicide and Life-Threatening Behavior, 7,* 67–74.

Nelson, F. L., & Farberow, N. L. (1982). The development of an indirect self-destructive behaviour scale for use with chronically ill medical patients. *International Journal of Social Psychiatry, 28*, 5–14.

Orbach, I. (1994). Dissociation, physical pain, and suicide: A hypothesis. *Suicide and Life-Threatening Behavior, 24*, 68–79.

Osgood, N. J. (1991). Prevention of suicide in the elderly. *Journal of Geriatric Psychiatry, 91*, 293–306.

Pagels, E. (1988). *Adam, Eve, and the serpent*. New York: Random House.

Rappaport, H., Fossler, R. J., Bross, L. S., & Gilden, D. (1993). Future time, death anxiety, and life purpose among older adults. *Death Studies, 17*, 369–379.

Rheingold, J. C. (1967). *The mother, anxiety, and death: The catastrophic death complex*. Boston: Little, Brown.

Richman, J. (1986). *Family therapy for suicidal people*. New York: Springer.

Richman, J. (1993). *Preventing elderly suicide: Overcoming personal despair, professional neglect, and social bias*. New York: Springer.

Shneidman, E. S. (1966). Orientations toward death: A vital aspect of the study of lives. *International Journal of Psychiatry, 2*, 167–200.

Shneidman, E. S. (1985). *Definition of suicide*. New York: John Wiley.

Stenback, A. (1980). Depression and suicidal behavior in old age. In J. E. Birren & R. B. Sloane (Eds.), *Handbook of mental health and aging* (pp. 616–652). Englewood Cliffs, NJ: Prentice-Hall.

Szanto, K., Prigerson, H., Houck, P., Ehrenpreis, L., & Reynolds, C. F. (1997). Suicidal ideation in elderly bereaved: The role of complicated grief. *Suicide and Life-Threatening Behavior, 27*, 194–207.

Toynbee, A. (1968). Changing attitudes towards death in the modern western world. In A. Toynbee, A. K. Mant, N. Smart, J. Hinton, S. Yudkin, E. Rhode, R. Heywood, & H. H. Price (Eds.), *Man's concern with death* (pp. 122-132). London: Hodder and Stoughton.

U. S. Department of Health & Human Services, Centers for Disease Control. (1996). Suicide among older persons—United States—1980–1992. *Morbidity and Mortality Weekly Report, 45*,(1), 3–6. Washington, DC: U. S. Government Printing Office.

Yalom, I. D. (1980). *Existential psychotherapy*. New York: Basic Books.

DEATH ATTITUDES IN OLDER ADULTS: EMPIRICAL FINDINGS

CHAPTER

5

Adrian Tomer

Death-Related Attitudes: Conceptual Distinctions

R. Jacob said: This world is like a vestibule before the world-to-come. Fix yourself up in the vestibule, so that you may enter the banqueting hall.

He used to say: Better one hour spent in repentance and good deeds in this world than the whole life in the world-to-come; and better one hour of bliss in the world-to-come than the whole life in this world.

—The Book of Legends (Bialik & Ravnitzky, 1992, p. 556)

The reader of the present volume is likely to encounter quite a "jungle" of attitudes related to death in multiple fashions. It is tempting to attempt a typology of death attitudes as an instrument designed to introduce some order in this thanatological chaos. I will resist this temptation and settle for a more modest endeavor. Instead of a typology I am rather offering a topology, a structure of concepts and distinctions that may help us to locate different types of death-related attitudes.

I start with a short examination of the concept of a "death attitude". Following it I consider the distinction between "my death" and death in general. A scheme of antecedents and consequences is further proposed as a type of conceptual space in which we can locate different species of attitudes related to the end of life. While the distinctions suggested here are not specific to old age, a life-span perspective is used to make the present analysis particularly relevant to the older adult.

☐ What is a Death-related Attitude?

It is of course a platitude that human beings, as distinct from other animals, have a concept of death. Developmental research, for example, shows that children start having a concept of death (albeit immature) around the age of three and arrive at a fairly mature concept of death, as final, irreversible, and universal, around the ages of 5 to 7 (e.g., Florian & Kravetz, 1985; Hoffman & Strauss, 1985; Speece & Brent, 1984, 1992). However death, in particular death of people close to us, as well as our own personal death, is problematic. While objectively we "understand" death, subjectively we tend to reject it and to be afraid of it. It is this tension between our objective understanding of death and the subjective problem that feeds the development of death-related attitudes. Those are ways of conceptualizing death, in general, and of thinking of our personal death, in particular, that go beyond the objective understanding of death and that typically have affective value or consequence. Death-related attitudes connect death to important aspects of our existence, to our main values and goals. For example, death may be perceived as the final loss of control and of power. Such a perception for an individual that values control and power constitutes a terrible threat. An examination of the contrast between the concept of "my death" and the concept of "death in general" can further elucidate this point.

☐ "My Death" versus "Death in General"

Let us assume that you just met a good friend that tells you about the death of his father. The father, almost a centenarian, died quietly in his sleep after living what many would consider a "good life." This death, the death of the other, does not strike you as problematic in any way. Your friend, on the other hand cannot hide from you not only his sadness (which normally will accompany such a separation) but also his anxiety. The death of a close relative is a close encounter of ourselves with our own death.

This illustration of the contrast between our own death (or the death of a close relative or friend), and death in general, has conceptual and methodological implications. We should always ask what concept we have in mind and what concept we measure. It is certainly conceivable to have a very accepting attitude toward death in general but, at the same time, to reject completely the notion of one's own death. Heidegger (1953/1996), in *Being and Time*, discussed the tendency to avoid one's death by adopting an "objective" approach in everyday life, by losing ourselves into the publicness of *das Man* (translated as "They" By Joan Stambaugh and as "One" by Macquarrie and Robinson). According to Heidegger, we (strictly speaking, Da-sein) only pretend that death is certain while at the same time we relegate it to a future where it cannot touch us. To quote, "death is postponed to 'sometime later' by relying on the so called 'general opinion'. Thus the they covers over what is peculiar to the certainty of death, *that is possible in every moment*" (p. 238).

☐ Death: Antecedents and Consequences

In this section I present a structure of antecedents and consequences that can help us to identify or locate different types of death-related attitudes. Attitudes have a cognitive or belief component and an emotional or affective component. Our emphasis is on the belief component. Affect may be considered as being a consequence or effect of the ways in which we think about death.

The rich variety of death-related beliefs can be systematized by locating them in a space of antecedents and consequences of death. Antecedents of death include processes that finish in death (or at least have a high probability of so finishing). Consequences of death refer to the impact our death may have on ourselves, our work and goals, and our relationships with others.

Antecedents: Illness, Disability, Aging

Our thinking of processes such as irreversible illness and aging, in general, tend to be colored by the perception that those processes have a clear direction. Old age and terminal illness, by definition, end in death. It would be, therefore, unwise to relegate death to the status of a contingent or accidental factor when one considers these processes. Therefore, we used to conceptualize attitudes toward aging or irreversible illness as reflecting in part an awareness of their general direction and as being, in this sense, death-related attitudes. It is certainly possible to take an even more radical perspective and to maintain that living is directed toward death from the very beginning and that a human being is not only a being that understands death but is also a being of whom death is a part. To quote Heidegger again: "Death is a way to be that Da-sein takes over as soon as it is" (p. 228). In this Heideggerian, radical sense, almost any attitude may be a death-related attitude.

The fact that the perception of time at our disposal is a powerful psychological factor was recently recognized by life-span theoreticians. Thus, Carstensen, in the formulation of her socioemotional selectivity theory (Carstensen, 1991; Carstensen, Isaacowitz, & Charles, 1999) argues that the perception of time as expansive or as limited affects the selection of life goals.

Consequences of Death: My Self, My Life, My Goals, My Work, My World

Death attitudes that relate to the certain or possible effects of death on our self and life can be considered "core attitudes" in the sense that they are related to the most important facets of ourselves that can be "touched" by death.

Consequences to Self

"Death is the loss of the self." This sentence articulates a possible death attitude that explains death fear or anxiety. Following Heidegger, we can view death anxiety as the reaction of the self to understanding the imminent annihilation of something about which the self cares intensely. Of course, other types of conceptualization of death vis-à-vis the self are possible. Religious doctrines tend to allow the self to endure and/or to be resurrected. In Judaism, immortality is achieved via resurrection of the dead by God or by Messiah. Resurrection of the dead in the Jewish tradition involves resurrection of the body and a similar belief is expressed in the Koran. In Christianity, we find in addition to the idea of resurrection, the platonic belief in the immortality of the soul (see Tipler, 1994, for an interesting discussion of these and other mechanisms of immortality). Other "mechanisms of immortality" might not require a divine intervention. One case in point is the old idea of the eternal return that was forcefully put forward by Nietzsche on physical grounds (see Tipler, 1994, for an analysis of Nietzsche's concept and justification of the eternal return). According to this idea, the universe is bound to return eventually to its previous states, to repeat them as a new cycle which itself will be repeated over and over. It follows that the self will repeat its birth, development, and, eventually, death innumerable times.

Consequences to "My Life"

Death can be considered as the final note in a musical piece, perhaps a symphony, perhaps a sonata and perhaps just a song. Recent life-span descriptions and theorizations have used the construct of the life story or personal narrative (Baumeister, 1991; Whitbourne, 1987). The construction of the life story provides individuals with the opportunity to satisfy their needs for meaning (e.g., Baumeister, 1991; Sommer & Baumeister, 1998) and to revise and consolidate their identities (Whitbourne, 1986, 1987). Death, as the end of life, deprives us of any opportunity for further revisions or additions. At the point of death we **are** our life. To quote Sartre: "At my limit, at that infinitesimal instant of my death, I shall be no more than my past." (Sartre, 1943/1966, p. 91). The "ontological" status of a finished life is somewhat unclear. Frankl (1962) believes that " . . . in the past, nothing is irrecoverably lost but everything irrevocably stored" (p. 122). Others will dispute this (e.g., Nozick, 1981). While it is not clear how such a debate can be resolved, our attitudes vis-à-vis our past life are death attitudes.

Of course, as was the case with the self, other views are possible. An afterlife may allow a relatively smooth continuation of our present life or may be the beginning of "a new and glorious" period that the individual may eagerly expect. The acceptance approach in the three component model of death acceptance formulated by Wong, Reker, and Geeser (1994) is based on such a belief. However, radical transformations and changes may be required in a "new life." A religious person who believes strongly in an afterlife may still be very anxious because of the possibility of radical change and perhaps punishment. Thus, for example, Florian and Har-Even (1983–1984) found high school students from religious schools in Israel to be especially afraid of punishment in the hereafter.

Consequences to "My Goals"

Another way to think about "my death" is to think about possible consequences to my important life goals or values. Baumeister (1991) formulated four needs for meaning: the need for (a) a sense of purpose; (b) efficacy and control; (c) value and justification, and self-worth. The first two clearly involve the idea of **a personal future**. Death, conceived as "the end of my life," denies by this very fact a possible satisfaction of the needs for meaning. The best thing we can say perhaps about this sad state of affairs is that, while these needs are not going to be satisfied (unless we subscribe to an afterlife doctrine), there is no one around to have the needs any more. It is also possible that, in old age, other needs for meaning become prominent. One candidate is the need for **a good closure**. The older person might be less interested in formulating new goals and more interested in finishing his or her life in a decent way. In Genesis, Abraham, Isaac, and Jacob die peacefully "full of years" (in literal translation "satiated of days") and are "gathered unto their people." The Hebrew expression "Arichut Yamim" (Length of Days) denotes a blessing that, according to the Talmudic literature, God bestows to those who obey him (The Israeli Encyclopedia of the Bible, 1995, p. 446). The secret here is to live long enough to satisfy your major goals in life and perhaps to adjust those goals to the length of life (Carstensen et al., 1999). Certainly the decline in death anxiety in old age is consistent with such a view and so are findings suggesting a convergence of present self and ideal self (Ryff, 1991).

Another possible need that may become more prominent in old life is the need to return to being an integral part of the cosmos rather than being an "individual." It seems to me that some recent research on the issue of gerotranscendence is consistent with this type of need as well (e.g., Tornstam, 1996, 1999).

Baumeister's formulation focuses on needs for meaning. It may be instructive to consider a more general system of values. An example is Schwartz's (1992, 1996) theory of integrated value systems. Schwartz defines values as goals that serve as "guiding principles' in people's lives. The theory specifies ten types of values. Some of them are focused on the individual as self-enhancement values (e.g., power, achievement) or as openness to change values (e.g., hedonism, stimulation, self-direction). Other values are focused on the society, on one's in-group and on relationships with others (e.g., conformity, tradition, security, benevolence). Still other values are oriented to the world in general (e.g., universalism). The importance of different values may differ from one society to another and from one individual to another. Death can be thought of as that event which may radically affect the attainment or pursuit of our most important values.

Self-enhancement values may suffer in particular. But not everything is negative. Death may bring an end to physical suffering and to continuous disability, consistent with our hedonistic needs. The "escape acceptance" approach to death is a result of the anticipated end to pain and suffering (Wong et al., 1994). Moreover the de-individuation related to death (as indicated by gerotranscendence) is consistent with the universalistic value. One consequence of this is that death may be appreciated or feared depending on the type of values that are important to the individual and depending on the effect of death on the realization of these values.

Consequences to "My Work" and to "My World"

While goals are future-oriented, "my work" is in the past. It may include any kind of product or accomplishment (e.g., a book, a theory, an invention, a workshop, a recording, a painting, a house, etc.). It includes symbolic achievements (e.g., being first in a competition), political achievements (e.g., helping to pass a law). It also includes our influences on others, for example on our children, perhaps even leaving children behind. A belief that "our work" will survive and perhaps will be continued after our death, tends to preserve meaning and allows for a more positive view of death. A life, on the other hand, that does not leave any valuable traces, is a life that is completely inconsequential and therefore meaningless (see, for example, Nozick's discussion of traces, Nozick 1981). A sense that our endeavor will be unraveled after our death may throw us into despair.

A specific type of such traces seems particularly effective in retaining meaning. These are generative traces. Generativity is a concept introduced by Erikson (1963) to characterize concern for future generations in middle age and it was extended by Kotre (1984), and by McAdams, de St.Aubin, and Logan (1993), to include a variety of types or dimensions and to be important at different points in life. McAdams et al. also documented the preservation of high generativity in old age as well as the connection to high life satisfaction and happiness. It is plausible that this effect of generativity is due to the ability to preserve meaning in the face of death. Indeed, death is very effective at destroying meaning by wiping out both the individual and his or her accomplishments (Nozick, 1981, p. 582). Generative traces, by being focused on the future generations, stand a better chance of preservation, at least for some time to come.

Generative efforts connect effectively between "my work," "my world," and the "future world." By engaging in generative actions, the individual manages to support his or her world so that this world remains intact and continues "in the right direction" even after the individual's death.

Points to Remember

Attitudes taken in relation to our anticipated death are death-related attitudes. These attitudes have a cognitive or belief component that connects death to our selves, to our lives, or to important aspects of our lives. Sometimes the relevant aspect of life is a process that brings us closer to death, for example an irreversible illness. Other times the aspect connected to death is work we have done in the past, experiences and situations that exist in the present (for example a painful disease), or goals that we would like to achieve in the future. Death may affect many of those, many times negatively, but sometimes positively. Life-span psychology has recently formulated a number of theories and concepts that help us to better understand the formation of death-related attitudes throughout the life span and particularly in older age.

☐ References

Baumeister, R. F. (1991). *Meanings of life.* New York: Guilford.

Bialik, H. N., & Ravnitzky, Y. H. (Eds.). (1992). *The book of legends—Sefer Ha-Aggadah* (W. G. Braude, Trans.). New York: Schoken Books.

Carstensen, L. L. (1991). Selectivity theory: Social activity in life span context. *Annual Review of Gerontology and Geriatrics, 11*, 195–217.

Carstensen, L. L., Isaacowitz, D. M., & Charles, S. T. (1999). Taking time seriously—A theory of socioemotional selectivity, *American Psychologist, 54*(3), 165–181.

Erikson, E. H. (1963). *Childhood and society.* New York: Norton.

Florian, V., & Har-Even, D. (1983–1984). Fear of personal death: The effects of sex and religious belief. *Omega, 14*(1), 83–91.

Florian, V., & Kravetz, S. (1985). Children's concepts of death: A cross-cultural comparison among Muslims, Druze, Christians, and Jews in Israel. *Journal of Cross-Cultural Psychology, 16*, 174–189.

Frankl, V. E. (1962). *Man's search for meaning.* Boston: Beacon Press.

Heidegger, M. (1996). *Being and time* (J. Stambaugh, Trans.). Albany, NY: State University of New York Press. (Original work published 1953)

Hoffman, S. I., & Strauss, S. (1985). The development of children's concept of death. *Death Studies, 9*, 469–482.

Kotre, J. (1984). *Outliving the self: Generativity and the interpretation of lives.* Baltimore: Johns Hopkins University Press.

McAdams, D. P., de St. Aubin, E., & Logan, R. L. 91993). Generativity among young, midlife, and older adults. *Psychology and Aging, 8*, 221–230.

Nozick, R. (1981). *Philosophical explanations.* Cambridge, MA: Harvard University Press.

Ryff, C. D. (1991). Possible selves in adulthood and old age: A tale of shifting horizons. *Psychology and Aging, 6*, 286–295.

Sartre, Jean-Paul (1966). *Being and nothingness* (H. E. Barnes, Trans.). New York: Citadel Press. (Original work published 1943)

Schwartz, S. H. (1992). Universals in the content and structure of values: Theoretical advances and empirical tests in 20 countries. In M. Zanna (Ed.), *Advances in experimental social psychology, Vol 25* (pp. 1–65). Orlando, FL: Academic Press.

Schwartz, S. (1996). Value priorities and behavior: Applying a theory of integrated value systems. In C. Seligman, J. M. Olson, & M. P. Zanna (Eds.), *The psychology of values: The Ontario symposium*, volume 8. Mahwah, NJ: Lawrence Erlbaum.

Sommer, K. L., & Baumeister, R. F. (1998). The construction of meaning from life events: Empirical studies of personal narratives. In P. T. P. Wong & P. S. Fry (Eds.), *The human quest for meaning* (pp. 143–161). Mahwah, NJ: Lawrence Erlbaum.

Speece, M. W., & Brent, S. B. (1984). Children's understanding of death: A review of three components of a death concept. *Child Development, 55*, 1671–1686.

The Israeli encyclopedia of the bible (1995). Y. Hoffman (Ed.). Israel: Modan.

Tipler, F. J. (1994). *The physics of immortality.* New York: Doubleday.

Tornstam, L. (1996). Gerotranscendence—a theory about maturing into old age, *Journal of Aging and Identity, 1*, 37–50.

Tornstam, L. (1999). Late-life transcendence: A new developmental perspective on aging. In L. E. Thomas & S. A. Eisenhandler (Eds.), *Religion, belief, and spirituality in late life* (pp. 178–202). New York: Springer.

Whitbourne, S. K. (1986). *The me I know: A study of adult identity.* New York: Springer.

Whitbourne, S. K. (1987). Personality development in adulthood and old age: Relationships among identity style, health, and well-being, *Annual Review of Gerontology and Geriatrics, 7*, 189-216.

Wong, P. T. P., Reker, G. T., & Gesser, G. (1994). Death Attitude Profile–Revised: A multidimensional measure of attitudes toward death. In R. A. Neimeyer (Ed.), *Death anxiety handbook: Research, instrumentation, and application* (pp. 121–148). Washington, DC: Taylor & Francis.

Barry V. Fortner
Robert A. Neimeyer
Bruce Rybarczyk

Correlates of Death Anxiety in Older Adults: A Comprehensive Review

It has been said that we may learn looking backward—we live looking forward. A person's thinking and behavior may be influenced more than we recognize by his views, hopes and fears concerning the nature and meaning of death (Feifel, 1959, p. 116).

As Herman Feifel suggested in the early morning of the contemporary death awareness movement, the way in which we conceptualize death may influence the way in which we engage our lives. In particular, how we anticipate our future death— with fear, equanimity, or eagerness—may shape the way we live and experience the present. While this symmetrical relationship may hold at any point in the life span, it may have special relevance for older persons, for whom life experiences such as diminishing health or the cumulative losses of peers or life roles can make the reality of their own mortality more salient. Our goal in the present chapter is to consider what is known about the death attitudes of older adults, with special emphasis on their fears and anxieties about their own mortality. While hundreds, even thousands of studies have addressed the causes, correlates, and consequences of death anxiety for younger adult samples (Neimeyer & Van Brunt, 1995), remarkably little of this research has examined factors associated with the unique death concerns of persons more advanced in age. Summarizing and evaluating this literature will be the primary aim of this chapter.

A secondary goal for the chapter will be considering the theoretical and practical implications of death anxiety among the elderly. On the one hand, developing a clearer idea of factors associated with discomfort about personal mortality could help refine existing theories of death anxiety (see Tomer, 1992) and other more general psychological theories, such as models of life span development and clinical geriatric psychology. Too often, such theories are offered as authoritative descriptions or even explanations of psychological trends in adult life, without being seriously evaluated for their "goodness of fit" with observed data.

On a practical level, studying death anxiety in older adults could suggest ways to improve the quality of life for this rapidly growing segment of the population. For example, individual studies suggest that living circumstances (e.g., Myska & Pasewark, 1978), psychological problems (e.g., Baum, 1983), and physical problems (e.g., Baum & Boxley, 1984) predict higher levels of death anxiety in elderly people. Establishing which factors are clearly associated with higher anxiety about the end of life could assist with the design of psychosocial interventions to help older adults live without unnecessary anxiety arising from factors as modifiable as housing conditions and as treatable as physical maladies and various forms of psychological distress.

Given the possible benefits of this research, it is surprising that little has been done to review the data available in published and unpublished literature. Previous reviews (Kastenbaum & Costa, 1977; Lester, 1967; Neimeyer & Fortner, 1997; Neimeyer & Van Brunt, 1995; Pollak, 1980; Wass & Myers, 1982) did little to distinguish findings of studies involving elderly participants from those involving participants of younger age groups. Only one death anxiety review in the published literature was devoted solely to findings derived from older adult samples (Neimeyer & Fortner, 1995), and the quantity of studies included in this review was limited by the relative brevity of an encyclopedia entry. Other death anxiety reviews covered studies involving elderly participants in small sections (Neimeyer & Fortner, 1997; Neimeyer & Van Brunt, 1995; Wass & Myers, 1982) or indiscriminately summarized studies of older people alongside those utilizing younger age cohorts (Kastenbaum & Costa, 1977; Lester, 1967; Pollak, 1980).

To compensate for this predominant focus on younger or mixed samples, we concentrated the present review on those empirical studies that examined only the experience of older adults. We then computed quantitative estimates of the reliability, direction, and magnitude of the relationship between death anxiety in this population and several practically and theoretically important constructs. Moreover, we examined a number of methodological variables bearing on the design of the studies and the nature of the measures used for their possible impact on the relationship between death anxiety and the respective predictors. Like comprehensive meta-analytic reviews of other literatures, the resulting quantitative findings were extensive, and have been reported exhaustively elsewhere for the reader interested in the statistical details of our analyses (Fortner & Neimeyer, 1999). In this chapter, we have tried to offer a cogent and readable discussion of the study and its main findings, representing important trends in the data and commenting on their significance in greater detail than was possible in the earlier report. In summary, we have attempted to provide an accessible evaluation of all that is currently known in the scientific literature about the death concerns of adults in late life, looking for theoretically and pragmatically important predictors of elevated death anxiety. We additionally tried to take into account the scientific quality of this literature, specifically examining the contribution of methodological rigor to the findings reported.

☐ Brief Description of the Quantitative Review Methods

Through an extensive literature search of diverse bodies of research literature, we located 28 published and 21 unpublished studies of death anxiety in older adults, which together included over 4,500 participants with an average age of 73. Characteristics of these studies are shown in Table 1. We selected studies that examined the relationship between death anxiety and at least one of the following constructs: age, ego integrity, gender, institutionalization, physical health, psychological health, and religiosity. *Death anxiety* included measures of the extent to which one experiences angst in reference to death. The theoretical distinctions between constructs related to death angst, such as "death anxiety" and "death fear," are debatable (Kastenbaum & Costa, 1977; Neimeyer & Van Brunt, 1995), and clear empirical distinctions of these terms have not been demonstrated. For this reason, we followed the convention of using "death anxiety" as a covering term to refer to a cluster of operational measures of subjective anxiety, fear, threat, and uneasiness associated with the prospect of personal mortality (Neimeyer, 1998a). *Age* referred to the chronological age in years of participants. *Ego integrity* referred to measures of Erik Erickson's concept of ego integrity (Erikson, Erikson, & Kivnick, 1986), including measures of life satisfaction, purpose in life, and measures of generativity and despair. *Gender* reflected whether participants were male or female. *Institutionalization* referred to whether participants lived in nursing homes or in less restrictive settings such as assisted-living facilities and independent residences. *Physical problems* consisted of measures of physical health and medical problems. *Psychological problems* included general or multi-modal measures of psychological

TABLE 1. Characteristics of Primary Studies

Study Characteristics	M	Range
Sample of Characteristics		
Mean age of participants (years)	72.68	61–87
Number of participants	91.98	16–293
Percent male participants	33.53	0–100
Methodology	No. of Studies	
Measured "death anxiety"	36	
Measures with known reliability	39	
Multiple item scales	37	
Random sample	4	
Involved a mixed sample of institutionalized participants	21	
Experimental design	2	
Publication status		
Published study	28	
Unpublished dissertation	16	
Unpublished thesis	5	

well-being and measures of anxiety, depression, and psychological distress. *Religiosity* consisted of measures of religious belief and religious behavior. "Religious belief" included measures of belief in an afterlife and measures that tapped the extent of commitment to belief. "Religious behaviors" included the frequency of behaviors associated with religious belief such as church attendance, Bible reading, and praying. As can also be seen in Table 1, we coded studies according to the methodology employed, including the use of an experimental design, measurement of the construct "death anxiety" in a strict sense (vs. more general measures of discomfort with death), use of measures with known reliability, use of multiple item scales, and the extent to which males and institutionalized participants were included.

In order to summarize findings across the studies, the results of the individual studies were converted to correlation coefficients (Rosenthal, 1994; Shadish, 1992; Shadish et al., 1993) for analysis. We aggregated the individual effects to obtain a weighted average correlation within each category and performed significance testing to determine if the average correlation was reliably different than zero and if there was more variation in the observed correlations than would be expected by sampling error alone. For those categories of weighted average correlations in which there was a great deal of variation we tried to account for the variation by taking into account the methods used by the individual studies through a regression method (Hedges, 1994). A number of methodological variables (e.g., percentage male, institutionalization, use of multiple item scales, measures of death anxiety versus other related constructs) were first reduced to three factors by a principal components analysis and these three factors were used to predict variation in the observed correlations between death anxiety and the other constructs of interest. Finally, if after the regression procedure there remained a significant amount of variation, we performed significance testing on the average correlation coefficient using a more conservative method for significance that takes into account the presence of excess variance (Shadish & Haddock, 1994).

☐ Summary of Study Findings

As can be seen in Table 2 and Table 3, higher levels of death anxiety in older adults was related to lower levels of ego integrity ($r = -.30$), more physical problems ($r = .19$), and more psychological problems ($r = .28$). There was also the suggestion that higher levels of death anxiety may be related to being institutionalized. In contrast, age, gender, and religiosity do not appear to predict death anxiety in the older age population. Furthermore, analysis of the methods used to measure death anxiety and the methods used to draw samples in respect to institutionalization and gender explained portions of the variation in study findings. Experiments that used multiple-item measures of "death anxiety" with known reliability and that drew balanced samples of male and female participants from institutionalized and noninstitutionalized populations tended to find larger correlations in expected directions. Given this brief summary of findings, we now turn to more

TABLE 2. Weighted Average Correlations by Predictor of Death Anxiety in Older Adults: Fixed Effects Model

Predictor	Number of Studies	r	SE	Q
Age	27	−.01	.02	34.7
Ego Integrity	20	−.30*	.02	59.46*
Gender	28	.07	.02	41.50*
Institutionalization	4	.33*	.05	31.50*
Physical Problems	12	.17*	.03	25.59*
Psychological Problems	8	.28*	.03	14.32*
Religiosity	13	−.03	.03	16.38

Note: Asterisks in column r indicate that the weighted average correlation coefficient is significantly different from zero at *p* < .05; asterisks in column Q indicate rejection of the test of homogeneity of effect size within category.

elaborate discussion of our findings for each predictor of death anxiety in the context of previous studies.

☐ Discussion of Predictors of Death Anxiety

Age

A number of studies have found that death anxiety is higher in middle-aged participants than in older adult participants (Bengtson, Cuellar, & Ragan, 1977; Feifel & Branscomb, 1973; Gesser, Wong, & Reker, 1988; Kalish & Reynolds, 1977; Keller, Sherry & Piotrowski, 1984), suggesting there is a negative linear relationship between age and death anxiety during the latter half of adulthood. Our study clarifies this trend by showing that this negative linear relationship with age does not hold within the elderly cohort. Taken together, our findings and those of previous studies imply that death anxiety tends to decline from middle age to older age and stabilizes during the final decades of life. This does not mean that all older people have low levels of death anxiety, but that as a group they have lower levels of death

TABLE 3. Weighted Average Correlations by Predictor of Death Anxiety in Older Adults: Random effects model

Predictor	Number of Studies	r	SE
Ego Integrity	20	−.32*	.04
Institutionalization	4	.34	.19
Physical Problems	12	.19*	.05

Note: Asterisks in column r indicate that the weighted average correlation coefficient was significantly different from zero at *p* < .05.

anxiety than middle-aged people. Moreover, the lack of association between age and death concerns in the studies we reviewed suggests that death anxiety does not continue decreasing with age within later life such that the old-old have less death anxiety than the young-old (Carstensen, Isaacowitz, & Charles, 1999). Our findings also suggest that researchers may do well to turn to other cohort-specific constructs such as perceived nearness of death or subjective passing of time (Bascue & Lawrence, 1977; Keith, 1982) and achievement of the developmental tasks of late adulthood (e.g., Erikson, 1963) to gain a clearer picture of psychological transitions in late life that may affect attitudes toward death.

Theories of late life psychological development, which emphasize increased maturity with age, would predict less death anxiety. Foremost among them is Erikson's theory emphasizing that healthy individuals move toward a greater acceptance of their past and, as a consequence, their mortality (see discussion below). Although they do not directly address death anxiety, other theories also posit a number of changes that would predispose older adults to being less fearful of death. These positive changes include an increased focus on the "here and now" (Carstensen et al., 1999), an accumulation of life experiences that leads to a greater tolerance of ambiguity and uncertainty (Rybash, Hoyer & Roodin, 1986), more complex and less extreme emotional experiences, both negative and positive (Schulz, 1982), and a tendency to become more introspective and philosophical in later life (Neugarten, 1977).

One cautionary note on the lack of a negative linear correlation with age in our study is the fact that the primary study samples were skewed toward the young-old age range (ages 65–75). Individuals in the oldest-old age group (85 years and older) were relatively scarce. In spite of the fact that the oldest-old are the fastest growing age group in the United States, thus far they have been neglected by behavioral science researchers generally (Niederehe, Cooley & Teri, 1995), and our review suggests that they have been neglected in death anxiety research as well.

Ego Integrity

Erikson's prediction (Erikson, 1963, 1982; Erikson et al., 1986) that awareness of death precipitates the *generativity versus stagnation* crisis in mid-life finds support in studies that show that death anxiety is higher in mid-life than old age (Bengtson et al., 1977; Kalish & Reynolds, 1977; Keller et al., 1984; Gesser et al., 1988). Erikson suggested that reaching the conclusion that one's chosen life was the best that it could be under the circumstances results in death losing its sting. Our findings corroborate Erikson's psychosocial theory by showing that there is a reliable, negative correlation between measures of ego integrity and death anxiety.

As a caution, it should be noted that most of the studies relevant to this category used measures of life satisfaction and purpose in life to operationalize ego integrity, even though the measures were not necessarily constructed on the basis of Erikson's theory. Only one study that met the inclusion criteria for this review used a measure specifically constructed to measure ego integrity in the strictest Eriksonian sense. Consequently, the finding that death anxiety is negatively correlated to life satisfaction and purpose in life in the elderly (as in younger cohorts, Neimeyer & Van Brunt, 1995) could also be interpreted as consistent with search-for-meaning theories (Bolt, 1978; Neimeyer, 1998b; Tomer, 1992) and less theoretically embedded assertions about quality of life.

Gender

A previous selective review (Neimeyer & Fortner, 1996) suggested that death anxiety is higher in older females than males. However, the present comprehensive review did not find gender to be a reliable predictor of death anxiety in the elderly. It may be that death anxiety is higher in females of younger age cohorts as noted by reviewers of this literature (Neimeyer & Van Brunt, 1995; Templer, Lester & Ruff, 1974), but such differences do not seem to generalize to the older adult population. Such a possibility deserves further empirical testing and theoretical explanation. It may also be that poor methodology is responsible for the negative finding for the older age cohort. Indeed the present review estimated a correlation in the expected direction of 0.21 under desirable methodological conditions (i.e., measured death anxiety, used measures with known reliability, used a multiple item scale, were unpublished), while a correlation of 0.00 is estimated under undesirable methodological conditions.

Another explanation for the absence of a gender effect in later life can be found in theories that suggest older adults are less differentiated by gender and exhibit a more androgynous gender identity (Gutmann, 1987; Jung, 1933; Neugarten, 1968). Studies suggest that this is a universal personality development process that begins at midlife and continues through the end of the lifespan. For example, Gutmann (see 1987 for summary) demonstrated that during the second half of the lifespan more stereotypically feminine responses to TAT cards are given by men in American, Mayan Indian, and Nomadic Galilean and Druze cultures.

Institutionalization

Our study suggests with some qualification that being institutionalized predicts higher levels of death anxiety. A more liberal method of analysis (i.e., fixed effects method) found that death anxiety tends to be higher among residents of nursing homes than among older people living in more independent settings, but when a more conservative method (i.e., random effects method) was used this relationship was not significant. The low number of relevant studies (n = 4) may explain the low reliability of this category of correlations; and, obviously, more studies are needed before we can have confidence in drawing conclusions about institutionalization as a predictor of death anxiety in older adults. Furthermore, future studies should test mediation models to "flesh out" variables such as forced relocation (Davis, Thorson, & Copenhaver, 1990; Thorson, 1988) that might account for a relationship between death anxiety and institutionalization. Special emphasis should be placed on those factors that carry implications for modification of nursing home conditions so that death anxiety is minimized for residents.

Due to the large representation of participants in institutional settings compared to the general population of older adults, the overall findings may say more about the factors that contribute to death anxiety in this segment of the population. Nonetheless, for a number of reasons, this is an important segment for psychologists and other mental health professionals to study. First, despite high rates of mental health problems found in nursing home residents (i.e., 30% of this populations have mental health disorder other than dementia; Lair & Lefcowitz, 1990), these facilities are often ill-equipped for treatment of these problems and only a small minority receive mental health services of any type (Smyer, Shea, & Streit, 1994). Therefore, it is incumbent on psychologists to study different ways to improve the environment, staff training, and consultative services provided in this setting. Second, even though only 5% of the older adult population resides in an institutional setting, a much larger segment of older adults will spend *some* time in a nursing home before they die (Spayd & Smyer, 1996). For example, Kemper and Murtaugh (1991) estimated that among the cohort of individuals who turned 65 in 1990, 43% would eventually use the services of a nursing home. Finally, understanding and humanizing institutional factors that exacerbate or assuage fears of death or dying are especially relevant given the growing reliance on nursing home services to provide residential care at the end of life, when personal mortality is likely to be more salient.

Physical Problems

Our findings suggested that relatively greater physical problems predict higher levels of death anxiety in the older adults. Only global measures of physical health were used in this review; therefore, future primary studies should tease out specific medical and somatic conditions in which death anxiety is higher for patients suffering from physical illness. For example, does pain, chronicity, terminality, or functional ability moderate this relationship? Identifying more clearly identifying which components of physical illness or distress are associated with elevated death fear could assist medical and psychosocial caregivers in targeting their interventions to ameliorate these factors. For example, there is evidence that persons receiving hospice care, with its emphasis on pain management and acceptance of death as a natural transition, experience significantly lower subjective threat about their own deaths, but slightly higher general depression relative to remitted cancer patients and patients in conventional hospitals (Hendon & Epting, 1989). Such findings suggest that interventions targeting specific domains of distress have specific effects, which deserve more research in the future.

Psychological Problems

Our study suggested that having more psychological problems predict higher levels of death anxiety in older adults. As with medical problems, this finding is limited to global measures of psychological problems, depression, and anxiety. Future primary studies should address the relationship between death anxiety and specific psychological problems such as panic disorder, in which fear of death is implicated in the diagnostic criteria. Moreover, findings such as those reported by Lester (1967), suggesting that suicidal people report higher levels of death anxiety, need to be extended to older populations, which are at heightened risk for suicide relative to younger groups (Leenaars, 1995). Finally, more research is needed on the heightened anxieties about personal vulnerability and mortality associated with exposure to traumatic events, such as assault, witnessing the murder or death of loved ones, and traumatic bereavement. Recent moves toward an integration of the traditionally distinct areas of traumatology and thanatology are promising in this respect (Figley, Bride, & Mazza, 1997).

Religiosity

Reviewers of studies of younger age cohorts suggest that people who are more religious report lower levels of death anxiety (Neimeyer & Van Brunt, 1995; Neimeyer & Fortner, 1995). The present study failed to find this relationship in studies of older adults. One possibility is that older Americans are relatively uniform on religiosity, restricting the variation of religiosity needed to correlate with varying levels of death anxiety. Alternatively, the broader literature (Neimeyer & Van Brunt, 1995) suggests that religious belief (e.g., intrinsic faith in God, belief in an afterlife) is predictive of lower death anxiety while religious behaviors (e.g., frequency of church attendance) are not. In order to test this possibility, we conducted a post hoc analysis to explore whether the inclusion of measures of religious behavior rather than belief was related to this unexpected outcome. The analysis supported the hypothesis that religious beliefs predicted higher correlations between death anxiety and religiosity than did religious behaviors. This finding implies that researchers should distinguish between measures of religious orthodoxy and belief on the one hand, and of church attendance and involvement in religious activities on the other, insofar as these have quite different implications for their death attitudes.

Methodology

Previous reviewers have consistently suggested that there are numerous methodological problems in this literature that may obscure a clearer understanding of the correlates of death anxiety (Kastenbaum & Costa, 1977; Kurlychek, 1979; Lester, 1967; Lester & Templer, 1993; McMordie, 1979; Neimeyer & Van Brunt, 1995; Pollak, 1980; Wass & Forfar, 1982; Wass & Myers, 1982). The present review partially confirms their concerns, alerting researchers to the possible effects of using poor methods, particularly the use of psychometrically unproven methods for measuring death anxiety.

We examined a number or methodological variables and study characteristics to determine if these factors accounted for variation in study findings. By submitting the methodological variables to factor analysis we found three reliable factors among the variables. The first factor was most closely related to those variables that reflected the way in which death anxiety was measured (i.e., measured death anxiety, used measures with known reliability, used a multiple item scale, were unpublished). The second factor was related to variables associated with the way in which researchers sampled from institutions. The third factor was most closely related to the representation of males in the samples. These methodological factors together accounted for a significant portion of the variance in the measurement of the relationship between death anxiety and ego integrity, gender, physical problems, and psychological problems, all of which had more variation in the observed correlations than would be expected by sampling error alone (see Fortner & Neimeyer, 1999, for details). A closer examination of the regression models suggested that the most compelling predictor of the variation in the study findings for these relationships was the way in which death anxiety was measured. Higher correlations between death anxiety and all three types of predictors were obtained in studies with the following characteristics: measured "death anxiety" in a stricter sense, used measures with known reliability, used a multiple item scale to measure death anxiety, and was unpublished.

In order to evaluate the importance of the methodological factors, we used the regression equation to predict what the average correlation would be for each of these categories of relationships under hypothetically desirable and undesirable methodological conditions. A hypothetically desirable study was defined as a published study, using multiple item measures of "death anxiety" with known reliability, administered to a randomly drawn sample of institutionalized and noninstitutionalized participants that were equally matched on gender. A hypothetically undesirable study was defined as an unpublished study, using a non-multiple item measure with unknown reliability of some construct other than "death anxiety." Furthermore, the undesirable study used a sample that consisted of only 10% males and contained purely non-institutionalized participants. The regression models predicted that the correlation would be greater in magnitude in the theoretically expected direction under desirable methodological conditions for ego integrity, gender, and psychological problems but would be less in magnitude for physical problems. Alternatively, the analysis showed that, when suboptimal methods were employed, predicted correlations for ego integrity and gender were reduced from large and medium size, respectively, to near zero for both categories. These findings reinforce the importance of relying on psychometrically adequate measures of death attitudes and sound experimental designs to achieve the clearest possible understanding of the causes, correlates, and consequences of death anxiety in adult life (Neimeyer, 1994).

As noted, however, the optimal methodological characteristics did not always predict larger correlations. In the case of physical problems and under undesirable methodological conditions predicted an average correlation coefficient of .19 with anxiety was predicted, while under desirable conditions the predicted correlation coefficient was .09. This highlights the possibility that positive, as well as null findings, may be related to poor methodology. In this case, it may be that using less reliable and valid methods of measurement and skewed samples may open the door for bias in the direction of researchers' expectation.

☐ Suggestions for Further Research

In closing, it is important to emphasize constraints on the inferences that we were able to draw about the predictors of death anxiety in older adults, owing to limitations intrinsic to the original studies on which this review was based. These limitations qualify the findings of the review to some degree and identify possible directions and considerations for future research. In particular, we were limited by the correlational nature of the research in this area, as few predictors of death anxiety have been experimentally manipulated in this relatively large literature. When feasible and humane, future primary studies should attempt to control experimentally the variables that this review highlights as related to death anxiety in the elderly, thereby permitting firmer conclusions about the factors causing elevated death fear in this segment of the population.

As one illustration of this recommendation, measures of death anxiety could be included in psychotherapy studies and medical treatment studies of the elderly to test the effects of these treatments on death fears, using the reduction of psychological problems and physical problems as mediators. For example, based on the demonstrated relationship with ego integrity, studies examining the efficacy of life review and reminiscence therapy interventions should include death anxiety as a key outcome measure. Life review therapy, as proposed by Butler (1963), is aimed at facilitating resolution of the ego integrity vs. despair crisis by making the process of coming to terms with one's past more conscious and deliberate.

A second limitation in this review that carries implications for future research concerns the role of scientific rigor in this literature. Although the relationship between methodological factors and the size of the resulting correlations between death anxiety and the predictor variables is interesting, this aspect of the review was limited because several methodological variables were poorly represented in the primary studies. For example, the review was unable to include the use of random sampling and experimental designs (as recommended by Neimeyer, 1994) as methodological variables because these methods simply were not used by the investigators who conducted the primary studies. Thus, our recommendation that future studies employ the strongest methods feasible (e.g., validated instrumentation, adequate sampling), while reasonable, is only partially supported by our findings.

Finally, the review was limited by the number of studies available for each category of relationships, which ranged from a high of 28 for gender to a low of 4 for institutionalization. The relatively low number of studies for some categories restricts statistical power. This minimizes the usefulness of finer grained follow-up tests of qualifying variables, such as those focused on differences in results depending on the various types of measures of death anxiety, ego integrity, or religiosity, that were used in the studies. Interestingly, the number of eligible studies was nearly doubled by including unpublished dissertations and theses; and, ironically, our findings suggested that unpublished studies were actually more likely to have used theoretically desirable methods for measuring death anxiety, making them an attractive source of information about the predictors of death anxiety in the elderly. Besides the obvious recommendation that graduate students and their mentors conducting research on death anxiety make greater effort to publish their

---

Points to Remember

1. Lower levels of ego integrity predict higher levels of death anxiety in older adults.
2. Higher levels of death anxiety in older adults are related to having relatively more physical problems.
3. Having psychological problems predicts higher levels of death anxiety in older adults.
4. Being institutionalized corresponds to relatively higher levels of death anxiety in older adults.
5. Religious belief but not religious behavior is related to death anxiety in older adults.
6. Age and gender are not related to death anxiety in older adults, although little research has been done on the old-old cohort of older adults.
7. Using valid and reliable measures of death anxiety makes it more likely that the theoretically predicted effect will be found in the studies of death anxiety in elderly people.

---

theses and dissertations, there may be a publication bias working in this area that inhibits the publication of death anxiety research. Regardless of the factors that left approximately half of the available scientific studies in this area unpublished, future death anxiety reviewers should consider unpublished literature as a significant source of studies despite the greater effort required to obtain and analyze these reports.

In summary, the present quantitative review represents the most comprehensive analysis of the correlates of death anxiety in older adults available to date. As more studies become available, future reviews should extend the analysis of this literature to additional theoretically relevant correlates (such as social support, bereavement status, and time perception), and test constructs that moderate the predictors identified in the present review. Such research should further clarify the physical, psychological, and social factors that contribute to exacerbated fears of death in older adults, and begin to suggest directions for efforts to ameliorate them.

☐ References

Bascue, L. O. & Lawrence, R. E. (1977). A study of subjective time and death anxiety in the elderly. *Omega, 8*(1), 81–90.

Baum, S. K. (1983). Older people's anxiety about afterlife. *Psychological Reports, 52*, 895–898.

Baum, S. K. & Boxley, R. S. (1984). Age denial: Death denial in the elderly. *Death Education, 8*(5–6), 419–423.

Bengtson, V. L., Cuellar, J. B. & Ragan, P. K. (1977). Stratum contrast and similarities in attitudes toward death. *Journal of Gerontology, 32*(1), 76–88.

Bolt, M. (1978). Purpose in life and death concerns. *Journal of Geriatric Psychology, 132*, 159–160.

Butler, R. N. (1963). The life review: An interpretation of reminiscence in the aged. *Psychiatry, 26,* 65–76.

Carstensen, L. L., Isaacowitz, D. M., & Charles, S. T. (1999). Taking time seriously: A Theory of socioemotional selectivity. *American Psychologist, 54*(3), 165–181.

Davis, R. E., Thorson, J. A., & Copenhaver, J. H. (1990). Effects of a forced institutional relocation on the mortality and morbidity of nursing home residents. *Psychological Reports, 67,* 236–266.

Erikson, E. H. (1963). *Childhood and society (rev. ed.).* New York: Norton.

Erikson, E. H. (1982). *The life cycle completed.* New York: Norton.

Erikson, E. H., Erikson, J. M., & Kivnick, H. Q. (1986). *Vital involvement in old age.* New York: Norton.

Feifel, H. (1959) Attitudes toward death in some normal and mentally ill populations. In H. Feifel (Ed.), *The Meaning of Death* (pp. 114–130). New York: McGraw-Hill.

Feifel, H., & Branscomb, A. B. (1973). Who's afraid of death? *Journal of Abnormal Psychology, 31*(3), 282-288.

Figley, C., Bride, F., & Mazza, J. (Eds.). (1997). *Death and trauma.* Philadelphia: Taylor & Francis.

Fortner, B. V., & Neimeyer, R. A. (1999). Death anxiety in older adults: A quantitative review. *Death Studies, 23,* 387–411.

Gesser, G., Wong, P. T. P., & Reker, G. T. (1988). Death attitudes across the life-span: The development and validation of the death attitude profile (DAP). *Omega, 18*(2), 113–128.

Gross, J. J., Carstensen, L. L., Pasupathi, M., Tsai, J., Gotestam Skorpen, C., & Hsu, A. (1997). Emotion and aging: Experience, expression and control. *Psychology and Aging, 12,* 590–599.

Gutmann, D. (1987). *Reclaimed powers.* New York: Basic Books.

Hendon, M. K., & Epting, F. R. (1989). A comparison of hospice patients with recovering and ill patients. *Death Studies, 13,* 567-578.

Jung, C. G. (1933). *Modern man in search of a soul.* New York: Harcourt, Brace and World.

Hedges, L. V. (1994). Fixed effects models. In H. Cooper & L.V. Hedges (Eds.), *The handbook of research synthesis.* New York: Russell Sage Foundation.

Kalish, R.A., & Reynolds, D. K. (1977). The role of age in death attitudes. *Death Education, 1,* 205–230.

Kastenbaum, R., & Costa, P. T. (1977) Psychological perspectives on death. *Annual Review Psychology, 28,* 225–249.

Keller, J. W., Sherry, D., & Piotrowski, C. (1984). Perspectives on death: A developmental study. *The Journal of Psychology, 116,* 137–142.

Keith, P. M. (1982). Perceptions of time remaining and distance from death. *Omega, 12*(4), 307–318.

Kemper, P., & Murtaugh, C. M. (1991). Lifetime use of nursing home care. *New England Journal of Medicine, 324*(9), 595–608.

Kurlychek, R. T. (1979). Assessment of attitudes toward death and dying: A critical review of some available methods. *Omega, 9*(1), 37–47.

Leenaars, A. A. (1995). Suicide. In W. Wass & R. A. Neimeyer (Eds.), *Dying: Facing the facts,* (3rd ed.). Washington, DC: Taylor & Francis.

Lester, D. (1967). Fear of death of suicidal persons. *Psychological Reports, 20,* 1077–1078.

Lester, D., & Templer, D. (1993). Death anxiety scales: A dialogue. *Omega, 26*(4), 239–253.

McMordie, W. R. (1979). Improving *measurement* of death anxiety. *Psychological Reports, 44,* 975-980.

Myska, M. J., & Pasewark, R. A. (1978). Death attitudes of residential and non-residential rural aged persons. *Psychological Reports, 43*(2), 1235–1238.

Neimeyer, R. A. (Ed.). (1994). *Death anxiety handbook: Research, instrumentation, and application.* Philadelphia: Taylor & Francis.

Neimeyer, R. A. (1998a). Death anxiety research: The state of the art. *Omega, 36,* 97–120.

Neimeyer, R. A. (1998b). *Lessons of loss: A guide to coping.* New York: McGraw Hill.

Neimeyer, R. A., & Fortner, B. V. (1995). Death anxiety in the elderly. In G. Maddox (Ed.), *Encyclopedia of aging: 2nd Edition,* New York: Springer.

Neimeyer, R. A., & Fortner, B. V. (1997). Death attitudes in contemporary perspective. In S. Strack (Ed.), *Death and the quest for meaning.* Northdale, NJ: Jason Aronson.

Neimeyer, R. A., & Van Brunt, D. (1995). Death anxiety. In H. Wass & R. A. Neimeyer (Eds.), *Dying: Facing the facts* (3rd ed.) (pp. 49–58). Washington, DC: Taylor & Francis.

Neugarten, B.L. (1968). *Middle age and aging.* Chicago: University of Chicago Press.

Niederehe, G., Cooley, S.G., & Teri, L. (1995). Research and training in clinical geropsychology: Advances and current opportunities. *The Clinical Psychologist, 48,* 37-44.

Pollak, J. M. (1980). Correlates of death anxiety: A review of empirical studies. *Omega, 10*(2), 97–119.

Rosenthal, R. (1994). Parametric measure of effect size. In H. Cooper & L. V. Hedges (Eds.), *The handbook of research synthesis* (pp. 231–244). New York: Russell Sage Foundation.

Roth, N. (1978). Fear of death in the Aging. *American Journal of Psychotherapy, 32*(4), 552–560.

Rybash, J.M., Hoyer, W.J., & Roodin, P.A. (1986). *Adult cognition and aging.* Elmsford, NY: Pergamon Press.

Saul, S. R., & Saul, S. (1973). Old people talk about death. *Omega, 4*(1), 27–35.

Schulz, R. (1982). Emotionality and aging: A theoretical and empirical analysis. *Journal of Gerontology, 37,* 42–51.

Shadish, W. R. (1992). Do family and marital psychotherapies change what people do? A meta-analysis of behavioral outcomes. In T. D.Cook, H. Cooper, D. S. Cordray, H. Hartmann, L. V. Hedges, R. J. Louis, & F. Mosteller (Eds.), *Meta-analysis for explanation: A casebook* (pp. 129–208). New York: Russell Sage Foundation.

Shadish, W. R., & Haddock, C. K. (1994). Combining estimates of effect size. In H. Cooper & L. V. Hedges (Eds.), *The handbook of research synthesis.* New York: Russell Sage Foundation.

Shadish, W. R., Montgomery, L. M., Wilson, P., Wilson, M. R., Bright, I., & Okwumabua, T. (1993). Effects of family and marital psychotherapies: A meta-analysis. *Journal of Consulting and Clinical Psychology, 61*(6), 992–1002.

Smyer, M. A., Shea, D. G., & Streit, A. (1994). The provision and use of mental health services in nursing homes: Results from the National Medicl Expenditure Survey. *American Journal of Public Health, 84*(2), 284–287.

Spayd, C. S., & Smyer, M. A. (1996). Psychological interventions in nursing homes. In S. H. Zarit & B. G. Knight (Eds.), *A Guide to psychotherapy and aging* (pp. 241–268). Washington, DC: American Psychological Association.

Templer, D. I., Lester, D., & Ruff, C. F. (1974). Fear of death and femininity. *Psychological Reports, 35,* 530.

Thorson, J. A. (1988). Relocation of the elderly: Some implications from the research. *Gerontology Review, 1*(1), 28–36.

Tomer, A. (1992). Death anxiety in adult life—Theoretical perspectives. *Death Studies, 16,* 475–506.

Wass, H., & Forfar, C. S. (1982). Assessment of attitudes toward death: Techniques and instruments for use with older persons. *Measurement and Evaluation in Guidance, 15*(3), 210–220.

Wass, H., & Myers, J. E. (1982). Psychological aspects of death among the elderly: A review of the literature. *The Personnel and Guidance Journal,* 131–137.

Wolff, K. (1967). Helping elder patients face the fear of death. *Hospital & Community Psychiatry, 18*(5), 26-28.

Adrian Tomer
Grafton Eliason
Jason Smith

The Structure of the Revised
Death Anxiety Scale
in Young and Old Adults

It is considered to be a truism that older age brings us closer to our death. In spite of this, and quite paradoxically, fear of death was not found to be stronger in older adults. Quite the contrary, fear of death was found in general to decline in older age after peaking either in adolescence or in middle age (e.g., Gesser, Wong, & Reker, 1987; Thorson & Powell, 1994). A possible interpretation of these cross-sectional data is that older adults find in themselves the resources necessary to deal more effectively with death anxiety than younger adults. This type of interpretation will certainly be consistent with theories of life-span development such as Erikson's psychosocial theory (e.g., Erikson, 1963), according to which wisdom is an achievement of a well-lived life. Eriksonian wisdom includes the ability to face personal death calmly and confidently. Other theories, such as the theory of wisdom as an expertise in uncertain matters of life (the Berlin wisdom paradigm) developed by Baltes and his colleagues (e.g., Baltes & Staundinger, 1993), as well as implicit theories of wisdom (e.g., Holliday & Chandler, 1986) are also consistent with the aforementioned interpretation. For example the explicit theory of wisdom developed within the Berlin wisdom paradigm requires the wise person's possession of insights into the nature of human condition and human life with a special focus on their uncertainties, limitations, and finitude (e.g., Staudinger, Lopez, & Baltes, 1997). Moreover, according to the same approach, the wise person is one who has come to terms with his or her condition—a mature person in whom knowledge, intelligence, and personality characteristics are well integrated (Staudinger et al., 1997). Acceptance of the inevitability of individual death seems to be implied by the description provided by the Berlin school.

  It is conceivable that the older person succeeds in dealing with the perspective of a relatively close death and annihilation by excluding or limiting as much as possible death self-awareness. However, some empirical findings make such an interpretation difficult. There is indeed evidence that older adults are likely to be exposed to death more often and to think more about it (e.g., Keller, Sherry, & Piotrowski, 1984).

This increase in the familiarity with death of the older adult may generate several speculations. It is plausible to assume that older adults, as a result of having to face death more frequently, form a more differentiated concept of death—one in which different dimensions are more clearly separated one from another. Moreover, we can expect to find this increased differentiation to be translated into a more complex structure of death anxiety. The result of this increased complexity and differentiation is that older adults' death-related fears are more specific whereas the younger adults' fears are more global in nature. This is indeed the major hypothesis in the study presented here, which is part of a project toward the development and testing of a comprehensive model of death anxiety (Tomer, 1994; Tomer & Eliason, 1996; see also Chapter 9 for a more comprehensive presentation of this study).

☐ The Multidimensionality of Death Attitudes and the Fear of Nonbeing

Structural questions regarding death anxiety (or, more generally, death attitudes) arise because of the view that death anxiety is multidimensional. The multidimensional view seems indeed to be universally accepted, at least in theory (e.g., Neimeyer & Van Brunt, 1995). For example, the *Death Anxiety Handbook* (Neimeyer, 1994a) includes, in the section on research instruments, six scales that measure death anxiety or death-related attitudes—all of them multidimensional. A comparison of these instruments, as well as others (e.g., Florian and Kravetz's fear of personal death scale; Florian & Kravetz, 1983), shows a great variety of factor structures. For example, the Multidimensional Fear of Death Scale (MFODS) developed by Hoelter (1979) and reviewed by Neimeyer and Moore (1994) was developed as in instrument that produces eight factors. On the other hand, the Revised Death Anxiety Scale (RDAS; see Nehrke, 1974; Thorson & Powell, 1994) generated in several samples a four factor solution. Florian and Kravetz (1983) reported a six-factor solution for their fear of personal death scale. These factors can be grouped into three components that can be considered then as higher order factors. A hierarchical structure was also reported by Moore and Neimeyer (1991) for the 40-item version of the Threat Index (see also Neimeyer, 1994). The structure is defined by a general, global threat factor and by three more specific threat factors. Differences between the instruments are, of course, not limited to the number of factors or to the existence of second order factors, or of a hierarchical structure. The nature of the factors is different from one instrument to another, reflecting differences in the theoretical frameworks used to construct the instruments as well as the specific selection of items. For example the Collett-Lester Fear of Death Scale (Lester, 1994; Collett & Lester, 1969) includes as its four factors (a) death of self, (b) dying of self, (c) death of others, and (d) dying of others, thus reflecting the double distinction (between self and others and between death and dying) that governed its creation. The MFODS, while including as one of the eight factors fear of the dying process, does not include any items that can measure anxiety regarding the death or dying of others and, consequentially, no factor like this is generated.

The comparison between the structure of different instruments also reveals at least one element of content common to most scales, although at different degrees of clarity and either as one or as multiple factors. This common element (or elements) is fear of nonbeing or self-annihilation, or fear of the unknown, which appears to be at the core of the concept of death anxiety. For example, Thorson and Powell (1994) report a four-factor solution for a subgroup of the sample characterized by high overall death anxiety. The first factor was denoted "not being." The first factor in the subsample characterized by low death anxiety was somewhat different and was characterized as a factor dealing with uncertainty. Another example is the Collett-Lester Fear of Death Scale (Collett & Lester, 1969; Lester, 1994). The Death of Self Subscale (Collett & Lesser, 1969) loads on several items, some of which deal with the ideas of never thinking, not being anymore, or with the uncertainty of death. Consistent with the view of a core element of death anxiety, current theorization on death anxiety such as the Terror Management Theory (e.g., Greenberg, Solomon, & Pyszczynki, 1997; see also Chapter 3 of this volume) or our own Comprehensive Model of Death Anxiety (Tomer & Eliason; also see Chapter 1) seem to have this concept in mind (but see Florian & Mikulincer, 1997, for a different position). Death anxiety, as pure fear of nonbeing or fear of the unknown, has a long philosophical descent that goes back to the existential concepts of anxiety in the writings of St. Augustin, Pascal, Kierkegaard, and more recently, Heidegger and Becker.

☐ The Investigation of Structure

Given the assumption of the multidimensionality of death attitudes and the concept of structure, questions arise regarding the similarity of the structures in different populations. Indeed comparisons of means of groups assume, in order to be valid, that structures are identical across groups. Investigations of structures have received an extraordinary impetus with the development of confirmatory factor analysis (CFA), particularly in the form defined in (the more general) structural equation models (SEM; see, for example, Bollen, 1989) and implemented by computer programs such as LISREL (Jöreskog & Sörbom, 1989, 1996) or EQS (Bentler, 1989). Given an assumption of a particular structure, (typically including number of factors, and the specification for each factor of the items that load on it) this structure can be tested (under certain assumptions such as identifiability) as for its fit to data, meaning its ability to reproduce a matrix of variances–covariances (or, occasionally, correlations) among the items. The SEM approach is particularly useful in comparisons of structures among different populations, such as a population of younger and a population of older adults. Analyses of stability of structure over time also may benefit tremendously from the SEM approach (e.g., Tisak & Meredith, 1990). Typically, the researcher will define several models indicating degrees of similarity of structures. These models specify the latent variables (factors), the relationships among them (variances–covariances) and the relationships between the latent variables or factors and items (loadings). For example, two structures may be similar (a) by having: the same relationships between factors and items (same loadings) or (b) by satisfying the first condition but also having, in addition, the same relationships between the factors themselves (identical covariances) (see, for example, Bollen, 1989; Jöreskog & Sörbom, 1989). This approach will be applied by making a comparison between the structure of the RDAS instrument (Thorson & Powell, 1994) for younger and older adults.

☐ The Structure of the RDAS and the Present Analysis

Exploratory factor analyses of the RDAS reported either four or seven factors (e.g., Thorson & Powell, 1994), with differences in structure between high-anxiety individuals and low-anxiety individuals (see above). In the present study, the RDAS (together with other instruments) was administered to a sample of younger and to a sample of older adults. The general strategy was to determine a certain structure in older adults using an exploratory technique (principal component analysis) and then to fit this structure to both samples simultaneously. A reduction in complexity of the death anxiety structure in young adults should be expressed by an increase in factor intercorrelations in this population, corresponding to a less clearcut distinction among the factors. A structural equation model that will force correlations (or, more precisely covariances) among factors to be equal across groups should fit the data less well than a model that does not impose this constraint. It is also possible that the number of factors in the young population be reduced, as the younger adults may make fewer distinctions than older adults.

☐ Method

Participants and Tests

The samples included 102 younger adults and 89 older adults. The young subjects were college students who volunteered to participate in the study and who received academic credit for their involvement. Their mean age was 19.98, (SD = 3.07) and most of them (92.2%) had finished two or more years of college. The sample of older adults was composed of volunteers from communities (including retirement communities) in Central Pennsylvania, aged 55 or more (M = 69.04, SD = 9.73), who agreed to participate in the study. Most of them (58.1%) had at least some college education and 17.4% of them had a second academic degree or higher. The distribution by gender was the following: among young adults 68.6%

were females; among older adults 79.8% were females. Most participants defined themselves as practicing religion in some way. Thus, for example, two thirds of the young subjects and 85.9% of the older subjects reported that they "engage in prayer or meditation".

A set of questionnaires was administered to young subjects in groups and to older subjects either in groups or individually. Besides the RDAS (Thorson & Powell, 1994), the set included additional tools dealing with death attitudes, beliefs about the world, and beliefs about the self. A background questionnaire was also administered to measure level of education, religiosity, and death salience. Young subjects finished completing the questionnaires in 35 to 50 minutes. Older subjects took longer, between 55 minutes and two hours.

Religiosity was determined using three questions dealing with: (a) participation in worship services; (b) engaging in prayer and/or meditation; and (c) reading religious texts. An overall index was based on the answer to these questions and on the frequency at which participants engaged in different activities. The index ranged from 0 (very low religiosity) to 12 (very high religiosity). Participants were asked to report how frequently they think about death (more than once a week, once a week, once a month, or once or a few times a year). Additional questions dealt with their inclination to think about specific circumstances of their possible death and about how the world would be after their death. Other background variables included gender, age, and level of education. We distinguished between five levels of education: (a) have not finished high school, (b) have finished high school, (c) have finished some college, (d) have a four year degree from college, or (e) have an advanced degree (Master's, Ph.D., etc.).

A full presentation of the instruments used is provided in Chapter 9 of the present volume.

☐ Results

Preliminary Analyses

We conducted a few preliminary analyses focused on frequency of thinking about death and on gender and age differences in death anxiety scores. The results regarding frequency of thinking about "your own death" are presented in Table 1. Clearly, older adults in our sample tended to think more frequently about their own death than younger adults did: Close to one half of them think about death at least once a week versus less than a fifth of the younger adults.

Additional preliminary analyses were conducted to examine the relationship between RDAS scores (calculated on the basis of 25 items after appropriate transformations of some of the scales to ensure that a high score indicates high death anxiety—see Thorson & Powell, 1994) and background variables—age and gender. RDAS scores by age and gender are presented in Figure 1.

The highest death anxiety scores were obtained by young females followed by young males, older females, and older males. A factorial analysis of variance con-

TABLE 1. Frequency of Thinking about Death in Young and Old Participants

| | Frequency | | | | | | | |
Group	More than once/week %	N	Once/week %	N	Once/month %	N	Once or a few times a year %	N
Young	5.9	6	12.7	13	33.4	34	48.0	49
Old	30.6	26	16.5	14	22.4	19	30.6	26
All	17.1	32	14.4	27	28.3	53	40.1	75

Note. The difference between the distributions of young and old Ss is significant, $\chi^2(3, N = 185) = 22.48, p < .0001$.

firmed that both gender and age are significant factors: $F = 8.75, p < .01$ for gender and $F = 15.61, p = .00$ for age. No significant interaction between age and gender was found.

Statistical Analyses—General Approach

A four step approach was used to investigate the main hypothesis of interest—the assumption that death anxiety has a more complex structure in older adults. The steps were the following:

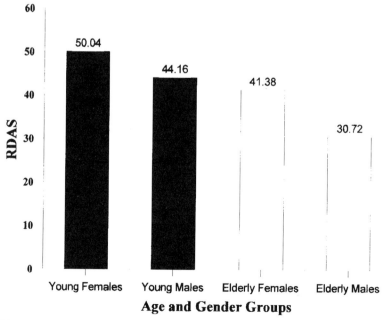

FIGURE 1. RDAS scores as a function of age and gender.

1. A principal component analysis (PCA) was conducted on the sample of older adults.
2. LISREL (Jöreskog & Sörbom, 1996) analyses were conducted exploratorily with the purpose of achieving a relatively simple structure of the Revised Death Anxiety Scale. LISREL 8 and the Maximum Likelihood Procedure of estimation (see for example Bollen, 1989) were used here and in the next structural analyses (steps 3 and 4).
3. Simultaneous analyses were conducted by applying the simple structure determined on step 2 to both samples.
4. Finally, based on the results of the previous step, a Confirmatory Factor Analysis Model was applied to the sample of younger adults.

Exploratory PCA and Exploratory LISREL Analyses

A principal axis factor analysis with a Varimax rotation was first used in the sample of older adults (N = 89) as a step toward generating a Confirmatory Factor Analysis model. The analysis showed the existence of four components (eigenvalue > 1), in general agreement with Thorson and Powell's (1994) findings. Several items tended to load on more than one component. LISREL analyses were performed by assigning items to each one of the four factors according to their highest loadings. Modification indices were used to determine items that tended to load on more than one factor and those items were eliminated. Eventually, fifteen items were retained as shown in Figure 2. The four factors were labeled Nonbeing, Pain, Regret, and Body. Nonbeing is measured in this model by six indicators, whereas each one of the other three factors has three indicators (see Figure 2). The loadings and the general fit of this four-factor model are also of interest and are presented in Table 2.

This model achieved a decent fit: $\chi^2(84, N = 89) = 171.24$, producing a χ^2/df ratio of 2.04, somewhat high but still acceptable (e.g., Bollen, 1989). Indices of fit (GFI = .82, CFI = .84) show a somewhat less than desirable fit (a more satisfactory index would be of about .90). Nevertheless the fit was considered good enough to retain

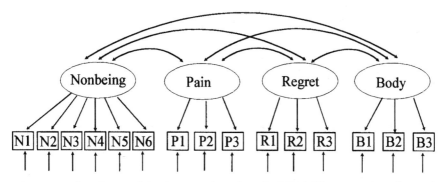

FIGURE 2. A four-factor of death anxiety based on the RDAS (Thorson & Powell, 1994).

TABLE 2. Standardized Loadings on Four Factors of the RDAS Scale in Older Adults

Item Number	Abbreviated Description	Non-being	Pain	Regret	Body
N1	Not knowing what the next world is like troubles me	.71			
N2	Never thinking again frightens me	.65			
N3	I hate to think about losing control	.74			
N4	The subject of life after death troubles me	.78			
N5	I hate the idea that I will be helpless after I die	.68			
N6	I am worried about what happens after we die	.72			
P1	I fear dying a painful death		.74		
P2	I dread to think about having an operation		.56		
P3	The pain involved in dying frightens me		1.01		
R1	I am troubled that my body will decompose			.72	
R2	That I will be missing out on so much disturbs me			.83	
R3	I will leave careful instructions			.51	
B1	I am not anxious about what happens to my body				71
B2	I do not mind being shut in a coffin				.76
B3	What happens to my body does not bother me				.55

Note. χ^2 (84, N=89) = 171.24. The LISREL goodness-of-fit index (see Jöreskog & Sörbom, 1996), GFI = .82. The comparative index of fit (see Bentler, 1989), CFI = .84.

the model for further analyses. Further tinkering with the model would have resulted in too few variables, as indicators, per factor. The estimated loadings (technically those are standardized estimates of Lambda-X coefficients; see Jöreskog and Sörbom, 1996) on the Nonbeing factor have a magnitude of about .7, indicating that about 50% of the variances of the indicators (the square of the loadings) is explained by the corresponding factor. The loadings for the other factors vary more widely, indicating perhaps less "pure" dimensions. One anomaly, a loading of 1.01, was obtained for the Pain factor. Most items are consistent with the label assigned to the factors. Thus, Nonbeing is represented by items such as "The idea of never thinking again after I die frightens me". The factor Pain is represented by items such as "I fear dying a painful death". The factor labeled Regret is represented by items such as "The feeling that I will be missing out on so much after I die disturbs me" and the factor labeled Body by items such as "What happens to my body after I die does not bother me". While the factors are reasonably pure, it is still the case that an item like "I am troubled by the thought that my body will decompose in the grave," which should belong (from a substantive point of view) to Body, ended loading on the Regret factor.

LISREL Analyses in Young and Old Adults

The structure of RDAS as presented in the previous section was obtained using structural equation modeling techniques in an exploratory (rather than confirmatory) way. The question arises whether the four-factor structure that was achieved exploratorily is adequate to describe the structure of RDAS in the young population. An additional question is whether the different dimensions of RDAS are intercorrelated in this population in the same way as in the older population. To investigate these issues, the obtained four-factor model was fit simultaneously to younger and older adults under different sets of constraints. One set of constraints (Model 1) imposed equal loadings of the variables on the factors as well as equal error variances for the variables, but not equal correlations. A more restricted Model 2 also imposed equal correlations among the four factors in addition to the previous constraints. The Models were again estimated using LISREL 8 and Maximum Likelihood. The restricted Model 2 was found to have an unsatisfactory fit, as indicated by a large χ^2/df ratio (much larger than 2 or 3 that are usually considered as the threshold for acceptance) and by very low indices of fit. The statistics were the following: $\chi^2(204, N = 191) = 959.65$, $GFI = .61$, $CFI = .20$. The fit was much better for Model 1, $\chi^2(198, N = 191) = 387.00$, $GFI = .82$, $CFI = .80$. The correlations among the factors for the older adults and for the younger adults, as estimated in Model 1, are presented in Table 3. The correlations are higher in the young group, except for the correlation between Pain and Nonbeing. In fact the .99 correlation between Nonbeing and Regret obtained in the young sample strongly suggests that these two factors collapse in the young population for which a three factor model may be more appropriate. This three-factor model, with Nonbeing and Regret collapsed into one factor, was then fitted to the younger sample generating the estimates shown in Table 4. The fit of this model as indicated by a ratio χ^2/df of 1.85 (< 2) and by indices of fit, GFI and CFI, of above .8 is reasonably good, providing evidence for a somewhat simpler structure in the younger population. Instead of four dimensions, three dimensions are sufficient to explain the pattern of correlations (or covariances) among the items of RDAS.

Regressions of the Four Factors on Background Variables

The previous analysis has shown the existence of four distinct factors in old subjects and three distinct factors in young subjects. We can anticipate these factors to show different patterns of relationships with background variables. To investigate these patterns, we conducted a series of regression analyses in which scores

TABLE 3. Correlations Among RDAS Factors in Older and Younger Ss

Factor	Old	N = 89			Young	N = 101		
	1	2	3	4	1	2	3	4
1. Nonbeing	—				—			
2. Pain	.40	—			.38	—		
3. Regret	.67	.44			.99	.69		
4. Body	.39	.12	.09	—	.67	.44	.71	—

TABLE 4. Standardized Loadings on Three Factors of the RDAS Scale in Young Adults

Item Number	Abbreviated Description	Nonbeing/ Regret	Pain	Body
N1	Not knowing what the next world is like troubles me	.70		
N2	Never thinking again frightens me	.74		
N3	I hate to think about losing control	.55		
N4	The subject of life after death troubles me	.42		
N5	I hate the idea that I will be helpless after I die	.71		
N6	I am worried about what happens after we die	.72		
P1	I fear dying a painful death		.78	
P2	I dread to think about having an operation		.68	
P3	The pain involved in dying frightens me		.46	
R1	I am troubled that my body will decompose	.59		
R2	That I will be missing out on so much disturbs me	.60		
R3	I will leave careful instructions	.30		
B1	I am not anxious about what happens to my body			.76
B2	I do not mind being shut in a coffin			.59
B3	What happens to my body does not bother me			.12

Note. χ^2 (87, N = 101) = 160.86. The LISREL goodness-of-fit index (see Jöreskog and Sörbom, 1996), *GFI* = .83. The comparative index of fit (see Bentler, 1989), *CFI* = .83

calculated for each dimension by summing the appropriate items served as dependent variables. In one series of analyses, the whole sample was used to regress each one of the four factors on four background variables: age, gender, education, and religiosity. Two additional series of regressions were conducted separately in older and younger subjects, using four factor scores in the first case and three in the second.

The four factors showed different relationships with the background variables—age, education, gender, and religiosity, as indicated by a multiple regression analysis conducted in both samples combined (see Table 5). Thus, age and education seem to be important when one considers fear of bodily deterioration, with younger people and less educated people being more afraid of it than older people and more highly educated people. Gender, on the other hand, is related to three of the four factors: females are more afraid of pain and decomposition of body and tend to have more regret associated with death. Religiosity, as one would predict, is associated with less fear of nonbeing and a lesser tendency of feeling regret. These relationships between the factors and the background variables are plausible, providing some degree of external validity to the factorial structure found in the samples.

☐ Discussion

The present analyses provide evidence for the existence of both similarity and differences between the structures of RDAS in older and younger subjects. Two

TABLE 5. Regression of Four Dimensions of the RDAS Scale on Background Variables

	Dimension							
	Nonbeing		Regret		Pain		Body	
Predictor	ß	P	ß	P	ß	P	ß	P
Age[a]	−.07	.322	−.00	.966	−.15	.048	−.28	.000
Gender[b]	−.14	.063	−.19	.010	−.34	.000	−.19	.007
Education[c]	−.08	.238	−.02	.760	−.07	.310	−.16	.021
Religiosity[d]	−.27	.001	−.31	.000	−.07	.327	−.11	.146
R^2 for equation	.10	.001	.13	.000	.10	.001	.16	.000

[a]Was entered as a dichotomous variable, Young = 1 and Old = 2.
[b]Female = 1, Male = 2.
[c]Level of education was coded as following: Has not finished high school = 1, High school = 2, Some college = 3, Finished college = 4, and Advanced degree = 5.
[d]The index of religiosity was based on frequency of participation in worship service, frequency of engaging in prayer, and frequency of reading religious writing, and could take values from 0 (no participation in any of those activities) to 12 (participation of more than once a week in all three activities).

factors, Pain and Body, were maintained intact by the structural equation modeling whereas two other factors, Nonbeing and Regret, were found to combine into one factor in the young population. This latter finding suggests a somewhat less complex structure in the young adults. Whereas this result is based on cross-sectional data, it is plausible to provide a developmental interpretation: with increased age individuals may make more cognitive distinctions which are then translated into a more complex structure of death anxiety (as measured by RDAS). While the study has not provided direct evidence for a cognitive refinement in the concept of death, such an interpretation is made plausible by the finding of more frequent thinking about death in older participants than in younger ones, consistent with the literature (e.g., Keller et al., 1984).

It can be also argued that, in general, the ability to make distinctions between different aspects of "death" may allow an individual to consider positive or neutral aspects related to it and, by doing so, to reduce the **overall** anxiety associated with it. Such an interpretation is consistent with the a general decrease in the overall level of anxiety in the older versus the younger subjects. Moreover, the tendency of less anxious individuals to approach death positively and to find meaningfulness in it (e.g., Holcomb, Neimeyer, & Moore, 1993; Neimeyer, 1994b; Wong, 1998; Wong, Reker, & Gesser, 1994,) can be understood developmentally as the formation of a more elaborate concept of death. The two factors that are differentiated in the elderly, Nonbeing and Regret, are directly related to the idea of nonexistence and thus represent a "core component" in any death anxiety construct. Interestingly, in terms of the Comprehensive Model of Death anxiety presented in Chapter 1, future related regret is one of the determinants of death anxiety. Future-related regret is close to the Regret factor in this version of the RDAS. Thus, finer distinction in older age may happen at the same time that developmental processes change the level of future-related regret in a positive direction of less regret.

In addition to these theoretical implications, the existence of differential structures in old and young adults has methodological and practical implications. From a methodological viewpoint, comparisons in **levels** of death anxiety implicitly assume structural invariance. The existence of different structures may complicate comparisons across age. Those comparisons have to be restricted to either "overall anxiety" or to dimensions of anxiety that have the same "meaning" (in terms of the loadings of specific items on a given dimension) across structures.

Finally, from a more applied viewpoint, findings regarding both levels and structure of death anxiety present interesting questions to death education programs. It can be argued that an important goal of death education programs should be the formation of a more complex concept of death, not necessarily the reduction of death anxiety to a minimal level (cf. Neimeyer, 1994; Warren, 1989).

Additional research, using other multidimensional scales, is required to further examine the possibility of different structures of death anxiety in young and old individuals. It is important in this respect to keep in mind the limitations of the present study that result from the specific samples and tools used. It would be interesting to investigate the structural issues using other tools and different populations.

The importance of a multidimensional view of death anxiety was also reinforced by the finding of relationships between dimensions of anxiety and other variables (such as religiosity, gender, and education) that differ according to the particular dimension. In particular, the finding of an inverse relationship between religiosity and the two factors, Nonbeing and Regret (but not Pain and Body), makes substantive sense and is consistent with other findings in the literature (e.g., Wong, 1998). Religious belief, in particular belief in an afterlife, whether constructed as a defense mechanism or not, should offer some protection by the very fact that it denies, in fact, the existence of a basis for fear of complete annihilation and provides the perspective of an eternal life that can compensate for the problems we face in "earthly" life. Moreover, religiosity may serve to provide meaning to one's life and to increase the acceptance of death as, in a sense, a part of life (e.g., Wong, 1998; Wong et al., 1994). The relationship between religiosity and death anxiety, specifically fear of nonbeing, is further examined in Chapter 9 of this volume.

Age differences in death anxiety (controlling for the other variables) were found for the dimensions Pain and Body, with older adults scoring lower on those dimensions. Controlling for the other variables in the regression equation, in particular for religiosity, had the effect of eliminating the relationship between age and the dimension of nonbeing (older subjects scored significantly lower on this dimension than younger subjects). It is plausible therefore that the finding of reduced death anxiety in older adults is "mediated" in part by religiosity, in particular when a core dimension of death anxiety, such as nonbeing, is involved. This topic is examined in depth in Chapter 9.

The relationship between death anxiety and gender, as evidenced by the regression analyses, is certainly consistent with the literature, in particular with the lit-

---

Points to Remember

1. Older adults were found to think about death more frequently than younger adults.
2. Use of the Structural Equation Models approach and of the LISREL program generated exploratorily a relatively simple structure for the Revised Death Anxiety Scale (Thorson & Powell, 1994) in older adults.
3. This structure has four factors: Nonbeing, Regret, Body, and Pain.
4. There is evidence that the first two factors, Nonbeing and Regret collapsed into one factor focused directly on the outcomes of the end of life in younger adults.
5. The final result can be interpreted to suggest a more elaborate structure of death anxiety in older persons.

---

erature based on the DAS scale (see Neimeyer & Van Brunt, 1995). It is interesting however that the finding of higher death anxiety in women was replicated only when the factors Regret, Pain, and Body are considered but not when Nonbeing is considered. (Although a probability of .063 can be considered "borderline"). The tendency for the female participants to be more concerned about their body is consistent with the finding of gender differences in health care-seeking behavior across age groups (e.g., Wyke, Hunt, & Ford, 1998). Nevertheless the relationship between gender and death anxiety is in need of further clarification. Generalizing the present findings by using a variety of death anxiety measures, as well as a variety of samples, might shed additional light on this issue.

☐ References

Baltes, P. B., & Staudinger, U. M. (1993). The search for a psychology of wisdom. *Current Directions in Psychological Science, 2,* 75–80.

Bentler, P. M. (1989). *Structural equations program manual.* Los Angeles, CA: BMDP Statistical Software, Inc.

Bollen, K. A. (1989). *Structural equations with latent variables.* New York: John Wiley & Sons.

Collett, D., & Lester, D. (1969). The fear of death and the fear of dying. *Journal of Psychology, 72,* 179–181.

Erikson, E. H. (1963). *Childhood and society* (2nd ed.). New York: Norton.

Florian, V., & Kravetz, S. (1983). Fear of personal death: Attribution, structure and relation to religious belief. *Journal of Personality and Social Psychology, 44,* 600–607.

Florian, V., & Mikulincer, M. (1997). Fear of death and the judgment of social transgressions: A multidimensional test of terror management theory. *Journal of Personality and Social Psychology, 73,* 369–380.

Gesser, G., Wong, P. T. P., & Reker, G. T. (1987). Death attitudes across the life-span: The development and validation of the Death Attitude Profile (DAP). *Omega, 18,* 109–124.

Greenberg, J., Solomon, S. & Pyszczynki, T. (1997). Terror management theory of self-esteem and cultural worldviews: Empirical assessments and conceptual refinements: In M. Zanna (Ed.), *Advances in Experimental Social Psychology, Vol. 29* (pp. 61–139). New York: Academic Press.

Hoelter, K. W. (1979). Multidimensional treatment of fear of death. *Journal of Consulting and Clinical Psychology, 47,* 996–999.

Holcomb, L. E., Neimeyer, R. A., & Moore, M. K. (1993). Personal meanings of death: A context analysis of free-response narratives. *Death Studies, 17,* 299–318.

Holliday, S. G., & Chandler, M. J. (1986). *Wisdom: Explorations in adult competence.* Basel: Karger.

Jöreskog, K. D., & Sörbom, D. (1989). *LISREL 7: A guide to the program and applications* (2nd ed.). Chicago: Scientific Software International.

Jöreskog, K. D., & Sörbom, D. (1996). *LISREL 8: User's reference guide.* Chicago: Scientific Software International.

Keller, J. W., Sherry, D., & Piotrowski, C. (1984). Perspectives on death: A developmental study. *Journal of Psychology, 116,* 137–142.

Lester, D. (1994). The Collett-Lester Fear of Death Scale. In R. A. Neimeyer (Ed.), *Death anxiety handbook: Research, instrumentation, and application* (pp. 45–60). Washington, DC: Taylor & Francis.

Moore, M. K., & Neimeyer, R. A. (1991). A confirmatory factor analysis of the Threat Index. *Journal of Personality and Social Psychology, 60,* 122–129.

Nehrke, M. (1974). *Actual and perceived attitudes toward death and self concept in three-generational families.* Paper presented at the 27th annual scientific meeting of Gerontological Society, Portland, OR.

Neimeyer, R. A. (Ed.). (1994a). *Death anxiety handbook: Research, instrumentation, and application.* Washington, DC: Taylor & Francis.

Neimeyer, R. A. (1994). The threat index and related methods. In R. A. Neimeyer (Ed.), *Death anxiety handbook: Research, instrumentation, and application* (pp. 61–101), Washington, DC: Taylor & Francis.

Neimeyer, R. A., & Moore, M. K. (1994). Validity and reliability of the multidimensional fear of death scale. In R. A. Neimeyer (Ed.), *Death anxiety handbook: Research, instrumentation, and application* (pp. 103–119), Washington, DC: Taylor & Francis.

Neimeyer, R. A., & Van Brunt, D. (1995). Death anxiety. In H. Wass & R. A. Neimeyer (Eds.), *Dying: Facing the facts* (pp. 49–88). Washington, DC: Taylor & Francis.

Staudinger, U. M., Lopez, D. F., & Baltes, P. B. (1997). The psychometric location of wisdom-related performance: Intelligence, personality and more? *Personality and Social Psychology Bulletin, 23*(11), 1200–1214.

Thorson, J. A., & Powell, F. C. (1994). A revised death anxiety scale. In R. A. Neimeyer (Ed.), *Death anxiety handbook: Research, instrumentation, and application* (pp. 303–381). Washington, DC: Taylor & Francis.

Tisak, J., & Meredith, W. (1990). Longitudinal factor analysis. In A. von Eye (Ed.), *Statistical methods in longitudinal research, Vol.1* (pp. 125–149). Boston: Academic Press.

Tomer, A. (1994). Death anxiety in adult life—Theoretical perspectives. In R. A. Neimeyer (Ed.), *Death anxiety handbook: Research, instrumentation, and application* (pp. 3–23). Washington, DC: Taylor & Francis.

Tomer, A., & Eliason, G. (1996). Toward a comprehensive model of death anxiety. *Death Studies, 20,* 343–365.

Warren, W. G. (1989). *Death education and research: Critical Perspectives.* New York: Haworth.

Wong, P. T. P. (1998). Spirituality, meaning and successful aging. In P. T. P. Wong & P. S. Fry (Eds.), *The human quest for meaning* (pp. 359–394). Mahwah, NJ: Lawrence Erlbaum.

Wong, P. T. P., Reker, G. T., & Gesser, T. (1994). Death attitude profile-revisited: A multidimensional measure of attitudes toward death. In R. A. Neimeyer (Ed.), *Death anxiety handbook: Research, instrumentation, and application* (pp. 121–148). Washington, DC: Taylor & Francis.

Wyke, S., Hunt, K., & Ford, G. (1998). Gender differences in consulting a general practitioner for common symptoms of minor illness. *Social Science and Medicine, 46*(7), 901–906.

James A. Thorson
F. C. Powell

Death Anxiety in Younger and Older Adults

Two women well-known in nearly all parts of the world died in the summer of 1997. One, Mother Theresa of Calcutta, founder of the Missionaries of Charity, an order of some 3,000 nuns devoted to care of the poor and the dying, was 87 years of age and passed away from natural causes on September 5, 1997. She had received the Nobel Peace Prize in 1979. Her death resulted in an outpouring of reaction throughout the world; heads of state issued news releases as to what a loss to us all this represented, important people publicly admired her piety, and there were calls to begin the process that would eventually lead to proclaiming her a saint. Perhaps because she was so widely known and admired, and because she had remained actively involved in her good works nearly until the time of her death, the reaction to the death of Mother Theresa was almost without precedent—at least for the death of a person of her advanced age.

It took place, however, in the shadow of another death, and it probably did not dominate public attention as it might have because of the event that had taken place a week earlier. The reaction might be said to have been somewhat muted because of the death of another individual—a 36 year-old, who had died in an automobile accident on August 31, 1997. That death had engendered a world-wide outpouring of expressions of grief that was still going on, and a funeral that had been televised that week to over two billion people throughout the world. As an expression of their bereavement and concern, ordinary citizens piled heaps of flowers at the site of her death, in front of her home, at British consulates in cities throughout the world. There subsequently were record-breaking sales of a song performed at her funeral by rock star Elton John. As media events go, the death of Diana Spencer, Princess of Wales, was at least as big as the murder trial of O. J. Simpson had been two years earlier. As a gauge of just how big it was, one needs merely browse the literally thousands of memorial pages still devoted to Princess Diana on the World Wide Web.

Students of popular culture will be gratified, by the way, to learn that as early as September 26, 1997, less than a month after the tragic deaths of the nun and the princess, a company called "Velvet Embraces" advertised on a Web page that copies of a painting entitled *Jesus and Elvis Meet Diana and Mother Theresa at the Gates of Heaven* were for sale:

> The original is on a plush black velvet canvas with even more of a striking appearance than can be reproduced on your screen! A limited number of these were painstakingly and lovingly created by Jean Maguetinez deJesus Latino and now you can own one to treasure for eternity! You CAN take it with you!

No doubt, the differential expressions after the deaths of these two individuals reflected in some way the relative value placed upon their lives by the public. One was an old lady who was expected to die. Although her life had been admirable and was almost unique in terms of accomplishment, it was felt that because of her age, her race had pretty much been run. The other, a beautiful young woman who had really begun to hit her stride as a media personality, had life cut short—stupidly. To judge the magnitude of her status as a personality, one might argue that Princess Di was among the few elite individuals whose first name was immediately recognizable by readers of the headlines in the supermarket tabloids, joining the panoply of names such as Oprah, Liz, Jackie, and Demi in mega-stardom.

☐ Different Deaths—Different Attitudes

The first thing one needs to recognize about attitudes toward death among young and older people is how very different they should be expected to be. Robert Kastenbaum makes this point: "...the young, the middle aged, and the old person might well be influenced by their differential perceptions of probable life expectancy" (1992, p. 4). Younger and older people have differing expectations of how much life is left as well as what the quality of that life may be. Thus the value of life differs. An everyday example of this can be seen when a young person dies. The community's expression of grief is expansive, especially in comparison to the death of an older person, where it is said, "He led a full life," or "We're glad her suffering is over," or similar platitudes meant to lessen the perception of the impact of the loss—or the worth of the life that has just ended. We value the lives of the young, and by comparison we devalue the lives of the aged. So do they.

This concept provides a plot device for John Hersey's novel, *A Bell for Adano* (1946). As an act of vengeance, an occupied Italian village is required by the Germans to yield up one of their own for execution; they select the oldest man in the village, and they stuff his cheeks and color his skin so he will not appear to be such a valueless offering. He is vastly amused at the trick the villagers are playing on the Nazis.

For younger people, it would not be unreasonable to anticipate a future of perhaps sixty or seventy more years of an interesting, rewarding life yet to come.

Aside from the often-recognized maxim that young people think that they are immortal—they don't often conceptualize their deaths very well if at all—it is entirely true that young adults for the most part have a bank of high-quality future years that they can depend upon. Older people have used up the capital in that bank, and the future for them may mean isolation, disability, and hardship. While younger people who are terminally ill no doubt contemplate what death means to them, it would be a singular older person who has not spent some mental time anticipating the end. Young people may think of death as missing out on so many things, but older people might look at death as something else entirely, perhaps even a release from suffering.

Further, the inevitability of death is impressed upon people as they age. Year after inexorable year, they see friends and loved ones pass away. At some point even the most oblivious must quit kidding themselves. One does not see a spouse and brothers and sisters die without having the thought come to mind, "Pretty soon that will be happening to me." In *The Republic*, Plato quotes the merchant Cephalus: "Know well, Socrates, that when a man faces the thought that he must die, he feels fear and anxiety about that which did not trouble him before" (1960, p. 330). The elderly have faced those fears and anxieties, and for the most part they have resolved them. Younger people, on the other hand, have yet to face the fears and anxieties associated with death.

☐ Related Studies

The greatest influences on feelings toward death are related to social circumstances. It should be expected that groups at opposite ends of the life course, older and younger adults, should have different social circumstances; equally, they should have different attitudes toward death. This has been demonstrated in numerous studies of death anxiety, with older adults typically scoring lower, despite the instrument or inventory used to measure death anxiety (DePaola, Neimeyer, Lupfer, & Fiedler, 1994; Kurlychek & Trepper, 1982; Lester, 1994; Neimeyer & Moore, 1994; Shusterman & Sechrest, 1973; Stevens, Cooper, & Thomas, 1980; Thorson & Powell, 1988, 1994; Wong, Reker, & Gesser, 1994). Lonetto and Templer (1986) note that a lack of relationship between death anxiety and age in many studies is most likely explained by a lack of older subjects in a particular sample. Those studies that do have older participants have generally found a negative relationship between death anxiety and age. Perhaps this is because of older persons having a higher level of psychosocial maturity (Rasmussen & Berms, 1996), having accomplished their goals in life (Quinn & Reznikoff, 1985), having accomplished a life review process (Butler, 1963; Thorson & Powell, 1988), because of their greater religiosity (Thorson & Powell, 1990), or because they merely have had the opportunity to adjust to the natural order of death coming inevitably in later life.

An interesting expression of the differential in attitude toward the death of a young person in comparison to the death of an elderly person can be found in mortality rates among widowed people. Here one needs to recognize the effects of age, gender, and socialization. It has been known for some time, for example, that people who lose a spouse themselves have higher mortality rates.

A classic study of bereavement published in 1963 followed 4,486 widowers aged 54+ for the year after the death of their wives. During the first six months, there was an increase of death of almost 40 percent from the rate that might have been anticipated among men in the same age group. This elevated death rate trailed off rapidly thereafter and was back to the normal rate by the end of the first year (Young, Benjamin, & Wallis, 1963). One outcome of this research was that it was thought for many years that the stress of the loss of one's spouse led to higher than anticipated levels of illness and death among survivors. It was only in 1981 that this apparent mortality effect was clarified. Knud Helsing and his colleagues did a 12-year follow-up of a sample of 4,032 adults and found that mortality rates were about the same for widowed women as for married ones (Helsing, Szklo, & Comstock, 1981). The rates, however, were significantly higher for widowers compared with married men. Mortality among widowers who remarried was much lower than it was among those who did not remarry. No significant difference was found, however, among widows. This left unanswered the question of why older men seemed to adapt more poorly to the loss of a spouse than did older women.

A third epidemiological study of widowhood, social networks, and mortality provided some of the answers. Teresa Seeman and her colleagues (Seeman, Kaplan, Knudsen, Cohen, & Guralnik, 1987) reported on a 17-year study of seven thousand adults. They found widows' relative mortality to be the highest among those aged 38 to 49. Death rates were lower among women who lost their spouse in later years, going down to the expected rate among those aged 60 to 69, and being only slightly higher among those 70 and older. The greatest difference found had to do with the existence of a social network. Those of both sexes who had a large number of contacts with friends and family and who belonged to church groups and voluntary organizations were much less likely to die after the loss of a spouse. It was explained that women develop and maintain social networks better than men do; one might conclude that this is why older widows have a lower mortality rate after the death of a spouse than older widowers. Perhaps, though, the relative value of the loss may have something to do with the difference in reaction.

A study in Finland followed 1,580,000 married people aged 35 through 84 for five years (Martikainen & Valkonen, 1996). The researchers were able to analyze a total of 9,935 deaths and calculate excess mortality by age, length of bereavement, and cause. Unexpectedly high rates of post-bereavement deaths were found among men at younger ages and during the first six months after the death of a spouse. While the excess mortality for most causes of death was about 15 percent, for alcohol-related diseases it was a very large excess of 140 percent. Suicide accounted for the largest excess mortality—131 percent for men and 74 percent for women. Violent deaths in the form of accidents were also elevated: "In the first six months of widow(er)-hood, mortality from accidents and violence is 153 percent and 133 percent higher among widowed than nonwidowed men and women correspondingly. After the first six months, the excess is only 37 percent among women but 82 percent among men" (p. 1091). The elevated mortality by age was particularly seen among young men who had lost their wives, an excess almost 70 percent higher than what might have been anticipated; among younger women it was only 25 percent. Among the 65 to 74-year olds, however, total excess mortality was only about 20 percent among males and 10 percent among females. In those 75 and older, excess mortality was only about 10 percent among widowers and it was nonexistent among widows. Again, the data demonstrate that the greatest relative loss—demonstrated in the death of the surviving spouse—happens in the younger years, perhaps when greater value is placed upon the individual who has died.

These findings have been partially confirmed by a study in the United States that assessed relative risk by age and whether or not the death was expected or unexpected (Smith & Zich, 1996). It was found that the greatest excess mortality was found among younger widowers whose wives died unexpectedly. Older widows whose husbands died after an extended illness actually had a significant *reduction* in their risk of mortality. Thus the elements of anticipation and caregiver burden are both folded into the equation, along with perceptions of relative value of the individual who has died.

Reaction to the loss of another is related to reaction to the loss of one's self. As our lives are intertwined with those of others, feelings about their deaths parallel our own attitudes toward death. And, just as it should be anticipated that there will be a greater sense of loss to the community when a young person dies, there should be a similar sense of personal feeling when forming attitudes toward one's own death. For the young person contemplating death, the loss may seem to be infinite. For the older individual, perhaps death may be seen as a release.

☐ Developmental versus Cohort Effects

Perceptions, reactions, and attitudes toward death can be seen to be quite different when the perspective of age is factored into the equation. And, it should be anticipated that individual feelings toward death among the young and among the elderly should be very different. In the literature reviewed thus far, it has been established that young and old vary in terms of the value placed upon the amount of life left, their reaction to the deaths of others, and in basic attitudes toward death. What is not clear is whether these attitudes are developmental or the result of cohort effects.

Attitudes toward one's own death probably change over time, as we have argued that circumstances change over time and influence other attitudes, including attitudes toward death. There is the possibility, though, that cohort effects have some influence upon attitude formation.

The usual example of the difference between developmental effects and cohort effects given in the gerontological literature deals with the importance of religion in the lives of older people. It is an apt example for this discussion, since religiosity most likely influences attitudes and feelings toward death. Older people typically score higher than younger people on various measures of religiosity. Have they become more religious as they aged, or did they begin life in a society that placed greater importance on religion? That is, did they start out high in religiosity and simply stay that way throughout life?

Without longitudinal data it would be impossible to give a definitive answer to these questions, but it would seem that a number of things are going on. First, it is true that socialization toward religion probably was more important sixty or seventy years ago than it is now. Cultural norms placed a greater importance on the extrinsic aspects of religiosity: good people went to church. However, the quest for meaning represented by the life review may have religious implications; there may be some increase in religiosity that has been influenced by this contemplative process. The prospect of facing the end of life does get one thinking, as Cephalus said to Socrates. Additionally, there is some data that would show that people high in religiosity tend to be survivors, that religiosity is a correlate of longevity. Perhaps the irreligious have been weeded out, so to speak, and are no longer available to be surveyed; or, it might simply be that church-goers also tend to live lives of moderation and have fewer health risks (Powell & Thorson, 1991; Thorson, 1991; Thorson & Powell, 1990; Thorson, Powell, Abdel-Khalek, & Beshai, 1997). So, it could be argued that life style influences survival, and that both cohort effects and developmental processes influence level of religiosity in later life.

There may be similar influences on death anxiety differences between young and old people. We have already discussed the differential value placed upon remaining life. Older people may become more fatalistic, seeing their peers die off, and reason that their time is coming soon. Attitudes and feelings toward death no doubt are influenced by the value placed on additional life if that life means social isolation, chronic disease, poverty, pain, disability, or institutionalization. And, the life review process theoretically should moderate death anxiety; it is, after all, brought on by a realization of impending death (Butler, 1963). These might all be seen as developmental processes taking place late in life.

Or, it might be argued that older people were born in an era that was less death-denying. The spirit of the times was less consistent on promoting a pervasive insistence on health and wellness. Older adults grew up in a society where death was a constant companion, and thus it was seen as a natural process that could happen at any time, to anyone. We have noted that a woman born in 1912 once mentioned that going to funerals was a principal social occupation of her youth in a small American town (Thorson, 1995). These factors accounted for by early socialization could be described as cohort effects. The meaning of death for old and young has changed because death itself changed over the course of the 20th century.

No doubt death attitudes are shaped by environmental factors such as early socialization, a will to survive that probably is genetic, and developmental factors such as life reviewing. Again, we can merely acknowledge these variables; without longitudinal information, we can only speculate on the influences that cause attitudes toward death to differ among the generations. We can, however, do a better job of identifying these differences. Just how do older and younger people differ in how they feel about death and dying?

☐ A Comparison of Younger and Older Peoples' Attitudes Toward Death

For the purposes of this chapter, we drew data from two samples, one of younger adults 16 to 35 years of age, and from older people—a group ranging in age from 65 to 92. There were 215 males and 363 females in the younger sample; the mean age of the younger group was 21.6 years (standard deviation = 3.2 years). The older sample consisted of 123 males and 130 females; the mean age of this group was 77.3 years with a standard deviation of 7.3 years. Both samples completed paper-and-pencil versions of the Revised Death Anxiety Scale (Thorson & Powell, 1994), the scale of Intrinsic Religious Motivation (Hoge, 1972), and the Center for Epidemiological Studies-Depression scale (Radloff, 1977).

The Revised Death Anxiety Scale (RDAS) is a multidimensional scale that assesses several elements of death anxiety: fear of pain, not being, isolation, being left out, loss of control, and the uncertainty of an afterlife. It has 25 items scored on a five-point Likert basis, with 0 = strongly disagree and 4 = strongly agree. The neutral score is 2.0, which is assigned to any blanks; there are several items stated as negatives (e.g., "I am not particularly afraid of getting cancer"), the scores for which are reversed in the scoring process so that in every case a higher item score indicates higher death anxiety.

The scale of Intrinsic Religious Motivation (IRM) is a unidimensional scale designed to assess depth of belief (intrinsic religiosity) rather than extrinsic religiousness (i.e., churchgoing activity). It has been shown to adequately assess religious feeling across denominations and across cultures (Thorson et al., 1997). It has ten items, scored on a similar five-point Likert scale; three negatively phrased items are reversed in scoring; in every event a higher score indicates higher intrinsic religiosity.

The Center for Epidemiological Studies-Depression scale (CES-D) has 20 items, scored on a four-point Likert scale (0 = rarely or never, 1 = occasionally, 2 = some of the time, 3 = most of the time), with positives (e.g., "I enjoyed life") reversed. A higher score on the CES-D indicates a higher level of depression. We have found the CES-D to reliably assess five different factors: (a) depressed affect—blues, restless, depressed, crying spells, and feeling sad; (b) somatic factors—loss of appetite, exhaustion, and sleeplessness; (c) interpersonal factors—talked less, feel lonely, people seem unfriendly, and people dislike me; (d) positive affect—hopeful, happy, and enjoying life; and (e) self-worth—just as good as others, feelings of failure, and being fearful (Thorson & Powell, 1993).

Overall, the younger people scored much higher on the RDAS (mean = 50.66, SD = 15.42) than did the older respondents (mean score = 42.43, SD = 12.71), a difference that was statistically significant (t = 7.26, p < .0001).

The scores from the younger sample (mean = 22.48, SD = 7.27) were significantly lower than those of the older sample (mean = 26.82, SD = 7.03) on Hoge's scale of Intrinsic Religious Motivation (t = 7.00, p < .0001).

And, the younger group was higher (mean = 16.50, SD = 11.24) than the older sample (mean = 11.47, *SD* = 7.92) on the Center for Epidemiological Studies-Depression scale. Again, the difference was significant (*t* = 5.74, p < .0001).

Correlations were in the expected direction. Age was significantly related to scores on all three scales: with RDAS (*r* = –.26, p < .01); with IRM (*r* = .28, p < .01); and with CES-D (*r* = –.23, p < .01). That is, as age went up, death anxiety went down. As age went up, religiosity also went up; and, as age went up, depression went down.

As in previous studies (Thorson & Powell, 1990; Thorson et al., 1997), scores on the RDAS and IRM correlated (*r* = –.20, p < .01); as religiosity went up, death anxiety went down. Scores on the measure of death anxiety also correlated with depression in the expected direction (*r* = .30, p < .01); as death anxiety went up, so did scores on the CES-D. Interestingly, religiosity was *not* related to depression; the correlation coefficient of IRM with CES-D was an insignificant –.06.

What to make of all this? First, we can see additional evidence in this analysis consistent with the findings cited above: Again, we see that older people were much lower than younger people in death anxiety and depression in a large, heterogeneous sample, and they were also much higher in religiosity. Death anxiety scores were related in a logical way to scores on other psychological tests; those with higher death anxiety were higher in depression, those with higher religiosity scores were lower in death anxiety. Age, however, is the topic of this chapter, and it is in the realm of generational differences that we need to give the data greater scrutiny.

It is clear from these data and many other studies cited that there are differences between old and young in death anxiety. The balance of our analysis deals with just where those differences lie. Let us look, then, at scores for the older and the younger samples on the individual items of the RDAS. An item analysis might give us better insight as to exactly where these 578 younger individuals differed from the 253 older people in their thoughts and feelings about death.

In the listing below we present the individual item score for each of the groups in terms of means and standard deviations, along with the calculated *t* score for a test of the difference between group means, as well as the level of confidence achieved:

Item #1. *I fear dying a painful death.*
  Younger respondents: mean = 2.8, *SD* = 1.2
  Older respondents: mean = 2.2, *SD* = 1.2, *t* = 6.22, *p* < .0001
  It is clear that the younger people in the present study expressed a much higher fear of dying a painful death. There is some previous data to indicate that women are freer to express fears of pain, but regression analysis indicates that age, not sex, was the important source of the variance in this analysis, as it is with the comparison of the other items: age is more important than gender in analyzing RDAS item differences.

Item #2. *Not knowing what the next world is like troubles me.*
  Younger respondents: mean = 1.7, *SD* = 1.2
  Older respondents: mean = 1.4, *SD* = 1.1, *t* = 3.70, *p* < .0001
  Younger people express more anxiety about the uncertainty of an afterlife, or what that afterlife might be like. This item typically correlates highly with scores on the measure of intrinsic religious motivation.

Item #3. *The idea of never thinking again after I die frightens me.*
Younger respondents: mean = 1.8, *SD* = 1.2
Older respondents: mean = 1.2, *SD* = 1.1, t = 6.07, $p < .0001$
A "not being" item, this indicates that the younger people have significantly greater fears about not existing as a personality after death.

Item #4. *I am not at all anxious about what happens to the body after burial.*
Younger respondents: mean = 2.0, *SD* = 1.3
Older respondents: mean = 1.5, *SD* = 1.2, t = 5.00, $p < .0001$
A "decomposition" item, this is the first of the scale's items reversed in scoring, so that the higher item score means that yes, the respondent *is* concerned about what happens to the body after burial.

Item #5. *Coffins make me anxious.*
Younger respondents: mean = 1.5, *SD* = 1.1
Older respondents: mean = 1.4, *SD* = 1.1, t = 0.51
This is the first of five (of the 25) items on the RDAS where no significant differences were found between the two groups. Coffins, as a trapping of death, may be also thought of as symbolic of the isolation or claustrophobia associated with burial.

Item #6. *I hate thinking about losing control over my affairs after I am gone.*
Younger respondents: mean = 1.7, *SD* = 1.2
Older respondents: mean = 1.4, *SD* = 1.2, t = 3.44, $p < .001$
This item was designed to test for fear of loss of control; older people are significantly lower on it.

Item #7. *Being totally immobile after death bothers me.*
Younger respondents: mean = 1.7, *SD* = 1.2
Older respondents: mean = 1.2, *SD* = 1.1, t = 5.21, $p < .0001$
Not being able to move, being closed up or restricted, or being totally still are facets of death that younger people fear significantly more than do older people.

Item #8. *I dread to think about having an operation.*
Younger respondents: mean = 2.2, *SD* = 1.2
Older respondents: mean = 2.2, *SD* = 1.1, t = 0.53
One of the "fear of pain" items, there was no significant difference between the two groups on it, perhaps because the aged are more likely to have experience or expectations of having to undergo surgery.

Item #9. *The subject of life after death troubles me greatly.*
Younger respondents: mean = 1.3, *SD* = 1.1
Older respondents: mean = 1.2, *SD* = 1.1, t = 0.56
This is another item upon which the two groups did not differ; the prospect of an afterlife seemingly is not of much concern to either group.

Item #10. *I am not afraid of a long, slow, dying.*
Younger respondents: mean = 2.9, *SD* = 1.2
Older respondents: mean = 2.4, *SD* = 1.3, t = 5.49, $p < .0001$
The dying process and the pain involved in it received one of the highest anxiety scores from both groups. This is a negative reversed in scoring; a high score means that people *are* afraid of a long, slow dying. Younger people feared it more by a significant margin.

Item #11. *I do not mind the idea of being shut into a coffin when I die.*
   Younger respondents: mean = 2.1, *SD* = 1.2
   Older respondents: mean = 1.7, *SD* = 1.2, *t* = 3.33, *p* < .001
   Another reversal, this item gets at the claustrophobia factor better than Item #5 and parallels the fears assessed by Item #7. Younger people are more fearful of the idea of being closed up in a coffin.

Item #12. *I hate the idea that I will be helpless after I die.*
   Younger respondents: mean = 1.8, *SD* = 1.2
   Older respondents: mean = 1.5, *SD* = 1.2, *t* = 2.92, *p* < .01
   Another "helplessness" item similar to Item #6, the difference here is not so great; it is, however, statistically significant.

Item #13. I am not at all concerned over whether or not there is an afterlife.
   Younger respondents: mean = 2.7, *SD* = 1.2
   Older respondents: mean = 2.5, *SD* = 1.4, *t* = 2.56, *p* < .01
   Again, another small difference that is significant; a reversal, a higher score means that the respondent *is* concerned over whether or not there is an afterlife. This item has a problem in that it can be interpreted differently by different people. It might be possible, for example, for highly religious people to feel sure of an afterlife and thus mark a low response on the Likert scale. Conversely, they may reason that the existence of an afterlife is quite important in their lives, and thus strongly disagree: they *are* concerned with whether or not there is an afterlife. Likewise, someone high in death anxiety who is nevertheless certain that there is no afterlife may indicate a lack of concern on this item.

Item #14. *Never feeling anything again after I die upsets me.*
   Younger respondents: mean = 1.7, *SD* = 1.2
   Older respondents: mean = 1.4, *SD* = 1.2, *t* = 3.25, *p* < .001
   This item combines concepts of "not being" with the lack of physical stimulus associated with being dead. Younger subjects were higher on it.

Item #15. *The pain involved in dying frightens me.*
   Younger respondents: mean = 2.4, *SD* = 1.1
   Older respondents: mean = 2.2, *SD* = 1.1, *t* = 2.98, *p* < .01
   Another "pain" item, the differences are not so great here, but with such a large sample they are statistically significant at an acceptable level of confidence.

Item #16. *I am looking forward to a new life after I die.*
   Younger respondents: mean = 1.4, *SD* = 1.1
   Older respondents: mean = 1.3, *SD* = 1.6, *t*=1.39
   There was no significant difference between the two groups on this item. Note, however, the variability in the older subjects' responses; this item had the largest standard deviation of any in the scale.

Item #17. *I am not worried about ever being helpless.*
   Younger respondents: mean = 2.2, *SD* = 1.2
   Older respondents: mean = 2.3, *SD* = 1.3, *t* = 0.23
   This is an item on the RDAS upon which older people had a higher mean score, although the difference was not significant; this item contributes little to the variance measured by the scale.

Item #18. *I am troubled by the thought that my body will decompose in the grave.*
Younger respondents: mean = 1.6, *SD* = 1.1
Older respondents: mean = 1.2, *SD* = 1.11, *t* = 4.19, *p* < .0001
Clearly, the younger people in the present study had much higher fears of body decomposition and loss of bodily integrity.

Item #19. *The feeling that I will be missing out on so much after I die disturbs me.*
Younger respondents: mean = 1.9, *SD* = 1.2
Older respondents: mean = 1.4, *SD* = 1.2, *t* = 5.51, *p* < .0001
Similar to Items #3 and #14, this again demonstrates younger subjects' much higher fears of "not being."

Item #20. *I am worried about what happens to us after we die.*
Younger respondents: mean = 1.9, *SD* = 1.2
Older respondents: mean = 1.4, *SD* = 1.1, *t* = 5.6, *p* < .0001
This item may combine concepts of not being with decomposition; younger people were much higher on it.

Item #21. *I am not at all concerned with being in control of things.*
Younger respondents: mean = 2.3, *SD* = 1.1
Older respondents: mean = 1.9, *SD* = 1.1, *t* = 4.54, *p* < .0001
A reversal; higher score indicates that the respondent *is* concerned with being in control. These data again demonstrate younger peoples' higher fears of becoming helpless.

Item #22. *The total isolation of death is frightening to me.*
Younger respondents: mean = 1.8, *SD* = 1.2
Older respondents: mean = 1.3, *SD* = 1.1, *t* = 5.53, *p* < .0001
Being closed in, being isolated, not being able to interact with others—this item again differentiates younger and older peoples' feelings about bodily death.

Item #23. *I am not particularly afraid of getting cancer.*
Younger respondents: mean = 2.9, *SD* = 1.1
Older respondents: mean = 2.2, *SD* = 1.2, *t* = 7.54, *p* < .0001
Another item reversed in scoring; a higher score is indicative of being afraid of getting cancer. This item's score is the highest on the scale, along with being afraid of a long slow dying, indicating younger peoples' fears of chronic, disabling terminal illness.

Item #24. *I will leave careful instructions about how things should be done after I am gone.*
Younger respondents: mean = 2.4, *SD* = 1.1
Older respondents: mean = 2.6, *SD* = 1.0, *t* = 2.59, *p* < .01
A small difference, but an important one; this is the only item on the entire RDAS upon which older subjects scored significantly higher. It indicates their greater sense of the need to take care of unfinished business—the practical considerations associated with the end of a life.

Item #25. *What happens to my body after I die does not bother me.*
Younger respondents: mean = 2.1, *SD* = 1.2
Older respondents: mean = 1.4, *SD* = 1.1, *t* = 7.19, *p* < .0001
The greatest difference among all of the items on the scale, this loss of bodily integrity item clearly differentiates the younger from the older participants in this study.

☐ Summary and Conclusions

Older people were significantly higher on only one of the RDAS items analyzed, a "taking care of business" item—the desire to leave careful instructions on what needs to be done after they are gone. This is a natural inclination, and a helpful one. They have spent years giving guidance to younger people; now that they are about to pass the torch they need to make one final effort at leaving instructions on how to light it. There were insignificant differences on five of the 25 scale items. On the remaining 19 items, younger people scored significantly higher than did the older people. Their total score on the Revised Death Anxiety Scale was a great deal higher than that achieved by the people aged 65 and above. This is consistent with our previous research using the RDAS among large, heterogeneous groups with a broad age span (Thorson & Powell, 1988, 1990, 1994). We feel that a persuasive body of evidence has been presented in this regard, and we are prepared to conclude that younger people have much higher death anxiety in comparison to the attitudes generally held by older individuals, when comparing large groups over time.

Just where those differences lie appears to be related to fears of loss of things that young people feel are important: being, activity, control, and especially physical aspects represented by fears of pain and decomposition. It might be said that the great social movement toward health and wellness seen in the American population in the current generation is an explication of those fears and anxieties related to morbidity and mortality. Perhaps these attitudes will be perpetuated in years to come as the generations move across the life course.

Society places greater worth upon the lives of younger people, and so do they. Beyond this social value factor, though, it might be said that higher levels of religiosity moderate older peoples' death anxiety. As that may well represent a cohort effect, it will be interesting to observe whether or not a more secular society in the future will also represent an aging population with higher levels of fear of death.

Points to Remember

1. Older people tend to fear death less than younger people do.
2. This age difference in approach to death may be due to what we called the "relative value of the loss," defined by the expected quality and quantity of one's future. This relative value is reflected in people's reaction to bereavement as well as in the greater worth the society places on younger people's lives.
3. Intrinsic religiosity (which is higher in older people) moderates death anxiety levels.

☐ References

Butler, R. N. (1963). The life review: An interpretation of reminiscence in old age. *Psychiatry, 26,* 65–76.

DePaola, S. J., Neimeyer, R. A., Lupfer, M. B., & Fiedler, J. (1994). Death concern and attitudes toward the elderly in nursing home personnel. In R. A. Neimeyer (Ed.), *Death anxiety handbook: Research, instrumentation, and application* (pp. 201–216). Washington, DC: Taylor & Francis.

Helsing, K. J., Szklo, M., & Comstock, G. W. (1981). Factors associated with mortality after widowhood. *American Journal of Public Health, 71,* 802–809.

Hersey, J. (1946). *A bell for Adano.* New York: The Modern Library.

Hoge, D. R. (1972). A validated intrinsic religious motivation scale. *Journal for the Scientific Study of Religion, 11,* 369–376.

Kastenbaum, R. (1992). Death, suicide and the older adult. *Suicide and Life-Threatening Behavior, 22,* 1–14.

Kurlychek, R. T., & Trepper, T. S. (1982). Accuracy of perception of attitude. *Perceptual and Motor Skills, 54,* 272–274.

Lester, D. (1994). The Collett-Lester Fear of Death Scale. In R. A. Neimeyer (Ed.), *Death anxiety handbook: Research, instrumentation, and application* (pp. 45–60). Washington, DC: Taylor & Francis.

Lonetto, R., & Templer, D. I. (1986). *Death anxiety.* Washington, DC: Hemisphere.

Martikainen, P., & Valkonen, T. (1996). Mortality after the death of a spouse: Rates and causes of death in a large Finnish cohort. *American Journal of Public Health, 86,* 1087–1093.

Neimeyer, R. A., & Moore, M. K. (1994). Validity and reliability of the Multidimensional Fear of Death Scale. In R. A. Neimeyer (Ed.), *Death anxiety handbook: Research, instrumentation, and application* (pp. 103–119). Washington, DC: Taylor & Francis.

Plato. (1960). *The republic: Translated into English by B. Jowett.* New York: Vintage Books.

Powell, F. C., & Thorson, J. A. (1991). Life, death, and life after death: Meanings of the relationship between death anxiety and religion. *Journal of Religious Gerontology, 8*(1), 41–56.

Quinn, P. K., & Reznikoff, M. (1985). The relationship between death anxiety and the subjective experience of time in the elderly. *International Journal of Aging and Human Development, 21,* 197–210.

Radloff, L. S. (1977). The CES-D scale: A self-report depression scale for research in the general population. *Applied Psychological Measurement, 1,* 385–401.

Rasmussen, C. A., & Berms, C. (1996). The relationship of death anxiety with age and psychosocial maturity. *The Journal of Psychology, 130,* 141–144.

Seeman, T. E., Kaplan, G. A., Knudsen, L., Cohen, R., & Guralnik, J. (1987). Social network ties and mortality among the elderly in the Alameda County study. *American Journal of Epidemiology, 126,* 714–723.

Shusterman, L. R., & Sechrest, L. (1973). Attitudes of registered nurses towards death in a general hospital. *Psychiatry in Medicine, 4,* 411–426.

Smith, K. R., & Zich, C. D. (1996). Risk of mortality following widowhood: Age and sex differences by mode of death. *Social Biology, 43,* 59–71.

Stevens, S. J., Cooper, P. E., & Thomas, L. E. (1980). Age norms for Templer's Death Anxiety Scale. *Psychological Reports, 46,* 205-206.

Thorson, J. A. (1991). Afterlife constructs, death anxiety, and life reviewing: Importance of religion as a moderating variable. *Journal of Psychology and Theology, 19,* 278–284.

Thorson, J. A. (1995). *Aging in a changing society.* Belmont, CA: Wadsworth.

Thorson, J. A., & Powell, F. C. (1988). Elements of death anxiety and meanings of death. *Journal of Clinical Psychology, 44,* 691–701.

Thorson, J. A., & Powell, F. C. (1990). Meanings of death and intrinsic religiosity. *Journal of Clinical Psychology, 46*, 379–391.

Thorson, J. A., & Powell, F. C. (1993). The CES-D: Four or five factors? *Bulletin of the Psychonomic Society, 31*, 577–578.

Thorson, J. A., & Powell, F. C. (1994). A Revised Death Anxiety Scale. In R. A. Neimeyer (Ed.), *Death anxiety handbook: Research, instrumentation, and application* (pp. 31–43). Washington, DC: Taylor & Francis.

Thorson, J. A., Powell, F. C., Abdel-Khalek, A. M., & Beshai, J. A. (1997). Constructions of religiosity and death anxiety in two cultures: The United States and Kuwait. *Journal of Psychology and Theology, 25*, 374–383.

Wong, T. P., Reker, G. T., & Gesser, G. (1994). Death Attitude Profile Revised: A multidimensional measure of attitudes toward death. In R. A. Neimeyer (Ed.), *Death anxiety handbook: Research, instrumentation, and application* (pp. 121–148). Washington, DC: Taylor & Francis.

Young, M., Benjamin, B., & Wallis, C. (1963). Mortality of widowers. *Lancet, 2*, 454.

CHAPTER 9

Adrian Tomer
Grafton Eliason

Beliefs about Self, Life, and Death: Testing Aspects of a Comprehensive Model of Death Anxiety and Death Attitudes

A Comprehensive Model of Death Anxiety (CMDA) was proposed by Tomer and Eliason (1996). According to this model (see Chapter 1), death anxiety, defined as fear of death conceptualized as annihilation of the self, is related directly or indirectly to several types of belief: beliefs about the meaningfulness of death (or "death attitudes"), beliefs about the self, and beliefs about the world. These belief systems are interconnected. In particular, the conceptualization of death is a function of one's beliefs about oneself and about the world. Also, death anxiety, in addition to being directly related to one's cognitive perception of death, is related directly to two types of regret—past-related and future-related regret. Death salience, the extent to which one thinks about his or her potential death, is assumed to play an important role in activating diverse coping processes and in affecting the belief systems. This model, although intuitively plausible and consistent with existing findings, requires empirical confirmation.

The study presented here attempts a partial investigation of the death anxiety model. A somewhat simplified model served for this purpose (see Figure 1).

Death attitudes (e.g., the belief that death is natural) together with attitudes about the self (e.g., self-esteem, locus of control) and the world (e.g., belief in a just world) are hypothesized to influence the level of death anxiety of an individual either directly or indirectly, by affecting death attitudes. Death salience and religiosity may also affect death anxiety directly or indirectly. Finally, other background variables—gender, age, and education—may be related to death attitudes and to other beliefs about the self and the world, or may affect DA directly. This model represents a simplification of the integrative death anxiety model, in particular because it does not consider the two types of regret that play an important

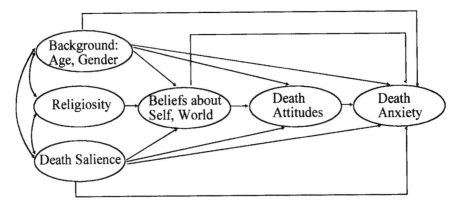

FIGURE 1. A simplified model of death anxiety.

role in the comprehensive model. This model was examined in two samples, one of young adults and one of older adults. Generally speaking, we expected more positive attitudes (e.g., more acceptance of death) to translate into a lesser level of death anxiety. We also expected positive attitudes about oneself and the world to reduce death anxiety. A strong sense of coherence, a strong internal locus of control, a sense that the world is a just place, and a higher degree of self esteem are likely to reduce death anxiety either by having a direct effect or by affecting one's attitudes about death.

☐ Method

Subjects

The samples included 102 young and 89 old adults. The young participants were college students (Mean age = 19.98, *SD* = 3.07) who volunteered to participate in the study and who received academic credit for their involvement. The old participants were volunteers, most of them from communities (including retirement communities) in Central Pennsylvania, aged 55 or more (Mean age = 69.04, *SD* = 9.73). There were 68.6% females among the young and 79.8% among the older adults. Protestantism is the predominant religious belief in this area.

Tests

A set of questionnaires was administered, in groups or individually. The tests and measures based on them were the following:

1. A measure of death anxiety was constructed on the basis of the Revised Death Anxiety Scale (RDAS; Thorson & Powell, 1994). The scale contains 25 items

and Thorson and Powell report a internal consistency of about .8 (measured by Cronbach alpha) in a young sample of students and adults and also in heterogenous sample of adults aged 18 to 88. (Thorson & Powell, 1990). The factorial structure changed somewhat among studies and a somewhat different structure based on a four-factor solution is reported for high death anxiety and for low death anxiety subjects by Thorson and Powell (1994). The first factor in both groups loads mainly on items related to "not being" and to losing control. In a previous factor analysis conducted on the subjects of the present study, we obtained a four factor solution in older subjects with the first factor being fear of non-being. The first factor in the sample of young subjects also loaded on items denoting regret or fear of missing out on things (see Chapter 7). For purposes of comparability across age groups we decided to use a score based on the items loading highly on the non-being factor in the older adults group. Fear of non-being reflects anxiety related to the prospect of not being able to think again, losing control, etc. (see Chapter 7).

2. Two questionnaires were used to define death attitudes—the Death Attitude Profile-Revised (DAP-R; see Wong, Reker, & Gesser, 1994) and the Death Transcendence Scale (DTS; Hood & Morris, 1983; VandeCreek & Nye, 1993). Three subscales of the DAP-R were used to measure three types of acceptance in accordance with the three-component model defined by Wong et al. (1994). The three are neutral acceptance, approach acceptance, and escape acceptance. The authors report alpha coefficients of internal consistency of .65, .97, and .84, respectively. Stability coefficients over a month period were of similar magnitude. Neutral acceptance reflects the view that death is a part of the process of life and therefore "natural." Approach acceptance is mainly based on a belief in a happy, glorious afterlife and reflects the conviction that heaven is a "much better place than this world" (p. 134). Escape acceptance is measured by items dealing with death as relief from the pain, suffering, and burden of this world.

   The DTS was the basis for two dimensions, mysticism and belief in an afterlife, that were used as additional "death attitudes." The two dimensions were defined based on the results of a principal component analysis of the DTS. The mysticism dimension was based on 5 items that were found by Hood and Morris to define the first factor. An example is: "I have had an experience in which I realized the oneness of myself with all things." A Belief in an afterlife factor was based on 6 other items such as "I believe in life after death." This factor corresponded almost entirely to the religious factor (second factor) in Hood and Morris's three-factor solution and was also very close to the second factor obtained by VanDecreek and Nye. Vandecreek and Nye reported a Cronbach alpha of .84 for the Mysticism factor obtained in a sample of middle age, predominantly female participants.

3. Measures that focused on beliefs about the world and the self included The Sense of Coherence Questionnaire (SOC; Antonovski, 1987), generated measures on the three dimensions—Meaningfulness, Comprehensibility, and Manageability. The first dimension, Meaningfulness, reflects the conviction that

one's life is worth living. The Comprehensibility dimension reflects the belief that one understands his or her life, and that life is "coherent" cognitively. Finally, Manageability indicates a belief in living the life that one wants. This questionnaire was shown to have good psychometric properties in a variety of samples. For example, Steiner et al. (1996) reported an average Cronbach alpha (measuring internal consistency) of .89 for 26 studies that included a wide range of ages. They also reported a Cronbach alpha of .77 for the short version of the SOC in a sample of older community-dwelling persons. The factorial structure of the instrument was examined empirically in a number of studies. Feldt and Rasku (1998), using three large samples of about 1,000 people each (belonging to different occupational groups) and a confirmatory factor analysis, were able to show that a first-order 3-factor structure fit the data. Other studies obtained different results (e.g., Saudell, Blomberg, & Lazar, 1998, who reported a 2-factor structure). In the present study, we used the three components as defined by Antonovsky (1987) as variables in the model investigated.

In addition to the SOC, we administered the Global Belief in a Just World Scale (Lipkus, 1991), the Self-Esteem Scale (Rosenberg, 1965), and Lumpkin's (1988) brief version of Levenson's (1974) Locus of Control Scale that has a multidimensional structure. The three factors—Internal Control, Chance, and Powerful Others—reflect strength of belief in the source of control over one's life: the person himself or herself, luck or chance, or others in position of power and authority. Lumpkin (1988) reported rather low Cronbach alpha coefficients of .51, .42, and .46, respectively, for the Internal Control, Chance, and Powerful Others dimensions in a sample of older persons.

4. Three questions were asked dealing with: (a) participation in worship services; (b) engaging in prayer and/or meditation; and (c) reading religious writings. Since several studies have shown the importance of making a distinction between extrinsic and intrinsic religiosity (Allport & Ross, 1967; Donahue, 1985; Thorson & Powell, 1990) we created, in addition, two indices based on the frequency with which participants engaged in the above mentioned activities. One index reflected the frequency of participation in worship services, from no participation to participation of more than once a week (range from 0 to 4). A second index was based on the questions dealing with frequency of prayer and reading religious texts (range 0 to 8). We named the first index "religious attendance" and the second index "religious devotion".

5. Salience of death was determined based on the answer of participants to two questions dealing with their inclination to think about specific circumstances of their possible death (from "never" to "many times") and with their thinking about how the world would be after their death (again from "never" to "many times"). Those two questions generated an index ranging from 0 to 6.

6. Background variables included gender, age, and level of education. We distinguished between five levels of education: (a) have not finished high school, (b) have finished high school, (c) have finished some college, (d) have a four year degree from college, or (e) have an advanced degree (Master's, Ph.D., etc.).

☐ Analyses and Results

Bivariate Analyses

Relationships among variables were first analyzed by computing Pearson correlation coefficients. The coefficients quantify relationships among pairs of variables without controlling for other variables in the set. The main results are presented in Tables 1 to 4. For convenience of reference and comparison we included fear of non-being and neutral acceptance of death in all tables. We chose only one type of death attitude, neutral acceptance of death, since further analyses (regression and path analyses) only retained this type in the model and eliminated others. We provide here only a summary description of the main patterns.

The correlations among death attitudes (see Table 1) show that the three types of acceptance of death, neutral, approach, and escape, are positively correlated with a particularly high correlation (about .6) between escape acceptance and approach acceptance. The three types of acceptance are also connected to fear of non-being in the expected direction: increases in any form of acceptance are connected to a decrease in fear (although the correlation between fear of non-being and escape acceptance does not reach significance). Belief in an afterlife is significantly and positively related to all three types of acceptance, but particularly so to approach acceptance. This is not surprising, given the common content of these two variables, the belief in an afterlife.

Correlations among the three components of locus of control, internal control, chance, and powerful others, are presented in Table 2. Internal locus of control is correlated negatively to powerful others but only weakly. As expected, the two external control dimensions, chance and powerful others are positively correlated (about .3). Also, fear of non-being correlates positively with all sources of control but only the correlations with the two dimensions of external control, chance and powerful others, attain significance.

The relationships between the three components of the sense of coherence,

TABLE 1. Pearson Correlations Among Dimensions of Death Attitudes and Fear of Non-being

Dimension	Neutral Acceptance	Approach Acceptance	Escape Acceptance	Belief in Afterlife	Mysticism
Fear of non-being	−.26*	−.16*	−.12	−.13	.09
Neutral Acceptance		.39**	.30**	.33**	.01
Approach Acceptance			.61**	−.02	.64**
Escape Acceptance				.33**	−.11
Belief in afterlife					.01

*p < .05. **p < .01.

TABLE 2. Pearson Correlations Among Three Dimensions of Locus of Control, Fear of Non-being and Neutral Acceptance of Death

Dimension	Neutral Acceptance	Internal Control	Chance	Powerful Others
Fear of Non-being	−.26*	.13*	.22**	.20**
Neutral Acceptance		.13	.23**	−.01
Internal Control			−.18*	−.22**
Chance				−.31**

*p < .05. **p < .01.

comprehensibility, manageability, and meaningfulness, are presented in Table 3. All the correlations are positive and of either moderate or large magnitude.

Particularly high is the correlation between meaningfulness and manageability (about 7) These two components tend to be positively connected to neutral acceptance and negatively to fear of non-being.

The independent variables in the model are age, gender, education, extrinsic and intrinsic religiosity, and salience of death. The correlations among them and neutral acceptance of death and fear of non-being are presented in Table 4.

Fear of non-being is correlated positively to salience of death and negatively to age and to the two types of religiosity, religious attendance and religious devotion. Older subjects tend to score lower on fear of non-being than younger subjects. This significant connection is preserved when we replaced age as a continuous variable with age as a dichotomous variable including two possible values, young and old. In the latter case, the point biserial correlation is -.16. Neutral acceptance of death correlates positively to devotion and education. Intercorrelations of exogenous variables are also of interest. The correlation between the two types of religiosity was high and positive in this sample, .711.

TABLE 3. Pearson Correlations Among Three Components of the Sense of Coherence, Fear of Non-being and Neutral Acceptance of Death

Dimension	Neutral Acceptance	Meaningfulness	Manageability	Comprehensibility
Fear of Non-being	.26**	−.18*	−.12	−.18*
Neutral Acceptance		.14*	.17	−.02
Meaningfulness			.73**	.46**
Manageability				.58**

*p < .05. **p < .01.

TABLE 4. Pearson Correlations between Background Variables, Death Salience and Religiosity Measures and Fear of Non-Being and Neutral Acceptance of Death

Variable	Neutral Acceptance	Gender	Age	Education	Religious Attendance	Religious Devotion	Death Salience
Fear of Non-being	−.26**	−.05	−.18*	−.08	−.19**	−.26**	.33**
Neutral Acceptance		.08	.09	.21**	.11	.22	−.02
Gender			−.14*	.03	−.23**	−.27**	−.22**
Age				.04	.36**	.42**	−.10
Education					.01	−.06	−.03
Religious Attendance						.71**	−.04
Religious Devotion							−.04

*$p < .05.$ **$p < .01.$

Regression Analyses

To reduce the number of variables in the final analysis, a series of regressions were conducted. First, we regressed non-being on death attitudes. Only neutral acceptance reached significance and was retained for further analyses. Second, we regressed fear of non-being as well as neutral acceptance on all other variables. We retained for further analyses (path analyses conducted using the LISREL program), only those variables that reached significance in at least one of those two regressions. The variables retained were the three dimensions of locus of control and the three dimensions of the sense of coherence, as well as, the following exogenous or independent variables: education, death salience, and religious devotion. The result of eliminating some of the variables was a small decrease in the amount of variance explained in fear of non-being. Thus the regression of non-being on neutral acceptance and all other variables produced an R square of .366 (36.6% variability explained). This percentage declined to 33.5% in the regression in which the more restricted set of predictors was used.

Simultaneous Path Analyses—the Choice of a Model

To further investigate the model, simultaneous path analyses were conducted in the two age groups using LISREL 8 (Jöreskog & Sörbom, 1996). These analyses were based on the final variables in the regression equation: neutral acceptance, the three dimensions of locus of control, the three dimensions of sense of coherence, and the background variables including religiosity, death salience, and education. Age of course was not a variable since the path analyses were conducted simultaneously with the two genders. Three models were formulated that imposed restrictions of different degrees of stringency. The most restrained Model 1 imposed equal raw path coefficients in the two age groups. A more relaxed Model 2 imposed this equality for relationships among the dependent or endogenous variables (including the locus of control components, the sense of coherence components, neutral acceptance, and fear of non-being), but not for the relationships between the independent or exogenous variables and the dependent ones. The latter that included the paths between education, religious devotion, and death salience on one hand, and all the other variables on the other hand, were estimated independently by the LISREL program in each one of the two age groups. Finally, a completely relaxed Model 3 estimated all coefficients independently within each age group. In all three models, we allowed for independent estimation of covariances among the exogenous variables. In all cases variance-covariance matrices and the Maximum Likelihood Method of estimation were used.

A comparison between the first two models is provided in Table 5. In general the more stringent model produces reasonably good goodness of fit indices. One exception is the RMSEA, that exceeds the recommended limit of .05 (Brown & Cudeck, 1993). Moreover, restricting some of the equality constraints in Model 2, as explained above, resulted in a significant improvement in chi-square: the difference between the two chi-squares is 38.05, which is significant at a .05 level. We retained, therefore, this model and we report in the next section the result of its estimation.

Simultaneous Path Analyses—Estimation

The path coefficients were estimated for the young and for the old subjects. Figures 2 and 3 present the results in each group in a standardized form that uses standard deviations for each group. Because of this last feature, path coefficients restricted to be equal in both groups are not exactly equal in their standardized form presented here.

TABLE 5. A Comparison of Two Models of Death Anxiety Estimated in a Group of Young and in a Group of Old Adults

Model	Description	χ^2	df	P	NFI[1]	GFI[2]	RMSEA[3]
1	Corresponding paths are equal across age group	54.53	37	.032	.90	.96	.066
2	Paths among endogenous variables are equal across age group	16.48	13	.22	.97	.98	.049

[1] Normed Fit Index (Bentler & Bonett, 1980).
[2] Goodness-of-fit index (Jöreskog & Sörbom, 1989).
[3] Root Mean Square Error of Approximation (Browne & Cudeck, 1993).

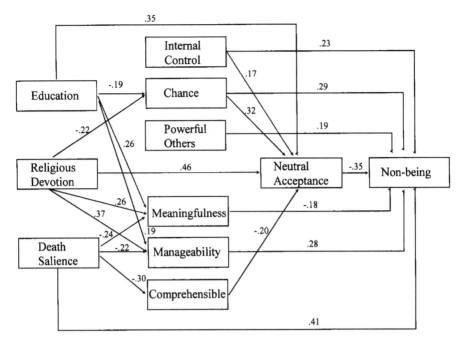

FIGURE 2. Significant path coefficients for a model of death anxiety estimated in old adults. Covariances between the exogenous variables (education, religious devotion, death salience) are not represented.

For both groups viewing death as natural (neutral acceptance) was strongly and negatively connected to fear of non-being, so that a strong belief that death is a natural process and a part of the process of life was related to decreased fear of death. Second, an increased sense of meaningfulness was also related to a reduced fear of non-being whereas, surprisingly, increased manageability tended to bring about more fear. Also, scoring highly on any of the three dimensions of locus of control, internal control, chance, or powerful others, appears to make a person more likely to report fear of non-being. Comprehensibility connected to fear of non-being only through neutral acceptance. Internal control and chance also had an indirect effect on fear of non-being, mediated by neutral acceptance. This effect went in a direction opposite to that of their direct effect.

The exogenous variables in the model affected fear of non-being directly and/or indirectly, and somewhat differently in the two age groups. A higher education promoted neutral acceptance in both groups and increased the tendency to see one's life as meaningful in older subjects. A higher salience of death results in more fear of non-being in both groups, but this connection is both clearer and stronger in older subjects in which salience of death had a direct effect on fear of death. In young subjects, salience of death was connected to a higher internal locus of control and to a decreased sense of meaningfulness.

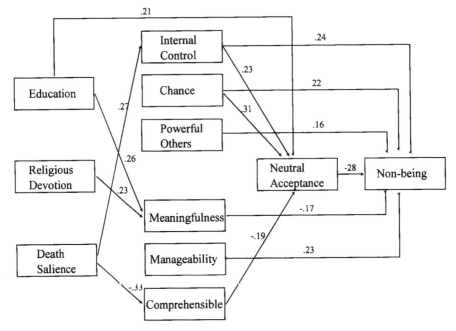

FIGURE 3. Significant path coefficients for a model of death anxiety estimated in young adults. Covariances between the exogenous variables (education, religious devotion, death salience) are not represented.

Finally, religious devotion increased the sense of meaningfulness of one's life in both young and old subjects. In addition, it decreased the strength of the belief in pure chance and it increased belief in the tendency to display neutral acceptance of death in older adults.

☐ Discussion

The estimation of the model in the two age groups has generated complex results. We divide the following discussion into sections, according to the type of relationship considered. We conclude by trying to present an overall view on the model and by trying to draw lessons for future investigations.

Death Anxiety and Death Attitudes

The reader may remember that the regression of fear of non-being on three types of death attitudes, neutral acceptance, approach acceptance, and escape acceptance left only the neutral acceptance of death "in the game." Our expectation was that a high score on any of the three should make one likely to score low on death anxiety. Particularly surprising is the fact that a high approach acceptance did not predict lower death anxiety. On the other hand, and as expected, accepting death as an integral part of life had a lowering effect on fear of non-being.

From the view of the death anxiety model that was our point of departure this finding emphasizes the need to specify the type of death attitudes and the kind of conceptualization that are conducive to a lower death anxiety. Attitudes that express a reintegration of death into life are likely to have an ameliorative effect. Moreover, such a result is certainly consistent with the findings regarding the relationship between death anxiety and the discrepancy between self and death as measured by the Threat Index (Krieger, Epting, & Leitner, 1974; Neimeyer, Dingemans, & Epting, 1977). Thus Neimeyer and Chapman (1980) found that subjects who showed a larger discrepancy between the self and the ideal self on the TI reported more death anxiety on the DAS (Templer, 1970) and less fear of death of self on the Collett-Lester Fear of Death Scale (Collett & Lester, 1969).

The Sense of Coherence Concept, Death Attitudes and Death Anxiety

The sense of coherence (SOC) in Antonovsky's (1979, 1987) conceptualization is a global orientation of the individual vis-à-vis life and world that includes the three components of meaningfulness, comprehensibility, and manageability. We expected the three components to relate to death attitudes and to death anxiety in similar ways, reflecting more positive attitudes and less anxiety with an increased sense of coherence. The estimation of the model, however, generated path coefficients that indicate different patterns of connection for the three components. Only meaningfulness was connected, in fact, in the way we anticipated. Meaningfulness is the component that is seen by Antonovsky as the "motivational component" (p. 18) of SOC and refers to "the extent to which one feels that life makes sense emotionally, that at least some of the problems and demands posed by living are worth investing energy in" (p. 18). A sense of meaningfulness reflects a good feeling about life. In our model it connects directly to fear of non-being in the expected direction. More appreciation of life's challenges and intriguing or enjoyable aspects is connected to less fear of non-being. This result is consistent with Antononvsky's view of SOC, in particular meaningfulness, as playing an important role in the process of mobilizing resources in dealing with stress and tension (e.g., Antonovsky, 1987). According to Antonovsky, one way to deal with stressors is to redefine "the boundaries of what is meaningful in one's life" (p. 139) so that the stressor is excluded as something that one does not care about any more. Another way of coping is to make sense of the stressor by seeing a positive side of it. Both ways may bring one to a secondary appraisal (Lazarus & Folkman, 1984). In the present context, having a strong sense of one's life as meaningful may encourage an appraisal of death as an unavoidable price that one has to pay for a meaningful life and may encourage one to focus on one's life and important life goals. Antonovsky's view was, in general, supported by a large number of studies. For example, Struempfer, Gouws, and Viviers (1998) reported that, in samples of nursing students and managerial life insurance personnel, SOC correlated positively with positive affectivity and negatively with negative affectivity. That a high SOC may serve as a kind of buffer against psychological dysfunction (e.g., depression, anxiety), which may be precipitated by illness, natural disaster, etc., was suggested by many studies (i.e., Erikson & Lundin, 1996; Forsberg & Bjoervill, 1996; Kaiser, Sattler & Bellack, 1996; Mullen, Smith, & Hill, 1993; Ying & Akutsu, 1997). Still, other studies failed to find such an effect and there are questions regarding the ability of SOC to predict negative health, as opposed to positive health (see Korotkov, 1998).

A sense that one's life is meaningful is also connected to (influenced by) religiosity, as religious devotion, and to salience of death as measured by frequency of thinking about possible circumstances of one's death. As expected, however, these two influences are of opposite sign: higher religiosity tends to further a sense of meaningfulness, whereas high salience of death tends to decrease meaningfulness. The connection between meaningfulness and religiosity is consistent with other findings in the literature. For example Donahue (1985), in a meta-analysis of the literature, found that intrinsically religious individuals tend to be high in a "sense of purpose" in life.

Locus of Control and Death Attitudes

In this study locus of control was measured using a multidimensional scale that makes a distinction between three dimensions: internal control, control by chance, and control by powerful others. The three scales measure strength of beliefs that one's life is affected or controlled, respectively, by the individual himself or herself, by chance, or by powerful others. Multidimensional scales were developed because the original internal–external locus of control scale developed by Rotter (1966) was found in several studies to depart from unidimensionality. For example, it was found that internality and externality are not real opposites: the correlation between them is negative, but low (e.g., Collins, 1974). In the results presented here, the three dimensions also displayed low intercorrelations. Moreover, all three had positive path coefficients for the direct paths leading to death anxiety. In other words, being high on internal control predisposes one to score highly on death anxiety, but so does a high score on the chance scale and a high score on control by powerful others. The literature presents a rather confusing and inconsistent picture regarding relationships between locus of control and death anxiety. Some of the results are consistent with our findings and some other results are not. Hunt, Lester, and Ashton (1983) found that a stronger belief in control by chance and/or by powerful others is connected to increased fear of personal death measured on the Collett-Lester Fear of Death Scale (abreviated CL; Collett & Lester, 1969). Similarly, Hayslip and Stewart-Bussey (1987) found that a belief in control by chance correlates positively to death anxiety as measured by Templer's Death Anxiety Scale (although not with the death-of-self component based on the CL). In this last study, a belief in powerful others correlated positively with covert measures of death anxiety (based on completion of sentences) but not with overt ones. Also, internal control, which was hypothesized in the Hayslip and Stewart-Bussey study (as well as in the present study) to correlate positively to fear of death-of-self, was found to be negatively correlated to this component. The relationship in our study was positive, perhaps indicating that a person with a strong belief in his or her ability to control life events may associate death with an increased sense of loss of control. A different interpretation is needed for relationships between external control and death anxiety. Individuals whose beliefs in chance or powerful others are strong may feel more threatened by death because they *already* believe that they don't have control over their lives.

It is also important to mention that the pattern of relationships presented in Figures 2 and 3 is very complex since beliefs in internal control and in control by chance influence one's tendency to accept death as a natural part of life. By doing so these two components tend to reduce fear of non-being. However, this indirect influence is less important in magnitude than the influence along the direct path to fear of non-being.

Religiosity and Death Attitudes

We measured religiosity in this study by using behavioral characteristics. Consistent with the distinction between extrinsic religiosity (or religiousness, see Donahue, 1985) and intrinsic religiosity, we distinguished here between a "superficial" behavior—church attendance—and behaviors that reflect how important religion is in one's life, such as praying or reading religious texts. This last dimension was named religious devotion and was retained by the regression analyses and estimated in relation to other variables in the path analysis.

Generally speaking, we found religious devotion to be connected to fear of non-being indirectly. In both old and young subjects, it translates into an increased sense of meaningfulness and through it into a reduced fear of non-being. In older persons, religiosity also has an effect on death attitudes, "encouraging" a neutral approach which also translated in less fear of non-being. A negative effect on the sense that one is controlled by pure chance is also conducive to a reduced fear of non-being. A third effect of religiosity in the direction of an increased sense of manageability eventually acts on death anxiety in an aggravating direction. Nevertheless, the sum of all those four indirect effects is clearly negative: more devotion means less fear of non-being. This result is consistent with other studies. For example, Thorson and Powell (1990) found that high death anxiety subjects scored tended to be younger and to obtain lower scores on an Intrinsic Religious Motivation Scale than low death anxiety subjects. A negative correlation between intrinsic religiosity and general anxiety was also reported by Ellison, Gay, and Glass (1989). Reviewing this literature, Neimeyer and Fortner (1997) reached the conclusion that religious commitment, perhaps by offering a buffer in the form of a belief in an afterlife, tends to have a ameliorative effect on conscious death anxiety.

These findings provide additional support to the general thesis regarding the importance of religiosity as a source of meaning and as a buffer from death anxiety. This finding is particularly forceful in older adults, where religiosity has a direct effect on death acceptance. Together with additional evidence suggesting a positive effect of religion and spirituality on the physical health of individuals (see Wong, 1998 for a review), the findings corroborate Wong's (1998) view that spirituality and religion are an important resource in achieving successful aging.

Death Salience and Death Anxiety

A tendency to think frequently about possible circumstances of one's death is found to be related to a fear of nonbeing in both groups, but the "mechanism" is different and the "net result" is also different. In older subjects, death salience directly affected fear of non-being, increasing it. In addition, it reduced the sense of coherence of the individual: all three components, meaningfulness, manageability, and comprehensibility are reduced. The indirect effects tend to cancel one another leaving the direct effect (which is also much larger) as most important. In younger adults, on the other hand, death salience tends to increase neutral acceptance by having an effect on the sense of internal control and by decreasing comprehensibility. This functions in the direction of decreasing fear of non-being. However, due to the direct path between internal control and fear of non-being, death salience also has a positive effect in the sense of increasing fear. The sum of all three indirect effects on fear of non-being is still positive (indicating more fear with increased death salience) but very small (.031, to be precise). The relationship of death salience to internal control is puzzling. Why should death salience increase the sense of internal control rather than decrease it? It is indeed conceivable that a need to control everything, including the process of one's dying, can make one engage in frequent thinking about concrete circumstances of his or her demise. If this is the case, there should be an effect of internal control on death salience, rather than the other way around. Of course, such an effect was not estimated since our model assumed a particular direction of causality, in accordance to the general model that served as point of departure. If our speculative interpretation here is correct, it may point to the need to modify the model by allowing for some reciprocal paths among variables.

The Comprehensive Model of Death Anxiety Revisited

The Comprehensive Model of Death Anxiety (CMDA) was helpful in delineating the "testable" model presented in Figure 1. Even this model, however, left unspecified the specific variables that should be indicated in a comprehensive model as well as the specific paths of influence. For this reason we selected the variables based on a sequence of regressions. Notwithstanding this lack of specificity the conceptual model proved to be a useful tool as a heuristic device that allows one to commit oneself to a plausible causal model and to estimate and test this model.

The strategy followed here was one of simultaneous estimation in young and old subjects. Ideally, assuming the generality of the model across age groups, we should be able to show the same pattern of relationships and perhaps even the same magnitude of path coefficients. Such a result would increase our confidence in the model. The model that we retained was close to this ideal: it stipulated the existence of equal path coefficients between the variables of control, sense of coherence, acceptance of death, and death anxiety. This model fit the data very well. The paths that were estimated independently in the two groups also showed partial consistency. Overall, education, religious devotion, and death salience have similar effects on fear of non-being. On the other hand, the differences obtained in the magnitude of those effects and in their specific pattern should not be ignored. Those differences point to the need to improve the model. This may be done by incorporating additional variables and/or paths among variables. A full investigation of the model should also use multiple indicators for the concepts. We should remember that the conceptual variables in the model of death anxiety are better formalized as "latent variables" and these should be measured using multiple indicators for each (ideally four or more). In conjunction with large samples of young and old subjects, this approach will allow a better estimation of the relationship among variables and, eventually, a better chance at approaching a specific model that can be confirmed across various populations. It is also possible that somewhat different models explain death anxiety in young and old adults.

Points to Remember

1. The way death is conceptualized and accepted by young and old adults has an impact on the level of fear of death conceived as disappearance or "non-being." In particular, a view of death as a natural part of life is related to a reduced level of fear.
2. A strong sense of meaningfulness, the tendency to see one's life as worth living, is conducive to less fear of non-being in both young and old adults.
3. A strong belief in external control in the form of chance or powerful others is related to more fear of non-being in both young and old adults. On the other hand, a strong belief in internal control may also predispose one to fear death.
4. The study pointed to several "resources" that older adults in particular have at their disposal in dealing with fear of non-being. Religious devotion tends to increase a sense of meaningfulness and to promote acceptance of death. A higher education also encourages (neutral) acceptance of death.
5. Thinking frequently about circumstances of one's death is related to a higher level of anxiety, in particular in older adults.

For example, religiosity was found to be a very important factor in the older sample but a less important factor in the young sample. In the old sample religiosity as religious devotion, determined to a great extent neutral acceptance of death by the person. In the young sample this path was not significant. Whether or not this is a "real difference," or rather one resulting from an incomplete model, remains to be further investigated.

☐ References

Allport, G. W., & Ross, J. M. (1967). Personal religious orientation and prejudice, *Journal of Personality and Social Psychology, 5,* 432–443.

Antonovsky, A. (1979). *Health, stress and coping: New perspectives on mental and physical well-being.* San Francisco: Jossey–Bass.

Antonovsky, A. (1987). *Unraveling the mystery of health.* San Francisco: Jossey-Bass.

Bentler, P. M., & Bonett, D.G. (1980). Significance tests and goodness of fit in the analysis of covariance structures. *Psychological Bulletin, 88,* 588–606.

Bergin, A. E., Masters, K. S., & Richards, P.S. (1987). Religiousness and mental health reconsidered. A study of an intrinsically religious sample. *Journal of Counseling Psychology, 34,* 197–204.

Browne, M. W., & Cudeck, R. (1993). Alternative ways of assessing model fit. In K. A. Bollen & J. S. Long (Eds.), *Testing structural equation models.* Newbury Park, CA: Sage.

Collett, L. J., & Lester, D. (1969). The fear of death and the fear of dying. *Journal of Psychology, 72,* 179–181.

Collins, B. E. (1974). Four separate components of the Rotter I.E. Scale: Belief in a difficult world, a just world, a predictable world, and a politically responsible world. *Journal of Personality and Social Psychology, 29,* 381–391.

Donahue, M. J. (1985). Intrinsic and extrinsic religiousness: Review and meta-analysis. *Journal of Personality and Social Psychology, 48,* 400–419.

Ellison, C. G., Gay, D. A., & Glass, T. A. (1989). Does religious commitment contribute to individual life satisfaction? *Social Forces, 68,* 100–123.

Erikson, N. G., & Lundin, T. (1996). Early traumatic stress reactions among Swedish survivors of the m/s Estonia disaster. *British Journal of Psychiatry, 169,* 713–716.

Feldt, T., & Rasku, A. (1998). The structure of Antonovsky's Orientation to Life Questionnaire. *Personality and Individual Differences, 25,* 505–516.

Forsberg, C., & Bjoervell, H. (1996). Living with cancer: Perceptions of well-being. *Scandinavian Journal of Caring Sciences, 10,* 109–115.

Hayslip, B., Jr., & Stewart-Bussey, D. (1986-1987). Locus of control–levels of death anxiety relationships. *Omega, 17,* 41–50.

Hunt, D. M., Lester, D., & Aston, N. (1983). Fear of death, locus of control and occupation. *Psychological Reports, 53,* 1022.

Hood, R. W., & Morris, R. J. (1983). Toward a theory of death transcendence. *Journal of the Scientific Study of Religion, 22,* 353–365.

Jöreskog, K. D., & Sörbom, D. (1989). *LISREL 7—A guide to the program and applications.* Second edition. Chicago: SPSS Publications.

Jöreskog, K. D., & Sörbom, D. (1996). LISREL 8: User's reference guide. Chicago: Scientific Software International.

Kaiser, C. F., Sattler, D. N., Bellack, D. R., & Dersin, J. (1996). A conservation of resources approach to a natural disaster: Sense of coherence and psychological distress. *Journal of Social Behavior and Personality, 11,* 459–476.

Korotkov, D. (1998). The sense of coherence: Making sense out of chaos. In P. T. P. Wong & P. S. Fry (Eds.), *The human quest for meaning* (pp. 51–70). Mahwah, NJ: Lawrence Erlbaum.

Krieger, S. R., Epting, F. R., & Leitner, L. M. (1974). Personal constructs, threat, and attitudes toward death. *Omega, 5,* 299–310.

Lazarus, R. S., & Folkman, S. (1984). *Stress, appraisal and coping.* New York: Springer.

Levenson, H. (1974). Activism and powerful others: distinctions within the concept of internal-external control. *Journal of Personality Assessment, 38,* 377–383.

Lipkus, I. (1991). The construction and preliminary validation of a global belief in a just world scale and the exploratory analysis of the multidimensional belief in a just world scale. *Personality Individual Differences, 12,* 1171–1178.

Lumpkin, J. R. (1988). Establishing the validity of an abbreviated locus of control scale: is a brief Levenson's scale any better? *Psychological Reports, 63,* 519–523.

Mullen, P. M., Smith, R. M., & Hill, E. W. (1993). Sense of coherence as a mediator of stress for cancer patients and spouses. *Journal of Psychosocial Oncology, 11,* 23–46.

Neimeyer, R. A., & Chapman, K. M. (1980). Self/ideal discrepancy and fear of death: The test of an existential hypothesis. *Omega, 11,* 233–240.

Neimeyer, R. A., Dingemans, P., & Epting, F. R. (1977). Convergent validity, situational stability and meaningfulness of the Threat Index. *Omega, 8,* 251–265.

Neimeyer, R. A., & Fortner, B. (1997). Death attitudes in contemporary perspective. In S. Strack (Ed.), *Death and the quest for meaning—Essays in honor of Herman Feifel.* Northvale, NJ: Jason Aronson.

Rosenberg, M. (1965). *Society and the adolescent self-image.* Princeton, NJ: Princeton University Press.

Rotter, J. B. (1966). Generalized expectancies for internal vs. external control of reinforcement. *Psychological Monographs, 80,* 1–28.

Saudell, R., Blomberg, J., & Lazar, A. (1998). The factor structure of Antonovsky's Sense of Coherence Scale in Swedish clinical and nonclinical samples. *Personality and Individual Differences, 24,* 701–711.

Steiner, A, Raube, K., Stuck, A. E., Aronow, H. U., Draper, D., Rubenstein, L. Z., & Beck, J. C. (1996). Measuring psychosocial aspects of well-being in older community residents: Performance on four short scales. *The Gerontologist, 36,* 54–62.

Struempfer, D. J. W., Gouws, J. F., & Viviers, M. R. (1998). Antonovsky's Sense of Coherence Scale related to negative and positive affectivity. *European Journal of Personality, 12,* 457–480.

Templer, D. I. (1970). The construction and validation of a death anxiety scale. *Journal of General Psychology, 82,* 165–177.

Thorson, J. A., & Powell, F. C. (1990). Meanings of death and intrinsic religiosity. *Journal of Clinical Psychology, 46,* 379–391.

Thorson, J. A., & Powell, F.C. (1994). A revised death anxiety scale. In R. A. Neimeyer (Ed.), *Death anxiety handbook: Research, instrumentation, and application* (pp. 303–381). Washington, DC: Taylor & Francis.

Tomer, A., & Eliason, G. (1996). Toward a comprehensive model of death anxiety. *Death Studies, 20,* 343–365.

VandeCreek, L., & Nye, C. (1993). Testing the death transcendence scale. *Journal for the Scientific Study of Religion, 32,* 279–283.

Wong, P. T. P. (1998). Spirituality, meaning and successful aging. In P. T. P. Wong & P. S. Fry (Eds.), *The human quest for meaning* (pp. 359–394). Mahwah, NJ: Lawrence Erlbaum.

Wong, P. T. P., Reker, G. T., & Gesser, T. (1994). Death attitude profile-revised: A multidimensional measure of attitudes toward death. In R. A. Neimeyer (Ed.), *Death anxiety handbook: Research, instrumentation, and application* (pp. 121–148). Washington, DC: Taylor & Francis.

Ying, Y. W., & Akutsy, P. D. (1997). Psychological adjustment of southeast Asian refugees: The constriction of sense of coherence. *Journal of Community Psychology, 25,* 125–139.

ATTITUDES TOWARD THE OLDER ADULT AND END OF LIFE DECISIONS

CHAPTER

Nancy J. Osgood

Ageism and Elderly Suicide: The Intimate Connection

As we begin the twenty-first century, two trends that characterized the last part of the last century will continue: an increase in the number and rate of suicides in those 65 and older; and increasingly louder cries for the "right to die" and legalization of physician-assisted suicide. Ageism is a factor influencing both trends. In this chapter we will examine the problem of elderly suicide, focusing on major factors related to this issue. We will also discuss attitudes and values that are fueling the current debates over an individual's right to self-determination and the pros and cons of legalizing physician-assisted suicide (PAS) in this country. The issue of elderly suicide and current debates about suicide and assisted suicide will be examined within the context of ageism in America.

It is no coincidence that arguments for the right to die and the right to self-determination and calls for legalization of PAS are gaining momentum at the same time that we are witnessing phenomenal growth in our nation's older and more dependent populations. Older adults, especially those 85 and up, place unprecedented demands on limited economic and health care resources in this country. We glorify and worship youth and beauty and denigrate aging and old people in America.

If PAS is legalized in several states and we adopt the value system that views some lives as less valuable than others, how will the growing number of older adults fare in the next century in America? What effect will such changes have on the rate of elderly suicide in years to come? Is it conceivable that in future years older adults living in America will feel an obligation to die in order to save valuable resources for younger people? In the next century, is it possible that choosing

Portions of this chapter were previously published in *Suicide in Later Life Recognizing the Warning Signs* by N. J. Osgood. Copyright 1992 by University Press of America, New York, NY.

suicide will be considered the most honorable and patriotic of acts in America? These and other questions will be examined in this chapter.

☐ The Problem of Elderly Suicide

Compared to other age groups, people 65 and older are the age group most "at risk" for completing suicide. Currently, in the United States, approximately 31,000 annual deaths are recorded as suicides. Among these, approximately 6,000 are carried out by adults 65 and older (Peters, Kochanek, & Murphy, 1998). Older adults commit one out of every five suicides in America. The rate of suicide for adults 65 and up is 50 percent higher than the suicide rate of individuals 15–24 years of age. In 1996, those 65 and older made up 12.8% of the U.S. population, but committed 18.9% of the suicides. By comparison, in 1996 those 15–24 years of age made up 13.7% of the U.S. population, and committed 14.1% of the suicides (Peters, Kochanek, & Murphy, 1998).

White males 85 and older have a rate of suicide 6 times higher than the national suicide rate. Every day 18 people 65 and older commit suicide in this country. This figure represents one elderly suicide every hour and a half. Firearms is the major method of suicide for older adults. Since we have kept statistics on suicide in this country, older adults have always had the highest rate of completed suicide. From 1980 to 1988 the number of suicides among people 65 and older increased 50 percent and the suicide rate for this age group increased 25 percent. Since 1992, rates of suicide among those 65 and older have declined slightly. Compared to other age groups, older adults are at greatest risk of suicide. Those 85 and older have the highest rate of suicide.

Although it is impossible to predict future suicide rates, we do expect that they will increase. Today there are approximately 32 million adults 65 and older in the U.S. population. By the year 2020 when many current "baby boomers" will be 65 and older, this figure is expected to increase to 52 million. As the number of older adults' increases, the number of elderly suicides will also increase. Even if there is no increase in the *rate* of suicide for people 65 and up, the *number* of suicides in this population will increase dramatically.

Some groups of older adults are more vulnerable to suicide than others. Older males are at greater risk than older females. At all stages of the life cycle, males are more likely to commit suicide than females, and are three times more likely to die from suicide. In the oldest age group (85 and over) males are 12 times more likely to commit suicide than females. The suicide rate increases linearly into the last decades of life for males, whereas the female rate peaks in midlife and then declines.

White elderly males are more likely to commit suicide than are minority males. For minority males, suicide rates peak in young adulthood; for whites, suicide rates peak in old age. Compared to black males and white females, aged white males in American society suffer the most severe loss of social status, power, and money. That loss represents one possible explanation for their dramatically higher rates of suicide. By comparison, women in general and minority males, two groups that traditionally have held lower status positions, have less to lose after retirement than do white males and thus tend to have lower rates of suicide than white males.

The "old old"—those aged 85 and over—represent an at-risk population, confirmed by their rate of suicide, which is much higher than those aged 65 to 74. Based on their study conducted in Arizona, Robert Kastenbaum and Richard Coppedge (1985) found such dramatically higher suicide rates among the "old old" compared to the "young old" that they referred to the situation among the "old old" as a countertrend—a reversal of the prevailing trend of decreasing suicide rates among the old.

Many factors increase the risk of suicide in late life. Loss is a factor. Older adults suffer many losses: loss of physical health and mobility; sensory losses; loss of money; loss of social roles, particularly the roles of worker and spouse; cognitive loss; loss of loved ones and pets; and loss of respect and dignity. Loss is a major factor producing stress in older adults, who are already more vulnerable and less resistant to stress. Loss and stress may increase the risk of depression and/or alcoholism in late life. Figure 1 portrays a model of the relationship between aging, loss, stress, depression, alcoholism, and suicide.

Depression and alcoholism are major factors in late-life suicide. Depression is the major factor in most suicides of younger and older individuals. It is estimated that up to 50% of all individuals who commit suicide suffer from major depression, and that this percentage may be even higher in older age groups (Conwell, 1994). In a recent study of suicide among 73 people ages sixty-five and older who died by suicide, Clark (1991) found that only 23% were chronically or severely medically ill and only 14% were terminally ill at the time they chose to end their lives. The majority of those who committed suicide were depressed or substance abusers or both. Large community-based psychological autopsy studies (Barraclough, Bunch, Nelson, & Saninsbury, 1974; Beskow, 1979; Chynoweth, Tonge, & Armstrong, 1980; Rich, Young, & Fowler, 1986) have confirmed the relationship between major mental disorder and death by suicide. These studies found major affective disorder and/or substance use disorder present in 57% to 86% of all suicides. Clinical studies (Elkin et al., 1989; Jarvick, Mintz, Steuer, & Gerner, 1982; Kramer, 1987) have revealed that older depressed people are more prone

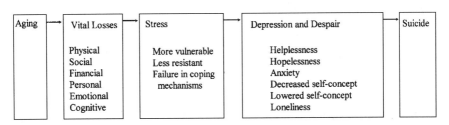

FIGURE 1. A model of the aging process and suicide. Source: N. J. Osgood, *Suicide in the Elderly: A Practioner's Guide to Diagnosis and Mental Health Intervention*. Rockville, MD: Aspen, 1985, p. xliv. Copyright by Osgood, 1985. Reproduced by permission.

than younger depressed people to take their own lives during an acute depressive episode.

Depression, alcoholism, and suicide represent a deadly triangle. Older alcoholics are at greater risk of depression and suicide. Depressed elders are at greater risk of alcoholism and suicide. Figure 2 depicts the relationship between depression, alcoholism, and suicide in late life.

☐ Ageism in America

Robert Butler's entry on ageism in *The Encyclopedia of Aging*, Second Edition, (1995) defines ageism in the following way:

> Ageism is defined as a process of systematic stereotyping and discrimination against people because they are old, just as racism and sexism accomplish this for skin color and gender. Older people are categorized as senile, rigid in thought and manner, and old-fashioned in morality and skills . . . Ageism allows the younger generation to see older people as different from themselves; thus they suddenly cease to identify with their elders as human beings and thereby reduce their own sense of fear and dread of aging. Such stereotyping and myths surrounding old age are explained in part by a lack of knowledge and insufficient contact with a wide variety of older people. But there is another factor operating—a deep and profound dread of growing old . . . Ageism is manifested in a wide range of phenomena; on both individual and institutional levels—stereotypes and myths, outright disdain and dislike, or simply subtle avoidance of contact; discriminatory practices in housing, employment, and services of all kinds; epithets, cartoons, and jokes. At times ageism becomes an expedient method by which society promotes viewpoints about the aged in order to relieve itself from the responsibility toward them, and at other times ageism serves a highly personal objective, protecting younger (usually middle-aged) individuals—often at high emotional cost—from thinking about things they fear (aging, illness, and death) . . . (p. 35)

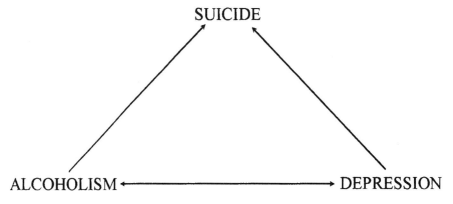

FIGURE 2. The deadly triangle. Source: N. J. Osgood, *Suicide in Later Life Recognizing the Warning Signals.* New York, NY: Lexington Books, 1992, p. 88. Copyright 1992 by University Press of America. Reproduced by permission.

In *Growing Old in America*, Fischer (1977) traces the historical development of ageism in America. According to Fischer, in the nineteenth century there was a revolution in age relations and views of older people. Two factors resulted in increasing contempt for the old and glorification of youth. The first trend, declining birth and death rates and increasing life expectancy, resulted in an increase in the number of older people and the proportion of elders in the nation's population. When there were few old people in our country, they were revered and respected. When they rapidly increased in number and proportion of the population, they became a threat to younger people, many of whom feared that they would consume scarce resources, and who did not want to see disease, dependence, and death, which are more common in older people.

The second trend, which began in the colonial period, was the acceptance of ideas of liberty and equality. In earlier times land, economic resources, status, and power were concentrated among the old. Under the new value system, which emphasized freedom and equality, older adults were associated with the "old order." The emphasis on freedom and equality resulted in an individual achievement orientation, which has dominated our society for the last 170 years. It places a high value on activity, personal productivity through work, materialism, success, individual achievement, independence, and self-sufficiency. Older adults, who are no longer able to produce due to physical and mental changes or to social policies that remove them from gainful employment (such as mandatory retirement), are at a distinct disadvantage in a society dominated by such a value orientation.

Our ideas about age are inherited from the classical Greeks, who viewed aging as an unmitigated misfortune and terrible tragedy. The Greeks believed "those whom the gods love die young." Youth was the only period of life of true happiness. During the heroic age, manhood was measured by the standards of physical prowess. Old age robbed the person of such prowess and the ability to fight like a valiant warrior and robbed males of sexual powers. Early Greek and Roman writings were filled with images glorifying youth and beauty. *Oedipus Rex*, written in the middle of the fifth century, depicted old age as a time of decline in physical and mental functioning. The image of the strong, young man also dominated Greek art and sculpture from the fifth through seventh centuries B.C. The love of youth is evident in the statues of young men and women of the Archaic period, the Parthenon frieze, and the well-known statue of the discus thrower that accentuates the strong, young, muscular physique of an athlete at the peak of his physical powers. Except in the Hellenistic period (323–227 B.C.), Greek sculptors never portrayed older figures.

America is also a country in which youth and beauty are highly valued. The glorification of youth and development of the youth cult in America began in the nineteenth century and grew rapidly in the twentieth; and it now flourishes in our present atmosphere of narcissism. Youth is associated with vitality, activity, and freshness. To be young is to be fully alive, exciting, attractive, healthy, and vigorous. Old age, on the other hand, is associated with decline, disease, disability, decrepitude, dependence, and death rather than wisdom, inner place, and other positive qualities.

Psychological factors influence ageism in our culture. The youth cult grows out of a profound fear of growing old. Through the ages, few fears have cut as deeply into the human soul as the fear of aging. Americans especially have a stark terror of growing old. Old age is associated with loss of independence, physical disease, and mental decline, loss of youthful vitality and beauty, and finally death. Old people are reminders of our own mortality. Because many people have limited contact with healthy, vibrant old people and lack accurate knowledge about the aging process, their fear escalates.

Ageism is manifested through stereotypes and myths about old people and aging. In medical circles older patients are stereotyped as "crocks" or "vegetables." Other common terms for older people are *"old fuddy duddy," "little old lady,"* and *"dirty old man."* Old people are thought of as being fit for little else but sitting idly in a rocking chair. Older women are referred to as *"old witch," "old bag," and "old biddy."* Old men are stereotyped as *"old geezers," "old goats," and "old codgers."* Common stereotypes of aging view the old as "out to pasture," "over the hill," and "all washed up."

In American culture, several mechanisms perpetuate and communicate ageist images, stereotypes, and myths: common aphorisms, literature, the media, and humor. Aphorisms about aging and older people permeate American culture. Some of the most common include: "You can't trust anyone over forty"; "You're only as old as you feel"; and "Age before beauty." These common sayings convey the idea that age is something to be denied or feared and allude to imagined losses accompanying the aging process.

The Western heritage in literature is replete with negative images of old age, beginning with medieval works. Foolish lust in older women is described in the works of Chaucer and Boccaccio. Physical ugliness and disgusting behavior in the old were frequently highlighted in fairy tales such as "Hansel and Gretel" and "Snow White," where women are portrayed as wicked witches. Emptiness in old age is a major theme in American literature. In the poem "Gerontion," T. S. Eliot (1970) provides a description of the empty misery of an old man, "a dry brain in a dry season." In his works Eliot describes old age as an empty wasteland.

In every culture humor conveys attitudes about the aged. In our own society these attitudes are expressed through jokes, cartoons, comic strips, and birthday cards. Predominant themes include the decline of physical appearance; lessening of sexual ability; decline in mental and physical abilities; loss of attractiveness; and denial of aging. The old become the brunt of many negative and cruel jokes. Jokes, cartoons, the media, and other cultural sources portray older people as sexless and senile, cranky and grumpy, non-productive, and an economic burden to be borne by younger members of society.

Ageism has many negative effects on older people in America. As they come to see themselves as old, with all of the negative connotations surrounding the status of the old in American culture, many feel they are abnormal, deviant, or marginal members of the culture. As Pat Moore described in *Disguised* (1985), they feel like an uninvited, unwelcome guest at the family reunion. To use sociologist Erving Goffman's term, they feel they have a "spoiled identity" (Goffman, 1963). As a result, many disengage from participation in civic, social, and other groups and become isolated. Ageism contributes to a sense of helplessness and powerlessness among older adults. If they accept the negative stereotypes and myths about old people, they may come to see themselves in negative terms. They believe they can no longer effectively live life and influence people and their environment.

☐ Death Debates in Context

Bioethics is the "disciplined examination of value dilemmas in health care" (Moody, 1992, p. 395.) As Moody points out in a recent chapter entitled "Bioethics and Aging": "The most dramatic questions of bioethics are the ethical dilemmas of death and dying . . . " (p.395). In bioethics, some of the major questions addressed are: Is it better to prolong life or to terminate it? When have people lived a full life that is long enough? Is it fair for members of the oldest age groups to over-consume scarce economic and health care resources at the expense of younger members of society? Does all life have equal meaning and value? Can an individual outlive his or her usefulness in a culture? Should limited health care procedures and resources be rationed on the basis of age or closeness to death? Has the time come when we should make death control as available as birth control currently is? These and other important questions and end-of-life issues form the social context in which current death debates are waged.

As we move into the twenty-first century, two debates will continue to occupy center stage: the debate over an individual's right to self-determination; and the debate over whether or not physician-assisted suicide (PAS) should be legalized in America. Both of these debates are taking place within a particular historical and sociocultural context. In other societies and in earlier historical time period in America these debates would not be occurring.

In this section we will examine current demographic and social conditions, economic concerns, and value orientations, which characterize America in the twenty-first century, and which have influenced and impacted current debates. End-of-life issues, particularly suicide and assisted suicide, will be overriding ethical issues of the twenty-first century.

Several changing societal conditions impact current attitudes about death and dying and impact current debates about suicide, assisted suicide, and other end-of-life issues. Foremost among these changing societal conditions are: the unprecedented technological development of medicine; the change in status of the physician from private practitioner to employee earning a salary in a bureaucracy; the increasing number and percentage of the very old (those 85 and over); the increased costs of health care in general; and the disproportionate amount of medical resources consumed by the very old population.

Dramatic medical advances have greatly increased life expectancy, but also have increased the period of chronic illness and disability. There are currently many more old individuals in our population than at any other previous time in history. Since 1900 the number of people 65 and older has increased 10 times. There are approximately 31 million people 65 and older in the United States population. The number of those over the age of 65 exceeds the number of teenagers in the United States. It is projected that the number of elderly will double in twenty years to 60 million. The oldest-old cohort (85 plus) are the fastest-growing age group in the country and are expected to triple in number during that same time span. The rate of increase in the oldest-old population has truly been impressive. For example, there are now twenty times as many people over age 85 as there were in 1900. It is estimated that by the year 2050, people 85 and older will number 19 million and make up 24% of the elderly American population, 5% of the total population, (Bureau of the Census, 1998). At the present time people 65 and over comprise 13% of the U.S. population, but account for approximately 35% of health care expenditures. Fifty percent of all Medicare expenditures occur during the last six months of life. A rapidly growing population of older people places considerably greater financial demands on society. In 2040, when the elderly will comprise 21% of the population, it is expected that they will consume 45 percent of all health care expenditures in the United States (Callahan, 1987).

We spend more of our national wealth on health care for all segments of the population than any other advanced nation. In 1986, the United States spent 11.1% of its gross national product (GNP) on health care. By contrast, Britain spent 6.2% on health care; Japan, 6.7%; West Germany, 8.1%; France and Canada, 8.5%; and Sweden, 9% (New York Times, 1988, p.12). In reviewing overall health care costs in the United States, the disproportionate utilization of the system by the elderly often becomes the focus for advocates of budget cutting, reevaluation of priorities, and redistribution of resources.

The increase in the number of older adults noted earlier, has been accompanied by a phenomenal increase in their health care costs, and in projections that this cost will continue to rise. In the early 1960s, less than 15% of the federal budget was allocated to those 65 and over; by 1985 that percentage had ballooned to 28% (Maddox, 1988). In that same year, the elderly cohort that represented 11% of the total population consumed 29% of all health care expenditures. In the year 2040, when the elderly will comprise 21% of the population, it is expected that they will consume approximately 50% of all health care resources in America. Manton and Soldo (1985) affirm that although various factors contributing to the severity and ultimately terminal outcome of chronic diseases have been controlled, the diseases themselves have not been eliminated. If the onset of these illnesses and disabilities is not delayed, they predict that the rates of dependency and lingering death will rise.

We are currently living in an era of "entrepreneurial medicine," which focuses on productivity, "units of service," and profit marking (Caine & Conwell, 1993). Health care rationing, cost containment, and other money saving strategies has assumed major importance in our health care system. As Prado (1998) noted recently, "Given the burden put on resources by a rapidly aging population, it's an undeniable fact that 'suicide is cheap'. The practice of preemptive suicide in advanced age obviously would have important economic benefits for government-supported health care systems" (pp. 12–13).

Spiraling health care costs in America have prompted rhetoric and policy changes aimed at promoting health care cost containment. Daniel Callahan (1987) argues for health care rationing on the basis of age. Marshall Kapp (1989) rightly points out that the call by Callahan and others for an explicit public policy of age-based health care rationing fits within the "intergenerational equity" movement. The rallying cry of the movement is that a public dollar spent on older persons is a dollar diverted away from the young. Age-based rationing of health care is, according to Kapp, an official policy of discrimination against older persons. These and other influential individuals are proposing arguments and social policies, which are blatantly, ageist. Many see the growing population of elders, many of whom are ill and/or dependent, as a major threat to their economic security.

Advanced medical technology has changed the time people die and the place where they die, as well as our views of death and dying. Phillipe Aries (1981) in his history of death in Western civilization, discusses a change from Medieval times to the present. In the past death was seen as a normal conclusion to a life, and the dying process was important. By contrast, in modern times death is feared and people prefer a quick death. In his book, *Seduced by Death*, Hendin (1998) states it this way: "We seem to be the last country to accept that dying is an inevitable part of the aging process, not simply the product of a disease that can be prevented or cured" (p. 245).

In America we see death as the enemy. We are terrorized by death and the dying process. A society that highly values youth and beauty, vitality, independence, success, and progress has no place for death. Toynbee called death "un-American." In modern America 80% of all people die in a hospital, nursing home, or other health care facility, away from home and family. Many are hooked to respirators and other machines, surrounded by doctors and nurses who are trained in the medical model, which emphasizes cure. Death has become medicalized, another health care "product" in a managed health care system. Emphasis is on the physical aspects of dying. In such a system the spiritual meaning of death and dying tend to get lost. Physicians are trained to cure, not to care, in an emotional supportive way, for dying patients. According to the American Medical Association's report on medical education, only 5 medical schools in the U.S. require a separate course in care of the dying; only 17 percent offer a hospice rotation (Hill, 1995).

Viewed in this historical context of limited economic and health care resources and calls for cost containment, and in which death and dying are feared and stripped of existential meaning, certain groups of individuals are vulnerable to pressures to die quickly and spare our society the social, emotional, and economic burden of caring for them at the end of life. Older adults are one of the most vulnerable groups.

Our society is characterized by social inequality. Some groups such as women, the poor, ethnic minorities, the disabled, and older adults are ostracized, oppressed, disenfranchised, and discriminated against. In America people have unequal access to health care and health care resources. Many Americans have inadequate health care. Approximately 34 million Americans do not have health insurance. Medical care in America is a privilege, not a right. Many individuals who are old and poor and many members of low-income ethnic minorities do not have the means to good medical care, appropriate pain management, or hospice care.

In a recent article Wardle (1987) referred to particularly vulnerable groups such as the poor, minorities, the disabled, the aged, and the infirm as the "new illegitimates," and suggested that these people will be at greater risk of having their lives ended pre-maturely by physicians and family members, who encourage them to "choose" rational suicide. According to Gil (1992), devalued populations, such as older adults, may not receive rigorous protection, assessment, and treatment.

In America we have a two-tiered or three-tiered system of health care. Some groups receive excellent health care and receive adequate management of physical pain, and have access to good psychiatric care, hospice care, and often-important mental and physical health services. Others are not so fortunate. The "new illegitimates" are not treated the same. They do not get first rate medical care. Many do not receive good mental health assessments and treatment. They are not offered the option of hospice care. If PAS is widely legalized in the U.S., it will also be practiced unequally. Poor people, ethnic minorities, disabled adults, and older individuals will be very vulnerable to losing their lives.

Investigators have recently found that the level of health care for the elderly in general, and nursing home patients in particular, is not up to the same high standards of medical care available to the patients of other age groups and other treatment locations. Kapp and Bigot (1985) report, for example, that "Physicians often attempt to avoid visiting their patients once they have entered a nursing home and, when a visit is made, frequently rush through their examination and treatment" (p. 115). In a study, Chu et al. (1987) found that of 1,680 women with breast cancer who were treated in 17 community hospitals, there was a linear trend for older patients to receive fewer services such as: biopsies prior to definitive treatment, number of lymph nodes examined, chemotherapy, or radiation therapy.

Older adults and other "disenfranchised" groups in America who do not have access to good health care may see suicide or PAS as their only option to escape untreated pain or untreated depression. As Professor Giles Scofield (1995), articulates:

> The moral issues of our day is not whether to enable or prevent a few individuals dying in the comfort of their home in the presence of their private physicians. The moral issue of our day is whether to do something about our immoral system of care, in which treatment is dispensed according to a principle best characterized as that of economic apartheid. (p. 491)

☐ Ageism by Any Other Name . . .

It is in the context of ageism and fear of aging and dying that we must hear the current death debates echoing in America. Arguments in favor of the right to die, the right to self-determination, and physician-assisted suicide take place within the sociocultural context of America in the twenty-first century. Any arguments offered must be viewed within the context of phenomenal increase in longevity and the numbers of people living past the age of 65 and 85; rising medical costs; advances in medical technology, and the increased medicalization of death and dying; and social inequality.

Gerontophobia, or an unrealistic fear of growing old and of older people, is common in our culture. Older people remind us of our own mortality and physical vulnerability. Looking at older people is like looking into a mirror of our future. Americans do not want to face the fact that eventually we all grow older and suffer physical, emotional, economic, and other losses. Americans, who glorify youth and beauty, are disgusted by old faces and old bodies, afraid of becoming disfigured, disabled, or ugly, and terrorized by the possibility of dying and death.

Prado (1998) argues for "preemptive suicide" in advanced age, justifying suicide as a way to avoid the physical and mental deterioration of advanced age. In his book, *The Last Choice*, Prado writes:

> I believe that elective death in advanced age should be recognized as a justifiable alternative to demeaning deterioration and stultifying dependency. My belief is supported by evidence that much of the historically recent increase in elderly suicides is due to growing unwillingness by the old to endure the very mixed benefits of increasingly dependent and debilitated survival. (p. 5)

According to Prado, aging results in erosion of reasoning, interpretive flexibility, and mental proficiency to the point that the individual in advanced age is no longer the person he or she used to be. Prado proposes that individuals should commit suicide, and society should provide the means to facilitate this act, before old age robs him/her of his/her personhood. It seems that Prado's solution to the problems of aging and old age is to commit suicide earlier in life.

Prado's argument is more extreme than most other arguments in favor of suicide and PAS; however, many proponents of the right to self-determination and legalization of PAS offer similar ageist arguments. Some supporters of sanctioned assisted suicide for the old, especially those who are senile or terminally ill, put forth what might be termed the social burden argument. Viewed from this perspective, old people are seen as a burden to their families and to society. The argument is made that soon we, as a society, will no longer be able to afford to care for this ever-increasing, non-productive segment of our population.

In her "Apologia for Suicide," Barrington (1969) argues that a disabled elderly individual in poor health and in need of constant care and attention may feel a burden to the younger person(s) who must provide that care. This situation may be such that the young person is in "bondage" whether willingly or unwillingly. The elderly person may want to "release" the young person but has no real choice but to continue to live on. Barrington argues for the option of voluntary termination of life. In a similar vein, Slater (1980; quoted in Hendim, 1995, p. 239) states: "If a chronically sick man dies, he ceases to be a burden to himself, or his family, on the health services and on his community." The social burden argument in favor of legalized PAS has a familiar ring to it. In previous centuries in many cultures, suicide of the old was obligatory and institutionalized. In such cultures as the Yuit in the St. Lawrence Islands in northern Canada and the Amassalik Eskimoes in Greenland, living conditions were harsh and there was not enough food and other resources to go around. The old, which were a burden on the social group, were forced to commit suicide so that children and parents could live.

Battin (1996), Prado (1998), Hendin (1995), Richman (1998), Smith (1999), and others point out that there is a very real possibility that older people, who are perceived by family members, physicians, and the society as a burden, will be coerced or manipulated into committing suicide or requesting PAS.

Older people, living in a suicide-permissive society characterized by ageism, may come to see themselves as a burden on their families or on society and feel it is incumbent upon them to take their own lives or receive assisted suicide. As C. Everett Koop (1985) suggests, uncaring or greedy family members may pressure others into assisted suicide. Those who need expensive medical technology to live may be denied help and die. The right to die then becomes not a right at all, but rather an obligation which robs some members of our society of their legal right to live.

Physicians, who are in a much more powerful position in the doctor/patient relationship than old, sick patients, could also inadvertently or intentionally pressure older patients to die. In our current system of managed care, older patients are expensive and consume a lot of health care resources. Physicians are encouraged and rewarded financially in a managed care system for denying expensive medical procedures, medical tests, and medical treatments to patients.

As Prado (1998) points out, at the present time in America we are coming to see old age as synonymous with dependency and being a social burden. He notes a major change in how we view living and dying in America:

> However, another part is the growing conviction that some lives aren't worth living, and not only because of untreatable pain. Some lives are seen as not worth living because they are wholly dependent and allow only what can be done with the help and cooperation of others. An aging population is putting increasingly onerous pressure on our healthcare system, and there's a good chance that the sea change in society's attitudes is more pragmatic than altruistic. Some regard the change as an ominous turn. They worry about 'where we're headed as a society with respect to health care,' and fear 'that assisted suicide is not going to be the option of last resort—it's going to be the attractive solution of first resort'. What this means for reflective aging individuals, in practical terms, is that they will be less tolerated in society and they'll face growing expectations that they 'should do the responsible thing' and end their lives before becoming costly burdens. Reflective aging individuals now have to take into account how continued life likely will be more unattractive than previously because of societal disapprobation of dependency. Deliberation of preemptive suicide must be qualified by how living dependent lives will be harder. Life in advance age will include not just the deterioration and afflictions that may make life less than worth living but increasingly grudging societal support, more difficult access to health care, and the stigma of appearing to deprive others of scarce resources simply by being old and continuing to live. (p. 36)

Suicide takes place within a particular socio-cultural context; and the predominant cultural values about the meaning and value of life and death, disability and dependency, and aging influence life and death decisions of peoples lives in the culture. Suicide is a culturally-determined act. Cultural shaping is a reality. As Prado (1998) points out: "We're seeing an essential change that turns on its being accepted as normal that some lives shouldn't be lived, aren't worth living, at least not to their ends" (p. xiv).

In a culture such as ours, older people may feel it is their obligation to die to relieve family, physicians, and society of the burden of caring for them and spending limited health care dollars to treat them. In such a culture, to exit early is the noble and courageous thing to do. Elderly suicide may be seen as the most patriotic of acts. In her response to the 1996 court decision in California lifting the ban on assisted suicide, Rita Marker, executive director of the Anti-Euthanasia Task Force, has this to say: "If this decision is permitted to stand, it will not be long before the 'right' to death will place every medically vulnerable person in the position of having to justify not 'choosing' this new medical lethal option" (quoted in *USA Today*, March 8, 1996).

Robert Kastenbaum (1972), well-known gerontologist and thanatologist, also is concerned about our current views about aging and death and dying. He points out that as a society we do not like death. We see it as something disgusting and distasteful. It is not progressive; and in our technologically sophisticated, achievement-oriented culture, material progress is very highly valued. Kastenbaum believes that in our society we abandon our dying, socially neglect them, and even try to hasten their deaths. "From the view that it is natural for the aged to die, it is not difficult to 'conclude' that they ought to die . . . ", Kastenbaum wrote (p. 118). Kastenbaum even suggests that if such notions aren't challenged vigorously, suicide could become the "preferred way of death in America." Arguing in a similar vein, Kasimar (1993) wrote:

> In a suicide-permissive society, in a climate in which suicide is the 'rational' thing to do, or at least a 'reasonable' option, will it become the unreasonable thing not to do? The noble thing to do? In a society unsympathetic to justifying an impaired or dependent existence, a psychological burden may be placed on those who do not think their illness or infirmity is reason for dying. The presence of a socially approved option becomes a subtle pressure to request it. (Quoted in Hendin, 1995, p. 214)

☐ Conclusion

Ageism results in the use of older adults as scapegoats for all of the social, political, and economic problems of the day. Arguments go something like this: The reason the federal deficit is so large is that we pay too much money out in Medicare and Social Security payments to those aged sixty-five and older. The reason the health care industry is in such a mess is that sick old people are draining all the health care resources. By categorizing the old negatively, younger members of society can see the old as different, deviant, not quite as good as the young, and possibly even as less than human. Ageism makes it easier for society to ignore the old and to shirk its economic and social responsibility to older citizens. Ageism blinds us to the many problems older men and women face and keeps older people from receiving the social, economic, and spiritual services they need and deserve. It facilitates control of younger people in power over older people by rationalizing their subordination, exploitation, and devalued status. By labeling the old as different or abnormal, it is easier for other members of the society to deny older citizens access to health care and societal resources and thus retain for the young power, status, wealth, and authority.

Certainly, as the aging population continues to expand rapidly and as we as a nation continue to spend more dollars on health care costs and advanced medical technology that are disproportionately utilized by the elderly, the need for budget cutting, health care rationing, and redistribution of health and other resources becomes more pressing. Older adults are viewed as an emotional and financial burden to be borne by the younger members of society. Cries for rational suicide, the right to die, and legalized assisted suicide grow louder. It seems easier to eliminate the problem of having too many expensive old people to care for by encouraging elderly suicide rather than facing hard moral choices about our financial spending as individuals and as a society and our obligations to the older members of the society. As John McIntosh (1999) recently pointed out:

> In a broader sense, the acceptance of suicide among the elderly, simple because they are long-lived and have fewer years left in their lives, leads to a devaluing of the elderly as a group and of the years of life remaining to them. The old are seen as expensive burdens, who contribute little; this is a movement backward in time with respect to ageistic practice and societal attitude. (p. 192)

In an earlier work, Harry Moody (1984) expressed a similar concern when he wrote:

> But do we really want a society in which our best answer to the 'meaningless' existence of old age is an encouragement for old people to kill themselves? Does this attitude itself not betray contempt for dependency, a feeling that the lives of old people are somehow less than human, and, finally, a secret despair over the last stage of the life cycle? (p. 89)

Most elders who commit suicide are not suffering intense physical pain or dying from a terminal illness. Rather, they are leading lives of desperation and despair, aching from loneliness, lack of social contact, and rejection and abandonment by a youth-oriented society. The fact that we have created a society that is so harsh to its old that ever-increasing numbers are choosing suicide as a solution to their problem is a sad commentary on America. To argue for the right to suicide and assisted suicide for the old is a symbol of our devaluation of old age and our own ageism and fear of aging. This position endorses the belief that the answers to the problem of old age is suicide. Moreover, it may in fact be setting up conditions that rob older people of their right to live. In a society, which devalues old age and old people, in which older adults are seen as "expendable" and as an economic burden on younger members, older people may come to feel that it is their social duty to kill themselves. As in more primitive societies in earlier historical periods, the old in America may be sacrificed for the good of the society.

Points to Remember

1. Elderly suicide is an acute problem in the US, particularly among old-old males.
2. Our culture is characterized by a devaluation of the older individuals (ageism) and by a fear of growing old (gerontophobia).
3. Limited resources, together with the increase in the numbers of older adults, are likely to increase ageism in the future. In particular, present tendencies to legalize physician assisted suicide (PAS) can evolve in the direction of putting pressures on the older, dependent individual to do his or her "patriotic" duty and "bow out" of life "in the interest" of the society.

Masquerading as benevolent protectors whom offers many new "rights"—the right to "die with dignity," the right to self-determination, and the right to a "living" will—advocates of suicide, sanctioned assisted suicide, euthanasia, and limited availability of life-prolonging medical technology for the old are promulgating a dangerous new medical ethic that proposes to save money and other resources by letting nonproductive people die or by sanctioning their suicides. We are witnessing the emergence of a medical ethic that says, essentially, "Don't waste scarce time and medical and economics resource on those who would be better off dead."

In light of our current level of ageism, our fear of aging and death, our advanced medical technology which robs death of its meaning and relegates it to just another health care "product," a new value system, which accepts and encourages rational suicides, and increasingly accepts legalized PAS, older adults are at risk for death. Do we really want to live in a society that sends its older members the message that: Some lives are more worthy of being lived than others. Your life is a dependent, useless one. By continuing to live, you are robbing younger people of scarce economic and health care resource. You should die quickly and early to save your family and society the burden of taking care of you and watching you die. Do the patriotic thing and exit early!

☐ References

Aries, P. (1981). *The hour of our death*. New York: Knopf.
Barraclough, B. M., Bunch, J., Nelson, B., & Saninsbury, P. (1974). 100 cases of suicide: Clinical aspects. *Br. J. of Psychiatry, 125*, 355–373.
Barrington, M. (1969). Apologia for suicide. In M. Barrington & A. B. Downing (Eds.), *Euthanasia and the right to die* (pp. 152–172). London: Peter Owen.
Battin, M. P. (1996). *The Death debate: Ethical issues in suicide*. Englewood Cliffs, NJ: Prentice-Hall Inc.

Battin, M. P. (1980). Manipulated suicide. *Bioethics Quarterly, 2,* 123–134.

Beskow, J. (1979). Suicide and mental disorder in Swedish men. *Acta Psychiatrica Scandinavica, 1,* 78–84.

Bureau of the Census, U.S. Department of Commerce, Economic, and Statistics Administration (1998). *Sixty-five plus in the United States.* (Current population reports special studies 23–100). Washington, DC: U.S. Government Printing Office.

Butler, R. N. (1995). Ageism. In G. L. Maddox (Ed.), *The Encyclopedia of Aging* (2nd ed., pp. 35–36). New York: Springer.

Caine, E., & Conwell, Y. (1993). Self-determined death, the physician, and medical priorities. *Journal of the American Medical Association, 270,* 875–876.

Callahan, D. (1987). *Setting limits.* New York: Simon & Schuster.

Chu, J., Diehr, P., Feigl, P., Glaefke, G., Begg, C., Glaicksman,A., & Ford, I. (1987). The effect of age on the care of women with breast cancer in community hospital. *Journal of Gerontology, 42*(2), 185–190.

Chynoweth, R., Tonge, J. I., & Armstrong, J. L. (1980). Suicide in Brisbane: A retrospective psychosocial study. *Australian and New Zealand Journal of Psychiatry, 14,* 37–45.

Clark, D. (1991). *Elderly suicide: Final report 2-3 submitted to the Andrus Foundation,* Washington, D.C.

Conwell, Y. (1994). Suicide in elderly patients. In L. S. Schneider, C. F. Reynolds, B. D. Lebowitz, & A. J. Friedhoff (Eds.), *Diagnosis and treatment of depression in late life* (pp. 397–418). Washington, DC: American Psychiatric Press.

Eliot, T. S. (1970). Gerontion. In E. San Juan, Jr. (Ed.), *A Casebook of Gerontion* [no 3]. Columbus, OH: C. E. Merill.

Elkin, I., Shea, M. T., Watkins, J. T., Imber, S. D., Sotsky, S. M., Collins, J. F., Glass, D. R., Pilkonis, P. A., Leber, W. R., Docherty, J. P. , Fiester, S. J., & Parloff, M. B. (1989). National Institute of Mental Health Treatment of depression collaborative research program: General effectiveness of treatments. *Archives of Gen. Psychiatry, 45,* 971–982.

Fischer, D. (1977). *Growing old in America.* New York: Oxford University Press.

Gil, C. J. (1992). Suicide intervention for people with disabilities: A lesson in inequality. *Issues in Law & Medicine, 8,* 37–53.

Goffman, E. (1963). *Stigma: Notes on the management of spoiled identity* (pp. 449–479). Englewood Cliffs, NJ: Prentice-Hall.

Hendin, H. (1995). *Suicide in America.* New York: W.W. Norton & Co.

Hendin, H. (1998). *Seduced by death: Doctors, patients, and assisted suicide.* NY: W.W. Norton & Co.

Hill, T.P. (1995). Treating the dying patient: The challenge for medical education. *Archives of Internal Medicine. 155,* 1265–1269.

Jarvick, L. F., Mintz, J., Steuer, J. L., & Gerner, R. (1982). Treating geriatric depression: A 26-week interim analysis. *Journal of the American Geriatrics Society, 30,* 713.

Kapp, M. B. (1989). Rationing health care: Will it be necessary? Can it be done without age or disability discrimination? *Issues in Law & Medicine, 5*(3), 337–352.

Kapp, M. B., & Bigot, A. (1985). *Geriatrics and the law.* New York: Springer.

Kasimar, Y. (1993). Are Laws against suicide unconstitutional? *Hastings Center Report, 23,* 32–41.

Kastenbaum, R. (1992). Death, suicide, and the older adult. *Suicide & Life-Threatening Behavior, 22*(1), 1-14.

Kastenbaum, R. (1972). While the old man dies: Our conflicting attitudes. In B. Schoenberg, A. O. Carr, D. Peretz, & A. H. Kutscher (Eds.), *Psychosocial aspects of terminal care* (pp. 116–125). New York: Columbia University Press.

Kastenbaum, R., & Coppedge, R. (1985). Suicide in later life: A counter trend among the old-old. In G. L. Maddox & E. W. Busse (Eds.), *Aging: The universal human experience* (pp. 301–308). New York: Springer Publishing.

Koop, C. E. (1985). *The right to live, the right to die.* Living Books Edition. Wheaton, Il: Tydale Health Publishers.

Kramer, B. A. (1987). Electroconvulsive therapy use in geriatric depression. *J. Nervous & Mental Disease, 233,* 175.

Maddox, G. L. (1988). 1987 Boettner Lecture. In *Aging and well-being* (pp. 1–21). Philadelphia: Boettner Research Institute.

Manton, K. G., & Soldo, B. J. (1985). Dynamics of health changes in the oldest-old: New perspectives and evidence. *Milbank Memorial Fund Quarterly, 63,* 206–285.

Marker, R. (1996, March 8). We must protect the ill. *USA Today,* vol. 14, p. 11A.

McIntosh, J. L. (1999). Arguments against rational suicide: A gerontologist's perspective. In J. L. Werth (Ed.), *Contemporary Perspectives on rational suicide* (pp. 188–193). Ann Arbor, MI: Braun-Brumfield.

Moody, H. R. (1984). Can suicide on grounds of old age be ethically justified? In M. Tallmer, E. R. Prichard, A.H. Kutscher, R. Debellis, M.S. Hale, & I. K. Golberg (Eds.), *The life-threatening elderly* (pp.64–92). New York: Columbia University Press.

Moody, H. R. (1992). Bioethics and aging. In T. R. Cole, D. D. Van Tassel, & R. P. Kastenbaum (Eds.), *Handbook of the humanities and aging,* (pp. 395–425). New York: Springer.

Moore, P. (1985). *Disguised.* Albuquerque: Word Books.

New York Times (1988). August 7, p. 12.

Peters, K. D., Kochanek, K. D., & Murphy, S. L. (1998). *Deaths: Final data for 1996. National Vital Statistics Report, 47*(9). Hyattsville, MD: National Center for Health Statistics (DHHS Publication No. (PHS) 99-1120).

Prado, C. G. (1998). *The Last Choice: Preemptive Suicide in Advanced Age* (2nd ed.).Westport, CT: Greenwood Press.

Rich, C. L., Young, D., & Fowler, R. C. (1986). San Diego suicide study, I: Young vs. old subjects. *Arch. Gen. Psychiatry, 125,* 355–373.

Richman, J. (1998). Euthanasia and physician-assisted suicide in America today: Whither are we going? In K. J. Kaplan & M. B. Schwartz (Eds), *Jewish approaches to suicide, martyrdom, and euthanasia* (pp.116–128). Northvale, NJ: Jason Aronson.

Scofield, G. R. (1995). Exposing some myths about physician-assisted suicide. *Seattle University Law Review, 18,* 473–491.

Slater, E. (1980). Choosing the time to die. In M. P. Batlin & D. Mayo (Eds.), *Suicide: The philosophical issues* (pp. 199–204). New York: St. Martins Press.

Smith, W. J. (1999). Rational Suicide as the new Jim Crow. In J. L. Werth (Ed.), *Contemporary perspectives on rational suicide* (pp. 54–62). Ann Arbor, MI: Braun-Brumfield.

Wardle, L. D. (1987). Sanctioned assisted suicide: "Separate but equal" treatment for the "New illegitimates." *Issues in Law & Medicine, 3*(3), 245–265.

11

CHAPTER

Victor G. Cicirelli

Older Adult's Ethnicity, Fear of Death, and End-of-Life Decisions

From the very beginnings of human existence, death has been an unpleasant fact of life, an event from which there is ultimately no escape and which most people regard as something to be feared and avoided for as long as possible. Over the past few decades, the topic of death has been of great interest to psychologists. Developmental psychologists have sought to determine how children develop concepts about death, and how such concepts change as children grow toward maturity. Other psychologists have investigated the fear of death in adulthood, the factors influencing it, and how it affects various aspects of personality and functioning.

However, considering the present multicultural society in the United States, it becomes important to extend present findings concerning fear of death to different ethnic groups. Also, the number of older adults in the population is increasing dramatically, so it is important to determine the death fears of older ethnic groups. Finally, older adults are nearing the end of their lives, and it is important to know how death fears might be related to their decisions about how their life should be ended. In the present chapter, two basic topics will be explored: (a) Does the fear of death in older adults differ for Whites and African Americans?, and (b) How do the death fears of older Whites and African Americans influence their views regarding end-of-life decisions?

☐ Does Fear of Death Exist Among Older Adults?

Before going on to compare fear of death among older African Americans and Whites, one first needs to consider whether older people in general do indeed fear death. Their advanced age increases older people's vulnerability to death. Yet some authors (e. g., Johnson & Barer, 1997) argue that older people have an acceptance of death and no longer fear it. However, this may depend on the particular aspect of fear of death that is involved.

Fear of death, or the anxiety associated with the anticipation of one's death, is widely recognized as a universal and normal human characteristic (Thorson & Powell, 1994). Although it was initially regarded as a unidimensional concept, most researchers now agree that it is multidimensional in nature. Templer's early Death Anxiety Scale (1970) was conceived as a single dimension, but has since been shown to have a diverse factor structure (e. g., Thorson & Powell, 1994). Other scales have also been constructed as multidimensional instruments, for example, the Collett-Lester Fear of Death Scale (Lester, 1994), the Leming Fear of Death Scale (Leming & Dickenson, 1985), the Death Attitude Profile (Gesser, Wong, & Reker, 1987–1988; Wong, Reker, & Gesser, 1994), and the Multidimensional Fear of Death Scale (MFODS; Hoelter, 1979a). The particular dimensions identified by the various researchers differ in number and content from one measure to the next. However, fears reflecting concerns about annihilation and the afterlife are common to most measures, as well as concerns about pain and suffering in the dying process, and about the destruction of the body. Despite recognizing the multidimensional nature of most fear of death instruments, many researchers report an overall fear of death score.

Various researchers have investigated whether the fear of death changes as death comes nearer in the latter part of life, and, if so, how it changes. Some existing studies suggest that the fear of death tends to decrease with age and be relatively low for older people (e.g., Bengtson, Cuellar, & Ragan, 1977; Gesser, Wong, & Reker, 1987–1988; Kastenbaum, 1992; Lonetto & Templer, 1986; Neimeyer, 1988). On the other hand, Mullins and Lopez (1982), in a study of nursing home patients, found that fear of death was greater among an older, sicker group than among those who were younger. Their conclusion was that when older people are actually closer to death, they may have more fear than they are aware of when in better health. Work by Viney (1984) and by Kureshi and Husain (1981) supports this finding. In a study using three age groups (18–26, 35–50, and 60 and older), a curvilinear trend was observed with death anxiety highest in the middle-aged group, lower in the young, and lowest in the older group (Gesser, Wong, & Reker, 1987–1988). Using the MFODS (Hoelter, 1979a) with a large sample ranging in age from 18 to 92, Neimeyer and Moore (1994) found that although scores on most fear dimensions declined with age, Fear of the Unknown increased with age.

Recent studies of the oldest old (those aged 85 and over), using unstructured interview techniques, have supported the view that fear of death is low in old age. According to Johnson and Barer (1997), the oldest old can accept death without fear. To them, death is no longer remote or abstract or something to avoid. What they fear is not death itself but the dying process, and dread a long illness in a nursing home and the thought of dying alone. In general, people of this advanced age have no unfinished business in life and many are bored with further living. Because they have less to lose, they can approach their death with equanimity; they feel prepared to die. Increasingly, they take death into account in daily tasks, viewing death without fear. Tobin (1996) also noticed a shift from a fear of non-being to a fear of the process of dying among the oldest old, as well as an acceptance of death. However, he concluded that acceptance of death depended on having completed life tasks with no unfinished business, citing examples of aged mothers still caring for mentally retarded offspring who did not accept the idea of their own death but actively resisted it. The conclusion reached by Johnson and Barer (1997) and by Tobin (1996) that fear of nonexistence declines among the oldest old while fear of the dying process increases appears to be at odds with the finding of Neimeyer and Moore (1994) that Fear of the Unknown increases with age. However, it is consistent with findings by Wong, Reker, and Gesser (1994) that fear of death declines with age while acceptance of death increases.

The preponderance of existing evidence indicates that fear of death is lower in old age. However, with the exception of Johnson and Barer's (1997) work, existing findings regarding the relationship of age to fear of death are based on cross-sectional studies. Certainly, longitudinal studies are needed to firmly establish age trends in fear of death. Nevertheless, the phenomenon of fear of death exists among older adults, although it may be low compared to younger adults. Given the difference in their life experiences, one would suspect that fear of death would differ for older Whites and African Americans.

☐ Why Expect That Fear of Death Will Differ for Whites and African Americans?

Psychologists have become increasingly interested in differences among various ethnic groups, particularly those differences between minority groups that have suffered discrimination in relation to the dominant cultural group. Not all groups who constitute a minority of the population (e.g., the Danish Americans) are discriminated against. However, African Americans are an ethnic minority group that has a long history of discrimination in the United States. As an ethnic minority group, they have been considered inferior by the majority, and discriminated against in terms of job opportunities, income, availability of adequate housing, availability of adequate nutrition, educational opportunities, accessibility of medical services, social acceptance, and so on (Johnson, Gibson, & Luckey, 1990; Smith & Thornton, 1993). Although civil rights legislation has led to improvements in all these areas in recent decades, the present generation of older African Americans was reared at a time when there was a high degree of prejudice and discrimination against them (Smith & Thornton, 1993). By comparison, the present generation of young African Americans grew up in changing times and experienced less prejudice and discrimination.

Obviously, discrimination has had an effect in shaping the values, beliefs, and lifestyles of older African Americans in order for them to adapt and survive (Jackson, Chatters, & Taylor, 1993). There is some evidence that they have become closer to the extended family and the church than many Whites, and have depended on them as support groups (Hatchett & Jackson, 1993; Sudarkasa, 1993).

In regard to death, African Americans have had experiences differing from those of Whites. Their life expectancy has been lower than that for Whites over this entire century, and was 71.8 years in 1994 as compared to 76.4 years for Whites, making them less likely to survive into old age. From childhood on, they were more likely to experience the death of a nuclear family member (a parent or a sibling) before age 15 than were Whites, and in adulthood were more likely to experience widowhood than were Whites in their age group (Kain, 1993). These differing mortality experiences within the nuclear family have led African Americans to place greater reliance on extended family relationships than do Whites, and imply different values and lifestyles (Hatchett & Jackson, 1993; Jackson et al., 1993; Sudarkasa, 1993).

As a result, it is of interest to consider the implications of experiences relating to discrimination and death for the way older African Americans feel about death as compared to Whites. All people have a biological urge to survive, as well as a fear of death (Becker, 1973). At first glance, one might expect African Americans to have a greater fear of death than Whites; African Americans have experienced a greater threat of death than Whites and have experienced greater losses of family members throughout life as a result of discrimination. On the other hand, those who have had to struggle the most to survive and have faced greater losses of family members have developed greater coping skills (Jackson et al., 1993) in order to survive and deal with death, and thus should have less fear of death. If this idea is correct, then one would expect African Americans to have less fear of death than Whites. Additionally, quality of life may have an effect on fear of death. Those who have had a quality of life typified by a struggle for survival may have less to lose and hence have less fear of death, whereas those who have a high quality of life may have more to lose and hence have a greater fear of death. On such arguments, one would expect that African Americans would have less fear of death than Whites.

☐ Does Fear of Death Differ for Older Whites and African Americans?

Ethnic differences in fear of death in old age have received little research attention, and the few existing studies have mixed results. Whereas some studies (Cole, 1978; Dodd & Mills, 1985; Sanders, Poole, & Rivero, 1980; Young & Daniels, 1980) reported that African Americans had a greater fear of death than Whites, others (Davis, Martin, Wilee, & Voorhees, 1980; Pandy & Templer, 1972; Thorson & Powell, 1994) found that African Americans had less fear of death than Whites. Still another study (Florian & Snowdon, 1989) found no difference between the two groups. Clearly a need exists to resolve these inconsistencies.

Study method

A recent study carried out by the author (Cicirelli, 1997, 1998) yielded new information on the effects of ethnicity on fear of death among older adults. The study sample consisted of 388 older adults at least 60 years of age who attended senior citizen centers in a large urban area (Indianapolis, Indiana) and a medium-sized city (Greater Lafayette, Indiana), who agreed to participate in the study, and for whom all data were complete. In all, 20 different centers were included in the study. Each study participant was asked to complete an interview-questionnaire which included the Multidimensional Fear of Death Scale (MFODS) (Hoelter, 1979a; Neimeyer & Moore, 1994), information on demographic background, and various other measures.

Participants ranged from 60 to 100 years of age. There were 285 women and 103 men, 265 Whites and 123 African Americans. A summary of the demographic characteristics of the White and African-American groups is presented in Table 1. The reader can observe that, compared to the African-American subgroup, the White subgroup has a greater proportion of women and married elders and is slightly older, better educated, at higher socioeconomic status levels, and in better health.

The MFODS consists of 42 5-point items yielding 8 subscales. The subscales include:

1. Fear of the Dying Process (including painful or violent deaths)
2. Fear of the Dead (including avoidance of human or animal bodies)
3. Fear of Being Destroyed (including cremation or dissection of the body for autopsy or organ transplants)
4. Fear for Significant Others (including apprehension about the impact of the respondent's death on others)
5. Fear of the Unknown (including fear of nonexistence and lack of knowledge about afterlife)
6. Fear of Conscious Death (including concerns about falsely being declared dead)
7. Fear for the Body after Death (including concerns about decay and isolation of the body), and
8. Fear of Premature Death (concerns about being unable to accomplish desired goals or experiences)

TABLE 1. Demographic Characteristics of White (*n* = 265) and African-American (*n* = 123) Elders in Study Sample

Variable	Whites			African Americans		
	Percent	Mean	SD	Percent	Mean	SD
Gender						
Males	24			33		
Females	76			67		
Marital status						
Married	33			29		
Widowed, divorced, etc.	67			71		
Age		73.95	4.46		69.85	7.58
SES		46.46	15.72		37.80	13.46
Health Rating		4.42	0.92		4.18	0.85

Appropriate items are summed to yield subscores, with items coded so that a high score indicates a greater fear of death on the scale. Neimeyer and Moore (1994) reported considerable evidence for the reliability and validity of the MFODS. Internal consistency reliabilities (Cronbach's alpha) for the subscales ranged from .65 to .82, and test-retest reliabilities determined over a three-week interval between testings ranged from .61 to .81. In addition, Neimeyer and Moore reported factor analytic evidence for the subscales as well as evidence for construct validity. Internal consistency reliabilities (Cronbach's alpha) computed for the participants in the present study ranged from .65 to .81 for the 8 subscales, values considered adequate for studies involving group comparisons.

Ethnic Differences in MFODS Scores

To determine whether African-American elders feared death more or less than White elders, means and standard deviations of the 8 MFODS subscores for the two groups were computed and are presented in Table 2. Because the subscores are composed of different numbers of items, an item mean (the average of the items making up the given subscore) is given in addition to the subscore mean and standard deviation. An examination of the table reveals that Whites reported greater fear than African Americans on 4 of the 8 MFODS subscales, and less fear than African Americans on the remaining 4 subscales. However, these differences were statistically significant only for Fear of the Dying Process, for which Whites reported greater fear than African Americans, and Fear of Conscious Death, for which African Americans reported greater fear than Whites. Differences between the two groups on the remaining 6 MFODS subscales were not large enough to be statistically significant.

A related question is whether different kinds of death fears predominate for

TABLE 2. Means and Standard Deviations of White (n = 265) and African American (n = 123) Elders on MFODS, with F-tests for Differences between the Groups

Fear of Death	Whites			African Americans			
	Item Mean	Mean	SD	Item Mean	Mean	SD	F
Of dying process	3.15	18.92	6.23	2.68	16.08	6.54	11.15**
Of the dead	2.62	15.74	4.77	2.63	15.78	5.22	0.15
Of being destroyed	3.20	12.80	4.74	3.39	13.56	3.88	3.16
For significant others	3.35	20.08	4.74	3.06	18.35	4.71	2.74
Of the unknown	2.06	10.28	4.51	2.07	10.33	4.64	0.02
Of conscious death	2.55	12.74	5.16	2.82	14.09	4.77	7.20**
For body after death	2.20	13.18	5.17	2.15	12.91	4.75	0.22
Of premature death	1.70	10.19	4.07	1.57	9.45	3.94	1.35

** $p < .01$; * $p < .05$

Whites and African Americans. If one looks at the item means in Table 2, one can get an idea of which fears are strongest and weakest for each group. Among the Whites, the strongest fear was Fear for Significant Others (M = 3.35), followed by Fear of Being Destroyed (M = 3.20) and Fear of the Dying Process (M = 3.15). Among the African Americans, the strongest fear was Fear of Being Destroyed (M = 3.39), followed by Fear for Significant Others (M = 3.06) and Fear of Conscious Death (M = 2.82). Among Whites, the weakest fear was Fear of Premature Death (M = 1.70), followed by Fear of the Unknown (M = 2.06) and Fear for the Body after Death (M = 2.20). Among African Americans, the weakest fear was Fear of Premature Death (M = 1.57), followed by Fear of the Unknown (M = 2.07), and Fear for the Body after Death (M = 2.15). It can be seen that, except for minor differences, there is considerable similarity between the two ethnic groups in regard to the fears they regard as their strongest and weakest.

☐ What Variables Are Related to the Death Fears of Older Adults and What Part Does Ethnicity Play?

The author's recent study (Cicirelli, 1987, 1988) also provided information on variables related to fear of death. Hierarchical multiple regression analysis was used to explore the relationship of various hypothesized predictor variables to fear of death. Four background variables and a single-item health rating were entered in the first step of the regression analysis. The background variables were marital status (0 = married, 1 = widowed, divorced, or unmarried), ethnicity (0 = White, 1 = African American), gender (0 = male, 1 = female), and age in years. A single-item self-rating of health was used, with ratings on a 6-point scale ranging from "1" (very poor) to "6" (excellent).

In the second step of the analysis, four psychosocial variables (religiosity, locus of control, self-esteem, and social support) and a measure of socioeconomic status (SES) were added to the hierarchical regression equation. Subjective religiosity of study participants was assessed by three items drawn from the work of Markides (1983) and Krause (1993). The externality score obtained from Levenson's (1981) Multidimensional Locus of Control measure was used as the measure of participants' locus of control beliefs. The Rosenberg (1965) Self-Esteem Scale was used as the measure of self-esteem. Perceived social support was assessed using the "circles" technique from Antonucci and Akiyama's (1987) Social Networks in Adult Life Survey; the total number of persons in the inner and middle circles was taken as the indicator of the elder's close support network. Finally, the measure of socioeconomic status level (SES) was Hollingshead's (1957) socioeconomic status index, with high scores indicating higher socioeconomic status levels.

Four interaction terms were entered in the third step of the hierarchical regression analysis: health by self-esteem, ethnicity by religiosity, ethnicity by socioeconomic status, and gender by social support. (Only those 2-way interaction terms identified as predictors of MFODS subscores in preliminary explorations were included in the final analysis.)

The hierarchical regression analyses for each of the MFODS subscores are summarized in Table 3, with β-coefficients (standardized partial regression coefficients) presented to indicate the strength of each of the predictor variables, and the squared multiple correlation coefficient R^2 indicating the amount of variance in the fear of death measure explained by the set of predictors. Values of R^2 after all three steps of the analysis indicated that from 14% to 32% of the variance in the MFODS subscores was explained by the set of predictor variables and their interactions.

Looking specifically at the relationship of ethnicity to fear of death revealed in Step 1 of the analyses (adjusted for the effects of other predictor variables), ethnicity was significantly related to Fear of the Dying Process, Fear for Significant Others, Fear of Conscious Death, and Fear of Premature Death. African Americans had less fear of death than Whites regarding Fear of the Dying Process, Fear for Significant Others, and Fear of Premature Death, but Greater Fear of Conscious Death.

TABLE 3. Summary of Hierarchical Regressions of MFODS Subscores on Demographic, Health, and Psychosocial Variables for Total Group (N = 388)

Variable	β-coefficient							
	Dying	Dead	Destr	Signi	Unkno	Consc	Body	Prema
Step 1								
Marital status	−.02	.05	−.01	.01	.10	−.03	−.03	.03
Ethnicity (ETH)	−.23**	.01	.05	−.18**	−.01	.12*	−.01	−.11*
Health (HEL)	−.05	−.09	−.16**	−.06	−.04	−.10	−.15**	−.09
Age	−.15**	−.06	−.03	−.05	−.02	.03	.07	−.11*
Gender (GEN)	.15**	.20**	.05	.15**	−.12*	.06	.10	.10
R^2	.08**	.06**	.03*	.06*	.02	.03	.04*	.04*
Step 2								
Externality	.20**	.23**	.09	.09	.27**	.25**	.22**	.23**
Social support (SUP)	.03	−.05	.07	.12*	−.11*	.04	−.09	−.01
Self-esteem (EST)	−.02	−.05	.07	.04	−.05	−.06	−.09	−.09
Religiosity (REL)	−.13*	−.06	.09	−.08	−.43**	−.10	−.05	−.14**
SES	.05	−.01	−.18**	.10	−.01	−.12*	−.07	.01
R^2	.14**	.13**	.08**	.09**	.31**	.14**	.13**	.12**
ΔR^2	.05**	.07**	.05**	.03*	.30**	.11**	.10**	.09**
Step 3								
HEL × EST	−.06	−.12*	−.11*	−.10*	.01	.01	−.09	−.16**
ETH × REL	−.02	.06	−.01	−.12*	−.08	−.03	−.03	−.01
ETH × SES	.14*	.12*	.24**	.16**	.00	.20**	.13*	.12*
GEN × SUP	.02	.17**	.05	.13	.05	−.03	−.04	.09
R^2	.16**	.17**	.14**	.14**	.32**	.16**	.16**	.17**
ΔR^2	.03	.04*	.06**	.05**	.01	.03	.02	.05*

** $p < .01$; * $p < .05$

Note. Dying = Fear of the Dying Process; Dead = Fear of the Dead; Destr = Fear of Being Destroyed; Signi = Fear for Significant Others; Unkno = Fear of the Unknown; Consc = Fear of Conscious Death; Body = Fear for the Body after Death; Prema = Fear of Premature Death.

Other predictors significantly related to MFODS scores in the first step of the analysis were health (with those in better health reporting less Fear of Being Destroyed and less Fear for the Body after Death), age (with older participants reporting less Fear of the Dying Process and less Fear of Premature Death), and gender (with women reporting greater Fear of the Dying Process, Fear of the Dead, and Fear for Significant Others than men, but less Fear of the Unknown).

Significant predictors in Step 2 of the analysis were externality (with participants with more external locus of control beliefs reporting greater Fear of the Dying Process, Fear of the Dead, Fear of the Unknown, Fear of Conscious Death, Fear for the Body after Death, and Fear of Premature Death than those with less externality), social support (with those who had more social support reporting greater Fear for Significant Others but less Fear of the Unknown), religiosity (with those with greater religiosity reporting less Fear of the Dying Process, Fear of the Unknown, and Fear of Premature Death than those with less religiosity), and SES (with those at higher SES levels reporting less Fear of Being Destroyed and less Fear of Conscious Death than those study participants at lower SES levels).

Looking finally at the interactions between MFODS predictors which were tested in Step 3 of the analysis, the ethnicity by SES interaction was significant for 7 of the 8 MFODS subscores (excluding only Fear of the Unknown). The method outlined by Aiken and West (1991) was used to probe the meaning of significant interaction terms in regression analysis. When the simple effect of SES was tested for the White subsample, those Whites at higher SES levels had significantly less Fear of Being Destroyed, Fear of Conscious Death, and Fear for the Body after Death than Whites at lower SES levels. Tests of simple effects for the African-American subsample revealed a different trend; African Americans at higher SES levels had greater Fear of the Dying Process, Fear of the Dead, Fear of Being Destroyed, Fear of Conscious Death, and Fear of Premature Death than African Americans at lower SES levels.

The ethnicity by religiosity interaction was statistically significant only for Fear for Significant Others. When simple effects of religiosity were examined for each ethnic group, the relationship was not significant for either Whites or African Americans, but among African Americans there was a tendency for higher religiosity to be associated with less Fear for Significant Others.

In summary, 7 of the 8 MFODS subscores depended on the ethnicity of the elders participating in the study, either as a direct effect of ethnicity or as the effect of an interaction with SES. For 3 of the 4 subscores for which the direct of ethnicity was significant, Whites had greater fear of death than African Americans; for the 4th subscore, African Americans had greater fear. In the interactions, the effect of SES on fear depended on whether Whites or African Americans were involved. In general for these interactions, Whites with higher SES had less fear of death, whereas African Americans with higher SES had greater fear of death. Several possible factors may help to explain these findings. First, the White subgroup had higher SES than the African Americans; second, religiosity tended to be greater among lower SES African Americans; and third, ethnic differences in mortality rates at different portions of the life span (Markides & Black, 1996) suggest that

African Americans in old-old age may be healthier and more robust than Whites. None of these factors, however, provides a clear explanation of the observed ethnicity by SES interaction effects on MFODS subscores.

☐ Do Whites and African Americans Differ in Their Views Regarding End-of-Life Decisions?

When one approaches death, various end-of-life decisions often need to be made, for example, whether to make every attempt to extend life for as long as possible or whether to refuse heroic medical treatments in hopes of an earlier death. The individual's biological urge to survive would lead some to make decisions to extend life, but low fear of death and poor quality of life might lead others to make decisions to shorten or to end life. If ethnic differences exist in fear of death, one might also expect older African Americans to differ from Whites in the kinds of end-of-life decisions they make.

Although the fear of death literature suggests that older people have some fear of death and have an urge to survive, more and more older people today find themselves to be afflicted either with a terminal illness or a nonterminal chronic condition which is accompanied by a low quality of life lasting for an indefinite period of time before eventual death. It is difficult to define just what constitutes a low quality of life, but it includes conditions (such as physical pain, mental suffering, immobility, and extreme dependency) which some individuals consider so onerous that death is viewed as a welcome alternative (Corr, Nabe, & Corr, 1997). According to Lawton, Moss, and Glicksman (1990), the number of older people for whom quality of life is low during the last year of life is not large. Nevertheless, many older people have sought ways to avoid such suffering.

Techniques of modern medicine make it possible to keep seriously ill people alive for extended periods without any hope of cure, and medical and health professionals have argued that they have an obligation to provide treatment to cure or prolong life (i.e., to prevent death) for as long as possible for their patients (e.g., Callahan, 1992; Hendin, 1995). On the other hand, others (e.g., Humphry & Wickett, 1986; Quill, 1993) have argued that individuals should have freedom of choice in deciding whether they should prolong life or not. To promote individuals' freedom of choice in making end-of-life decisions, various forms of advance directives (e.g., living will, durable power of attorney) are now available throughout the United States. A living will is a legal document that instructs medical personnel to withdraw or withhold certain treatments that would prolong life, in advance of a time when the individual concerned might become decisionally incapacitated. Durable power attorney is a legal document that designates another person to make end-of-life decisions in an incapacitated individual's behalf. In addition, the 1991 Patient Self Determination Act (Kastenbaum, 1995) acknowledge patients' rights to withdraw or withhold treatments, at least for those with a terminal illness and a low quality of life.

The empirical literature contains a number of studies of the kinds of end-of-life decisions people would want to make should they become terminally ill with a low quality of life. Some investigators (e.g., Cassel & Zweibel, 1987; Cohen-Mansfield, Droge, & Billig, 1992; Lee & Ganzini, 1992; Zweibel & Cassel, 1989) have sought to determine whether individuals presented with various end-of-life decision scenarios would accept certain life-extending treatments (e.g., cardiopulmonary resuscitation, tube feeding, dialysis) or would refuse the treatments with the prospect of an earlier death. In effect, these studies probed the kinds of treatment preferences people would include in an advance directive document. Overall, the more aggressive or invasive the treatment, the more likely respondents were to refuse the treatment (unless it led to greater comfort). However, High (1993) found that many older people did not care to specify treatment decisions in an advance directive, but preferred to leave such decisions to someone whom they trusted, such as a family member or their physician.

Only a few studies have considered ethnicity in relation to end-of-life decisions. A recent study (Eleazer et al., 1996; Hornung et al., 1998) of frail older persons enrolled in a comprehensive managed care program found that African Americans were more likely to prefer aggressive treatments than Whites, but were less likely to use a written document to express their preferences. About one-third of African Americans had designated an alternative decision-maker compared to only about 8% of the Whites. Another study of seriously ill hospitalized adults (Mattimore et al., 1997) found that overall about 30% indicated that they would rather die than live out the remainder of their lives in a nursing home; however, African Americans were more willing than Whites to live in a nursing home.

Other end-of-life decision alternatives involve the use of more active means to bring life to an end: suicide, assisted suicide, and voluntary euthanasia. The incidence of suicide among older Americans has been increasing ("Suicide rate," 1996), although the act of suicide is frowned on by society. There is an ongoing movement to legalize assisted suicide for the terminally ill in several states, and this option has been legalized in Oregon; however, this option is strongly opposed by many groups. The remaining option, voluntary euthanasia (in which an ailing individual asks another to end his or her life), has not been seriously considered in this country and perpetrators of such "mercy killing" may receive harsh penalties. The empirical literature pertaining to these options has been concerned with respondents' views concerning the legalization of assisted suicide and voluntary euthanasia. For example, Leinbach (1993) and Ward (1980) used large-sample survey data collected by the National Opinion Research Center. Ward found that 62% of those aged 18 to 85 were in favor of ending the life of an incurably ill patient, although only 49% of those over age 70 approved. Leinbach, examining data for successive cohorts of adults, found greater approval among more recent cohorts. African Americans had less favorable views on this issue than did Whites.

Author's Study

The author's study discussed earlier (Cicirelli, 1997, 1998) had as its main focus older individuals' views on various end-of-life decision options and the factors

TABLE 4. Percentages of Whites and African American Favoring Each of Seven End-of-Life Decision Alternatives (Averaged over 17 Decision Scenarios)

End-of-Life Decision Alternative	Percent Whites	African Americans
Striving to maintain life as long as possible	44.9	65.1
Refusing or withdrawing from treatment	56.4	29.8
Letting someone close decide	35.6	35.5
Letting the doctor decide	21.0	14.8
Suicide	9.5	2.7
Assisted suicide	14.9	5.9
Voluntary euthanasia	15.5	5.9

influencing such views. Study participants were asked to respond to each of 17 decision scenarios depicting elders with a variety of terminal and nonterminal conditions involving a low quality of life (for example, a patient with terminal bone cancer where chemotherapy was unsuccessful and side effects difficult, with only partial relief of pain). For each scenario, 7 decision options were presented: (a) to strive to maintain life; (b) to refuse medical treatment or request its withdrawal; (c) to allow someone close to decide what is best in the situation; (d) to allow the physician (or someone else) to decide to terminate one's life; (e) to commit suicide; (f) to ask for assistance in committing suicide; and (g) to ask the physician (or someone else) to end one's life. A 5-point response scale was used for each option, ranging from "would do" to "would not do," although responses were collapsed to a dichotomous scale for analysis. Scores for each option were summed over the 17 scenarios.

Table 4 presents the percentages of Whites and African Americans endorsing each decision option, averaged over the 17 scenarios. It can be observed that African Americans were more likely than Whites to want to maintain life, but less likely to want to refuse or withdraw from treatment, to want to commit suicide, to want assisted suicide, or to want voluntary euthanasia. Although the two ethnic groups did not differ on wanting someone close to decide what is best, African Americans were less likely than Whites to want the physician to make a decision to end life.

☐ Relationship of Fear of Death to End-of-Life Decisions

There is little available literature relating fear of death to end-of-life decisions, although Hoelter (1979b) found that college students who expressed more fear on the MFODS subscales Fear of the Dead, Fear of Conscious Death, and Fear of Being Destroyed found suicide to be less acceptable. However, it is not known just how fear of death is related to older adult's views regarding suicide and other end of life decision options, or whether such a relationship differs for Whites and African Americans.

In an attempt to understand how fear of death, ethnicity, and other variables contribute to older adults' end-of-life decision preferences, hierarchical regression analyses were carried out. As a preliminary step based on factor analysis (see Cicirelli, 1997) the 7 end-of-life decision scores were combined to yield three factors: (a) Maintain (striving to maintain life and *not* refusing or withdrawing from treatment), (b) Endlife (suicide, assisted suicide, voluntary euthanasia), and (c) Others (wanting someone close or wanting physician to decide). These three variables were regressed on ethnicity, gender, SES, marital status, age, and health status in the first step of the hierarchical regression, with MFODS subscores, externality, self-esteem, social support, religiosity, and quality of life values (adapted from a measure devised by Cohen-Mansfield et al., 1992). The results of these analyses are summarized in Table 12.5. (Only those MFODS subscores related to end-of-life decisions in preliminary analysis were included in the regression equation. Interactions between predictor variables, including interactions of ethnicity with fear of death, were tested but were not statistically significant and are not included in Table 5.)

Ethnicity was a significant predictor of all three end-of-life decision scores, with African Americans scoring higher than Whites on Maintain, but lower than Whites on Endlife and Others. That is, when ill and with low quality of life, African Ameri-

TABLE 5. Summary of Hierarchical Regression of End-of-Life Decision Factors on MFODS Subscale Scores, Ethnicity, and Other Psychosocial and Demographic Variables

Variable	Maintain	β-Coefficients Endlife	Others
Step 1			
Ethnicity	.41*	−.16*	−.14*
Gender	−.02	−.09	−.09
Socioeconomic status	−.06	.16*	−.15
Marital status	.03	−.06	−.04
Age	−.03	−.04	.11*
Health status	.15*	−.07	−.02
R²	.44*	.28*	.26*
Step 2			
Fear of the dying process	−.16*	.02	.07
Fear of being destroyed	.11*	−.24*	.05
Fear of the unknown	.08	.14*	−.03
Externality	−.02	−.02	.13*
Self-esteem	.12*	−.05	−.10
Social support	.02	.03	−.02
Religiosity	.10	−.19*	.14*
Quality of life values	−.30*	.11*	.14*
R²	.60*	.52*	.39*

* $p < .05$

cans were more likely to want to strive to maintain life for as long as possible, but less likely to want to use active means to end life or to want others to make a decision to end their lives. Stanford (1990) observed that many older African Americans are skeptical of anyone in a "power" position, which helps to explain their reluctance to allow their physician to make end-of-life decisions for them.

Three of the 8 MFODS subscores were significant predictors of the end-of-life decisions Maintain and Endlife. Those with less Fear of the Dying Process and with greater Fear of Being Destroyed were more likely to want to strive to maintain life. Those with less Fear of Being Destroyed and greater Fear of the Unknown were more likely to want to take active means to end life. However, these relationships of fear of death to end-of-life decisions did not depend on the elders' ethnicity.

The analysis does not provide any clear explanations for the relationship of ethnicity to end-of-life decisions, although the lack of significant interactions between variables suggests that these differences are not due to differences in SES or other study variables. However, the findings add support to Ward's (1980) suggestion that the cultural history of oppression of African Americans may have resulted in a strong will to survive regardless of hardship.

Points to Remember

1. African Americans and Whites are similar in most dimensions of death fear. However, Whites have more fear of the dying process than do African Americans.

2. African Americans differ from Whites in the kinds of end-of-life decisions they prefer, with more preferring to maintain life for as long as possible or depending on others to make end-of-life decisions for them and fewer seeking active means to end life. Overall, the majority of older adults seem to prefer end-of-life decisions that maintain or extend life for as long as possible. Nevertheless, many prefer to refuse or withdraw from life-extending treatments, and others would defer any end-of-life decisions to a close family member or friend. A sizable minority of older adults would seek some active means to end life under onerous conditions involving a low quality of life.

3. Practitioners counseling older adults about end-of-life decisions should take into account the ways in which their fears of death may affect their decisions. Those elders wanting to strive to remain alive as long as possible appear to have less fear of the dying process and more fear of being destroyed, while those wanting to actively end their lives have less fear of being destroyed but more fear of the unknown.

☐ References

Aiken, L. S., & West, S. G. (1991). *Multiple regression: Testing and interpreting interactions*. Newbury Park, CA: Sage.

Antonucci, T. C., & Akiyama, H. (1987). Social networks in adult life and a preliminary examination of the convoy model. *Journal of Gerontology, 42*, 519–527.

Becker, E. (1973). *The denial of death*. New York: Free Press.

Bengtson, V. L., Cuellar, J. B., & Ragan, P. H. (1977). Stratum contrasts and similarities in attitudes toward death. *Journal of Gerontology, 32*, 76–88.

Callahan, D. (1992). When self-determination runs amok. *Hastings Center Report, 22*, 52–55.

Cassel, C., & Zweibel, N. R. (1987). Attitudes regarding life-extending medical care among the elderly and their children. *The Gerontologist, 27* (Special Issue), 229A.

Cicirelli, V. G. (1997). Relationship of psychosocial and background variables to elders' end-of-life decisions. *Psychology and Aging, 12*, 77–83.

Cicirelli, V. G. (1998). Views of elderly people concerning end-of-life decisions. *Journal of Applied Gerontology, 17*, 187–204.

Cohen-Mansfield, J., Droge, J. A., & Billig, N. (1992). Factors influencing hospital patients' preferences in the utilization of life-sustaining treatments. *The Gerontologist, 32*, 89–95.

Cole, M. A. (1978). Sex and marital status differences in death anxiety. *Omega, 9*, 139–147.

Corr, C. A., Nabe, C. M., & Corr, D. M. (1997). *Death and dying, life and living* (2nd ed.). Pacific Grove, CA: Brooks/Cole.

Davis, S. F., Martin, D. A., Wilee, C. T., & Voorhees, J. W. (1980). Relationship of fear of death and loss of self-esteem in college students. *Psychological Reports, 42*, 419–422.

Dodd, D. K., & Mills, L. L. (1985). FADIS: A measure of the fear of accidental death and injury. *Psychological Record, 35*, 269–275.

Eleazer, G. P, Hornung, C. A., Egbert, C. B., Egbert, J. R., Eng, C., Hedgepeth, J. R., McCann, R., Strothers, H., III, Sapir, M., Wei, M., & Wilson, M. (1996). The relationship between ethnicity and advance directives in a frail older population. *Journal of the American Geriatrics Society, 44*, 938–943.

Florian, V., & Snowden, L. R. (1989). Fear of personal death and positive life regard. *Journal of Cross-Cultural Psychology, 20*, 64–79.

Gesser, G., Wong, P. T. F., & Reker, G. T. (1987–1988). Death attitudes across the life-span: The development and validation of the Death Attitude Profile (DAP). *Omega, 18*, 109–124.

Hatchett, S. J., & Jackson, J. S. (1993). African American extended kin systems: An assessment. In H. P. McAdoo (Ed.), *Family ethnicity: Strength in diversity* (pp. 90–108). Newbury Park, CA: Sage.

Hendin, H. (1995). *Suicide in America*. New York: W. W. Norton.

High, D. M. (1993). Why are elderly people not using advanced directives? *Journal of Aging and Health, 5*, 497–515.

Hoelter, J. W. (1979a). Multidimensional treatment of fear of death. *Journal of Consulting and Clinical Psychology, 47*, 996–999.

Hoelter, J. W. (1979b). Religiosity, fear of death, and suicide acceptability. *Suicide and Life-Threatening Behavior, 9*, 163–172.

Hollingshead, A. B. (1957). *Two-factor index of social position*. New Haven, CT: Author.

Hornung, C. A., Eleazer, G. P., Strothers, H., III, Wieland, G. D., Eng, C., McCann, R., & Sapir, M. (1998). Ethnicity and decision-makers in a group of frail older people. *Journal of the American Geriatrics Society, 46*, 280–286.

Humphry, D., & Wickett, A. (1986). *The right to die*. Eugene, OR: The Hemlock Society.

Jackson, J. S., Chatters, L. M., & Taylor, R. J. (1993). Status and functions of future cohorts of African-American elderly: Conclusions and speculations. In J. S. Jackson, L. M. Chatters, & R. J. Taylor (Eds.), *Aging in black America* (pp. 301–318). Newbury Park, CA: Sage.

Johnson, C. L., & Barer, B. M. (1997). *Life beyond 85 years: The aura of survivorship*. New York: Springer.

Johnson, H. J., Gibson, R. C., & Luckey, I. (1990). Health and social characteristics: Implications for services. In Z. Harel, E. A. McKinney, & M. Williams (Eds.), *Black aged: Understanding diversity and service needs* (pp. 69–81). Newbury Park, CA: Sage.

Kain, E. L. (1993). Race, mortality, and families. In H. P. McAdoo (Ed.), *Family ethnicity: Strength in diversity* (pp. 60–78). Newbury Park, CA: Sage.

Kastenbaum, R. J. (1992). *The psychology of death* (2nd ed.). New York: Springer.

Kastenbaum, R. J. (1995). *Death, society, and human experience* (5th ed.). Boston: Allyn and Bacon.

Krause, N. (1993). Measuring religiosity in later life. *Research on Aging, 2*, 170–197.

Kureshi, A., & Husain, A. (1981). Death anxiety and intropunitiveness among smokers and nonsmokers: A comprehensive study. *Journal of Psychological Research, 25*, 42–45.

Lawton, M. P., Moss, M., & Glicksman, A. (1990). The quality of the last year of life for older people. *Milbank Quarterly, 68*, 1–28.

Lee, M. A., & Ganzini, L. (1992). Depression in the elderly: Effect on patient attitudes toward life-sustaining therapy. *Journal of the American Geriatrics Society, 40*, 983–988.

Leinbach, R. M. (1993). Euthanasia attitudes of older persons: A cohort analysis. *Research on Aging, 15*, 433–448.

Leming, M. R., & Dickenson, G. F. (1985). *Understanding death, dying, and bereavement*. New York: Holt, Rinehart, & Winston.

Lester, D. (1994). The Collett-Lester Fear of Death Scale. In R. A. Neimeyer (Ed.), *Death anxiety handbook: Research, instrumentation, and application* (pp. 45–60). Washington, DC: Taylor & Francis.

Levenson, H. (1981). Differentiating among internality, powerful others, and change. In H. M. Lefcourt (Ed.), *Research with the locus of control construct* (Vol. 1, pp. 15–63). New York: Academic Press.

Lonetto, R., & Templer, D. I. (1986). *Death anxiety*. Washington, DC: Hemisphere.

Markides, K. S. (1983). Aging, religiosity, and adjustment: A longitudinal analysis. *Journal of Gerontology, 38*, 621–625.

Markides, K. S., & Black, S. A. (1996). Race, ethnicity, and aging: The impact of inequality. In R. H. Binstock & L. K. George (Eds.), *Handbook of aging and the social sciences* (4th ed., pp. 153–170). San Diego: Academic Press.

Mattimore, T. J., Wenger, N. S., Desbiens, N. A., Teno, J. M., Hamel, M. B., Liu, H., Califf, R., Connors, A. F., Lynn, J., & Oye, R. K. (1997). Surrogate and physician understanding of patients' preferences for living permanently in a nursing home. *Journal of the American Geriatrics Society, 45*, 818–824.

Mullins, L. C., & Lopez, M. A. (1982). Death anxiety among nursing home residents: A comparison of the young-old and the old-old. *Death Education, 6*, 75–86.

Neimeyer, R. A. (1988). Death anxiety. In H. Wass, F. M. Berardo, & R. A. Neimeyer (Eds.), *Dying: Facing the facts* (2nd ed) (pp. 97–136). Washington, DC: Hemisphere.

Neimeyer, R. A., & Moore, M. K. (1994). Validity and reliability of the Multidimensional Fear of Death Scale. In R. A. Neimeyer, R. A. (Ed.), *Death anxiety handbook: Research, instrumentation, and application* (pp. 103–119). Washington, DC: Taylor & Francis.

Pandy, R. E., & Templer, D. I. (1972). Use of the Death Anxiety Scale in an inter-racial setting. *Omega, 3*, 127–130.

Quill, T. E. (1993). *Death and dignity: Making choices and taking charge*. New York: Norton.

Rosenberg, M. (1965). *Society and the adolescent self-image*. Princeton, NJ: Princeton University Press.

Sanders, J. F., Poole, T. E., & Rivero, W. T. (1980). Death anxiety among the elderly. *Psychological Reports, 46*, 53–56.

Smith, R. J., & Thornton, M. C. (1993). Identity and consciousness: Group solidarity. In J. S. Jackson, L. M. Chatters, & R. J. Taylor (Eds.), *Aging in black America* (pp. 203–215). Newbury Park, CA: Sage.

Stanford, E. P. (1990). Diverse Black aged. In Z. Harel, E. A. McKinney, & M. Williams (Eds.), *Black aged: Understanding diversity and service needs* (pp. 33–49). Newbury Park, CA: Sage.

Sudarkasa, N. (1993). Female-headed African American households. In H. P. McAdoo (Ed.), *Family ethnicity: Strength in diversity* (pp. 81–89). Newbury Park, CA: Sage.

Suicide rate among elderly climbs by 9% over 12 years. (1996, January 12). *The New York Times,* p. A11.

Templer, D. I. (1970). The construction and validation of a death anxiety scale. *Journal of General Psychology, 82,* 165–177.

Thorson, J. A., & Powell, F. C. (1994). A Revised Death Anxiety Scale. In R. A. Neimeyer (Ed.), *Death anxiety handbook: Research, instrumentation, and application* (pp. 31–43). Washington, DC: Taylor & Francis.

Tobin, S. S. (1996). A non-normative old age contrast. Elderly parents caring for offspring with mental retardation. In V. L. Bengtson (Ed.), *Adulthood and aging: Research on continuities and discontinuities* (pp. 124–142). New York: Springer.

Viney, L. L. (1984). Concerns about death among severely ill people. In F. R. Epting & R. A. Neimeyer (Eds.), *Personal meanings of death* (pp 143–158). Washington, DC: Hemisphere.

Ward, R. A. (1980). Age and acceptance of euthanasia. *Journal of Gerontology, 35,* 421–435.

Wong, P. T. P., Reker, G. T., & Gesser, G. (1994). Death Attitude Profile-Revised: A multidimensional measure of attitudes toward death. In R. A. Niemeyer (Ed.), *Death anxiety handbook: Research, instrumentation, and application* (pp. 121–148). Washington, DC: Taylor & Francis.

Young, M., & Daniels, S. (1980). Born again status as a factor in death anxiety. *Psychological Reports, 47,* 367–370.

Zweibel, N. R., & Cassel, C. K. (1989). Treatment choices at the end of life: A comparison of decisions by older patients and their physician-selected proxies. *The Gerontologist, 29,* 615–621.

12
CHAPTER

Sara Carmel
Hanna Zeidenberg

Israeli Nurses' Attitudes toward End of Life of Middle Aged and Old Terminally Ill Patients

One of the basic principles in the ethical code of physicians and nurses as embedded in the Hippocratic Oath, and redefined by professional associations all over the world, is the universalistic approach towards patients. According to this principle, all patients have to be similarly treated, with no discrimination on the basis of age, sex, family status, medical condition, religion, political orientation, nationality, sexual inclination, socioeconomic status, race, or ethnic origin (Israeli Nurses Association Code of Ethics, 1994; Canadian Nurses Association Code of Ethics, 1997). This study examines the role of the patient's age in Israeli nurses' attitudes and feelings regarding treatment of terminally ill patients at the end stages of their lives.

☐ The Effect of the Patient's Age on Medical Treatment

Despite the universalistic approach expected from health care professionals in treating the ill, the professional literature indicates that health care professionals discriminate between old and young, and between terminally ill versus other patients. Differential treatment is noticed in communicating with patients, in the provision of medical treatment, and in caring practices. It is reported, for example, that physicians spend less time with their older patients than with their younger ones (Keeler, Solomon, Beck, Mendenhall, & Kane, 1982; Radecki, Kane, Solomon, Mendenhall, & Beck, 1988). Such findings of shorter physician–patient encounter time for elderly patients, in ambulatory settings and in the hospital, are startling since elderly patients suffer from multiple diseases, and use more medications than younger patients do. Elderly patients also need special attention due to sensory deficits and/or poor comprehension (Radecki et al., 1988). In contrast to physicians' behavior, there are indications in the literature that, similar to younger people, almost all elderly persons want to receive medical information (Beisecker, 1988). Furthermore, a significant majority of elderly persons prefer to be involved in medical decisions, including decisions regarding life-sustaining treatment at the end of life (Carmel & Lazar, 1997; Kelner, 1995). One of the explanations for this phenomenon is that physicians believe that elderly people prefer to be passive in regard to medical treatment and delegate medical decision-making authority to their doctors (Beisecker, Helmig, Graham, & Moore, 1994). This perception probably derives from the general negative stereotypes of elderly persons held by the public and medical personnel, which are difficult to change (Carmel, Cwikel, & Galinsky, 1992; Carmel, Galinsky, & Cwikel, 1992; Hazan, 1994). Elderly persons are perceived as lacking mental and physical resources, and therefore, powerless, passive, and dependent. Gaps in age, and in social and cultural backgrounds between health care providers and elderly patients are additional factors that negatively influence communication with elderly patients (Haug, 1996).

With regard to medical treatment, some studies report that physicians tend to give less intensive medical treatment to older patients in comparison to younger patients in similar health conditions. According to data from the New Mexico tumor registry, the proportion of patients diagnosed with cancer, at either local or regional stage, who received potentially curative therapy declined with age (Samet, Hunt, Kay, Humble, & Goodwin, 1986). For example, breast cancer patients receiving definitive treatment for regional stage cancer declined from 95% for those under age 55 to 81% for those over age 85. A similar trend was also found for treatment of local-stage breast cancer. In comparison to 99% of breast cancer patients under the age of 55 who were treated, 88% of those 85 or older were treated. These findings are disturbing considering reports which indicate that elderly patients are able to tolerate surgery and chemoteraphy with acceptable levels of mortality, morbidity, and toxicity (Begg, Cohen, & Ellerton, 1980). Furthermore, although studies have shown that elderly women can tolerate even radical mastectomy, Greenfield and his colleagues (Greenfield, Blanco, Elashoff, & Ganz, 1987) found that only 83% of breast cancer patients in the age range of 70 and older received appropriate surgery, in comparison to 96% of the patients aged 50–69, after controlling for tumor stage, functional status, comorbidity, and type of hospital. While only 6% of the younger patients with stage I or II breast cancer had no examination of lymph nodes, 22% of the older patients were not examined. They concluded that comorbidity status and age appear to affect treatment decisions independently. It is not clear, however, whether these results express the physicians' choice or the elderly patients' choice or both. It might be that elderly patients, after receiving all the information about possible treatments, are more likely to reject the suggested treatments than younger patients (Beisecker et al., 1994).

Findings indicating that elderly persons are less treated than younger persons are also reported with regard to other diseases. For example, Kjellstrand and Logan (1987), after analyzing data from a number of Western countries regarding treatment for renal failure, concluded that physicians connect elderly patients to dialysis less often than younger patients although renal failure is more prevalent among elderly persons. Other researchers from the U.S. and Germany report that even when there is no medical justification, older persons have significantly fewer chances to receive a kidney transplant (Kutner & Brogan, 1990; Schmidt, 1998). In the U.S., for example, elderly persons, women, and blacks are less likely to receive a kidney transplant than are younger persons, men, and whites (Kasiske et al., 1998).

The discrimination of different groups in medical treatment is more obvious when treatment is expensive and depends on scarce resources. In such cases selection criteria more clearly emerge, and findings indicate that value judgments, idiosyncratic considerations, and not just medical knowledge play a major role in determining provision of medical treatment to different patients. Furthermore, Bernnan and his colleagues (Bernnan et al., 1991), who investigated incidence of negligence in hospitalized patients in New York State, found a substantial amount of injury to patients from medical management, many of them resulting from substandard care. The percentage of adverse events due to negligence was markedly higher among elderly persons in comparison to others. In regard to nurses, Shelley, Zahorchack, and Gambrill (1987) found that nurses' attitudes toward care were less aggressive for the older patient, and also for the patient with Do-Not-Resuscitate orders than for others. Davis and Slater (1989) also reported that American nurses are more likely to justify providing resources to young than to elderly patients at the end stages of life. Such findings indicate that nurses have similar attitudes to those of the physicians.

☐ Emotional Distress in Caring for Dying Patients

Treating dying patients is especially difficult and demanding for health care providers because it confronts them with what is often perceived as a medical failure to sustain life. It is also difficult because it faces them with their own death and raises their death anxiety. Such associations, as well as the emotional distress that follows, cause medical personnel to avoid treating the dying, or to treat them in a detached way (Hazan, 1994; Hochschild, 1983; Mills, 1990). The discrimination in treatment and attention that health care personnel provide to dying patients probably is the reason that The Israeli Medical Association included a note in its position statement emphasizing that dying patients deserve the same medical help and attention as any other patient (Israeli Medical Association, 1997).

In this context, Garfinkle and Block (1996) report empirical findings about a strong relationship between the level of death anxiety and the experienced discomfort with treating the dying. Neimeyer and Van Brunt (1995), in two studies of nursing homes, report that nursing staff with high levels of death anxiety had significantly more negative attitudes toward the elderly than nursing staff with low levels of death anxiety. Considering the above findings, and the fact that old age itself is associated with death, the combination of old and dying patients probably affects most negatively the quality of care provided to such patients by health care providers. It is somewhat ironic that elderly persons, who are perceived as fragile and powerless, present a threat to younger persons' own existence (Hazan, 1994). Keeping distance and minimizing contact with dying and elderly patients, and treating them more as objects than as human beings, are some of the disturbing outcomes of the emotional burden that medical personnel find themselves experiencing when treating the dying. These emotional difficulties and patterns of behavior have been recognized by a number of researchers who interpreted the medical personnel's distant behavior in treating the dying as self-protective coping mechanisms (Gow & Williams, 1977; Kübler-Ross, 1969; Quint, 1967; Whitfield, 1998). The outcome of this situation is that nurses feel badly about avoiding their dying patients, and dying patients feel more abandoned than ever in the last stages of their lives.

Although nurses have little authority in medical treatment decisions (Hunt, 1987), they play a central role in treating dying patients. Nurses spend more time at the patient's bedside than physicians. They perceive themselves as advocates for patients and are determined in their efforts to recognize and uphold patients' rights to be involved in treatment decisions (Curtis & Flaherty, 1982). In caring for their patients they manage and provide the supportive care, follow the changes in the patient's medical condition and in the patient's specific needs, and try to help in controlling pain and suffering. As a result, they usually have also more contact with the patient and the family. The closeness between the nurse and the patient is thus of special importance to the patient, the family, and the medical service. Studies show that nurses can help dying patients to accept dying in a peaceful and dignified way by facilitating appropriate communication between the dying patient, his or her family and the health care providers (Samarel, 1995).

Awareness of the problems of health care providers in treating dying patients, and of the negative outcomes to the patients, brought about the development of special training interventions for nurses, mainly in hospice programs. Samarel (1991), for example, reports about an intervention for nurses focused on education for terminal care, development of a personal philosophy of living and dying, and mutual support. The intervention resulted in more effective and supportive treatment of dying patients, and in higher levels of work satisfaction, and lower turnover rates among hospice nurses. Rarely do general-duty nurses benefit from such programs. There are reports of programs which are successful in reducing nursing students' death anxiety (Lockard, 1989), and there is a dramatic increase in emphasis in nursing schools on death education and on preparation of nurses to effectively deliver quality care to dying patients (Dickinson, Cummer, & Durand, 1987). Still, however, most nurses are ill equipped to handle the human experience of death (Boyle & Carter, 1998). One of the purposes of this study was to learn about nurses emotional reactions—a neglected area in empirical studies (Boyle & Carter, 1998)—by assessing the intensity of different feelings experienced by nurses following the death of terminally ill old and young patients.

One of the most prominent and disturbing contemporary ethical and medical questions is whether patients have the right to control their own death, and to what extent health professionals ought to assist them in hastening death. The public debate regarding these morally problematic issues has become daily reality for medical personnel. Active euthanasia—doing something to hasten the patient's death—and physician-assisted suicide, are the extreme means of intervention, and are rarely used. However, health care providers are often confronted with decisions and actions regarding passive euthanasia—the withholding or withdrawing of medical treatment from patients at the end of life. Although physicians make such decisions, nurses often also play an important role in making the decisions and in the needed actions (Wilson, 1992). Since nurses are often closer to the patient and the family, they know more about their treatment preferences, and therefore, are either consulted by physicians or try to influence physicians' decisions in these issues by their own initiative. A number of studies show that nurses not only cooperate with physicians in committing active voluntary euthanasia and assisted suicide, but also perform it themselves without receiving permission from physicians or patients and families. These studies were conducted in the U.S., Australia, and the Netherlands, where the local Nurses' Associations clearly declared that nurses should not be involved in committing active voluntary euthanasia and assisted suicide (Asch, 1996; Kuhse, Singer, & Phil, 1993; Van der Arend, 1998). In some settings, such as long-term care hospitals, nurses make the decisions and carry them out without consulting physicians (Wurzbach, 1996). Studies of nurses and physicians employed in the same institutions also show significant differences between them in attitudes toward cancer treatment. Nurses are less likely to approve of aggressive treatment and more favorable of considering patient–family attitudes than physicians (Damrosch et al., 1993). It is thus clear that nurses, while not having the authority to make treatment decisions, are on the front line of caring for patients in severe medical conditions, and experience intrapersonal ethical dilemmas and interpersonal conflicts with physicians. It appears that, in such difficult situations, personal characteristics, such as age and religiosity, affect nurses' attitudes and decisions. In this regard, studies repeatedly indicate that the younger and more religious nurses have more negative attitudes toward hastening the death of terminally ill patients (Gow & Williams, 1977; Kitchener, 1998).

☐ Nurses' Dilemmas in Restricting Nourishment to Dying Patients

Among the most difficult decisions regarding withholding or withdrawing life-sustaining treatments is the decision to prevent fluids and feeding from being given to a dying patient. In spite of their accumulated medical experience which indicates that providing fluids and food artificially at the end stages of life often increases the patient's suffering (Wanzer et al., 1989), it seems that physicians and nurses find it difficult to be responsible for depriving a patient of these basic needs, and for letting him or her die from starvation (Carmel, 1996; 1999; Wurzbach, 1996). Only nurses who have much experience with the suffering and dehumanization that such interventions cause dying patients become morally convinced of the benefits of withholding or withdrawing such treatments. Once this happens, nurses are ready to withhold or withdraw feeding and fluids from dying elderly persons, and to convince the patients' families that it is the best course of action in order to prevent suffering for their loved ones and help them die peacefully (Wurzbach, 1996).

It has been suggested that, although moral certainty (conviction based on an absolute belief in the "rightness" of a course of action) causes no psychological conflict for the person taking the action, moral uncertainty causes negative feelings, such as loss of control, frustration, anger, depression, stress, and anxiety (Crisham, 1980; Quinn & Smith, 1987; Wurzbach, 1996). However, in our view, since nurses do not have direct responsibility for making decisions about withholding and withdrawing medical treatment from patients, they may experience such negative feelings both when they have moral certainty and when they are morally uncertain. Not only is it frustrating for nurses in those situations where they are asked to stop treatment and they are uncertain about this decision; it is also frustrating to see a dying patient who suffers from overtreatment, which the nurse cannot stop, in spite of being morally certain that it is the wrong decision. Lacking the authority to act according to their own ethical beliefs increases nurses' stress in treating patients at the end stages of their lives. Such dilemmas which are faced daily by nurses in Western countries, and affect work outcomes, such as satisfaction with work and burnout (Davis, 1986), are not sufficiently acknowledged by the medical institutions, physicians, and many of the nursing schools.

☐ The Israeli Medical System and the Nurse's Role

Justice and equity in the provision of health services are basic principles of the Israeli health care law, which was implemented in January 1995. According to this law, all Israeli citizens have the right to a basic health benefits package, including hospitalization. In general, patients are assigned to the different hospitals and the wards within them, according to the geographic regions in which they live. Patients who come to the emergency ward for the second or third time are directed to the same general medicine or oncology ward in which they were previously hospitalized. It is believed that under this system, patients with chronic diseases and repeated hospitalizations receive more efficient and effective medical treatment, in a familiar and supportive environment. Patients have, however, the right to choose services of other hospitals or wards. In the Israeli system primary care physicians who treat the patients in the community clinics do not work in the hospitals.

In regard to the cost of medical services, only during the last few years have physicians in Israel started to be aware of some restrictions in treatments due to cost considerations. Most of them still perceive financial considerations as contradicting the physician's role as exclusive guardian of the patient's health. The Israeli Medical Association recently declared that it opposes the financial pressure exerted by the sick funds and the Israeli government on physicians' practice, and will fight against cost-oriented considerations in regulating patients' treatment

(Belashar, 1998). In general, neither the patient nor the physician sees medical bills, or is aware of the costs of medical treatments. Economic concerns are, therefore, usually not a factor in the decision process regarding medical treatment.

The role of the nurse in Israel is significantly limited in spite of the last decade's developments in nursing education. In order to receive the degree of a registered nurse, students have to complete 4 years of post high school studies and a full baccalaureate. Today, most of the nursing schools are academic and nurses graduate with a B.N. degree. At work, however, not much has changed during the last decades. Nurses have little autonomy in medical settings, such as general hospitals, where physicians' supervision is close and permanent. Although new hospital roles, such as case managers and nursing clinical specialists, have been developed, nurses still function under two strictly hierarchic ladders. They are responsible for carrying out doctors' orders for treatment and medical examinations and orders of nurses in higher positions regarding managing and providing care and comfort services (Carmel, Shoham-Yakubovich, Azanger, & Zalteman, 1988; Shoham-Yakubovich, Carmel, Zwanger, & Zalteman, 1989). In regard to treating terminally-ill patients, some courses about death and dying and palliative care have been introduced to the curriculum of some of the nursing schools in Israel. Hospice nurses receive special training. These training programs for nurses are, however, rare in Israel. Most of the nurses who work in general hospitals, especially the senior nurses, have never received any training in treating the dying.

As in other countries, Israeli nurses spend more time than physicians at the patient's bedside, and often develop closer relations with the patients and their families, especially in long term hospitalizations, or repeated hospitalizations that are quite common among terminally-ill patients. The development and implementation of palliative care will increase nurses' responsibility and involvement in caring for people at the end stage of their lives. Learning about nurses' beliefs, attitudes, and feelings regarding these issues is, therefore, important for defining their role in treating such patients, for planning supportive interventions for nurses at the workplace, and for nursing education.

The purpose of our study was twofold: (a) To investigate attitudes of Israeli nurses toward the prolongation of life of middle-aged and old patients by the use of different life sustaining treatments, and (b) to examine nurses feelings in reaction to the death of terminally-ill middle-aged and old patients.

☐ Methods

Data for this study were collected from registered nurses that work in three general hospitals in Israel, in the general medicine, oncology, geriatrics, and intensive care wards. All the nurses in these hospital wards were asked to fill out anonymously a structured questionnaire that included closed-ended questions about their beliefs, attitudes, and feelings regarding treating dying patients. The questionnaire was pre-tested on 30 nurses who were not included in the study population. Three hundred and twenty questionnaires were distributed among the nurses in these wards, and 245 were completed—a response rate of 76.5%. Out of the missing 75 questionnaires, 10 were returned empty, 42 were not returned for unknown reasons, and 23 were only partly filled out, and therefore, not included. Fifty one percent of the nurses worked in the largest medical center, "Soroka" in Beer-Sheva, 22% in the "Shaare Tzedek" medical center, and 27% in the "Hadassa" medical center, the last two located in Jerusalem.

The distribution of nurses on sociodemographic characteristics is presented in Table 1. As can be seen, 91% of the respondents were women with an average age of 35.9 ($SD = 9.2$), 71% were married, and 70% had children. About half were born in Israel, 32% immigrated to Israel before 1988, and 17% immigrated to Israel since 1989, mainly from the former Soviet Union. Ninety-two percent of the nurses

TABLE 1. Socio-demographic Characteristics of the Nurses (N = 245)

	Percent	Mean	SD
Gender			
Women	91		
Age			
25 or younger	12		
26–45	71		
46 and older	17	35.9	9.2
Origin[a]			
Israel	52		
Former U.S.S.R.	22		
Asia-Africa	12		
Other countries	14		
Immigration status			
Born in Israel	51		
Immigrated before 1989	32		
Immigrated since 1989	17		
Religion			
Jewish	92		
Religiosity (among Jews)			
Secular	41		
Traditional	31		
Religious	28		
Marital status			
Married	71		
Number of children			
None	30		
1 to 3	57		
4 or more	13	1.9	1.5

[a]Based on the father's country of birth

TABLE 2. Professional Characteristics of the Nurses (N = 245)

	Percent	Mean	SD
Degree			
Academic degree	38		
No academic degree	62		
Nursing school attended			
Religious - in Israel	22		
Secular - in Israel	58		
Secular - out of Israel	20		
Ward			
General medicine and geriatric	42		
Intensive care	30		
Oncology	18		
Dialysis	10		
Position			
Administrative	32		
Years of professional experience			
5 or less	29		
6-10	19		
10 or more	52	13.2	10.0

were Jewish, and 8% were Moslem or Christian. Forty-one percent reported being secular, 31% traditional, and 28% religious.

The professional characteristics of the participants are described in Table 2. Thirty eight percent of the nurses had an academic degree, 42% of the nurses worked in general medicine or geriatric wards, 30% in intensive care, 18% in oncology, and 10% in dialysis. Fifty two percent of the nurses had at least 10 years work experience, the average being 13.2 (SD = 10). The majority of nurses (80%) completed their professional studies in Israeli nursing schools.

☐ Questionnaire

The data for this chapter is based on three sets of questions that referred to old versus young terminally ill patients.

A. Attitudes toward the use of life sustaining treatments (LST)

Nurses' attitudes toward the use of LST were elicited by presenting two vignettes, adopted from Carmel (1999) that differed only in the age of the patient. The vignettes read as follows:

A cancer patient of about 80 (or 40), with a severe metastatic cancer, and chances for only temporary improvement.

After each vignette the nurses were asked to respond, on a scale of 1 to 5 to the following three questions:

	Definitely yes				Definitely no
1. In your opinion, if he cannot eat, should he be connected to artificial feeding (not fluids) such as nasogastric tube or gastrostomy ?	5	4	3	2	1
2. If he cannot breath, should he be connected to a breathing machine?	5	4	3	2	1
3. If his heart stops beating, should he receive cardiopulmonary resuscitation (CPR)?	5	4	3	2	1

B. Attitudes toward the prolongation of life

The question regarding this issue was phrased as follows:

Suppose that you are a member of a committee that has to make decisions regarding terminally ill patients with a bad prognosis. You have to decide whether to prolong the life of a patient by using mechanical ventilation (MC) or not to start it and let the patient die. What will be your decision regarding:

	Definitely start MC				Definitely don't start MC
A patient of above 80 years old	5	4	3	2	1
A young patient, of about 40	5	4	3	2	1

C. Feelings regarding death of terminally-ill patients

Questions regarding this issue were presented as follows:

Following are a number of different feelings. To what extent do you feel them when a terminal patient, of *your age*, dies during your shift.

The same question was presented a second time, but instead of a women of the nurse's age, the question referred to a women of about 80 years of age.

Both questions were followed by a list of 7 different feelings in the following way:

	Strongly				Not at all
Relief	5	4	3	2	1
Failure and frustration	5	4	3	2	1

Pain	5	4	3	2	1
Anxiety	5	4	3	2	1
Anger	5	4	3	2	1
Withdrawal	5	4	3	2	1
Self-blame	5	4	3	2	1

The questionnaire also included questions about socio-demographic and professional characteristics, as specified in the first two tables. Included as well were the following questions about the nurses' education regarding treatment of terminally ill patients, and their need for such education in continuous education and supportive interventions:

• In your nursing studies did you learn how to deal with your feelings when treating terminally-ill patients?
• Are discussions intended to help personnel to cope emotionally with treating terminally ill patients held in your ward?
• In your opinion, is there a need to have team discussions and support groups to help nurses deal with caring for dying patients?

Responses to the three questions were provided on a five-point scale, from 5 = to a great extent to 1 = not at all.

Results

The results regarding attitudes toward the use of life-sustaining treatments (LST) are presented in Table 3. All the differences between the mean scores of the responses to each of the three questions regarding the use of a specific life-sustaining treatment for a young and an old person were found to be statistically significant. These findings clearly indicate that, in the same medical condition, no matter which life-sustaining treatment is used, nurses are more likely to believe that it should be used more for the young than for the old.

The results regarding these items also show that nurses differentiate between the different LST. High percentages among them (82% for the young patient and 72.6% for the old) think that artificial feeding should be provided to terminally ill cancer patients. A significantly lower percent believe that mechanical ventilation (45.2% and 27.3%, respectively) or cardiopulmonary resuscitation (33.1% and 11.8%, respectively) should be provided to such patients.

In order to evaluate the relationships between the demographic and professional characteristics of the nurses and their attitudes toward the use of LST in treating old versus young terminally ill patients, nurses were divided into subgroups according to background variables. The attitudes of each subgroup were separately examined. Table 4 indicates that the differences by age found in the general sample also hold in each of the subgroups. Religion, immigration status, years of work, and position at work have no significant effect on the attitudes of

TABLE 3. Nurses' Attitudes Regarding the Use of Life-sustaining Treatments for a Young and an Old Terminally-ill Cancer Patient[a]

| | Young Patient | | Old Patient | | |
	Mean	SD	Mean	SD	t
Should be fed through nasogastric tube or gastrostomy	4.3	1.0	4.0	1.2	−5.69*
Should be connected to mechanical ventilation	3.2	1.5	2.5	1.4	−9.51*
Should receive CPR	2.7	1.6	1.7	1.2	−10.70*

*$p<0.01$
[a]Responses were given on a five point scale, the higher the score, the stronger the attitude that treatment should be given.

the nurses about prolonging the life of young versus old terminally ill patients by the use of LST.

The responses to the questions regarding decisions, when functioning as a member of a medical committee, whether or not to prolong the life of a 80 or a 40 years old patient by the use of mechanical ventilation, showed similar results to those

TABLE 4. Socio-demographic and Professional Characteristics and Attitudes Regarding the Use of Mechanical Ventilation at the End of Life of Young and Old Patients

| | Young Cancer Patient | | Old Cancer Patient | | |
	Mean	SD	Mean	SD	t
Age					
35 or younger	3.24	1.46	2.70	1.49	−6.67*
36 or older	3.20	1.60	2.43	1.45	−6.90*
Religiosity					
Secular	3.20	1.49	2.50	1.41	−5.73*
Religious	3.17	1.56	2.56	1.52	−7.00*
Immigration status					
Veterans	3.04	1.54	2.47	1.49	−7.87*
New Immigrants (since 1989)	4.02	1.20	3.05	1.36	−5.91*
Years of work					
5 or less	3.01	1.52	2.60	1.50	−3.77*
6 or more	3.21	1.58	2.44	1.50	−4.40*
Position					
Non managerial	3.18	1.52	2.56	1.47	−8.03*
Managerial	3.21	1.58	2.44	1.50	−4.40*

*$p<0.01$

given in the previous set of questions. The average score for an old person was significantly lower than for a young person (Mean = 2.2, *SD* = 1.2 versus Mean = 3.3, *SD* = 1.37, *t* = 11.6, *p* = 0.01), which indicates that the data are reliable and consistent.

The nurses' reports regarding their feelings following a death of an old versus a middle-aged terminally ill woman are presented in Table 5. It is clear that nurses have significantly stronger negative feelings such as failure, pain, anxiety, anger, withdrawal, and guilt, in a reaction to the death of a woman their age, in comparison to the death of an old woman. The strongest feelings are pain, failure and frustration, and anxiety. Nurses also report feeling a relatively low level of relief, which is, however, significantly stronger following the death of an old terminally ill patient than the death of a younger patient.

To the question of whether they had received any education or training in treating dying patients in nursing schools, only 29% responded positively (4 or 5 on a 5-point scale) (Mean = 2.73, *SD* = 0.99). Only 21.5% responded positively to the question of whether discussions intended to help personnel to cope with treating terminally ill patients are held on the ward level (Mean = 2.30, *SD* = 1.27). A large majority of nurses (81.5%) expressed a strong need (Mean = 4.29, *SD* = 0.99) for team discussions and support groups in order to help them to deal with treating dying patients. Comparisons on these variables between older (over 35) versus younger nurses, and more experienced (6 and more years of work) versus less experienced nurses revealed no significant differences.

☐ Discussion

The findings of this study indicate that, in the same medical condition, nurses believe that more life support treatments should be provided to middle-aged com-

TABLE 5. A Comparison of Nurses Feelings Following the Death of a Terminally-ill Woman their Age versus and Old Woman[a]

| | Young Women | | Old Women | | |
	Mean	SD	Mean	SD	t
Pain	4.5	0.9	3.3	1.2	14.61*
Failure/frustration	3.3	1.4	2.1	1.1	13.07*
Anxiety	3.0	1.4	1.6	0.9	14.12*
Anger	2.8	1.4	1.7	1.0	11.96*
Withdrawal	1.7	1.1	1.5	0.9	4.64*
Self-blame	1.8	1.2	1.4	0.8	5.24*
Relief	2.5	1.4	3.6	1.3	−12.08*

*p<0.01
[a]Responses were given on a five point scale, so that the higher the score the stronger the feeling.

pared with old terminally ill patients. The same results were obtained in response to questions regarding attitudes about the use of different LST in a terminal cancer condition, and in a hypothetical situation in which the nurse is a member of a committee to decide about withholding mechanical ventilation from terminally ill patients. Our findings also indicate that nurses' age, religiosity, immigration status, work experience, and position at the hospital have no effect on this general strong distinction that nurses make between treating elderly versus younger terminally ill patients. Since these Israeli findings are in accordance with previous reports from Western countries (Shelley et al., 1987; Davis & Slater, 1989), it appears that the distinction made by nurses between treating old and young patients in similar medical conditions is a cross-cultural phenomenon. It seems that age is an independent criterion in decisions to withhold treatment, so that life support treatment is given less to elderly patients than to younger patients. It also appears that physicians and nurses in Israel agree with this principle (Carmel, 1996; Ziedenberg, 1997), even though neither patients nor physicians are troubled by the cost of life-sustaining treatments. This consensus among health care providers probably reflects the emphasis Western culture places on youth, and the notion that old persons are at the end of their lives, while young people have to continue living as long as it is still possible. This attitude might also derive from medical personnel's experience with dying patients. They might have witnessed the dying process of young and old patients and learned, as Kastenbaum (1991) suggests, that elderly terminally-ill patients comprehend death and are psychologically more ready to accept it than children or young persons.

Our results regarding nurses' feelings following the death of a patient their age versus the death of an old patient also suggest that nurses feel more threatened by the death of patients their age than by the death of an old patient. They probably more easily identify with such a patient and, therefore, report experiencing more intensively negative feeling when facing their own death. Out of the 6 negative feelings presented to them, they report experiencing mostly pain, failure or frustration, and anxiety. They also report feeling a moderate level of relief after the death of an old patient but a much lower level when facing the death of a patient their age. Although nurses report that all their negative feelings are stronger when a younger patient dies, the discrepancies are the largest on anxiety and pain. The comparative results regarding anxiety, although not specified in the questionnaire as death anxiety, might indicate that the death of an old patient arouses less death anxiety among nurses than the death of a patient their age. The relatively high levels of feelings of pain, failure, and anxiety indicate that nurses experience stress and emotional damage when confronting such work situations. Burnout is one of the negative outcomes of such accumulated stressful experiences. The present results should be considered in the light of our finding that nurses were poorly prepared in nursing school for treating dying patients, and they expressed a need for team discussions and support. Since nurses can be better prepared for treating the dying and handling negative feelings (Degner & Gow 1988; Lockard 1989; Samarel, 1991), we suggest that nurses, at least the nurses that are most likely to care for dying patients (e.g., in oncology, intensive care wards, etc.), should receive special training for treating terminally ill patients and continuous group support.

Our findings also indicate that nurses are more likely to want to provide artificial feeding than mechanical ventilation or CPR to their dying patients. This finding also holds for Israeli physicians, but contradicts elderly persons' preferences, who seem to perceive artificial nutrition as similar to mechanical ventilation (Carmel, 1999; Carmel & Mutran, 1997). Three possible explanations are suggested for these findings. First, such attitudes might derive from deeply rooted beliefs and associated feelings that feeding a patient is an integral part of basic caring and, therefore, should never be stopped. Second, they may also derive from nurses' lack of updated medical knowledge regarding the negative outcomes of artificially providing nutrition to dying patients, or, third, from their lack of experience with dying patients. Such experience would have allowed them to compare the dying process in patients who received artificial hydration and nutrition versus patients who did not receive them at the end of their lives. We suggest that all three explanations hold for our sample of nurses. It seems clear that, if change is desired regarding feeding the dying at the end stages of their lives, the reasons for these attitudes should be further studied. Such knowledge is necessary in order to plan and implement appropriate educational interventions to change beliefs, attitudes, and medical treatment at the end stages of patients' lives.

In summary, our findings indicate that Israeli nurses need more knowledge about treating dying patients, more open discussions on ethical issues such as treating differently aged patients with the same medical conditions, and more support in dealing with the emotional burden of caring for terminally ill patients. Such interventions are essential for the benefit of both the nurses and their patients.

Points to remember

1. Israeli nurses have different attitudes regarding life support treatments in old (80 year old) versus young (40 year old) terminally ill patients.
2. This result is not affected by controlling for various background variables such as nurses' religiosity or age.
3. Nurses tend to be more upset after the death of a younger person than after the death of an older person. In the last case they showed a moderate level of relief.
4. Consistency of these findings with other similar findings obtained in Western countries, and with results obtained from studies on physicians, makes plausible a cross cultural interpretation in terms of values prevalent in the Western society.

☐ References

Asch, D. A. (1996). The role of critical care nurses in euthanasia and assisted suicide. *The New England Journal of Medicine, 334,* 1374–1379.

Begg, C. B., Cohen, J. L., & Ellerton, J. (1980). Are the elderly predisposed to toxicity from cancer chemotherapy?: An investigation using data from the Eastern Cooperative Oncology Group. *Cancer Clinical Trials, 3,* 369-374.

Beisecker, A. E. (1988). Aging and the desire for information and input in medical decisions: Patient consumerism in medical encounters. *The Gerontologist, 28,* 330–335.

Beisecker, A. E., Helmig, L., Graham, D., & Moore, W. P. (1994). Attitudes of oncologists, oncology nurses, and patients from a women's clinic regarding medical decision making for older and younger breast cancer patients. *The Gerontologist, 34,* 505–512.

Belashar, Y. (1998). Physician autonomy. *Michtav Lehaver. Bulletin of the Israeli Medical Association, 60,* 4–6.

Bernnan, T. A., Leape, L. L., Larid, N. M., Hebert, L., Localio, A. R., Lawthers, A.G., Newhouse J. P., Weiler, P. C., & Hiatt, H. H. (1991). Incidence of adverse events and negligence in hospitalized patients. *New England Journal of Medicine, 324,* 370–376.

Boyle, M., & Carter, D. E. (1998). Death anxiety among nurses. *International Journal of Palliative Nursing, 4,* 37–43.

Canadian Nurses Association Code of Ethics—Codes and Declarations. (1998). *Nursing Ethics, 5,* 65–74.

Carmel, S. (1996). Behavior, attitudes, and expectations regarding the use of life-sustaining treatments among physicians in Israel: An exploratory study. *Social Science & Medicine, 43,* 955–965.

Carmel, S. (1999). Life-sustaining treatments: What doctors do, what they want for themselves and what elderly persons want. *Social Science & Medicine, 49,* 1401–1408.

Carmel, S., Cwikel, J., & Galinsky, D. (1992). An evaluation of changes in knowledge, attitudes and work preferences following courses in gerontology among medical, nursing, and social work students. *Educational Gerontology, 18*(4), 329–342.

Carmel, S., Galinsky, D., & Cwikel, J. (1990). Knowledge, attitudes and work preferences regarding the elderly among medical students and practicing physicians. *Behavior, Health and Aging, 1*(2), 99–104.

Carmel, S., & Lazar, A. (1997). Giving bad news: To what extent do elderly persons want to know, and to participate in the process of medical decision making? *Harefua: Journal of The Israel Medical Association* (Hebrew), *133,* 505–509.

Carmel, S., & Mutran, E. (1997). Preferences for different life-sustaining treatments among elderly persons in Israel. *Journal of Gerontology: Social Sciences, 52B,* S97–S102.

Carmel, S., Shoham-Yakubovich, I., Zwanger, L., & Zaltcman, T. (1988). Nurses' autonomy and job satisfaction. *Social Science & Medicine, 26,* 1103–1107.

Colaizzi, P. (1978). Psychological research as the phenomenologist views it. In R. Vale & M. King (Eds.), *Existential-phenomenological alternatives for psychology* (pp. 48–71). New York: Oxford University Press.

Corbin, R. M. (1980). Decisions that might not get made. In T. Wallsten (Ed.), *Cognitive processes in choice and decision behavior.* Hillsdale, NJ: Lawrence Erlbaum.

Crisham, P. (1980). Measuring moral judgment in nursing dilemmas. *Nursing Research, 30,* 104–110.

Curtis, L., & Flaherty, M. J. (1982). *Nursing ethics: Theories and pragmatics.* Bowie, MD: Prentice-Hall.

Damrosch, S., Denicoff, A. M., St. Germain, D., Welsch, C., Blash, J.L., Jackson, T., & Etzelmiller, J. (1993). Oncology nurse and physician attitudes toward aggressive cancer treatment. *Cancer Nursing, 16,* 107–112.

Davis, D. S. (1986). Nursing: An ethic of caring. *Humane Medicine, 2,* 19–25.

Davis, A. J., & Slater, P. V. (1989). U.S. and Australian nurses attitudes and beliefs about the good death. *Image–Journal of Nursing Scholarship, 21,* 34–39.

Degner, L. F., & Gow, C. M. (1988). Preparing nurses for care of the dying: A longitudinal study. *Cancer Nursing, 11,* 160–169.

Dickinson, G., Summer, E., & Durand, R. (1987). Death education in U.S. professional colleges: Medical, nursing and pharmacy. *Death Studies, 11,* 57–61.

Garfinkle, C. L., & Block, P. (1996). Physicians' interactions with families of terminally-ill patients. *Family Medicine, 28*(10), 692–693.

Gow, C. M., & Williams, J. I. (1977). Nurses' attitudes toward death and dying: A causal interpretation. *Social Science & Medicine, 11,* 191–198.

Greenfield, S., Blanco, D. M., Elashoff, R. M., & Ganz, P. A. (1987). Patterns of care related to age of breast cancer patients. *Journal of the American Medical Association, 247,* 2766–2770.

Haug, M. R. (1996). Elements in physician–patient interactions in late life. *Research On Aging, 18*(1), 32–51.

Hazan, H. (1994). *Old age: Constructions and deconstructions.* Cambridge, UK: Cambridge University Press.

Hochschild, A. R. (1983). *The managed heart.* Berkeley and Los Angeles: University of California Press.

Hunt, M. (1987). The process of translating research findings into nursing practice. *Journal of Advanced Nursing, 12,* 101–110.

Israeli Nurses Association Code of Ethics (1994). Tel-Aviv: Israel Nurses Association.

Israeli Medical Association. (1997, December). *The Dying Patient. Position statements.*

Kasiske, B. L., London, W., & Ellison, M. D. (1998). Race and sociodemographic factors in influencing early placement on the kidney transplant waiting list. *Journal of the American Society of Nephrology, 9,* 2142–2147.

Kastenbaum, R. (1991). *Death, society and human experience* (4th ed.). New York: Macmillan.

Keeler, E. B., Solomon, D. H., Beck, J. C., Mendehall, R. C., & Kane, R. L. (1982). Effect of patient age on duration of medical encounters with physicians. *Medical Care, 20,* 1101–1108.

Kelner, M. (1995). Activists and delegators: Elderly patients' preferences about control at the end of life. *Social Science & Medicine, 41,* 537–545.

Kitchener, B. A. (1998). Nurses characteristics and attitudes to active voluntary euthanasia: A survey in the Australian capital Territory. *Journal of advanced Nursing, 28,* 70-76.

Kjellstrand, C. M., & Logan, G. M. (1987). Racial, sexual and age inequalities in chronic dialysis. *Nephron, 45,* 257–263.

Kubler-Ross, E. (1969). *On death and dying.* New York: MacMillan.

Kuhse, H., Singer, P., & Phil, B. (1993). Voluntary euthanasia and the nurse: An Australian survey. *International Journal of Nursing Studies, 30,* 311–322.

Kutner, N.G., & Brogan, D. (1990). Sex stereotypes and health care: The case of treatment for kidney failure. *Sex Roles, 24,* 279–290.

Lockard, B. E. (1989). Immediate, residual, and long-term effects of death education instructional unit on the death anxiety level of nursing students. *Death studies, 13,* 137–159.

Mills, J. (1990). A study of the relationships between hospice nurses and college students in the area of death anxiety. University Microfilms International USA.

Neimeyer, R. A., & Van Brunt, D. (1995). In H. Wass & R. A. Neimeyer (Eds.), *Dying: Facing the facts* (3rd ed.) (pp. 49-88). Washington, DC: Taylor & Francis.

Quinn, C. A., & Smith, M. D. (1987). *The professional commitment: Issues and ethics in nursing.* Philadelphia: W. B. Saunders.

Quint, J. C. (1967). When patients die: Some nursing problems. *Canadian Nurse, 63*(12), 33–36.

Radecki, S. E., Kane, R. L., Solomon, D. H., Mendenhall, R. C., & Beck, J. C. (1988). Do physicians spend less time with older patients? *American Geriatrics Society, 36,* 713–718.

Samarel, N. (1991). *Caring for life and death.* Washington, DC: Hemisphere.

Samarel, N. (1995). The dying process. In H. Wass & R. A. Neimeyer (Eds.), *Dying: Facing the facts* (3rd ed.) (pp. 89-116). Washington, DC: Taylor & Francis.

Samet, J., Hunt, W. C., Kay, C., Humble, C. G., & Goodwin, J. S. (1986). Choice of cancer therapy varies with age of patient. *Journal of the American Medical association, 255,* 3385–3390.

Schmidt, V. H. (1998). Selection of recipients for donor organs in transplant medicine. *Journal of Medicine and Philosophy, 23,* 50–74.

Shelley, S. I., Zahorchak, R. M., & Gambrill, C. D. S. (1987). Aggressiveness of nursing care for older patients and those with Do-Not-Resuscitate orders. *Nursing Research, 36,* 157–162.

Shoham-Yakubovich, I., Carmel, S., Zwanger, L., & Zaltcman, T. (1989). Autonomy, job satisfaction and professional self-image among nurses in the context of a physicians' strike. *Social Science & Medicine, 28,* 1315–1320.

Taylor, S. E. (1995). *Health psychology* (3rd ed.) (p. 474). San Francisco: McGraw-Hill.

Van der Arend, A. J. G. (1998). An ethical perspective on euthanasia and assisted suicide in the Netherlands from a nursing point of view. *Nursing Ethics, 5,* 307–318.

Wanzer, S. H., Federman, D. D., Adelstein, S. J., Cassel, C. K., Cassem, E. H., Cranford, R. E., Hook, E. W., Lo, B., Moertel, C.G., & Safar, P. (1989). The physicians responsibility toward hopelessly ill patients: A second look. *New England Journal of Medicine, 320,* 844–849.

Whitfield, B. II. (1998). *Final passage: Sharing the journey as this life ends.* Deerfield Beach, FL: Health Communication Inc.

Wilson, D. M. (1992). Ethical concerns in a long-term tube feeding study. *Image–Journal of Nursing Scholarship, 24,* 195–199.

Wurzbach, M. E. (1996). Long-term care nurses' ethical convictions about tube feeding. *Western Journal of Nursing Research, 18,* 63–76.

Ziedenberg, H. (1997). *Nurses' attitudes regarding the prolongation of life for terminal patients.* Unpublished M. Med. Sc. dissertation, Ben-Gurion University of the Negev, Faculty of Health Sciences, Beer-Sheva, Israel.

Stephen J. DePaola
Mike Prewett
Rachel L. Hawkins

Death Anxiety in Nursing Home Personnel as a Function of Race

As the population of older people increases in the United States, many gerontologists have increased their interest in the impact of professional caregivers' age-related attitudes toward older patients (Bachelder, 1989; Gardner & Perritt, 1983; Houlihan, 1985). In fact, the National Institute on Aging (1987) anticipated that students in health care professions will be dedicating a major portion of their future efforts to the care of older persons. Roscow (1962) noted this phenomenon early on: "by now it should be clear that the crucial people in the aging problems are not the old, but the younger age groups who determine the status and the position of the older persons in the social order."

As the population of older people increases, concerns of giving and receiving quality care grow. Therefore, research of caregivers' attitudes toward older persons is of importance. For this reason, the central purpose of this investigation is to assess the relationship between death anxiety and attitudes toward older people held by nursing personnel in geriatric facilities. Unlike most past research, the present project will compare African-American and Caucasian nursing home personnel.

☐ Caregivers' Attitudes Toward Older Persons

Nurses' negative attitudes toward the aged often mar the care given to older persons (Martin & Buckwalter, 1984). The scarcity of geriatric curricula in nursing education and the fact that most nurses choose to work with patients of younger age groups is a reflection of these negative attitudes (Burnside, 1981). As a result, there is a need to explore the underlying influences on nursing staff's attitudes in order to improve the health care of older patients. In regard to negative attitudes, Eakes (1985) and Lester, Getty, and Kneisel (1974) have pointed out that negative attitudes toward older persons may be mediated by nurses' death anxiety. Consequently, the quality of nursing care provided by personnel who hold either positive or negative attitudes toward death and the aged are of interest for researchers.

☐ Professional Status of Nursing Home Personnel

Several researchers (e.g., Chandler, Rachal, & Kazelskis, 1986; Smith, Jepson, & Perloff, 1982; Taylor & Harned, 1978; Williams, 1982) have examined the attitudes held by different levels of nursing home personnel—registered nurses (RNs), licensed practical nurses (LPNs), and nurse aides (NAs)—toward older persons. However, the studies that have been conducted show mixed results. Williams (1982), in a survey of over 100 nurses who supplied different levels of care to older persons, found that 75% of nurses at all levels demonstrated negative attitudes toward older patients as measured by a test developed by Palmore (1977) called the Facts on Aging Quiz #1 (FAQ #1). Smith et al. (1982) took into account in their study the levels of nursing care (skilled, intermediate, or discharged) needed by older patients. Their results indicated that RNs exhibited more positive attitudes toward older patients than LPNs or nurse's aides. Equally important, Smith et al. found that all levels of nursing personnel exhibited more positive attitudes toward patients that were being discharged. Such attitudes may result from personal exposure to the demands of the nursing home environment or from a stereotype of old age (Almquist, Stein, Weiner, & Linn, 1981).

☐ Death Anxiety in Nursing Home Personnel

Several studies have found that nursing home personnel with high levels of death anxiety have significantly more negative attitudes toward the elderly as compared to nursing home personnel with low levels of death anxiety (Eakes, 1985; Vickio & Cavanaugh, 1985). Vickio and Cavanaugh (1985) reported that increased death anxiety was associated with greater personal anxiety toward aging. Furthermore, they found that employees who had experienced greater exposure to the deaths of the residents reported more comfort in thinking about and discussing death and dying with the patients. However, this same group of employees did not always have lower scores on Templer's (1970) Death Anxiety Scale (DAS). The researchers speculated that these employees may have had the ability to separate their own death anxiety from their desire to discuss concerns that the residents had about death and dying. The researchers also pointed out that the apparent multidimensionality of the DAS may have obscured the relationship between death experience and death anxiety.

A recent study investigated the relationship between death anxiety, attitudes toward the elderly, and personal anxiety toward one's own aging in a group of nursing home employees and a matched comparison group of participants who worked in non-death related occupations (DePaola, Neimeyer, Lupfer, & Fiedler,

1992). Their results indicated that nursing home personnel did not have higher levels of death concern on two dimensions of death anxiety (fear of the dead and fear of significant others dying). Nevertheless, the results also indicated that increasing levels of death anxiety were associated with greater anxiety toward one's own aging, especially in the nursing home sample. Surprisingly, nursing personnel displayed significantly less positive attitudes toward the elderly than controls. DePaola, Neimeyer, and Ross (1994) extended this line of research by examining death anxiety in nursing home personnel as a function of training. The results indicated that nursing professionals (i.e., registered nurses, licensed practical nurses) did not have higher levels of death anxiety when compared to nursing assistants. In fact, nursing assistants had higher levels of death anxiety on four components of death anxiety (fear of the dead, fear of the unknown, fear of consciousness when dead, and fear for body after death).

☐ Death Anxiety and Age

Another variable that influences the level of death anxiety for an individual is the age of the participant. Most studies indicate that age is negatively correlated with death anxiety (DePaola, Neimeyer, Lupfer, & Fiedler, 1992; DePaola, Neimeyer, & Ross, 1994; Keller, Sherry, & Piotrowski, 1984; Neimeyer, 1985; Neimeyer, Moore, & Bagley, 1988; Neimeyer & Van Brunt, 1995; Wong, Reker, & Gesser, 1994). However, sometimes in broader samples, a curvilinear trend was detected. For example, Gesser, Wong, and Reker (1987–1988) administered the Death Attitude Profile (DTP) to fifty participants in three age groups; the young (18–26); the middle-aged (35–50); and the elderly (60 and older). Their results indicated that death anxiety was high in young participants, higher in middle adulthood, and lowest in the elderly. Thus, it seems important to examine how the ages of nursing home personnel is related to both death anxiety and possible reactions to the aged as a group.

☐ Death Anxiety and Ethnicity

Race is another variable that influences the level of death anxiety in individuals. However, few researchers have assessed death anxiety in relationship to race in a meaningful manner (Cotton, 1997). In fact, many studies have simply described the racial composition of the sample without making any meaningful comparisons (e.g., Fiefel & Nagy, 1980; Hintze, Templer, Cappellety, & Frederick, 1994; Slezak, 1982; Rappaport, Fossler, Bross, & Gilden, 1993). The studies that have examined differences with respect to race are few, and the results are inconsistent from study to study. Even when researchers have attempted to examine race as a variable, they have done so in a superficial manner (Thorson & Powell, 1990, 1992). An earlier study conducted by Kalish and Reynolds (1976) assessed death anxiety in over 400 adults. In their sample, they included African Americans, Japanese Americans, Mexican Americans, and Caucasian men and women. Their results indicated that African Americans and Caucasians had lower levels of death anxiety when compared to Japanese Americans and Hispanic participants.

In contrast, other studies have found that African Americans report greater levels of death anxiety than Caucasians across diverse socioeconomic settings (e.g., Dodd & Mills, 1985). Many of these studies employed Templer's Death Anxiety Scale (DAS) and found that African American participants scored higher on the DAS when compared to Caucasian participants. However, other research employing multiethnic samples has not identified race as a significant predictor of death anxiety (e.g., Bengtson, Cuellar, & Ragan, 1977; Davis, Martin, Wilee, & Voorhees, 1978). Recently, Thorson and Powell (1998) found that Caucasian participants scored higher on 5 of the 25 questions compared to African-American participants who scored higher on 3 of the items. Because of these inconsistent findings, it is important to relate caregiver's race to both death anxiety and possible reactions toward the aged. The study reported here compares African American nursing personnel with Caucasian nursing personnel.

☐ Methodological Considerations

The research previously discussed was a step toward assessing death anxiety and attitudes held toward the elderly by nursing home personnel. However, these studies have presented several methodological problems and a number of questions are yet to be answered. Despite the promising leads offered by research into the relationship between death anxiety and a wide array of other important variables, many of these studies have failed to include a wide range of participants in their study. In particular, African American participants have typically been excluded in samples, making inferences about death anxiety precarious. This over-reliance on narrow databases has led death anxiety researchers to construct a biased image of death anxiety. Thus, for the present research, methodological pluralism seems imperative in researching death anxiety. Dattel and Neimeyer (1990) cautioned researchers in attempting to generalize results based on primarily Caucasian respondents.

Reliability and Validity

One limiting concern is the use of attitude measures with questionable reliability, validity (Collette-Pratt, 1976; Green, 1981; McTavish, 1971), and dimensionality (Hicks, Rogers, & Shemberg, 1976; Kafer, Rakowski, Lachman, & Hickey, 1980; Weinberger & Millham, 1975). More specifically, several researchers have suggested that attitudes toward one's own personal aging should be distinguished from attitudes to the aged as a group (Carp, 1967; Kafer et al., 1980; Kogan & Shelton, 1962). In addition, some researchers (e.g., Hoelter, 1979; Neimeyer, 1995) have recognized that attitudes toward death are also multifaceted, requiring more sophisticated assessment.

Measures of Attitudes

A second concern is that the Facts on Aging Quizzes (FAQ #1 and FAQ #2) are the most commonly used measures to identify positive or negative attitudes toward older persons (Palmore, 1980, 1981). Both scales were designed to assess basic physical, mental, and social facts about aging rather than attitudes per se. As such, both the FAQ #1 and FAQ #2 are only rough indicators of bias toward older people. Palmore (1980), the author of the instruments, has recommended that the FAQs be used only when instruments that measure attitudes toward older persons in a direct manner are unavailable. In contrast, the Aging Opinion Survey (AOS; Kafer et al., 1980) was designed specifically to address the issues of multidimensionality when measuring attitudes toward older persons. Although less frequently used, the AOS, which demonstrates adequate reliability, measures attitudes toward personal aging, aging in peers, and reactions to the general-other.

Measures of Death Anxiety

A third limitation is the lack of psychometric soundness of death anxiety measures. For example, the death anxiety measure that has been used in many previous studies of death attitudes in relation to attitudes toward older person is Templer's Death Anxiety Scale (DAS). Despite its popularity, the DAS has been increasingly criticized on methodological grounds (Neimeyer, 1988). A central problem with this instrument has been its susceptibility to social desirability response bias (Dattel & Neimeyer, 1990), along with its low interval consistency (Devins, 1979; Martin, 1982; Warren & Chopra, 1978). Moreover, the finding that the DAS measures not one, but several dimensions of death attitudes that shift from study to study complicates interpretation of the scale. This shift lead reviewers to recommend that its use be discontinued altogether (Durlak, 1982). Thus, a need exists to replicate the correlation between the caregivers' death anxiety and negativity toward older people (Neimeyer & Moore, 1989) using methodologically sound measures of death concern such as the Threat Index or the Multidimensional Fear of Death Scale (Hoelter, 1979).

As has been noted, a limitation of previous research is that most projects have not compared differences between African-American and Caucasian nursing home personnel. This over reliance on a narrow data base has lead researchers to construct a biased image of death anxiety. Only by analyzing for possible racial differences can researchers determine whether the relationship between the level of death anxiety and attitudes toward the older persons is a pervasive phenomenon in nursing home personnel or is rather specific to a particular racial group

The major purpose of this investigation was to assess the nursing home personnel's relationships between death anxiety and attitudes toward older persons. However, unlike previous studies, this study examines possible racial differences on the various measures. In addition, the present study uses a measure of death anxiety that is psychometrically sound: The Multidimensional Fear of Death

Scale. Along with this measure, this study uses the Aging Opinion Survey (Kafer et al., 1980) which was designed specifically to address the issues of multi-dimensionality when measuring attitudes toward older people. In response to the conflicting and tentative research of African-American nursing home staff, the study analyzes racial differences on the various measures without advancing, however, specific hypothesis about them.

☐ Method

Participants

The study was conducted in six nursing homes in Memphis, Tennessee. Despite efforts to recruit an equal number of White and African-American participants, the sample (respondents) was weighted toward African-American participants, reflecting the demographics of nursing home work. A total of 145 nursing personnel working in the six facilities took part in the data collection.

Measures

Demographics Form

This was a general information sheet on which the subject provided sociodemographic information needed for the analysis (i.e., age, education, job tenure).

The Multidimensional Fear of Death Scale (MFODS)

The MFODS (Hoelter, 1979) was used as the best available multidimensional measure of death fear that provides a broader assessment of death than the one obtained by using the Threat Index. The MFODS is a 48-item scale that is composed of eight distinct factors. The eight factors and their alpha coefficients (Hoelter, 1979; Walkey, 1982) are as follows: fear of the dying process (.80); fear of the dead (.72); fear of being destroyed (.81); fear for significant others (.76); fear of the unknown (.73); fear of conscious death (.65); fear for the body after death (.82); and fear of premature death (.72).

Social Value of the Elderly Scale (SVES)

The SVES (Kafer et al., 1980) is one of the 15-item subscales that comprise the Aging Opinion Survey (AOS; Kafer et al., 1980). The AOS is the only instrument to date that was developed on the basis of a multidimensional view of attitudes toward aging and the elderly. The SVES assesses several content areas, generally focusing on interpersonal relations and the place of older persons in the community (e.g., residential segregation, social responsibility, public policy, knowledge).

In fact, the SVES scale assesses a factor that has been identified in previous research as being an important component of negative attitudes toward the elderly (Hickey, Bragg, Rakowski, & Hultsch, 1979; Kapos & Smith, 1972). The items focus on perceptions of older persons as a group. Lower scores are indicative of less perceived social value. Coefficient alpha, an index of internal reliability, is .60 for this subscale.

Personal Anxiety toward Aging (PAA)

The PAA (Kafer et al., 1980) is a second 15-item subscale of the AOS designed to tap subjects' anxiety and fear concerning their own aging. Previous research has found that fear concerning one's own aging is associated with negative views of the elderly. The items comprising the scale cover a broad range of topic areas (e.g., finances, mobility, friends, family relationships). Lower scores on this scale are indicative of greater anxiety toward personal aging. The coefficient alpha for this subscale is .65.

☐ Results

Overview of Analyses

Descriptive statistics were calculated for both the African-American and Caucasian participants. Subsequently, an analysis of variance (ANOVA) was conducted on the MFODS comparing African American nursing home personnel with Caucasian participants. In addition, Pearson correlations were computed on all variables for the combined sample. Finally, a multiple regression analysis of independent variables was conducted to determine the best predictors of global death anxiety.

Descriptive Statistics for Both Groups

Table l presents means and standard deviations for each demographic variable for the nursing home and control groups. Despite efforts to recruit comparable samples, preliminary analyses indicated that the nursing home sample included more blacks, and more females, and was somewhat less educated when compared to Caucasian participants.

Analyses of Variance

An analysis of variance was conducted on all instruments comparing African-American nursing home personnel with Caucasian personnel. Table 2 presents the group means, F results, and significance levels for the death anxiety measures, anxiety regarding one's own aging, and attitudes toward the elderly. Results indi-

TABLE 1. Demographic and Descriptive Characteristics of Nursing Home Personnel

	African Americans (N = 108)	Caucasians (N = 37)
Sex		
Male	7 (6%)	2 (5%)
Female	101 (94%)	35 (95%)
Age		
Mean	32.3	44.1
Job Title		
NAS	96 (89%)	15 (40%)
LPNs & RNs	12 (11%)	22 (60%)

cated significant differences on the total MFODS scale and three of its subscales. The ANOVA for the total MFODS score revealed a significant difference, with Caucasian nursing home personnel (M = 130.0) scoring higher than African-American nursing home personnel (M = 120.0). The results also indicated a significant difference for the MFODS subscale measuring the fear of the unknown, with Caucasian personnel (M = 18.8) exhibiting more anxiety regarding the ambiguity of death when compared to African-American (M = 16.8) personnel. The results also

TABLE 2. Mean Scores on Death Anxiety and Aging Held by African American and Caucasian Nursing Home Personnel

	African-American Participants		Caucasian Participants	
	M	M	F	P
MFODS				
MFODS Total	120.0	130.0	4.36	.0386
F1 - Fear of Dying	14.9	14.7	.0231	.8794
F2 - Fear of the Dead	18.5	20.2	2.9	.0905
F3 - Fear of Being Destroyed	9.1	9.2	.0420	.8380
F4 - Fear of Significant Others	15.5	13.8	.6960	.4089
F5 - Fear of the Unknown	16.8	18.8	6.5	.0122
F6 - Fear of Consciousness when Dead	14.7	18.0	13.7	.0003
F7 - Fear for Body after Death	20.3	22.8	5.40	.0216
F8 - Fear of Premature Death	11.3	12.4	1.84	.1776
Anxiety Toward Aging	41.5	43.6	1.84	.1775
Attitudes Toward Elderly	53.0	49.1	6.9	.0094

Note: Higher scores on the Anxiety Toward Aging scale and the MFODS factors indicate higher levels of anxiety. A high score on Attitudes Toward Elderly scale indicates more negative attitudes toward the elderly.

indicated a significant difference for the MFODS subscale measuring fear of conscious death (e.g., I'm afraid of being buried alive). Again, Caucasian nursing home personnel (M = 18.0) displayed more death anxiety on this component when compared to African-American personnel (M = 14.7). In addition, the ANOVA for the Fear for Body After Death (e.g., "The thought of my body decaying after I die scares me.") revealed a significant difference with Caucasian nursing home personnel (M = 23.0) having more apprehension regarding this dimension of death anxiety as compared to African-American personnel (M = 20.3).

The ANOVA on the Social Value of the Elderly Scale reveled a significant difference between the two groups, with African Americans (M = 53.0) displaying more negative attitudes toward the elderly when compared to Caucasians (M = 49.2).

Pearson Correlations

Age

Age was negatively associated with the total score on the MFODS and six of the eight subscales of the MFODS. Nursing home personnel who were older displayed lower levels of death anxiety, which is consistent with past research.

Personal Anxiety Toward Aging

A positive correlation was found between personnel anxiety regarding one's own aging and the total score on the MFODS. In addition, five of the eight MFODS subsclaes were positively correlated with personal anxiety regarding one's own aging. Nursing home personnel who had higher levels of death anxiety were more distressed about their own aging.

Attitudes Toward the Elderly

Although a negative view of the elderly was not significantly correlated with the total score of the MFODS, three of the eight MFODS subscales were significantly associated with negative views of the elderly. Moderate correlations were found between fear of the unknown, fear of consciousness when dead, and fear for the body after death were correlated with negative views of the elderly. Finally, personal anxiety toward one's own aging was associated with negative views of the elderly.

Prediction of Death Anxiety

A multiple regression analysis was conducted to identify the statistical model that best explained death anxiety in nursing home personnel. The total score on the MFODS was the dependent variable. The independent variables were age of nursing home personnel, personal anxiety toward one's own aging, and negative attitudes toward the elderly. As shown in Table 4, age of nursing home personnel and

TABLE 3. Pearson Correlations of Death and Aging Attitude Measures for All Nursing Home Personnel ($N = 145$)

	Age	Elderly	Aging	MFODS	F1	F2	F3	F4	F5	F6	F7	F8
Age	—	-.18*	-.07	-.35**	-.04	-.30	-.02	-.19*	-.19*	-.28**	-.31**	-.23**
Value of elderly (Elderly)		—	-.18*	.12	-.10	.15	-.07	.05	.20*	.19*	.18*	.05
Anxiety toward aging (Aging)			—	.36**	.31**	.20**	.09	.08	.14	.28**	.32**	.39**

Note: F1 - Dying; F2 - Dead; F3 - Destroyed; F4 - Significant Others; F5 - Unknown; F6 - Consciousness; F7 - Body; F8 - Premature. Reverse scoring of the value of elderly, anxiety toward aging, and the MFODS scales were conducted for interpretive clarity.
*p < .05, all tests are two-tailed.
**p < .01, all tests are two-tailed.

TABLE 4. Multiple Regression Analysis Predicting Global Death Anxiety of the MFODS

Variables in the Equation	Beta	T	F
Anxiety toward one's own aging	.364838	4.686	21.96**
Age	.315555	4.282	21.47**

*Final model accounts for 23% of the variance in global death anxiety.
**$p < .001$.

personal anxiety toward one's own aging contributed significantly to the prediction of nursing home personnels' death anxiety. These two variables were significant predictors of the total MFODS score, accounting for 23 percent of the variance. Negative views of the elderly failed to add significantly to the total model.

☐ Discussion

Based on past research, it was expected that African-American nursing home personnel, when compared to Caucasian nursing home personnel, would have higher levels of death anxiety and consequently more negative attitudes toward the elderly. Contrary to this prediction, African-American nursing home personnel displayed lower levels of death anxiety, as assessed by the MFODS, when compared to Caucasian nursing home personnel.

One plausible interpretation for African Americans scoring low on global death anxiety may be that the African-American culture places greater importance on faith and religious involvement. Consequently, this religious background allows African-American nursing home personnel to interpret death as a non-threatening personal reality. In this context, religion assists African American personnel in understanding death and providing a cohesive philosophy.

Another interpretation for the above finding is that African Americans have more contact with family members who are dying. According to Brown (1990), the family is central to the care provided for the terminally ill among African Americans. Terminally ill care is perceived as a "public" function and the extended family includes friends and neighbors. African Americans are reluctant to place terminally ill individuals in a hospital or nursing home, preferring to keep them at home.

Caucasian nursing home personnel also displayed higher levels of death anxiety on three of the subscales on the MFODS. One of the most interesting findings was that Caucasian nursing home personnel were more anxious regarding the fear of the unknown when compared to African American personnel. The items on this scale specifically deal with issues regarding the existence of a life after death. One possible reason for this finding is that African-American nursing home personnel perceive death in relation to an afterlife of reward. Thus for African Americans, death leads to reward, personal justification, and benevolent eternity.

The results of this study also revealed that African-American nursing home personnel displayed more negative attitudes toward the elderly than did Caucasian personnel. One possible interpretation of this finding is that the African-American sample was composed mostly of nurses' aides, who spent a large portion of their day working with the elderly residents. Nurses' aides perform a variety of demanding tasks for a low amount of pay. As a result, patients may be perceived in very negative terms.

Another plausible interpretation is that many of the patients are Caucasians who grew up in a time when prejudice against African Americans was quite common. This may result in interpersonal tension between nurses' aides and patients, which is reflected in the aides displaying negative attitudes toward the elderly.

Lastly, African-American nursing home personnel may be experiencing ingroup–outgroup bias. The ingroup–outgroup bias is especially strong in situations where group memberships are salient (Mullen & Hu, 1989), as is the case in nursing homes. Moreover, this bias is particularly strong when the attributes do in fact characterize the outgroup (Lee & Ottati, 1993) and for trait dimensions that most distinguish the outgroup from the ingroup (Stangor & Ford, 1992). Consequently, elderly nursing home residents may be perceived more negatively.

Significant correlations were found between death anxiety and personal anxiety toward one's own aging. All the MFODS subscales were correlated with increased levels of personal anxiety toward one's own aging. Nursing home personnel who were more fearful of death were also more anxious about personal issues related to growing older. One possible interpretation of this result is that old age may be feared because of its proximity to death. Anxiety about growing older may be also the result of a third, unmeasured factor, such as locus of control.

Our results also indicated that age was negatively correlated with global death anxiety and six of the eight subscales on the MFODS. Older nursing home personnel were less death anxious than younger personnel. Lastly, age was negatively associated with negative views of the elderly. One possible interpretation of this result is that younger nursing home personnel may initially react to the chronic disorders and impairments suffered by the elderly in nursing homes in a negative manner.

The results of the current investigation highlight the need for researchers to continue to employ multidimensional measures of death anxiety. By using a multidimensional death anxiety scale we were able to identify significant differences between Caucasian and African-American nursing home personnel. Identifying these cultural differences could be important for developing educational programs aimed at improving attitudes toward death and the elderly. It is important for training programs to recognize that nursing home personnel attitudes toward death are impacted by social and cultural variables.

Lastly, the results of the current investigation highlight the need for investigators to employ multi-racial samples in order to gain a valid and accurate understanding of death anxiety of all ethnic groups in our society.

Points to Remember

1. The present project employed a multidimensional measure of death anxiety (MFODS) to investigate differences between African-American and Caucasian nursing home personnel.
2. Caucasian personnel was found to have a higher level of global death anxiety than African-American personnel.
3. African-American personnel displayed more negative attitudes toward older persons when compared to Caucasian personnel.
4. Nursing personnel more fearful of death were also more anxious about personal issues related to growing older.

☐ References

Almquist, E., Stein, E. S., Weiner, A., & Linn, M. (1981). Evaluation of continuing education for long-term care personnel: Impact upon attitudes and knowledge. *Journal of American Geriatrics, 29*, 117–122.

Bachelder, J. (1989). Effectiveness of a stimulation activity and perceptions of the elderly. *Educational Gerontology, 15*, 363–375.

Bengston, V. L., Cuellar, J. B., & Ragan, P. K. (1977). Stratum contrasts and similarities in attitudes toward death. *Journal of Gerontology, 32*, 76–88.

Brown, J. E. (1990). Social work practice with the terminally ill in the black community. In J. K. Parry (Ed.), *Social work practice with the terminally ill: A transcultural perspective.* Springfield, IL: Charles C. Thomas.

Burnside, I. M. (1981). Psychosocial issues in nursing care of the aged. *Journal of Geronotological Nursing, 7*, 689–693.

Carp, F. M. (1967). The applicability of an empirical scoring standard for a sentence completion test administered to two age groups. *Journal of Geronotological Nursing, 22*, 308–312.

Chandler, J. T., Rachal, J. R., & Kazelskis, R. (1986). Attitudes of long-term care nursing personnel toward the elderly. *Gerontologist, 26*, 551–555.

Collette-Pratt, C. (1976). Attitudinal Predictors of devaluation of old age in a multigenerational sample. *Journal of Gerontology, 31*, 193–197.

Cotton, A. (1997). Is there a relationship between death anxiety and engagement in lethal behaviors among African-American students? *Omega, 34*, 177–245.

Dattel, A. R., & Neimeyer, R. A. (1990). Sex differences in death anxiety: Testing the emotional expressiveness hypothesis. *Death Studies, 14*, 1–11.

Davis, S. F., Martin, D. A., Wilee, C. T., & Voorhees, J. W. (1978). Relationship of fear of death and levels of self-esteem in college students. *Psychological Reports, 42*, 419–422.

DePaola, S. J., Neimeyer, R. A., Lupfer, M. B., & Fiedler, J. (1992). Death concern and attitudes toward the elderly in nursing home personnel. *Death Studies, 16*, 537–555.

DePaola, S. J., Neimeyer, R. A., & Ross, S. K. (1994). Death concern and attitudes toward the elderly in nursing home personnel as a function of training. *Omega, 29*, 231–248.

Devins, G. M. (1979). Death anxiety and voluntary passive euthanasia. *Journal of Consulting and Clinical Psychology, 47*, 301–309.

Dodd, D. K., & Mills, L. L. (1985). FADIS: A measure of the fear of accidental death and injury. *Psychological Record, 35*, 269–275.

Durlak, J. A. (1982). Using the Templer scale to assess "death anxiety": A cautionary note. *Psychological Reports, 50*, 1257–1258.

Eakes, G. G. (1985). The relationship between death anxiety and attitudes toward the elderly among nursing staff. *Death Studies, 9*, 163–172.

Feifel, H., & Nagy, V. T. (1980). Death orientation and life-threatening behavior. *Journal of Abnormal Psychology, 89*, 38–45.

Gardner, D. L., & Perritt, L. J. (1983). Attitude changes toward the elderly: A national staff development program report. *Physical and Occupational Therapy in Geriatrics, 2*, 1983.

Gesser, G., Wong, P. T., & Reker, G. T. (1988). Death attitudes across the life span: The development and validation of the Death Attitude Profile (DAP). *Omega, 18*, 113–128.

Green, S. K. (1981). Attitudes and perceptions about the elderly: Current and future perspectives. *International Journal of Aging and Human Development, 13*, 99–119.

Hickey, T., Bragg, S. M., Rakowski, W., & Hultsch, D. F. (1979). Attitude instrument analysis: An examination of factor consistency across two samples. *International Journal of Aging and Human Development, 9*, 359–375.

Hicks, D. A., Rogers, C. T., & Shemberg, K. (1976). Attitudes toward the elderly: A comparison of measures. *Experimental Aging Research, I*, 199–224

Hintze, J., Templer, D. I., Cappelletty, G. C., & Frederick, W. (1994). Death depression and death anxiety in HIV-infected males. In R. A. Neimeyer (Ed.), *Death anxiety handbook: Research, instrumentatory and applications* (pp. 193–200). Washington, DC: Taylor & Francis.

Hoelter, J. W. (1979). Multidimensional treatment of fear of death. *Journal of Consulting and Clinical Psychology, 47*, 996–999.

Houlihan, N. (1986). Promoting attitude change toward older people: The effects of experimental and didactic presentations of information about aging. *Dissertation Abstracts International, 46*, 3219B.

Kafer, R. A., Rakowski, W., Lachman, M., & Hickey, T. (1980). Aging opinion survey: A report of instrument development. *International Journal of Aging and Human Development, 11*, 319–333.

Kalish, R. A., & Reynolds, D. K. (1976). *Death and ethnicity: A psychocultural study.* Farmingdale, NY: Baywood.

Kapos, A., & Smith, D. (1972, July). Identifying standard attitudes toward senescence. Paper presented at the 9th International Congress of Gerontology, Kiev, U.S.S.R.

Keller, J. W., Sherry, D., & Piotrowski, D. (1984). Perspectives in death: A developmental study. *Journal of Psychology, 116*, 137–142.

Kelly, G. A. (1955). *The psychology of personal constructs.* New York: Norton.

Kogan, N., & Shelton, F. C. (1962). Images of "old people" and "people in general" in an older sample. *Journal of Genetic Psychology, 100*, 3–21.

Lee, Y. T., & Ottati, V. (1993). Determinants of ingroup and outgroup perceptions of heterogeneity. *Journal of Cross-cultural Psychology, 24*, 298–318.

Lester, D., Getty, C., & Kneisel, C. R. (1974). Attitudes of nursing students and nursing faculty toward death. *Nursing Research, 23*, 50–53.

Martin, T. O. (1982). Death anxiety and social desirability among nurses. *Omega, 13*, 51–58.

Martin, M. E., & Buckwalter, K. C. (1984). New approaches to continuing education for gerontological nursing. *Journal of Continuing Education in Nursing, 15*, 53–57.

McTavish, D. G. (1971). Perceptions of old people: A review of research methodologies and findings. *Gerontologist, 11*, 90–101.

Moore, M. K., & Neimeyer, R. A. (1991). A confirmatory factor analysis of the threat index. *Journal of Personality and Social Psychology, 60*, 122–129.

Mullen, B., & Hu, L. (1989). Perceptions of ingroup and outgroup variability: A meta-analytic integration. *Basic and Applied Social Psychology, 10*, 233–252.

National Institute on Aging, Personal health needs of the elderly: Through the year 2020, DHH Publication No. 1988-735-736; 32533, 1987.

Neimeyer, R. A. (1985). Actualization, integration, and fear of death: A test of the additive hypothesis. *Death Studies, 9*, 235–244.

Neimeyer, R. A., & Epting, F. R. (1992). Measuring personal meanings of death: Twenty years of research using the threat index. In R. A. Neimeyer & G. J. Neimeyer (Eds.), *Advances in personal construct psychology* (Vol.2). Greenwich, CT: JAI Press.

Neimeyer, R. A., Moore, M. K., & Bagley, K. (1988). A preliminary factor structure for the threat index. *Death Studies, 12*, 217–225.

Neimeyer, R. A., & Moore, M. K. (1989). Assessing personal meanings of death: Empirical refinements in the threat index. *Death Studies, 13*, 227–240.

Neimeyer, R. A., & Van Brunt, D. (1995). Death anxiety. In H. Wass, & R. A. Neimeyer (Eds.), *Dying: Facing the facts* (3rd ed.) (pp. 49–88). Washington, DC: Hemisphere.

Palmore, E. (1977). Facts on aging: A short quiz. *Gerontologist, 17*, 315–320.

Palmore, E. (1980). The facts on aging quiz: A review of findings. *Gerontologist, 20*, 669–672.

Palmore, E. B. (1981). The facts of aging quiz: Part two. *Gerontologist, 21*, 431–437.

Rappaport, H., Fossler, R., Bross, L., & Gilden, D. (1993). Future time, death anxiety, and life purpose among older adults. *Death Studies, 17*, 369–379.

Roscow, I. (1962). Old age: One moral dilemma of affluent society. *The Gerontologist, 2*, 182–191.

Slezak, M. E. (1982). Attitudes toward euthanasia as a function of death fears and demographic variables. *Essence, 5*, 191–197.

Smith, S. P., Jepson, V., & Perloff, E. (1982). Attitudes of nursing care providers toward elderly patients. *Nursing and Health Care, 3*, 93–98.

Stangor, C., & Ford, T.E. (1992). Accuracy and expectancy—confirming processing orientations and the development of stereotypes and prejudice. In W. Stroeve & M. Hewstone (Eds.), *European Review of Social Psychology, 3*, 51–90. London: John Wiley.

Taylor, K. H., & Harned, T. L. (1978). Attitudes toward old people: A study of nurses who care for the elderly. *Journal of Gerontological Nursing, 4*, 43–47.

Templer, D. I. (1970). The construction and validation of a death anxiety scale. *Journal of Clinical Psychology, 82*, 165–177.

Thorson, J. A., & Powell, F. C. (1990). To laugh in the face of death: Games that lethal people play. *Omega, 21*, 225–239.

Thorson, J. A., & Powell, F. C. (1992). A revised death anxiety scale. *Death Studies, 16*, 507–521.

Thorson, J. A., & Powell, F. C. (1998). African- and Euro-American samples differ little in scores on death anxiety. *Psychological Reports, 83*, 623–626.

Vickio, C. J., & Cavanaugh, J. C. (1985). Relationships among death anxiety, attitudes toward aging, and experience with death in nursing home employees. *Journal of Gerontology, 40*, 347–349.

Walkey, F. W. (1982). The multidimensional fear of death scale: An Independent analysis. *Journal of Consulting and Clinical Psychology, 50*, 466–467.

Warren, W. G., & Chopra, P. N. (1978). Some reliability and validity considerations on Austrian data for the death anxiety scale. *Omega, 9*, 293–299.

Weinberger, L. E., & Millham, J. (1975). Multi-dimensional multiple method analysis of attitudes toward the elderly. *Journal of Gerontology, 30*, 343–348.

Williams, A. (1982). *Nurses' attitudes toward aging and older people.* Unpublished Doctoral Dissertation, University of Denver, CO.

Wong, P. T., Reker, G. T., & Gesser, G. (1994). Death Attitude Profile—Revised. In R. A. Neimeyer (Ed.), *Death anxiety handbook: Reasearch, instrumentation, and application* (pp. 121–148). Philadelphia: Taylor & Francis.

14
CHAPTER

Stephen R. Connor

Hospice Care and the Older Person

"The more complete one's life is, the more . . . one's creative capacities are fulfilled, the less one fears death . . . People are not afraid of death per se, but of the incompleteness of their lives."

—Lisl Marlburg Goodman

The vast majority of hospice patients are over 65 years old. Death mainly comes to us when we are older. This is as it should be in the ebb and flow of life. As such, hospice care is mainly concerned with care in the latter portion of life.

☐ Definition

The National Hospice Organization (NHO) defines hospice as "a coordinated program providing palliative care to terminally ill patients and supportive services to patients, their families, and significant others 24 hours a day, seven days a week. Comprehensive case managed services based on physical, social, spiritual, and emotional needs are provided during the last stages of illness, during the dying process, and during bereavement by a medically directed interdisciplinary team consisting of patients/families, health care professionals, and volunteers. Professional management and continuity of care is maintained across multiple settings including homes, hospitals, long term care facilities, and residential settings" (NHO, 1993).

This definition of hospice care in the United States is consistent with the philosophy of care rooted at St. Christopher's Hospice, the first modern hospice in the United Kingdom. A number of important tenants or characteristics were developed there that universally describe hospice programs. They include:

227

1. *The patient and family as the unit of care.* Hospices don't just admit patients; they serve the whole family and address the family's needs as well as those of the patient.
2. *Symptom management is the focus of treatment.* Rather than continuing attempts to cure the disease, hospice care focuses on control of symptoms of the illness through effective palliative care.
3. *Care is provided in the home and in inpatient facilities.* Hospice care is available in all settings. Though most care is provided in the patient's home, hospices have arrangements to deliver care in inpatient settings when patients are unable to be cared for in their own homes.
4. *Hospices care for the whole person including his or her social, psychological, physical, spiritual, and practical needs.* Rather than just focusing on physical care, hospice recognizes that social, psychological, spiritual, and practical needs are often critical to achieving good quality of life.
5. *Services are available 24 hours a day, seven days a week.* Dying patients have problems at all hours of the day. Hospices have to be able to respond to needs at all hours of the day or night.
6. *Hospice care is interdisciplinary, involving caregivers who can respond to all the patient's and family's needs.* Interdisciplinary care requires collaboration between all team members who have specialized expertise in the care of the terminally ill.
7. *Hospice care is physician directed.* All patients are under the care of a physician who can order all needed care. Hospice physicians work with the patient's physician to achieve optimal management.
8. *Volunteers are an integral part of hospice care.* They provide added emotional and compassionate support and relief for the family.
9. *Services are provided without regard to ability to pay.* Hospices have always believed that financial limitations should never prevent access to needed care.
10. *Bereavement services are provided based on need.* The provision of bereavement support to families before and after death has been a hallmark of hospice care. (Adapted from Connor, 1998)

Hospice is a philosophy of care as well as a program of care. It is based on a humanistic view and a family systems perspective. The hospice movement's roots are based on a belief in individual autonomy. Patients have a fundamental right to determine and participate in the course of their treatment. Each individual determines his or her goals for care and hospice supports their reaching them.

Humanism stresses acceptance of individual differences and unconditional positive regard. Hospice personnel work with people with all kinds of lifestyles and beliefs and must support each in dying in a way that is suitable for the individual and his or her family. We know that families influence each other greatly and understand how this can impact the way care needs to be delivered.

The hospice philosophy is to acknowledge death as a natural part of life. Hospices advocate neither hastening or postponing death. Patients are encouraged and supported in making end-of-life care decisions, issuing advance directives, and in participating in all decisions about their care. With appropriate care and support "patients and families may be free to attain a degree of mental and spiritual preparation for death that is satisfactory to them" (NHO, 1993).

☐ History and Background

The roots of the Hospice Movement lie in the Middle Ages. During the Crusades, travelers to and from the Holy Lands might stay at a hospice or way station during their journey. Some who were wounded or dying would be cared for there, as hospitals of the time refused admission to the dying. Some knights specialized in providing compassionate care for the dying as part of their religious obligations.

This concept of hospice, meaning to care for someone on life's last journey, was adopted in this century and developed by the founder of the modern hospice movement—Dame Cicely Saunders. Dame Saunders started St. Christopher's Hospice outside London in the 1960s to specialize in the care of the dying. She had background as a nurse, a social worker, and finally as a physician. Her vision of hospice included an interdisciplinary approach to care using the most up-to-date treatments in the management of symptoms. She established a research and teaching center along with patient-care facilities to promote palliative care, and has inspired professionals throughout the world to improve care of the dying. There are now over 5,000 hospices worldwide (Higginson, 1999).

☐ Hospice Programs

As of 1999 there were over 3,100 operational or planned hospice programs located in the 50 states, the District of Columbia, Puerto Rico, and Guam. Approximately 28% of hospices are independent hospice corporations, 59% are divisions of a corporation and 13% are unidentified. Of the 59% that are divisions, 30% are divisions of hospitals, 19% are divisions of home health agencies, 19% are divisions of hospice corporations, 1% are divisions of nursing homes, and 3% are "other" corporations (NHO, 1999a).

In 1998, 66% of hospices were non-profit corporations, 18% were for-profit, 4% were government entities, and 12% were unidentified. In terms of budget size, 24% of hospices have operational budgets less than $250,000, 12% have budgets between $250,000 and $499,999, 11% have budgets between $500,000 and $999,999, 15% have budgets between $1 million and $3.99 million, 3% have budgets between $4 million and $6.99 million, and 1% have budgets greater than $10 million; 33% are unidentified (NHO, 1999a).

In 1995, over 90% of hospices were Medicare certified. Twenty-eight percent also had Medicare certification for home health agency services. Almost 18% reported that they provided "pre-hospice" services under the Medicare Home Health Benefit. Most hospice programs (61%) reported that they had contracts with managed care organizations to provide hospice services, and over half had strategic alliances with other organizations (NHO, 1996a).

The average charitable contributions received annually by hospices reporting in 1995 was $128,608 out of an average total revenue of just under 2 million dollars. Hospices received almost 74% of their revenue from Medicare, 7% from Medicaid, 12% from private insurance companies, 1% each from self pay and public payor sources, and 5% from other sources. Responding programs reported that an average of just under 12% of funds went to care for people without the ability to pay (NHO, 1996a).

There is a trend for hospices to combine operations. As of July 1996, 3% of programs reported being purchased by another organization, and 7% reported merging with another organization. Twenty-five percent of programs reported that they were somewhat likely, very likely, or certain to merge or be purchased by another organization in the next 24 months (NHO, 1996a).

☐ Who is Served

An estimated 540,000 patients were admitted to hospice programs in the United States in 1998 (NHO, 1999a). Based on data from the last provider census in 1995, 60% had a diagnosis of cancer. Hospices cared for one out of every two cancer deaths in America. The remaining 40% of patients had various diagnoses including: heart disease, AIDS, lung diseases, liver or kidney diseases, dementia, stroke, motor neuron or other diseases (NHO, 1996a).

In 1995 the sources of payment for hospice care included Medicare 65%, Medicaid 8%, private insurance 12%, non-reimbursed indigent care 4%, and 11% other. There was little difference in the number of males (52%) and females (48%) admitted to hospices. Of male patients, 71% were 65 or older, 17% between 50–64, 10% were 18–49, and 1% were 17 or younger. Of female patients 74% were 65 or older, 17% between 50–64, 8% between 18–49, and 1% were 17 or younger. Racial breakdown in 1995 indicated that 84% of patients were white, 8% were African American, 3% Hispanic, and 6% identified as other (NHO, 1996a).

The average length of hospice care declined from 1992 to 1998. In 1992 the average length of stay was 64 days and the median stay was 34 days. In 1998 it had declined to a mean of 51 days and a median of 25 days (NHO, 1996b).

☐ Funding

Hospice care is funded primarily through Medicare/Medicaid payment. The Hospice Medicare Benefit was established in 1983 to provide a prospective payment system for hospice care. Under this system, each day of hospice care is paid at one of four levels of care. They are

1. routine home care
2. continuous home care
3. general inpatient care and
4. inpatient respite care.

The routine home care (RHC) rate is paid when one of the other three levels is not being used. The vast majority (96%) of hospice care occurs at the RHC level. General inpatient care accounts for 3%, while continuous home care and inpatient respite together account for 1%. The rate in 1999 for RHC was about $97 per day. All services, equipment, supplies, procedures, and medications must be covered under that rate.

If the hospice is able to deliver care for less than the set rate it makes a profit. If not it loses money. Many hospices must raise additional funds to cover the costs of caring for patients without coverage or for patients who cost more to care for than the per diem payment. Hospices are being forced to become more efficient and to have a larger population to serve in order to be able to handle the financial risks of prospective payment.

Hospices also care for younger patients who have private insurance or HMO coverage. The payment arrangements vary widely but are usually either on a fee-for-service basis or a per diem arrangement similar to Medicare/Medicaid. When paid a fee for service the insurer often will only cover those services similar to home health agency service, such as for the nurse and home health aide. Often the other disciplines are not covered and the hospice ends up providing the services for free in order to treat all patients the same regardless of coverage.

If the hospice negotiates a contract with the insurer, it often seeks a per diem all-inclusive payment. The hospice can educate the insurer that bundling all the hospice services together will often save the insurer money. If they purchase all the components separately it often is more expensive. In addition the Champus and Indian Health Programs both provide hospice coverage based on the Medicare model.

For those without any health coverage the hospice must determine a way to provide care. Some programs do not bill the patient for any services and instead just use donations to pay the expense of care. This can create problems under Medicare regulations so programs usually develop some type of sliding scale based on income to bill the patient, though they rarely pursue collection.

☐ Services

Hospice care usually includes a package of services that are provided to each patient and his or her family based on identified needs and a plan of care. The core services of hospice include nursing, physician services, volunteer services, social work, counseling, and spiritual support. In addition personal care and homemaker services can be provided by home health aides, and speech, occupational, and physical therapists can be arranged.

Nursing staff assess the patient's ongoing condition and serve as the eyes and ears of the physician. They make sure the patient's symptoms are controlled and spend a great deal of time educating family and caregivers about how to provide care. Social workers focus on the psychological and social needs of the patient and family. They help everyone prepare for the death both psychologically and practically by tapping community resources, helping make funeral plans, and getting affairs in order.

The attending physician and hospice physician are both members of the core hospice team. They are responsible for ensuring that the medical care of the patient is optimal by overseeing the care being delivered and by ordering all medications and treatments. Volunteers provide many different services in hospices. They are available to stay with the patient to give the family respite in the home, to form a friendship with the patient and family and to give a wide variety of practical assistance such as errands, cooking, cleaning, or just being there to listen. Volunteers also assist the hospice in administrative or community work.

Counseling can be provided by any of the hospice team members. While it is a primary responsibility of social workers; in most hospices nurses, aides and others help provide counseling through support and education. Hospices are uniquely positioned to provide for spiritual counseling for patients and families. This is most often provided through chaplains hired to work as part of the hospice team. Sometimes it is through a close working relationship with clergy in the community. All hospices work with the community clergy who are already involved in the lives of the patient and family.

A variety of therapists can be utilized through hospice to enhance the care of patients or to provide for special needs. Physical therapists can help to maintain function or to help with a temporary setback. Occupational therapists can assist in maintaining normal functioning for longer periods. Speech pathologists can help to extend the patients' ability to communicate especially in cases where stroke or other neurological impairment has limited speech communication. Hospices may use the services of clinical psychologists, music, art (expressive), massage, enterostomal, or other therapists as needed.

The home health aide is a central part of the hospice care team. These aides provide personal care to the patient including bathing, feeding, dressing, toileting, and grooming. Typically, when personal care is needed to help support the family, the aide visits about three times a week. Aides can also provide homemaker assistance to help with light housework chores.

Hospices arrange for durable medical equipment such as a hospital bed, wheelchair or walker, bedside commode, oxygen, or other items as needed. They provide all medications that are related to the terminal illness and any medical supplies or appliances needed. If laboratory or diagnostic imaging are needed the hospice must provide for them as well as any outpatient procedures or visits to the emergency room. If a treatment is deemed to be palliative (including chemotherapy and radiation therapy) and the hospice includes it in the plan of care it is a provided service.

Needed services must be available 24 hours a day, 7 days a week. Nursing staff are always on-call to respond to patient and family needs and must be available to visit the patient if symptoms are out of control. Medications, oxygen, and other needed items must be available when needed with minimal delay.

Grief experienced during the care of the dying person by the patient and family is responded to with support, education, and counseling. After the patient's death, hospices continue to provide bereavement support to the family for at least a year. This support includes group or individual counseling, education about the grief process, referrals for treatment, memorials, etc.

☐ Staffing

The interdisciplinary team is one of the secrets to the success of hospice care. Its blend of staff disciplines mirror the important dimensions of care for the terminally ill and their families. The amount of staffing for a hospice program is critical to its ability to achieve effective outcomes of care.

With a shorter and shorter length of stay hospice patients usually require more staff time to assess, evaluate, and educate everyone at the front end and to help deal with the stressful events around the time of death. The original assumptions of the Medicare Hospice Benefit assumed that there would be a considerable period of stability when the staff would need to visit less often. This is now rarely the case. To respond to these patients the nurse is needed daily around the time of death, the patient is more ADL dependent and in need of personal care, the family is in need of more emotional and spiritual support, and arrangements to get affairs in order are more urgent.

The National Hospice Organization recommends staffing ratios for full-time staff equivalents that generally call for a caseload of 8–12 for nurses and 15–25 visits per week; for social workers, a caseload of 20–30 patients and 15–25 visits per week; for chaplains, a caseload of 40–60 patients and 15–25 visits per week; and for home health aides a caseload of 12–15 patients with an average of 15–25 visits per week. A full-time volunteer coordinator would be needed for a daily census of 60–80 patients, and a full-time bereavement coordinator per 200–300 patient deaths per year. Ranges are affected by patient acuity, geographical area covered, use of volunteers, scope of practice, etc.

☐ The Process of Care

When a patient is referred to a hospice an effort to determine eligibility is made. If the referral is from a physician the hospice must still make sure the referral is appropriate, when necessary by review of the medical director. If the referral is from a non-physician the hospice must contact the patient's attending physician to determine if the patient is appropriate for hospice care. If physician approval is given an intake appointment is scheduled. This is usually within one working day of referral.

During the intake appointment a hospice staff person does an assessment of the patient and family's situation. Once the patient has been determined to meet all the eligibility criteria for hospice care he or she is admitted to the hospice program. The hospice core staff do comprehensive nursing, psychosocial, and spiritual care assessments; these assessments are done by the nurse, social worker, and sometimes the chaplain.

These assessments are used to develop an interdisciplinary team plan of care. The content of the plan of care includes at a minimum:

- patient and family problems and needs
- realistic and achievable goals and objectives
- the frequency and mix of services and the level of care to be provided
- agreed-upon outcomes
- prescribed and required medical equipment, and
- patient/family understanding, agreement, and involvement with the plan of care

☐ Management and Organization

Hospices have different organizational structures, which determine to some extent their organization. Independent "freestanding" hospice programs usually have a board of directors responsible for the operation. The Board hires an executive to administer the day-to-day operations of the program. The hospice administrator is responsible for ensuring that the program is in compliance with all laws and regulations pertaining to hospice care, that the program remains financially viable, and is responsible for hiring staff who are competent to provide care to all patients and families.

Hospital-based hospice programs are often a department of the facility they serve. The administrator is head of the department and reports to hospital administration. Depending on the ownership of the hospital the governing body may be a Board of Trustees or other responsible entity.

Home health agency-based hospice programs are often a specialized program of a larger home care agency. The administrator of the home health agency may also be the administrator of the hospice program. Separation of the hospice and the home health agency is necessary under Medicare rules. Some staff can overlap but they must keep separate records. Some freestanding hospices operate their own home health agencies as a program, usually for patients not eligible for the hospice benefit.

The size of the hospice program determines it's organizational structure. Large hospice programs may have a management team that includes a finance officer, clinical director, medical director, human resources head, public relations head, and chief operating officer. Smaller programs may have a team where the director provides many of these functions or where individuals have multiple responsibilities. In hospital-based programs the administrator is often a department manager reporting to an assistant hospital administrator.

However organized, the certified hospice must meet many Medicare regulations that require considerable capacity for administrative processes. Some of these requirements include: medical records management, quality improvement, utilization review, infection control activity, maintenance of corporate records, interdisciplinary team operation, assurance of an adequate number of competent staff and volunteers, and provision of all required services.

More and more hospice programs are seeking voluntary accreditation to demonstrate the quality of their programs. National accreditation programs such as the Joint Commission on Accreditation (JCAHO) and the Community Hospice Accreditation Program (CHAP) provide accreditation for hospice providers through demonstrated compliance with a set of standards and outcomes.

☐ Problems in the Growth of Hospice Care

Prognosis

A prognosis is a physician's judgement about the expected course of an illness. Accurate prognostication has always been more an art than a science. Deciding whether someone has less than six months to live is fraught with difficulty and will never be entirely accurate. Unfortunately, when hospice agreed to limit its coverage to a less than six month prognosis it created a dilemma.

Once the number of people living under the hospice benefit more than six months got to be large enough it attracted the attention of government regulators who are charged with seeing that health care providers meet all requirements. The regulators did a study of hospices under "Operation Restore Trust" and came to the conclusion that many of these patients who lived more than six months should not have been admitted to hospice and wanted the Medicare payments back.

The assumption was that the hospice ought to have known that the person was not terminally ill and was therefore negligent in admitting the patients and billing Medicare. The obvious problem here was the assumption that prognostication is a more precise science than it is. All these patients were judged by two physicians to be terminally ill in order to be admitted to hospice. The review physicians, most of whom had no training in palliative care, were second guessing.

This has been one of the factors leading to shorter lengths of stay in hospices. Hospice programs and physicians are reluctant to risk admitting patients unless they are very sure they will die reasonably soon. The NHO developed guidelines (NHO, 1996b) for determining prognosis in selected non-cancer diseases. These guidelines have helped the field make better decisions about admitting patients with uncertain prognoses but have now been made into more rigid medical review policies by the Medicare intermediaries and in some cases have led to less hospice access.

Nursing Home Care

A Medicare Hospice Benefit for terminally ill patients residing in nursing homes was added in 1988. The idea was that choosing to reside in a nursing facility (NF) ought not to deprive someone of access to the hospice benefit. Regulations were adapted to cover how the nursing facility and the hospice were to work together to treat the patient. This arrangement proved difficult in some cases as the requirements of the facility at times came into conflict with hospice care provisions.

For example, patients have a right to refuse medical treatment. At the same time nursing facilities are required to carefully monitor patients' weight and condition to prevent neglect. If the patient chose to forgo a feeding tube and was unable to eat he or she would lose weight and decline. This caused concern to the nursing facility but was part of the expected plan of care by the hospice.

In addition, there was some confusion over who had responsibility for which aspects of patient care. When done well this was clearly addressed in both the hospice's and NF's plans of care. However, with high staff turnover in NF's, procedures were not always undertaken according to plan. Sometimes the hospice would provide services that were the responsibility of the NF, leading to perceptions that the hospice was doing something in return for referrals from the NF.

Outcomes for hospice patients in NFs appear significantly better than for non-hospice patients, and since about 25% of people die in NFs, more hospice care ought to be encouraged in NFs. At present there is considerable variability to the availability of hospice care for NF patients.

Defining Treatment

Considerable latitude is allowed for the hospice team to determine which treatments are palliative in nature. This has led to considerable variability in the kinds of treatments allowed for hospice patients. In the past 16 years since the advent of the hospice benefit there have been many advances in treatments for the terminally ill. Some of these treatments are aimed at curing the illness. More often they are disease-modifying treatments whose aim is to prolong life. Some of these prolongative treatments are clearly palliative in that they relieve symptoms. Others can cause added distress to the patient. Most all of these new medicines or treatments are very expensive and were not adequately funded in the hospice benefit.

For hospices, providing many of these treatments is so burdensome that doing so could result in closure of the program. Yet if they meet the patient's goals for care or relieve distress patients ought to be able to receive them. It is unfair to force the terminally ill to chose between getting hospice care or getting a treatment of choice. Often the patient ends up waiting until the treatment is no longer effective before entering hospice, which is usually when death is near.

☐ Future Issues

The hospice movement in the U.S. faces a number of challenges in the coming years. The problem with shorter lengths of stay needs to be addressed, along with the issues of palliative/curative treatment distinctions, prognostic accuracy, and the need for more outcome data.

The optimal period of time for receiving hospice care is approximately three months. This allows time for the hospice team to establish a therapeutic relationship with the patient and family, to thoroughly assess the family system, to prevent the emergence of distressing symptoms, to fully educate caregivers, and to mobilize additional resources needed for caregiving.

To increase the length of stay in hospice to this level will require systemic changes. The most important changes will be to address the statutory requirement that patients have a documented prognosis of six months or less to live, and that they be required to discontinue all disease modifying curative therapy to be admitted to hospice care. The six month prognostic requirement has led to overzealous scrutiny by health care regulators who second guess attending and hospice physicians. This has caused concern among physicians afraid of being sanctioned for making a wrong judgement in an area where accuracy will always be difficult to attain.

In place of the six month prognostic requirement, signs and symptoms need to be researched that may predict terminal illness in populations of patients with incurable diagnoses. Reasonable room for error should be built in to the system for oversight. Those hospices who are 85–90% accurate in admitting patients who die within six months should not be penalized. Nor should the referring physicians.

The emergence of new disease-modifying therapies for the terminally ill has created a new class of patients, the chronically terminally ill, who need services and who should be able to receive hospice care. These therapies are not palliative or curative. They are mainly prolongative treatments and patients who want them should not be denied them. They are forced to make a terrible choice between the treatment they want and the services they need.

Hospice reimbursement was not designed to cover the cost of these treatments. Hospices either need a payment mechanism to cover this care or the cost of this care needs to be provided through another source. If this change occurred it would allow hospices to serve a much larger proportion of those who are dying. Hospices in the U.K. and Canada are free to serve those who are continuing to receive curative treatment. This distinction came about as a result of limitations placed on hospice in the U.S. when the Medicare Hospice Benefit was established. Prior to the Medicare Benefit hospices and NHO Standards viewed appropriate therapy as a combination of palliative and curative treatment.

Defining and measuring outcomes in hospice and end of life care presents some unique challenges. The NHO published a conceptual model for understanding the needs of patients and their families facing terminal illness (NHO, 1997). The model proposes three major end-result outcomes for hospice care (a) self determined life closure, (b) safe and comfortable dying, and (c) effective grieving. Work is now underway to operationally measure these outcomes. In addition the satisfaction of patients, families, and the cost of hospice care have been studied.

The United States faces a unique change in future demographics that will result in an unprecedented proportion of older persons in the population. The need for more effective caregiving options, especially for those with chronic illness, is growing. The hospice movement represents a potential source of skill in meeting the

---

Points to Remember

1. Hospice care is for terminally ill persons and is primarily provided in the home setting.
2. Hospices serve patients and their whole families. Families receive extensive education about caregiving, and support continues for at least a year after a death occurs.
3. Medicare, Medicaid, and most private insurers cover all or most of hospice care.
4. Care is provided by an interdisciplinary team of nurses, physicians, social workers, home health aides, volunteers, chaplains, counselors, and others as needed.
5. Symptom management (palliative care) is the focus of caregiving, allowing patients to enjoy quality of life and opportunities for growth and life closure.

---

needs of the seriously and terminally ill. Greater flexibility is needed in supporting the provision of hospice and palliative care in the health care system of the future.

☐ References

Connor, S. (1998). *Hospice: Practice, pitfalls, and promise.* Washington, DC: Taylor & Francis.

Higginson, I. (1999, June 26). Going to sea in a sieve—Evidence based policy making in palliative care. Lecture given at the 11th Annual Assembly of the American Academy of Hospice and Palliative Medicine. Snowbird, UT.

National Hospice Organization. (1993). *Standards of a hospice program of care.* Arlington, VA: Author.

National Hospice Organization. (1996a). *Census of hospice providers in the U.S.* Arlington, VA: Author.

National Hospice Organization. (1996b). *Medical guidelines for determining prognosis in selected non-cancer terminal illnesses.* Arlington, VA: Author.

National Hospice Organization. (1997). *A pathway for patients and families facing terminal illness.* Arlington, VA: Author.

National Hospice Organization. (1999a). *NHO fact sheet.* Arlington, VA: Author.

National Hospice Organization. (1999b). *National survey of length of stay in hospice.* Unpublished survey results. Arlington, VA: Author.

PART

IV

CONCLUSIONS

15
CHAPTER

Grafton Eliason

Spirituality and Counseling of the Older Adult

As we enter a new century, human beings will receive the benefits of educational, technological, and medical advances, including greater life expectancy. Concurrently, the United States and other nations have begun to witness the effects of an expanding elderly population, as the baby boom generation turns 65. The combination of increased population and life expectancy will result in the largest elderly ratio our society has ever experienced. By 2025, the elderly will comprise an estimated 20–25% of the United States population (Butler, 1977; Choi & Dinse, 1998; Nussbaum, 1997). The absolute and relative increase in the elderly population brings with it a need for a matching increase in services, including those that address psychological and spiritual well-being.

A review of the literature in the field of psychology and counseling reveals a need for research and application in two related areas: counseling of the older adult population and the incorporation of spirituality in the therapeutic process, specifically concerning death anxiety. Contemporary helping professions have been hesitant to embrace the integral role of spirituality in the healing process. Spirituality becomes particularly applicable in relation to death anxiety and issues concerning our older population. Specific therapeutic applications such as reframing, life review, life planning, and constructivist or existential theory can then be applied to the issues of death anxiety and the older adult.

I would like to thank Dr. Adrian Tomer for his friendship and assistance in editing this chapter. I would also like to thank Kimberly Colosimo, David Kirkland, and Nadine Garner, graduate students at Duquesne University, for their assistance on various aspects of this article.

☐ Death Anxiety and the Older Adult

As a result of a long life span, the elderly population has experienced extensive personal, peer, and societal changes. Death anxiety must be considered when counseling any older adult client. Specific issues regarding death anxiety are two-fold. The elderly experience greater death exposure, yet paradoxically, this may not result in increased death anxiety. A great number of elderly persons deal successfully with the anxiety associated with death. Neimeyer and Brunt (1995), in an extensive review of death anxiety studies that considered age, note that elderly subjects responded that they think about death more, but are less anxious about death.

The elderly fear death for varied reasons, including fear of the unknown, fear of punishment, the loss of self, or lost opportunities. Most have experienced the loss of loved ones, friends, and family. As individuals grow older, they move closer to death themselves. Existentially, humans must deal with the question of whether or not life has been meaningful. Erikson (1963) viewed the last stage of the life cycle to be the crisis of integrity versus despair. Individuals who feel that they have not met their aspirations, or that their lives have been meaningless, may fall into despair. Those who are happy with their lives and have resolved the differences between their ideal life and reality will experience more emotional integrity (Erikson, 1963; Wong, Reker, & Gesser, 1994).

Tomer and Eliason (1996) proposed the Comprehensive Model of Death Anxiety (CMDA) which considers these issues and relates death anxiety to three factors: past related-regret, future-related regret, and meaningfulness of death. Past-related regret refers to the client's inability to fulfill aspirations. Future-related regret refers to the client's knowledge of his or her limited time and the inability to achieve basic goals in the future. These goals may be related to the self, such as a client's wish to succeed in his or her profession, or it may be related to other individuals, such as concern for one's family after death or being unable to see future grandchildren. Meaningfulness of death refers to the client's perception of the life cycle and death. Is there purpose or meaning to the life and death experience, and is that meaning positive and fulfilling (Tomer & Eliason, 1996)?

Death anxiety may be reduced through the incorporation of coping mechanisms such as life review, life planning, identification with one's culture, self-transcending processes, and religiosity or spirituality. These activities can act as a buffer, or actually change one's self and world view. Coping mechanisms may also help individuals who are struggling to reconcile the stage of integrity versus despair by providing understanding into the human condition, personal meaning, and self-acceptance.

Professionals must deal with accompanying issues such as depression, nervousness, loneliness, and hopelessness. Counseling the elderly means counseling a diverse group of people. This group of people is not only culturally diverse, but they have simply done more living than others have. The final stage of life is a stage of change and transition. The elderly continue to experience the same needs: physical, psychological, and spiritual. Though a majority of individuals lead an independent life style, for some these needs are met by very different means, and at times, in ways individuals are not ready to accept. Family, caregivers, or residential facilities often provide physical needs such as food, shelter, and clothing. Many become more dependent, resulting in a change of living, as well as a change in emotional and psychological perception. It is a difficult transition to spend one's life striving for independence and providing care for others, and then having these roles reversed (Lapsley, 1993).

Each of us must deal with the stages of the life cycle, the aging process, and death. Individuals who have not dealt successfully with issues of life and death throughout the life stages are likely to experience higher death anxiety. If an individual is experiencing high death anxiety and has not processed this, the issue can be addressed in counseling. The counseling process can often be enhanced through the incorporation of spirituality to further promote the client's mental health and well-being.

☐ Spirituality and Religion

Current trends in the United States show that we live in a religious society. A recent Gallup Poll (1994) found that 93% of respondents indicated a religious preference. When asked about the importance of religion, 59% of respondents reported "very important," and 29% reported "fairly important." Through a random sample of American Psychological Association (APA) members, the results showed that 51% of psychologists responded that religion was "not very important." Conversely, 73% of those polled responded that *spirituality* was either "very important" or "fairly important" (Gallup, 1994, p. 72). A distinction was perceived, therefore, between the importance of spirituality and religion.

When spirituality is defined in philosophical, psychological, and religious terms it begins to incorporate the human capacity for self-transcendence. Within each religion, the basic components are similar and include what Buber (1970) refers to as the "I and Thou" experience, or the human and the Holy. Self-transcendence is the ability to go beyond oneself in wisdom, human relationships, and in the experience of the Holy, in whatever way the Holy is understood (Conn, 1993). Spirituality and religion share commonalities. However, they also have significant differences in meaning: spirituality points to self-transcendence, self-actualization, and our existential search for meaning, but most importantly, to the phenomenological experience of relationship.

Religion may be seen as the belief system and ritual practices of a sect or denomination of individuals. It differs from spirituality, in that religion refers to the organized practice of worship and ritual. Etymologically, the word religion stems from the Latin root *religio*, meaning piety, conscientiousness, or scrupulousness; and from *religare*, meaning to bind back or to bind together. It is the common belief system which binds a group of individuals together in worship, practice, and community. Webster's New World Dictionary defines Religion as an individual's or group's expression of belief through conduct and ritual in a divine power.

The word spirit originates from the Latin root *spiritus*, meaning breath, courage, vigor, the soul, life, and from *spirare*, to blow, or to breathe. In Hebrew and

Greek culture, the spirit was believed to be the breath of life. In Western cultures, spirit is that which is the sentient part of an individual, one's personality, dynamic drive, and creative response to the demands one encounters throughout the process of becoming. Spirituality is not only what gives us life, animation, and self-awareness, but it is that which is other than our corporeal body. It is our individual soul's connection with that which is other, our God. It is the essence of the I/Thou experience on all levels: our awareness of self, our empathic response to other humans, and our unique experience with God (Buber, 1970). Spirit was seen as the *psyche* in psychology.

The role of spirituality in counseling is multidimensional. On one level, the client explores his or her own spirituality and calls upon faith and the spiritual I/Thou relationship to act dynamically in the healing process. On another level, the counselor draws upon his or her spiritual faith to enhance the interaction and the I/Thou experience between counselor, client, and God (Buber, 1970).

☐ Spirituality in Counseling and Psychotherapy: Pastoral Counseling

There has been tension between science and religion throughout Western history. The synthesis of Judeo-Christian theology and contemporary social sciences is not an easy process. However, such a synthesis presents a worthwhile challenge on many interdisciplinary levels. The American Association of Pastoral Counselors (AAPC) notes that "a Gallup poll conducted in February 1992 found that when confronted with a personal problem needing counseling or psychotherapy, 66% of persons would prefer a therapist who represented spiritual values and beliefs, and 81% would prefer a therapist who enabled them to integrate their values and belief system into the counseling process" (AAPC, 1998).

Browning (1993) proposes significant reasons that support the need for spirituality, pastoral counseling, and the application of theoretical models. Theologically, humans may be viewed as both spirit and nature in that both free choice and conditions dictate our behavior. Humans are subject to physical needs and harms; yet spiritually, humans have the potential for individual choice, self-expression, self-reflection, and self-transcendence. Humans have the ability to conceptualize physical mortality and spiritual immortality, finite abilities, and infinite possibilities. Human problems result from a combination of misused freedom and the impact of historical, social, and psychological factors. Ultimately, God becomes the source of personal growth and redemptive change in our lives (pp. 8–12).

In a pluralistic society, it is important to acknowledge the social sciences as a tool for better understanding our human condition, while at the same time not allowing the sciences to become a religion unto themselves (Browning, 1987). It is up to the counselor to apply this tool appropriately within the Judeo-Christian context (Meier, Minirth, Wichern, & Ratcliff, 1997). From a psychological standpoint, "pastoral counselors are more truly helpful in mediating these transformative qualities—more truly able to increase a sense of self-cohesion, initiative, and freedom in those they help—if they are sensitive to and able to address the actual developmental and environmental blocks, conflicts, and ambivalences that are undercutting a person's capacities" (Browning, 1993, p. 12).

Pastoral care and counseling has become a recognized field within the disciplines of theology, counseling, psychology, and sociology. According to the AAPC, pastoral counseling is a major provider of mental health services accounting for over three million hours of treatment in both institutional and private settings and offering individual, group, marital, and family therapy. The AAPC also points to a study by The Samaritan Centers which indicates that pastoral counselors have treatment success rates comparable to those of quality mental health services throughout the nation (AAPC, 1998).

From historical and ecumenical perspectives, pastoral care and counseling has always been a central part of the Protestant, Catholic, and Jewish traditions. However, we can no longer mesh the varied aspects of pastoral care and counseling into a single category. Current trends in specialization, training, certification, and licensure have had a positive effect on the field of pastoral counseling. These trends have also forced us to delineate the varied forms of pastoral care and counseling.

Browning (1993) distinguishes three distinct levels of practice: pastoral care, pastoral counseling, and pastoral psychotherapy. Each type of practice has relied upon and integrated aspects of other disciplines including theology, psychology, counseling, and sociology. Today, individuals with diverse training and specializations practice pastoral counseling on a variety of levels. The clergy, counselors, and psychologists each approach pastoral counseling from a unique perspective.

Pastoral care refers to the more generalized and less structured work within the religious community. This takes place in common activities and discussions. Pastoral care may include hospital visitations, participation in funerals, or dialogue in less specific situations.

Pastoral counseling pertains to a more structured relationship, which may include the designation of a time, place, and subject. The focus is placed on an individual, couple, or family and a specific psychological and/or religious issue. "The major new development that has motivated the founding of the pastoral counseling movement has been the insight that most human problems are various mixtures of both conflicted human freedom and moral and religious discernment" (Browning, 1993, p. 6).

Pastoral psychotherapy is a more specialized practice. The practitioner often has extensive training in both theology and psychology or counseling. Pastoral psychotherapy maintains a structured time, place, and subject like pastoral counseling; however, it also entails a specialized setting and concentrates specifically on psychological dimensions of the clients' problems, within a spiritual or religious context (Browning, 1993, p. 6).

Although each aspect of pastoral care and counseling has a different focus, each also contains elements of the Judeo-Christian tradition, ethics, psychology, and counseling. "Pastoral counselors combine the spiritual dimension of human life with the technical skills of modern psychotherapy to address the wholeness of the person in ways unmatched by other disciplines" (AAPC, 1998).

According to Strunk (1993, p. 14), "Pastoral counseling is as old as the church and as new as the birth of psychoanalysis." In a very general sense, psychotherapy becomes pastoral when it takes place within "the moral and religious assumptive world associated with the Judeo-Christian tradition" (Browning, 1993, p. 6). These assumptions are established by the faith of the traditions and encompass shared views of morality, human nature, and existence. It is within this context that psychotherapeutic theories can enhance our understanding of human development. This understanding can then help to facilitate awareness, growth, and change in the individual. Once the client becomes aware of his or her freedom to live and to choose, moral or religious values should not be forced upon the client. The client must choose his or her own path on life's journey (Browning, 1987, 1993).

☐ Ethics

The counseling profession is built upon a foundation of ethical guidelines, which protect both the client and the counselor. It is inherent in the nature of this profession that counselors work with clients who are vulnerable and, in this way, counselors allow themselves to become vulnerable as well. In fact, it is only through vulnerability, genuineness, and openness to the I/thou experience (Buber, 1970) that a trusting therapeutic relationship may be established (Rogers, 1951). Age, physical health, changes in living situations, and experiences of loss contribute to the emotional vulnerability of the elderly population. It is in the understanding and application of these ethical guidelines, that a measure of safety exists, paradoxically in the presence of vulnerability.

Ethical guidelines are presented in a number of different frameworks throughout the counseling field which cover a broad spectrum of concerns. The first framework to consider is our current legal system, which generates laws and court judgments that ultimately govern our interpretation of acceptable ethical standards. The second framework to consider is comprised of professional and state organizations upon which accreditation, certification, and licensure are based. The third framework includes our educational institutions and current literature on the topic. The fourth, and perhaps most important framework, is the individual.

Each counselor must establish his or her own ethical belief system from which to work and live. By establishing an ethical belief system, a counselor may become more secure in the knowledge that he or she has and will act in an ethical and personally "right" manner. Though this might not lessen the ambiguity one must face when working with a variety of clients and issues, it will provide a secure standpoint from which to practice. This may also become a benefit in lowering the anxiety associated with the sense of vulnerability felt by both the counselor and the client. As a member of the counseling profession, it is the counselor's responsibility to gain an understanding of the ethical guidelines, as well as, an awareness of his or her own personal issues so that the therapeutic relationship may be a positive experience for both the counselor and client.

☐ Constructivist Theory and Therapeutic Foundations

When working with clients of any age group, the therapist needs to explore his or her own spiritual belief system and develop a congruent personal theory of counseling. The therapist can then enter into a genuine client relationship from a centered perspective. In the continuous process of spiritual development, the therapist must attend to the common threads echoed throughout philosophy, theology, and the human sciences. The goal of pastoral counseling is to facilitate the client's spiritual and psychological growth, while counselors continue to grow themselves. To counsel is to participate in the I/Thou experience on an individual, relational, and spiritual level.

"Constructivism has captured the interest of those who understand the individual as an 'active agent seeking order and meaning in social contexts where his or her uniquely personal experiences are challenged to continue developing' " (Mahoney, 1996, as cited in Goncalves, 1997). Constructivist theory, existentialism, and phenomenology are first based on the philosophies of Kant, Sarte, Heidegger, Tillich, and Buber. Constructivism is more than an academic approach; rather, it becomes a philosophy of life. Constructivist theory incorporates the concepts of freedom, personal choice, non-determinism, and the search for meaning and self-awareness. Philosophically, each of us is ultimately alone, and each of us will die; yet, we are urged to search for personal meaning and to continuously ask the question "why?" Meaning and self-awareness are found through the sharing of experiences and ultimately the I/Thou experience.

In therapy sessions, primary emphasis is placed on the relationship between counselor and client. The I/Thou relationship allows all individuals involved to express their own past, present, and future experiences and hopes in the counseling session. The interactions between individuals become the dynamic for personal understanding and change. Techniques such as active listening, clarification, and the use of metaphor enhance the significance of the narrative. Genuine empathy and feedback aid in self-awareness and change. The counseling session becomes a new experience unto itself, and as a result, both counselor and client change in some way through the process of interaction. Ultimately, the most important aspect of any true learning and growth experience is the relationship between participating individuals.

☐ Specific Applications

Upon entering into a therapeutic relationship with an elderly person, the therapist must first understand where the client is on his or her life and faith journey in the present, how he or she arrived at this point and, if possible, where the client would like to go emotionally and spiritually. The therapist also needs to understand the client's faith in order to define a common ground from which to proceed. Psychologically, it is important to examine how the client's current emotional and spiritual state is manifested in his or her affect and actions. The therapist can then draw from this information to develop a treatment plan with the client, which would facilitate personal growth.

Though many therapeutic techniques may be used effectively throughout the counseling process, three specific applications—life review, life planning, and constructivist or existential therapy correspond well with Tomer and Eliason's (1996) three determinants of death anxiety, and may be incorporated as effective coping mechanisms through individual (Viney, 1995), family, or group (Stones, Rattenbury, & Kozma, 1995) counseling.

Sartre's (1966) nihilism suggests that death limits our abilities and negates our future possibilities. It reduces our existence to meaninglessness—nothing. A more positive interpretation suggests that an individual's final identity is defined by one's experiences, or by whom he or she has been (Neimeyer & Chapman, 1980). Continuing this line of reasoning, Wong, Reker, and Gesser (1994) build upon Frankl's (1965) perspective that individuals are motivated to search for personal meaning. Thus, death anxiety not only results from the inability to complete one's goals, but "from the failure to find personal meaning for one's life and death" (Wong et al., 1994, p. 123).

Elderly clients may seek counseling to better deal with issues of anxiety, depression, or dissatisfaction in their lives. These feelings may be intensified when individuals are faced with their own mortality and when the elderly begin to take inventory of their lives, seeking meaning or "putting their lives in order" (Butler, 1995). Often the ideal self does not match reality. Individuals may experience past-

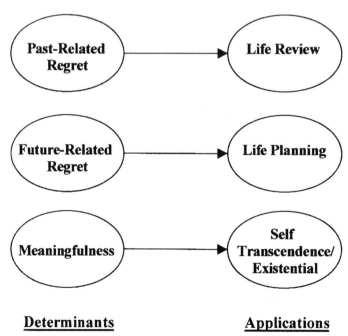

Determinants   **Applications**

FIGURE 1. Three determinants of death anxiety with corresponding therapeutic applications.

related regret or future-related regret if they are not content with their lives to the present point. Clients may harbor a sense of failure or loss if they have not fulfilled basic goals and realize that they will not be able to fulfill these goals in the future (Tomer & Eliason, 1996; Butler, 1995). Individuals may also possess feelings of guilt or remorse if they have not led a life with which they are comfortable morally or spiritually. They may begin to question belief systems concerning the meaningfulness of death. If individuals are not able to live in the present, but rather focus on the past or future, anxiety may rise when contemplating death or when undergoing a stressful life change related to age or loss. Life review and life planning, in the context of existential therapy, can help the client to better deal with issues of past-related regret, future-related regret, and personal meaning through self-awareness and reframing.

Reframing

The process of self-awareness and reframing may help one better understand oneself as human and reintegrate one's personal identity. As a result of finding a sense of ego integrity and coming to grips with one's fear of the unknown, an individual's death anxiety should be reduced, and one might then view one's existence as a fulfilling experience. Reframing past and present regrets may provide a sense of hope in the client, as well as, a focus on living more spiritually in the present. The concepts of life review and reminiscence (Butler, 1963, 1995; Romaniuk, 1981), biography construction (Marshall, 1980), and reframing (Capps, 1984, 1990, 1995) become an integral part of the process of personality reintegration and the life cycle.

Donald Capps (1984, 1990, 1995) incorporates the technique of reframing in pastoral care and counseling. The concept of reframing is to look at oneself, or one's situation, from a different angle, perspective, or from another viewpoint. When an individual is able to reframe his or her view of a situation, a paradigm shift occurs resulting in not only a different view of the situation, but also a new view of life and action. A negative situational view may be more positively understood from another perspective. Capps refers to Judeo-Christian parables to illustrate reframing:

Parables contain five structural elements, which facilitate the reframing event:

1. The parable involves a conflict, usually interpersonal.
2. The relationship between characters is changed by the end of the story.
3. The meaning is found in the story itself.
4. The parable is open-ended.
5. The parable emphasizes the importance of perceiving what is not readily apparent. (Capps, 1984, p. 96)

The parabolic event can include pastoral interaction through counseling, the use of metaphor and parables, or it can consider an individual's own life as a parable. This would incorporate an individual's intrapersonal perception of his or her life, autobiography, history, and self-worth. Through reframing, one's perception of God's activity in our lives and in the world shifts. Capps (1984) applies Ricoeur's (1976) theory of textual criticism to the parabolic event. The event moves the individual from his or her narrow personal view of the world, *umwalt*, and awakens the individual to the multidimensions of his or her spiritual world, *walt*, or the I/Thou experience (Capps, 1984, pp. 21, 97; Ricoeur, 1976, p. 37; Buber, 1970).

In this context, life review becomes a significant aspect of the counseling process. An individual, who suffers from many past-related regrets and does not find life or death to be a meaningful or fulfilling experience, may find hope through this counseling technique. The parable of the prodigal son can be used as a metaphor for the client's life. A young man takes his portion of an inheritance, leaves his family, and spends it foolishly. He humbly returns home and is welcomed back joyfully by his father. The son's poor judgment and actions were not wasted time; rather, this experience became the impetus for his understanding, repentance, and ultimate peace. An older adult with regrets can find comfort in reframing his or her own life as a process of learning. Peace and meaning can then be found through spiritual reconciliation.

Capps (1990) expands the application of reframing in pastoral counseling in his book, *Reframing: A New Method in Pastoral Care*. Here he applies Watzlawick, Weakland, and Fisch's concept of first order change (change within a system) and second order change (change which alters the system itself). Additional techniques are also suggested as potential interventions in the counseling and reframing process. These techniques include: paradoxical intention, dereflection, confusion, advertising, the Belloc ploy, the "why should you change?" question, benevolent sabotage, the illusion of alternatives, providing a worse alternative, relabeling, preempting, prescription, and the surrender tactic (Capps, 1990, pp. 9–51).

Life Review

A number of motivations for life review may be considered. Life review acts as a mechanism of coping with developmental changes throughout one's life span. It may also act more specifically as a mechanism of coping with one's past-related regret, death anxiety, or the threat of death. This is particularly true in later life or with the terminally ill, when the threat becomes more distinct. Butler (1963) originally coined the phrase "life review," describing it in the following manner:

> I conceive of the life review as a naturally occurring, universal mental process characterized by the progressive return to consciousness of past experiences, and, particularly, the resurgence of unresolved conflicts; simultaneously, and normally, these revived experiences and conflicts can be surveyed and reintegrated. Presumably, this process is prompted by the realization of approaching dissolution and death, and the inability to maintain one's sense of personal invulnerability. It is further shaped by contemporaneous experiences and its nature and outcome are affected by the lifelong unfolding of character. (Butler, 1963, p. 66)

Not long ago, reminiscence was viewed as a sign of senility and aging—living in the past. It is now believed that reminiscence may help to resolve unfinished business and to reintegrate these past events in a positive manner (Butler & Lewis, 1977). However, life review is not limited to only the last developmental stages, but corresponds with Erikson's (1963, 1982) psychosocial model as a whole. Though Butler emphasizes that life review is usually "prompted by the realization of approaching dissolution and death," (Butler, 1963, p. 66) he also acknowledges that it may occur as a result of other life crises. Life review may then be prompted by Erikson's (1964) concept of epigenetic crises, occurring as an individual moves from one developmental stage to another.

Butler (1974) emphasizes life review in old age because one has experienced the life cycle completely, and one is more acutely aware of one's time and place in the seasons of life. This emphasis fits well with Erikson's (1963, 1982) concept of ego integrity in the final stages of generativity versus stagnation, and integrity versus despair. An individual, who reviews his or her life experiences and finds his or her life to have been meaningful, would gain a sense of integrity and positively resolve the crises of this stage. Conversely, a person who sees a meaningless life upon reflection would experience a higher fear of death (Tomer, 1994).

Fortunately, the verdict is not so black and white. Life review not only affords one an occasion to look in a mirror, but to come to grips with the reflection at hand. It provides an individual the opportunity to move from a sense of despair to a feeling of integrity through reframing and the parabolic experience. Each person has regrets and misgivings. Some might be able to deal with their past failures on a concrete level. More often, one is forced to deal with one's past on a more internal and less tangible level. One must accept one's own humanity, and in so doing, all that is perfect and imperfect. More importantly, one must accept one's place in relation to God and humankind. This results in becoming a more selfless individual, or experiencing what Erikson (1959) refers to as identity diffusion, as one begins to lose one's boundaries. Somewhat different than the integrated self, one transcends the self—a transition from ego-integration to ego-separation—or the selfless self (Dickstein, 1977).

Quality of the life experience is more important than longevity. Wong, Reker, and Gesser (1994) look at life review from an existential framework. They find this to be consistent with both Erikson's (1963) concept of epigenetic crisis in the last developmental stage of integrity vs. despair, and with Butler's (1963, 1975) view that individuals are more fearful of a meaningless existence than of death itself.

Merriam (1995) notes that research has been inconclusive regarding the adaptive value of reminiscing and its relationship to the aging adult (Merriam, 1995). Wong, Reker, and Gesser (1994) conclude that studies on life review and death attitudes tend to support Butler's view. Accordingly, individuals who participate in life review and have achieved a measure of satisfaction and integrity in their past experience show decreased death denial, decreased fear of death, increased death acceptance, and seem to be more healthy and happy in general. Conversely, those who lack a sense of purpose and direction in their lives may have higher levels of death anxiety (Wong et al., 1994, p. 123). From a therapeutic standpoint, the advantages of participating in life review seem to outweigh the possible disadvantages, especially if it is experienced in a structured counseling environment.

Wong and Watt (1991) found that two types of six reminiscence categories are helpful as therapeutic adaptive processes for the older adult. The six categories are as follows: integrative, instrumental, transmissive, escapist, obsessive, and narrative (Wong, 1995, p. 24). One, *integrative reminiscence,* includes: "acceptance of self and others, conflict resolution and reconciliation, a sense of meaning and self-worth, and the integration of the present and past" (p. 24). The second type, *instrumental reminiscence,* includes: "remembering past plans and goal-directed activities, drawing from past experience to solve present problems, and recalling how one coped with past difficulties" (p. 25). Each of these aspects can be addressed in a therapeutic setting.

Life Planning

Just as an individual reframes his or her present self and past-related regrets through life review, he or she must also consider issues regarding future-related regrets and life planning. If an individual projects his or her self worth into the future via potential goals or accomplishments, the prospect of death can have an anxiety producing effect. An older adult may realize that there is no longer enough time available to fulfill specific dreams or goals. Such goals vary drastically between individuals and can range from hopes of a successful business, to dreams of seeing grandchildren. Death anxiety can increase or decrease, depending on the personal importance of future goals, or the emotional extent of future-related regret. An individual must begin to reconcile the ideal future-self with the reality of one's present-self.

Levinson (1978), Baltes and Baltes (1990), and Smith (1996) each stress the importance of evaluating and redefining future possibilities during times of change and transition in one's life. This is particularly important for the older adult experiencing future-related regrets. Baltes and Baltes use the term "selective optimization with compensation" to describe three components of their model for successful aging. The older adult must learn to deal not only with decreased physical, mental, and social resources, but with the limited resources of time as well. The first component, *selection,* implies that an individual must adjust his or her expectations and concentrate on domains of high priority physically, emotionally, and environmentally, including future goals. The second component, *optimization,* refers to process of augmenting one's general abilities in order to maximize one's quality of life. The third component, *compensation,* is used if specific capacities are lost or fall below a functioning range. Other abilities, strategies, or technology may be incorporated to supplement lost functionality (Baltes & Baltes, 1990, pp. 21–22). Carstensen, Isaacowitz, and Charles (1999) complement this concept by applying socioemotional selectivity theory to time and the older adult. They suggest that the elderly are primarily concerned with the present and that time boundaries create the framework in which individuals regulate and prioritize goals.

The process of life planning can incorporate reframing much the same as life review. Levinson (1978) refers to this process in mid-life as "modifying the dream."

Points to Remember

1. Death anxiety should be considered when counseling any older adult client due to increased death salience.
2. Death anxiety can be related to an individual's perception of meaning, as well as, past-related or present-related regrets.
3. Death anxiety may be reduced through the incorporation of coping mechanisms and counseling techniques such as reframing, life review, life planning, spirituality, and constructivist or existential therapy.
4. Spirituality points to self-transcendence, self-actualization, and our existential search for meaning. Most importantly, spirituality leads to the phenomenological and existential experience of the I/Thou relationship.
5. Reframing may include parabolic events and paradigm shifts in perception.

Smith (1996) focuses on the social aspects of life planning, pointing out that many plans are dependent on and must be synchronized with the plans of others in our lives. Many might perceive that life planning eventually comes to the ultimate question of "What would I do if I only had so much time left in my life?" However, by reframing one's point of self-reference, the question becomes "What should I do now?" If one is able to reconcile past and future regrets, one's view of world and time shifts to focus more on the immediacy of life in the present and the I/Thou experience.

☐ Conclusion

The concept of death anxiety includes emotional issues of regret, grief, and loss. Yet, meaning may be drawn from these very concerns through a process of reframing, life review, and life planning. A positive counseling experience can result in lowered death anxiety for the older adult client. More importantly, the individual has an opportunity to reframe his or her existential view of life. The incorporation of spirituality in the counseling process facilitates transcendence, the I/Thou experience, and a focus on life in the present.

☐ References

American Association of Pastoral Counselors. (1998). The pastoral counselor in an era of managed care. *American Association of Pastoral Counselors* [On-line]. Available: www.metanoia.org/aapc/.

Baltes, P. B., & Baltes, M. M. (1990). Psychological perspectives on successful aging: The model of selective optimization with compensation. In P. B. Baltes. & M. M. Baltes (Eds.), *Successful aging: Perspectives from the behavioral sciences.* Cambridge, UK: Cambridge University Press.

Browning, D. S. (1987). *Religious thought and the modern psychologies: A critical conversation in the theology of culture.* Philadelphia: Fortress Press.

Browning, D. S. (1993). Introduction to pastoral counseling. In R. J. Wicks, R. D. Parsons, & D. Capps (Eds.), *Clinical handbook of pastoral counseling: Vol. 1* (expanded ed., pp. 5–13). New York: Paulist Press.

Buber, M. (1922/1970). *I and thou.* New York: Charles Scribner's Sons.

Butler, R. N. (1963). The life review: An interpretation of reminiscence in the aged. *Psychiatry, 26,* 65–76.

Butler, R. N. (1974). Successful aging and the role of the life review. *American Geriatric Society, 22,* 529–535.

Butler, R. N. (1977). *Why survive? Being old in america.* New York: Harper & Row.

Butler, R. N. (1995). Forward. In B. K. Haight & J. D. Webster (Eds.), *The art and science of reminiscing: Theory, research, methods, and applications.* Washington, DC: Taylor & Francis.

Butler, R. N., & Lewis, M. I. (1977). *Aging and mental health: Positive psychosocial approaches.* Saint Louis, MO: The C. V. Mosby Company.

Capps, D. (1984). *Pastoral care and hermeneutics.* Philadelphia: Fortress Press.

Capps, D. (1990). *Reframing: A new method in pastoral care.* Minneapolis, MN: Augsburg Fortress.

Capps, D. (1995). *Agents of hope.* Minneapolis, MN: Fortress Press.

Carstensen, L. L., Isaacowitz, D. M., and Charles, S. T. (1999). Taking time seriously: A theory of socioemotional selectivity. *American Psychologist, 54*(3), 165–181.

Choi, N. G., & Dinse, S. (1998). Challenges and opportunities of the aging population: Social work education and practice for productive aging. *Educational Gerontology, 24,* 159-173.

Conn, J. W. (1993). Spirituality and personal maturity. In R. J. Wicks, R. D. Parsons, & D. Capps (Eds.), *Clinical handbook of pastoral counseling: Vol. 1* (expanded ed., pp. 14–25). New York: Paulist Press.

Dickstein, E. (1977). Self and self esteem: Theoretical foundations and their implications for research. *Human Development, 20,* 129–140.

Durlak, J. A. (1972). Relationship between individual attitudes toward life and death. *Journal of Consulting and Clinical Psychology, 38,* 463.

Erikson, E. H. (1959). Identity and the life cycle. *Psychological Issues Monograph, 1*(1) (Whole Issue), 50–100.

Erikson, E. H. (1963). *Childhood and society* (rev. ed.). New York: Norton.

Erikson, E. H. (1964). *Insight and responsibility: Lectures on the ethical implications of psychoanalytic insight.* New York: W. W. Norton.

Erikson, E. H. (1982). *The life cycle completed.* New York: W. W. Norton.

Frankl, V. E. (1965). *The doctor and the soul.* New York: Knopf.

Gallup, G., Jr. (1994). *The Gallup poll: Public opinion 1993.* Willmington, DE: Scholarly Resources.

Georgemiller, R., & Maloney, H. N. (1984). Group life review and denial of death. *Clinical Gerontologist, 2*(4), 37–49.

Goncalves, O. F. (1997). Forward. *Constructivist thinking in counseling practice, research, and training.* New York: Teachers College, Columbia University.

Lapsley, J. N. (1993). Pastoral care and counseling of the aging. In R. J. Wicks, R. D. Parsons, & D. Capps (Eds.), *Clinical handbook of pastoral counseling: Vol. 1* (expanded ed., pp. 5–13). New York: Paulist Press.

Levinson, D.J. (1978). *The seasons of a man's life.* New York: Ballantine Books.

Lewis, M. I., & Butler, R. N. (1974). Life review therapy: Putting memories to work in individual and group psychotherapy. *Geriatrics, 29*(11), 165–173.

Marshall, V. W. (1980). *Last chapters: A sociology of aging and dying.* Monterey, CA: Brooks/Cole.

Mahoney, M. J. (1996). Constructivism and the study of complex self-organization. *Constructive Change, 1,* 3–8.

Meier, P. D., Minirth, F. B., Wichern, F. B., & Ratcliff, D. E. (1997). *Introduction to psychology and counseling: Christian perspectives and applications* (2nd ed.). Grand Rapids, MI: Baker Books.

Merriam, S. B. (1995). Reminiscence and the oldest old. In B. K. Haight & J. D. Webster (Eds.), *The art and science of reminiscing: Theory, research, methods, and applications.* Washington, DC: Taylor & Francis.

Neimeyer, R. A., & Chapman, K. M. (1980). Self/ideal discrepancy and fear of death: testing an existential hypothesis. *Omega, 11,* 233–240.

Neimeyer, R. A. & Van Brunt, D. (1995). Death anxiety. In H. Wass, & R. A. Neimeyer (Eds.), *Dying: Facing the facts* (3rd ed.) (pp. 49–88). Washington, DC: Hemisphere.

Nussbaum, P. D. (1997). Introduction. In P. D. Nussbaum (Ed.). *Handbook of neuropsychology and aging* (pp. 1–4). Cambridge, MA: Perseus Publishing.

Quinn, P. K., & Reznikoff, M. (1985). The relationship between death anxiety and the subjective experience of time in the elderly. *International Journal of Aging and Human Development, 21,* 197–209.

Ricoeur, P. (1976). *Interpretation theory: Discourse and the surplus of meaning.* Fort Worth, TX: The Texas Christian University Press.

Rogers, C. (1951). *Client-centered therapy.* Boston: Houghton Mifflin.

Romaniuk, M. (1981). *Reminiscence and the second half of life. Experimental Aging Research, 7,* 315–336.

Romaniuk, M., & Romaniuk, J. G. (1981). Looking back: An analysis of reminiscence functions and triggers. *Developmental Aging Research, 7,* 477–489.

Sartre, J. P. (1966). *Being and nothingness: An essay on phenomenological ontology* (H. Barnes, Trans.). New York: Citadel Press. (Original work published 1943)

Sexton, & Griffin, (1997). *Constructivist thinking in counseling practice, research and training.* New York: Teachers College, Columbia University.

Smith, J. (1996). Planning about life: Toward a social-interactive perspective. In P. B. Baltes & U. M. Staudinger (Eds.). *Interactive minds: Life-span perspectives on the social foundations of cognition.* Cambridge, UK: Cambridge University Press.

Stones, M. J., Rattenbury, C., & Kozma, A. (1995). Group reminiscence: Evaluating short- and long-term effects. In B. K. Haight & J. D. Webster (Eds.), *The art and science of reminiscing: Theory, research, methods, and applications.* Washington, DC: Taylor & Francis.

Strunk, O., Jr. (1993). A prolegomenon to a history of pastoral counseling. In R. J. Wicks, R. D. Parsons, & D. Capps (Eds.), *Clinical handbook of pastoral counseling: Vol. 1* (expanded ed., pp. 14–25). New York: Paulist Press.

Tomer, A. (1994). Death anxiety in adult life: Theoretical perspectives. In R. A. Neimeyer (Ed.), *Death anxiety handbook: Research, instrumentation, and application* (pp. 121–148). Washington, DC: Taylor & Francis.

Tomer, A., & Eliason, G. (1996). Toward a comprehensive model of death anxiety. *Death Studies, 20,* 343–365.

Viney, L. L. (1995). Reminiscence in psychotherapy with the elderly: Telling and retelling their stories. In B. K. Haight & J. D. Webster (Eds.), *The art and science of reminiscing: Theory, research, methods, and applications.* Washington, DC: Taylor & Francis.

Wass, H., & Neimeyer, R. A. (1995). *Dying: Facing the facts.* Washington, DC: Taylor & Francis.

Watzlawick, P., Weakland, J., & Fisch, R. (1974). *Change: Principles of problem formation and problem reslution.* New York: W. W. Norton.

Wong, P. T. P. (1995). The process of adaptive reminiscence. In B. K. Haight & J. D. Webster (Eds.), *The art and science of reminiscing: Theory, research, methods, and applications.* Washington, DC: Taylor & Francis.

Wong, P. T. P. , Reker, G. T., & Gesser, G. (1994). Death Attitude Profile-Revised: A multidimensional measure of attitudes toward death. In R. A. Neimeyer (Ed.), *Death anxiety handbook: Research, instrumentation, and application* (pp. 121–148). Washington, DC: Taylor & Francis.

Wong, P. T. P., & Watt, L. (1991). What types of reminiscence are associated with successful aging? *Psychology and Aging, 6,* 272–279.

CHAPTER

Robert Kastenbaum

Death Attitudes and Aging in the 21st Century

What is the significance of crossing a border? The answers vary, but usually tell us much about the minds that have conceived and interpreted the border in the first place. "Great news," bellows Father as he bursts into the family's hovel, almost as cold inside as out. "We have just been told we live in Poland. *Poland!* No more of those terrible Russian winters!" This was one of my father's favorite jokes (judging by the number of times he retold it). Even a young child could understand that redrawing a border did not convert a freezing into a balmy land. The funny part was that some people might think it did. Later I would learn that borders can be consequential even—or especially—if they are more mental than topographical features. And these consequences are not necessarily harmless or amusing.

Three borders converge as we consider death attitudes and aging in the 21st century: the crossings from (1) adulthood to old age, (2) old age to death, and (3) the 20th to the 21st century, gateway to a new millennium. We have been approaching the first two border crossings as individuals, but we have proceeded *en masse* to Y2K and beyond. It will be useful, then, to attend to all three borders both from objectivistic and interpretative perspectives (not that either of these perspectives is independent of the other). Our task must also include at least a basic comprehension of the power of ritual in endowing border crossings with much of their significance. Let's start there.

☐ Ritual, Passage, and Borders

Human behavior and experience have been subjected to the influence of ritual for as long as the historical record can tell us anything. Anthropologists and historians often hold that ritual developed from the need to explain the inexplicable and control the uncontrollable. Perhaps religion developed from ritual, or ritual from religion; in either case, there was an intimate connection. Ritual also provided people with the opportunity to interact in predictable ways. Life was plenty dangerous; ritual prescriptions and practice offered some protection.

It can be difficult to distinguish between ritual and routine. Both are characterized by a fixed sequence of actions which may also include stereotyped verbal and nonverbal communications. Two office workers passing in the Monday morning corridor may greet each other with "Same old, same old" as indeed they do repeat the sequence of behaviors they have performed for many a preceding Monday. Ritual is more than routine, though. The action sequence is thought to embody a sacred principle and to affirm a relationship with the gods. We will often see more symbolism in ritual performances, but some individuals so enhance their obsessive routines with idiosyncratic symbols and gestures that the distinction may be blurred.

The emerging field of ritual studies owes much to the pioneering work of Arnold Van Gennep whose classic work of 1909, *Rites of Passage*, became available to a new and receptive generation in 1960, "Liminality," one of Van Gennep's core concepts, has since been further developed by Victor Turner (1967). For sake of brevity, we will restrict ourselves to these basic concepts and their implications for death attitudes and aging in the 21st century.

There is something fundamentally the same within all ritual sequences, whether on a macro or a micro scale. This was Van Gennep's insight after many observations, and it will be a working assumption here although it is not immune from criticism. His rites of passage theory certainly is not lacking for conceptual sweep. Van Gennep first asks us to think of territorial passages. It may be easier to focus on one individual, though the model applies to small and large groups as well. A person leaves his/her own people and place. This is *separation,* the first phase of passage. It is fraught with significance and peril. One is no longer protected by the gods of the hearth and the company of like-minded people. One's life is divided between the past self living in a familiar setting and the new, more vulnerable self venturing further out into the world. During *transition,* the second phase of passage, one is travelling as a stranger through and to strange lands. The sojourner will probably pass through wild and unclaimed territory in which identities and interactions are ambiguous and uncertain until reaching zones where claims and boundaries exist. This is certainly how it was back in those days when much of the world was still open territory. There were already established routes of passage and these were marked into zones, each of which had implications for the traveller's safety.

> The prohibition against entering a given territory is intrinsically magico-religious. It has been expressed with the help of milestones, walls, and statues in the classical world, and through more simple means among the semi-civilized. . . . A bundle of herbs, a piece of wood, or a stake adorned with a sheaf may be placed in the middle of the path or across it. (Van Gennep, p. 183)

The passage is completed when one has reached the destination and becomes *incorporated* into the new setting. A subtle distinction is implied although not elaborated by Van Gennep. The traveller may simply be there or may really become part of the culture of the destination group. Rituals are enactments and elaborations of a special kind of territorial passage. The person has shed his or her previous identity and status in favor of a new place in life.

When territorial passage becomes ritual, the middle phase of the passage is often challenging and perilous. This is particularly striking in those adulthood rituals where youths must demonstrate skill and valor under stressful circumstances. The passage from one status to another is often a major cultural event. It is intended to make a big impression on the novice. With coming-of-age rituals, the basic message is: "You are no longer a child. You now have the privileges but also the responsibilities of adulthood."

A special case—but also a universal certainty—is the passage from the world of the living to the realm of the dead. In contemporary culture we usually speak of the transition in terms of dying or terminal illness. Improved care of terminally ill people has become a much higher priority in recent years, as most clearly demonstrated in the hospice or palliative care movement. Many people, though, also regard aging as transition to death. The interpretive melding of aging and dying is a phenomenon to which we will want to return later. Most rites of passage in most cultures had priorities different from our own. There was less focus on the transition from healthy-to-dying person. Perhaps this was because of the rapid transition from alive to dead and the limited expectancy for growing old. The most elaborate ritual-driven ceremonies and practices were concerned with ushering the dead into their new status. By contrast, today, mainstream society gives relatively little attention to the incorporation of the deceased into the culture of the dead. (It should be noted that this perspective is limited to society's orientation toward the fate of the developing, aging, or dying person. The fate of society itself after a member has moved on requires a different kind of analysis.)

The concept of liminality helps to bridge the spheres of magico-religious ritual and the interactions that occur in industrial and postindustrial societies. Van Gennep introduced this term in delineating the rites of passage:

> I propose to call the rites of separation from a previous world, *preliminal* rites, those executed during the transitional stage, *liminal* (or *threshold*) rites, and the ceremonies of incorporation into the new world *postliminal* rites (Van Gennep, 1909, p. 11)

Turner's many contributions have emphasized those situations in which individuals or groups are caught in between two fixed positions. Examples would include the young person who is no longer a student, but not yet in the work force. In such a situation a person's status might be described as "statusless." If Turner were to have examined current issues in health care, he would have probably included the person in a persistent vegetative state as caught between the traditional status dichotomies of "alive" and "dead." Turner recognizes the complexities of societal arrangements. A person may be secure within several fixed status categories while at the same time experience anxiety and confusion in another sphere. "I don't know whether I'm coming or going" is one of the ways a person might describe the ambiguity of transition or liminality.

For our purposes here, it may be useful to remind ourselves that aging people often find themselves in just such a combination of fixed and liminal situations. Some status indicators are age-irrelevant (e.g., citizenship and, hence, credentials for full cultural participation); some could be subject to change (e.g., spouse to widow or widower); and others are likely to change (e.g., employed or retired, recognizing as we must the ambiguity in both of these terms). People with aging and death on their horizons are likely to have some fixed positions to call upon for material and emotional support while at the same time experiencing the stress and ambiguity of life course passage.

Turner's model has at least two seminal implications for the exploration of aging, dying, and death now and in the future. First, he extrapolates liminality into our everyday world. This seems fair enough. Ritual originated in the challenges of everyday life. We do not have to confine ourselves to established magico-religious rituals: often we are dealing with the perils and opportunities of status passage in work, family, and social interaction. Secondly, liminality seems to be one of the core features of our life experiences at this point in history. Many of us are betwixt and between in several spheres of our lives. One might even argue that life at the interstice of the 20th and 21st centuries is mostly about transition, about passage from—well, where are we, exactly?—to where we are going (and what might that be?).

Aging and dying are formidable enough processes in their own right. They become even more formidable with the concepts of ritualistic passage and life course liminality in mind. As Grimes (1995) observes, the *liminar*—the person in transition—is not only unclassifiable, but is located at just those societal zones in which there is uncertainty, openness, and potential. The rules of order do not apply as securely and firmly to liminars—which is to say, to all of us as we age and face death. And all of this ambiguity and ferment does not even reckon with the passing of a century and a millennium!

We will look first at conditions and constructions of aging, then do the same with dying and death before attempting to integrate both into an imagining of what might occur in the 21st century and beyond. There will not be a strict separation of aging, death, and futurity, but each will have its turn as the salient. We distinguish between conditions and constructions along the same lines that Stephen Jay Gould distinguishes between the natural and the arbitrary (1997). As he notes, there is an objective basis for recognizing a day of approximately 24 hours, but a week of 7 days is a convention dear to some societies but not to others. A distempered epistemologist could insist that nothing in cognition and language is free of constructivism. That caveat is OK by me. However, I will proceed on my bias that there is something "in reality" that answers to such terms as aging, dying, and death. We will therefore have a little to say about both conditions and constructions.

Aging: Conditions and Constructions

What conditions have influenced our attitudes toward aging up to this point in time? If we have any success in answering this question we will be that much closer to anticipating the attitudes that might prevail when conditions change. Here are a few of the conditions that are worth considering.

Wearing Out Too Soon

Historical evidence suggests that many societies have known at least a few people who went deep into age. There is no reason to doubt that the occasional person reached or exceeded "three score and ten." Evidence also points, though, to the foreshortened lives that were the lot of most people in most societies—foreshortened when compared with average life expectancies in developed nations today. There is another fact that is perhaps even more relevant to our exploration: Those who did not die young often aged young. This phenomenon was still common in the early years of the 20th century.

Arnold Lorand, M. D., an Austrian physician who is among the pioneers of modern geriatric medicine, was hopeful about the prospects of postponing the onset of old age. "We need no longer grow old at forty or fifty" (Lorand, 1912, p. iii.) Old at forty or fifty? In making this observation Lorand was simply reporting the status quo. There had been many advances in health care throughout history. As recently as the turn of the 20th century, however, many people exhibited pronounced characteristics of physical aging at the period that we regard today as midlife. Lorand was among the optimists, as indicated by the title of his book: *Old Age Deferred*. There was some substance to his hopes. Medical science was discovering that some people old at 40 were suffering from thyroid deficiency. There were remarkable rejuvenations with thyroid replacement therapy, which has remained an effective procedure to this day.

The success of this limited rejuvenation encouraged and intensified efforts to conquer aging completely. The quest for eternal youth had been a powerful motivating force since antiquity (Kastenbaum, 1995). Alchemists invested at least as much energy and ingenuity in attempting to maintain or renew youth as they did in transmuting lead into gold. A century ago, though, there was a new spirit of excitement and anticipation: the breakthrough must be just around the corner. Perhaps the most captivating notion was rejuvenation through "monkey glands" therapy. This fantasy lingered in some circles long after it had been rejected scientifically. More modest but also more realistic advances were slowly being made, though, as physicians and others concerned with hygiene, nurturance, and healthy living started to emphasize the ways in which people could keep mind and body in good repair throughout the adult years. Lorand, for example, called attention to the harmful cardiovascular effects of excessive eating of red meat, the longevity benefits of a contented marriage, and the avoidance of intellectual labors before bed time if "brain workers" are to enjoy a good night's sleep.

"Wearing out too soon" had several implications for our attitudes toward age and aging:

1. *Age comes too soon, and is therefore more of a threat and imposition.* One has just barely moved into parenthood, career, and the opportunities of full adulthood before starting to experience the downward phase of the cycle.
2. *Security and control needs were intensified for adults who were being worn down prematurely.* It was important to command the support and obedience of the younger generation as their own physical health and vigor declined. Some of the authoritarianism and rigidity demonstrated by parental generations could be attributed to their need to channel the vitality of the young into their own (and family) preservation. Children and grandchildren were the social security in a still-mostly-agrarian society, but the urge to keep a tight grip on the young was intensified by the premature grip of aging on one's self. To some indeterminate extent, "family values" meant that the personal goals and hopes of the young were secondary to the obligation to support parents who we would say were old before their time.
3. *The rhetoric was gender-biased, and in a direction that was controverted by the facts.* From ancient times forward, the quest for perpetuation or renew of youth was primarily a masculine pursuit. Both mythic and protoscientific endeavors usually featured men who were trying to preserve or rejuvenate their sexual vigor. The monkey glands adventure was just one more episode. In reality, though, women were more likely to be worn out earlier in their adult years through mutiple pregnancies, inadequate maternal care, and overwork.

There were remarkable exceptions to this general picture. Some people were vigorous throughout their long lives, setting examples that would be impressive at any period of history. Vigorous adulthood and a long life tended to be associated with superior biological heritage and acquired skills in a society with many hazards and few safety nets. Fewer people would be nursed along into their 50s and 60s, let alone 80s or 90s despite frailties.

A Short Life and a Hard One

One of the first things I learned from elderly men and women was their lack of expectation and, therefore, of preparation for old age. This was true both for people residing in the community and for those in geriatric facilities. Most had concentrated on getting through their lives as best they could, day by day, from challenge to challenge, from crisis to crisis. There was little reason to do otherwise. From the crowded tenements and shops of the port cities to the hard labor and precarious economics of the farms and to the health hazards and dangers of the mining industry many people had all they could do to make a life for themselves and their families.

The United States was still a young country when these elders were in their childhood. Only four percent of the population was 65 or older, and a mere 0.2 percent were 85 or older. There were relatively few living models of people at an advanced age. One might be taken aback by this statement. The image of "the good old days" often includes a much valued grandparent at the center of the family circle. There were such fortunate elders in such fortunate families, of course. However, the actual sparse survivorship of elders was disguised to some extent by the premature aging phenomenon that has already been noted. Furthermore, also as noted, survival was more selective than it is today, so in all likelihood the elders a child would come to know were especially hardy and resourceful people. Two other points should be added: the rarity of truly aged people enhanced their social value, and there were invariably useful chores and responsibilities that could be carried out even by a partially disabled family elder. By 1950, the percentage of elders in the population (at both 65 and over, and 85 and over) had doubled, and society started to worry about a surplus of aged and dependent people. The social economics of rarity no longer worked in favor of elders, and this trend has continued to increase over the past half century. Additionally, the social value of an elder in the home declined with the introduction of labor saving devices and the fading of the home as the indisputable center of family life.

The stereotype of a secure, respected, and valued elder often has had a plaintive quality. Scriptures and moralists repeatedly have urged that society not abandon its elders—for the very good reason that elders often have been abandoned in hard times. Those who were children around the turn of the 20th century had to notice that all was not well with the situation of aged people. Subsisting on charity or being removed to "the poor house" was not an appealing prospect. Aging and impoverished widows were at particular risk for being consigned to the furthest margins of society.

All of this added up to some potent attitudinal effects on young people in past generations:

1. *There was no point in spending much effort in preparing for old age.* Chances are they would not have a very long life, and there was so much to deal with now.
2. *Consequentially, one was likely to enter the later adult years without a life program or agenda and with little immediately available to reconstruct one's identity.* This contributed to the folly of denying change. Although appealing in its show of independence, this attitude impaired both the ability to adjust and to explore further developmental potentials. Elders who did not accept or know what to make of their unexpected status tended to make growing older an unattractive proposition in the eyes of the young.
3. *Growing old has been interpreted as so negative a prospect that many felt it would be better to die young.* I am certain that many other gerontologists have also heard people say, "I never want to get that way. I'll kill myself first," or words to that effect. The dread of aging takes many forms of expression in midlife, and sometimes even earlier. Preoccupation with staying young can dominate a person's life to the exclusion of other obligations and opportunities. Abuse of alcohol and drugs can become an escape channel. Perhaps most insidiously, suicidal ideation may accompany the individual throughout the adult years, waiting for signals of aging to cue an attempt.
4. *Most people quickly learned to hold the required attitude that elders are to be sup-*

ported, protected, and cherished. This sets up a conflict, though, when the elder in question is seen as rigid, rejecting, overdemanding, or, as some put it, "just plain mean." Realistic coping was made more difficult by the code of ritual deference that discouraged open communication.

There are So Few of Us

The relatively small number of elderly people in the past has already been mentioned. What may be overlooked, though, are the implications of a limited peer group. Generally, one becomes less powerful and secure in transitioning from a larger to a smaller peer group. For example, suicide rates tend to increase for those who are in an occupation that is decreasing in numbers. The major exception is when one is achieving a higher rung in a power hierarchy. There are fewer on top, but they have most of the clout. Seniority in Congress and some other organizations confers additional privileges and parameters of influence. In some societies gerontocracy has been an established general principle, including family relationships. Mostly, though, becoming an elder in the United States has meant a reduction in perceived status and power. The most typical situation, until recent years, saw relatively few people move with age into a smaller and weaker peer group. Furthermore, there was little public recognition or little individual awareness of elders *as* a peer group. The Gray Panthers and other consciousness-raising peer advocacy groups were still well off into the future.

Moving from a larger and relatively powerful to a smaller and less powerful peer group has had several implications for attitude formation, as can be seen through the rites of passage model.

1. *Separation from adult to elder, the first part of the process, was seldom marked by robust and effective rituals.* Some major life transitions were not only celebrated but also laden with guidelines, expectations, and vital meanings. "You are no longer a child," for example, and "you are no longer a single person" were part of rituals in which separation from a previous status was welded to incorporation in a new status. Few people received a ritualistic send-off into old age that was equal to the challenge. With the growth of big business and industry, retirement became the de facto marker for many people, but this seldom elicited a strong and supportive ritualistic response. For women—much underrepresented in the mainstream work force for so many years—there was even less to mark the transition. One did not so much become an elder as to lose much of what one had been without acquiring a clear and positive new status.

2. *The lack of formal ritual and group support contributed to ambiguity.* Was a person old because one zone of activity had been concluded? Or when others started making decisions without consultation? Or, without any particular notice, started to exclude one from previous patterns of interaction? Or when a change in physical appearance or functional ability became evident—or even just sus-

pected? It was difficult to take up the duties and privileges of age when the markers were often so unclear, incomplete, and even contradictory.

3. *The poorly ushered transition to a smaller, weaker, and less articulated peer group led to the possibility of anomie.* Some found ways to cope with this situation. People who were accustomed to being useful could still be valuable contributors if the situation permitted. Nevertheless, attitudes toward aging featured the theme that what elders did seldom amounted to anything. Professional and scientific attitudes were cut from the same cloth.

Loved, Respected, and Needed

Much of the foregoing has painted a grim picture of attitudes toward aging and the aged in years gone by. There was also a bright side, especially for those upon whom fortune shined. Elders in general benefited somewhat from their scarcity. The problem of "surplus elders" that started to engage societal concern around the middle of the 20th century had not yet arisen. To have reached three score and ten was to have achieved a status given to few. It could be comforting to have an elder or two within the family circle. This status often was strengthened by the nostalgia and sentimentality that had made its way into American life in the waning decades of the 19th century and the place of honor given to elders in religious teachings. As already noted, pious expressions of respect for elders sometimes resulted only in ritualistic deference and perfunctory actions. There were people, though, who believed deeply in respecting and caring for elders and this belief could more readily translate into actions when the aged were not yet conceived as a massive burden for a high pressured, high-tech society.

Attitudes even more positive developed around those elders who had something to offer that society clearly needed and cherished. These were the people who could pass on knowledge and skills desired by the younger generation. Many powerful stories had eager listeners, notably those associated with first-person memories of The War Between the States, and emancipation from slavery. The whole identity of the nation was in the process of fundamental review and revision and, in this project, the words of the elders played a significant role. There was also much how-to-do-it information to supply to young homemakers, farmers, and craftsmen. Practical information and a living cultural heritage were resources that articulate and accomplished elders could share. In years to come—and in the years still to come—what elders know best no longer is likely to be found indispensable by society.

Some elders earned high status on the basis of their life-long achievements. The woman who had helped others through illness and hardship might well be venerated in her advanced years, as would the tireless doctor who never pressed for his fee. Others may not have been loved for themselves, but commanded power and respect because of their position in family or community. Ethnic traditions in which power was vested in either paternalistic or maternalistic family lines were still dominant. Getting to be the senior male or female assured a status that had to be reckoned with.

The dread of aging itself contributed to the appeal of those elders who some-how managed to relieve society's anxiety. Some elders accomplished this feat by conforming to the stereotype of "the sweet old lady," embroidering as she sat peace-fully in her rocking chair, if she was not out in the kitchen baking those pies only she could make. Others became embodiments of the saint or the sage (Kastenbaum, 1994). The losses associated with advanced age could be transcended by an ex-alted level of virtue, holiness, or wisdom. The average person could not expect to achieve this extraordinary status, but the simple existence of a few aged people elevated above the common run of humanity offered a glow of dignity and rever-ence. And it was important that there were just a few saints and sages at any particular time. For all their symbolic importance, the saint and sage often were not comfortable folk to have around, and too many would pose a distinct threat. Curiously, perhaps, there was also admiration mingled with the disapproval of those who answered to the title, "son of a bitch." (The sexist implications here cannot be shed without also shredding the concept.) People often had a sneaking admiration for the thoroughly rambunctious, norms-defying, and selfish elder who "won't take nothing from nobody." In his own way, the S.O.B. made old age seem a more tolerable stage of life—a forerunner of Dylan Thomas' elegant plea, "Do not go gentle into that good night."

The attitudes and experiences we have reviewed here did not have equal sa-lience through all moments in our history. Age-related themes surged, faded, and melded into new configurations as our population mix continued to change, the economy leaped or faltered, emerging technologies assisted some and harmed others, epidemics raged or subsided, and many other events altered the spirit of the times. We have no reason to believe that the incessant and perhaps inherently unpredictable pattern of change will end with the cross-over to a new millennium. When we conclude shortly with some guesswork about the future of attitudes toward aging, then it might be more realistic to think of dynamic patterns rather than a single new and enduring configuration. But first, there is death to enter into the equation.

☐ **Death: Conditions and Constructions**

Thoughts and feelings about death are strongly influenced by maturational level, culture-mediated beliefs, and personal experiences. There may also be something universal in the human response to death. For example, the difference between a living and a dead body has raised questions and aroused fears that have stimu-lated the development of ritual, religion, art, science, and linguistic structures (Foucault, 1984; Sheets-Johnstone, 1990). All societies have had to come to terms with mortality as best they could. Some observers go so far as to conclude that sociocultural institutions have been shaped largely by the motive to control death by a configuration of symbolic, magical, and pragmatic means (Becker, 1973). It would be reasonable to expect, then, that attitudes toward death in the years ahead will be marked by continued variations on ancient themes. We will first identify some influential past conditions and constructions of death. This done, we will then be in a position to think about the future of attitudes toward aging and death.

The Shadow of Grief

"I just realized. I don't know anybody who's died. " This observation by a medical student in her mid twenties stands in contrast to my parents' memories of brothers and sisters who did not survive their youth—and to the life stories I have heard from many other people who came into this world while contagious diseases and opportunistic infections brought death into many a household. Young children died of diptheria and other prevalent diseases; the frail and aged were scythed by seasonal waves of pneumonia; women were still dying of "childbed fever" and other complications; and epidemics of cholera, smallpox, and yellow fever continues to ravage some areas of the country. Most of today's elders have brought memories of grief and loss along with them through their life journeys. There is more than one way to respond to grief and loss, so it would be a mistake to generalize about the effects of early and multiple bereavement on adult personality and adaptation. Nevertheless, a serious attempt to understand the character of current and past generations of elders would need to take into account their frequent exposures to the deaths of loved ones.

Dying at Home and Hospital

The loss of a unique and valued relationship is one thing. Watching a person die is something else. It is only in recent years that ending one's life in a hospital or other set-apart facility has become so prevalent, and care entrusted to strangers (Rosenberg, 1987). A fog of nostalgia has obscured the reality of home deaths. Although much has been written about the impersonality of institutional care for terminally ill people, the home experience often was far from idyllic. Helpless and frightened family members witnessed the ever-tightening grip of death on a child, sibling, or parent. One might be haunted forever by memories of a loved one suffering unrelieved pain, delirium, and other symptoms. The image of the hospital as a place where sick people go to get better took a long time to emerge. Most of today's elders and the generations before them viewed the hospital as a house of death. One might be among the fortunate few who do recover, but admission to a hospital was pretty much admission that the case was hopeless.

Life-or-Death Crisis

People seldom lingered in a life-threatening situation. Feverishly struggling against infection or trauma, a person would either manage to pull through, or would die within a few days or even hours. There were many episodes that could be accurately described as life-or-death crises. Physicians had limited pharmaceutical and other resources to affect the outcome. Dramatic scenes developed. There were truly situations in which the family and perhaps its compassionate physician would companion the patient, doing what little they could, and saying their very best prayers. These actual events became the stuff of widely disseminated dramatic images and representations of dying. In our own time the "trajectory" of dying (Glaser & Strauss, 1968) more often takes the shape of a long and lingering decline. At its extreme, a person who would have died at a much earlier time is maintained on life support. Before this extreme is reached, however, there is often an extended period of time in which it may not be clear whether the person's condition is most accurately described as "chronic-progressive" or "terminally ill." In the case of elderly people, decline has often been dismissed as the normal course of aging. We are becoming ever more separated from the past, then, in our construction of dying as a lengthy and complex process as contrasted with a quick hammerblow from Fate.

Cheerful Flowers and Noble Memorials

There was at least one saving grace in death. The suffering person was now out of his or her misery. The emerging professional funeral industry labored to craft a peaceful look. People of faith added the belief that the loved one was in a better place and, frequently, the conviction that they would be reunited when the time came. Several social movements converged to create a new era of "cheerful flowers and noble memorials" as described by some advocates. Although these movements were closely interwoven, each can be separately identified:

1. *The continuing reaction against the devastation and losses of The War Between the States.* There was a widespread impulse to honor and respect the dead and to somehow mitigate the trauma. The federal government contributed to this movement by establishing national cemeteries for veterans and setting a model for dignity and respect that had not been typical of all burial grounds.
2. *The ascendance of "the age of sentiment."* Hearts and flowers . . . soothing poetry . . . delicacy in manners . . . genteel speech . . . "sensitivity of soul" . . . These were among the traits of a veneer of sentimentality that was applied to all spheres of life. Coarse human appetites and vulgarity were cast out. Death—all too physical, smelly, and depressing—also had to be made over. This could be accomplished through more artistic funeral and memorial practices. Carefully coded verbal and nonverbal communication could prevent offending each other with unpleasant truths.
3. *A return to nature movement.* Like other rapidly industrializing nations, the United States was paying the price of progress through slums and environmental ravages. A determined and competent advocacy developed to preserve the environment and counteract the growing estrangement from nature.
4. *Public health and hygiene awareness.* A strenuous effort was also being made to educate people about the value of sound hygiene practices and the need to

eradicate menaces to public health. Neglected and improperly designed burial grounds were on everybody's list of risk factors for epidemics. The forbidding and often derelict burial ground quickly gave way to comforting park-like environs as these movements coalesced. Mount Auburn Cemetery (Cambridge, Massachusetts) became the first to provide spacious and inviting grounds, a concept rapidly embraced by communities across the nation. The development of the memorial park has not completely erased the local cemetery with its "been there forever" anchoring of a community. The local cemetery is perhaps unique in its perservation of community history. Taken along with the larger and more elaborate memorial parks, the local burial ground has, for many years, affirmed society's belief that the dead have their place. A dapper octogenarian in a small industrial city made it a point to show me the cemetery that now is surrounded by dilapitated industrial buildings in what was once a thriving neighborhood. "I look after them. It's the right thing to do. This will be my place, too, but who will look after me?"

Making Sense of Death

That organisms die is not especially puzzling to biologists. That births and deaths continue to occur year after year is not a cosmic mystery to statisticians. Deaths are expected, although timing, modes, and conditions will vary. Not so for the individual—and not so for intimate groups of individuals such as the family. The permanent loss of a relationship and the prospect of one's own death pose questions that one must either studiously avoid or take as the subject of serious inquiry.

Several interpretations of death competed for favor as the United States entered the 20th century. The first two interpretations identified below may be considered as paired polarities, representing opposite extremes of the Christian message. The next interpretation represents mainstream Christian beliefs as they took shape in American culture. The other interpretation identified here bears the marks of modernization and its discontents. We will see that all these views remain part of the mix a century later.

1. *Death is punishment for a life of sloth or sin.* This was a familiar message in pre-mass media America where channels of communication tended to be narrow and intense. The belief that we are in danger of eternal damnation made death a central theme in everyday life. One should avoid temptations of the flesh and not become too attached to this imperfect life on earth. Seeing life through the lens of death and possible damnation was a heritage from the *Ars moriendi* tradition that flourished in the plague-and-calamity stricken Europe of the later middle ages, culminating in Jeremy Taylor's *Holy Dying* (1651/1977). In the 19th century there were still many people who believed that catastrophes were punishment for our failure to live in unsullied purity and faith. The imagery of the medieval deathbed scene featured a tormented, despairing person who was surrounded by demons

and angels as his soul hung in the balance. The demons and angels had become less visible by the 19th century, but for some people the deathbed scene remained fraught with significance. Would this soul find salvation or damnation? Many a child grew up with the frightening image of the agonies of the damned on their deathbeds.

2. *Death brings deliverance from misery.* Some people reached this conclusion based upon their personal experiences with pain, hardship, loss, and disappointment. A mother, aged beyond her years by multiple pregnancies and burdened with the grief of multiple bereavements, might pray for an end to her suffering. A man who had left the farm for the big city might be ashamed of his failure to succeed and enraged at the cruel treatment he had received and witnessed. The temporary escapes into alcohol might no longer seem enough. Superimposed on personal experiences of distress was a belief system that flourished in some churches and communities. Death was release from misery, but it was also something far greater—a joyous delivery into an incomparably higher form of life. This conception provided hope for African Americans in a century that saw the brutal institution of slavery give way to the long struggle for opportunity and respect. The dignity and freedom one did not experience in this life would find more than ample compensation in the next. Much of what would become established as America's own music (spirituals, blues, jazz) was created within a subculture that found ways to celebrate life and joy through embracing death as delivery. The traditional New Orleans funeral with its dirge en route to the cemetery and the boisterous "When the Saints Go Marching In" on the way back is one of the most familiar examples of this attitude.

3. *Death is the natural end to this life, but also the beginning to a better life that we can hardly imagine with our limited knowledge.* God knows, and that's all we really have to know. This view was not dominated by fear of God's wrath. Mainstream Christianity had become a rather gentle, comforting, and feminized endeavor in yesterday's America (Friedman, 1997). The raw edges of messianic Christianity had been smoothed in many homes and churches by an emerging middle-class appreciation of an ordered and secure life. Jesus loves us, so we need not either live or die in fear unless we have been very wicked people indeed. The next life is greatly to be desired, with anticipations of reunion with those who have gone before and a more intimate relationship with God. But, just as one did not have to live every day in terror of death, so there was also no compulsion to go too soon. Life had become more promising and rewarding in many ways; we might as well enjoy what we have before moving on to our final destination. This conception, holding life and death in a judicious balance, did provide moral guidance. One should meet obligations, treat others fairly, and do the right thing. Separation would still be difficult as loved ones passed away, but the parting would only be temporary. Dying might be painful, but we were in God's hands and all would be for the best. As long as one's faith remained secure, a person could live with death.

All three of these interpretations were variations on the Christian theme as developed by people with different backgrounds and experiencing different situations. Despite their important differences, these views had in common the assumption of an ordered universe in which human lives count for something. The interpretation that follows is one that gradually emerged through science, technology and its attendant changes in the environs as well as the quality of life. The prehistory of this belief system can be traced back to Democritus' explanation of the universe as the mindless consequence of one or more capricious atoms colliding with another. There is no cosmic story in which humans play a featured role, hence our deaths as well as our lives have little if any significance.

4. *Death is the junkyard for the failed, worn, and obsolete.* Humans made the machine and the machine became first a subtle, than an increasingly pervasive model for humans. This has become a commonplace observation of industrialization and its effects. We can see some of the evidence for ourselves in the blank faces of fatigued workers serving their machines in photographs of past generations, and listen to the evidence from elders who perceive themselves as suffering the same fate as machines that have outlived their usefulness. There is not much place for God or for any source of either intrinsic or transcendental meaning. The typical attitude is not one of hostility to religion, but, rather, a feeling of abandonment. This was expressed, for example, some years ago by a woman in her nineties who had toiled in a sweatshop through what should have been her childhood. "God was very busy elsewhere," she said quietly. Competitive, fast-paced mass society has in fact used up many people and thrown them away. It was difficult to believe in one's own value when society undercut that hope at every turn. Death, then, became for some people the meaningless ending to an essentially meaningless life. No demons, no angels, just fadeout. Physicians by this time were moving rapidly toward a more scientific orientation and elevating their expectations for effective treatment. Soon patients became the flawed machines, and physicians the expert mechanics. The dying person became assimilated into this image as the machine that was beyond repair. The cost efficient mechanics became increasingly less motivated to waste their time with such machines and thereby also be forced to recognize the limits of their expertise.

These four interpretations all had their advocates who, sometimes, coalesced in uneasy combinations. They have been brought forward in our own time through the experiences of many long-lived people, and will be influential in the future, though themselves being vulnerable to influence, as we will see.

☐ Reconstruction of Attitudes toward Aging and Death in the 21st Century and Beyond

We are ready now to chance some thoughts about the reconstruction of attitudes toward aging and death as we move into the new millennium. The rites of passage model will be called upon as our general frame of reference. We begin, therefore, with the question of ritual.

More or Less Ritualization for Aging?

There is a useful distinction between rituals and ritualization, useful, that is, so long as we do not get too rigid about it. We commonly think of rituals as fairly elaborate structured sequences through which a shared purpose is expressed and fulfilled. Weddings and funerals are clear examples. Ritualization, however, is the process of converting ordinary actions and practices into a sequence that is more repetitive and predictable than the functions seem to require. Watch a few baseball players step into the batters box, for example, and we will witness a variety of personal ritualizations as each goes through an idiosyncratic set of maneuvers to prepare for the challenge. Baseball, in fact, is a game where players, umpires, and fans ritualize not only the action sequences, but also the pauses and interruptions. By contrast, spontaneous play—and doing almost anything for the first time— usually does not have this ritualistic quality. We want to understand the articulated rituals associated with aging and death, but we also want to be alert to the ritualization that often takes place without reference to established ceremonies.

A couple of points can be offered for consideration regarding both rituals and ritualization:

1. *The ritualized avoidance of dying and death discourse will be further moderated and transformed.* This trend will also moderate the discomfort with elders as living reminders of mortality. Much of the early literature in the death awareness movement (starting to make its mark in the 1960s) emphasized the need to say the word and hear the word. Herman Feifel (1959) rallied this cause with his diagnosis of our society as having afflicted itself with a taboo on death. Today this taboo no longer has its former strength. Death education courses are abundant, supported by a thriving literature on dying, grief, suicide, and related topics. Hospice programs, themselves a source of death education, have also stimulated much dialogue. It is likely that the severe ritualization of dying and death discourse will continue to lose its hold, giving way to open dialogue, more informed minds, and more positive attitudes. However, a closer reading of death-related communications suggests that ritualized avoidance has sometimes only changed its rhetoric. One notes, for example, that for the most part in medical discourse *people* still do not *die.* Instead, there is an end-phase to terminal illness. Those who must continue to protect themselves against authentic awareness of death will continue to be resourceful in this endeavor. We will see, then, both a true deritualization of dying and death discourse, and new patterns of ritualized avoidance that recognize just that much of mortality that cannot be completely disguised or dismissed.
2. A broader spectrum of transition rituals will help to mark and ease the transition to elder status. As already noted, established customs have provided little in the way of rituals to guide people through separation from midlife adult responsibilities to a new status as valued elder. From a rites of passage standpoint, there has been weakness at every phase, from separation through liminal journey to incorporation into a new phase of life. It is not likely that the

adjustment will come in the form of a single major ceremony. More probable is the emergence of a variety of diverse acknowledgments that contribute incrementally to an improved image of aging and the aged. A forerunner already has won wide acceptance: the senior discount. Some may scoff at this commercial device, seeing little connection with the coming-of-age rituals so frequently described by anthropologists. Ethnographers, however, have also identified practices in which special privileges are reserved for elders, partially in respect, partially in compensation (e.g., the tortoise may be eaten only by elders who are less likely to catch the hare). Furthermore, as a capitalistic society reviled and admired by much of the world, we take money seriously as a badge of personal worth. In its limited but effective way, the senior discount offers respect and welcome to people who are just crossing the still tenuous age boundary. The Tooth Fairy has compensated many a child for the loss of a body part that nevertheless signified a small step in growing up. The Senior Discount Fairy is one of what should prove to be many resourceful ways in which society tells its members that there are some compensatory gains, along with the losses and discontinuities that often are attendant upon advancing age.

A much different and potentially more powerful approach is offered by the emerging movement to celebrate ascendance to the status of crone. Centuries of abuse have debased this term ("that nasty old crone!"). Advocates point out, however, that crone (and similar terms in other cultures) refers to a woman who has reached a higher level of maturity and social value through years of deepening wisdom. At this point it is difficult to know how many women have actually participated in crone ceremonies, but this is probably less important than the growing recognition that (a) some people achieve higher levels of development through their later adult years and should therefore be recognized by society, and, more specifically (b) women often are deserving of this status regardless of whether or not they have compiled productive records in the mainstream work force.

It is becoming increasingly more difficult to establish a clear point of separation from previous adult status. Many people now enjoy multiple careers. Instead of staying at the same position in the same line of work until retirement, an increasing number of people move in and out of various career lines, so that separation from a previous activity has lost some of its usefulness as a termination marker. This trend may be expected to continue and expand. Furthermore, the stereotyped lines of demarcation between adult children and their parents will also continue to weaken. In fact, "act your age!" is an injunction that has already become much less powerful in recent years. This phenomenon is usually noted with respect to "under age" youth that take sexual activity as their right and otherwise intrude upon realms of activity previously reserved for adults. However, the reverse is also evident: an increasing number of middle-aged and elderly adults see no reason to adopt an "oldster" lifestyle and give up their previous pleasures and pursuits. In both the social and work spheres there will be increasing flexibility and ambiguity regarding just when an adult has become an elder. To the extent that this boundary is blurred, no ritualization will be needed. On a more subtle level we may see new rituals develop that affirm the *continuity* of role and value through the later adult years. For example, the consumer role may so unite generations that the age difference counts for little. "Mom and I are world-class shoppers!" a fiftyish woman announces, and so they well might be.

Rituals of incorporation will probably undergo significant change and development. These rituals will be contingent upon the ways in which elders define themselves and are defined by society in the years ahead. The health and vigor of long-lived people has already contributed to the decline of the worn-out-and-useless stereotype. We will look at another facet of this change when we touch on social and parasocial integration.

More or Less Ritualization for Death?

Throughout much of the 20th century there was a spirited reaction against elaborate, expensive, and by-the-book funerals. Memorial societies proliferated as an alternative. This movement was in part a specific counterattack against what was seen as the exorbitant cost of funerals conducted through commercial establishments. It was also, however, part of a larger movement toward efficiency and objectivity and away from the burden of sentimentality as well as the centrality of death. Yes, people died and that was sad, but, no, this passing did not require us to invest so much time, money and energy that could be put to better use. Around mid-century, the consumerism movement started to encompass "last things," providing further support for the deritualization of death.

As we move further into the 21st century both of these well established attitudes will continue to guide practice. Some people will endorse traditional funeral and memorial practices because nothing else seems quite right. Others will decide that a simple and functional disposition of the corpse has its own dignity and does not add to the survivor's grief. I do think, however, that the traditional approach will not regain its former compass, and that the "simple funeral" approach is already losing some ground as more people feel more need for some kind of meaningful ritualistic process. We see many advance signs in the number of families who expect funeral directors to vary their customs in order to have more resonance with the family and the deceased—and the slowly increasing number of funeral directors who are willing to oblige. An example: the funeral director in a small Midwestern city had everything under control until one of the adult children of the deceased protested that "Father would not be caught dead in a suit and tie. He always said he wanted to wear his red jump suit." The funeral director was appalled and resistant, but the daughter was able first to engage the support of the rest of the family and then to browbeat the funeral director into complying. A few days after the event, the funeral director appeared humbly at the family's door. "You were right. Thanks for teaching me a lesson. I won't forget it."

We can expect more activity on the part of the public when a particular death touches their feelings with depths of sorrow and or anger. Spontaneous memorialization now occurs frequently when lives are lost to senseless murder and violence (Haney, Leimer, & Lowery, 1997), as in the Oklahoma City bombing but also in many smaller-scaled tragedies. The AIDS quilt is another striking example of the public's increasing readiness to participate in death-related rituals. The professional funeral director will continue to have an important role in death rituals, but we can expect more participation and an expanding variety of responses from the public. We will also see a wider use of rituals within the health care field to acknowledge deaths that have long been shunted away. Some families who have suffered neonatal deaths have already benefited from "memory kits" and the more communicative and supportive approach that nurses have innovated in receptive hospital settings. It is probable that this simple but valuable ritualization will become increasingly available (unless blocked by hospital control and expense concerns). We should look now for more development of effective rituals upon the death of nursing home residents. Here there are still educational and attitudinal challenges to overcome. A few medical schools have devised rituals to honor and respect the people who they will meet as cadavers. This innovation has met with resistance from some senior faculty and administrators who have spent their careers in careful avoidance of death-related emotions, but has been welcomed by the medical students and is likely to become a more common practice in the years ahead.

On the Future of Death Anxiety

History strongly suggests that death anxiety has always been with us, and common sense suggests this will continue to be so. Empirical research on death anxiety is copious but not entirely illuminating. Among the limitations is the fact that almost all studies sample a self-report of death anxiety at one or at the most two closely related points in a person's life. We still know little about the origins and vicissitudes of death anxiety within the life course of an individual, and even less about the whole configuration of death-related feelings within a culture at a particular time and its possible changes over time (Kastenbaum, 2000). Nevertheless, one might look for variations in our culture's death anxiety in several regards.

1. *Less unlived life to arouse frustration and despair.* More people reach "four score and ten" and beyond than ever before. This trend toward a longer life is expected to continue for some time. As already noted, there are now also more people in reasonable health from their middle years forward. The component of death anxiety that arises from a sense of incompletion or deprivation should become less salient as time goes by. By contrast, more people are around to cope with the challenge of finding themes, agendas, and relationships that will carry them through the "bonus" years. Less death anxiety, then, but more suicidality among those who have difficulty in dealing with their later years in a meaningful and satisfying way.
2. *More anxiety about becoming a victim of violence.* Statistics sometimes do and sometimes do not bear out the fear of sudden death by murder or accident.

(For example, the general accidental fatality rate has actually declined in recent decades.) Nevertheless, there is enough reality and perhaps more than enough media presentation of violence to increase anxiety among those who have already become sensitized through insecurity, fantasy, or personal experience.

3. *Less anxiety about damnation and eternal punishment.* We would not want to underestimate the hardiness of this belief system. It will certainly accompany us for some time to come. The most broadly-based developments in religious attachments, however, are of a far more comforting and congenial nature. "New Age" (a term rejected by many to whom it is applied) philosophy softens the distinction between life and death or, rather, between one life and the next. Blending selected facets of Buddhist and Christian thought, New Agers report they have nothing to fear from a judgmental and avenging God, and little if anything to fear from death itself.

4. *More anxiety about being caught in a state suspended between life and death.* The precursors of this fear go back to the "buried alive" anxieties prevalent throughout the 19th and early 20th century. The current fears—and revulsions—center on being kept in a persistent vegetative state or helplessly suffering and awaiting a death that is all too slow to arrive. This set of fears has already been consequential in their sparking of "right to die" education, court decisions, and legislation, as well as their invocation of the physician-assisted death controversy. There are also less obvious manifestations of the dread often felt when we contemplate somehow being alive and dead at the same time. For example, the cryonic suspension movement has met with more apathy and resistance than one might have expected in a society that thrives on technological innovations and constantly seeks ways to elude death. From what I have been able to determine, most people are repelled by the basic idea even if it should happen to prove feasible (as has not yet happened). The dark corners of the imagination explored by Edgar Allan Poe may generate even more death-related anxiety in the future as technology continues to outstrip social philosophy and control.

Social or Parasocial Integration?

Gerontologists have an abiding concern about the social integration of the aged. The hospice movement is responding to concern about the social integration of the dying. Thanatologists perhaps should be as concerned about the social integration of the dead, who have been losing their place in urban cultures for some time now (Kastenbaum, 2000). A more educated public is likely to recognize that aging and dying are not the same, but that people in either or both categories should remain socially integrated. The future fate of the dead will not be explored here, other than noting that videotape and internet are already giving the dead new opportunities to be among the living (or, more accurately, perhaps, the living now have new opportunities to call upon the dead on demand).

We will focus instead on the following possibilities.

1. *Parasocial integration is an attractive but unreliable substitute.* The term *parasocial* is occasionally used in communication studies to refer to relationships that exist more in fantasy than reality. Most commonly it is applied to the belief that celebrity that is adoringly seen on television is also looking at them (i.e., that by viewing and thinking about a famous person that person becomes a real part of our own life). The term can also be extended to the fan that wears "team gear" and lives through the exploits of a favorite player or team. I use the term even more broadly: parasocial integration is a symbolic alternative to actual participation in core social relationships, obligations, and responsibilities. It has become increasingly easy for people to imagine themselves linked to society through spectatorship, emblems, and uncritical imagination. The present generation of elders has known enough human reality to temper this inclination. One can admire and cheer, if one so chooses, but real life is still with real people and real relationships in real places. Succeeding generations of elders, however, will have had a more thoroughgoing parasocialization. People who have come to rely more on computers and internetworking may be members in good standing of a virtual community, but there is little sustenance here when faced with life or death issues. The increasing popularity of a parasocial form of integration may well give rise to increasing panic, helplessness, and suicidality that is not moderated by direct and devoted human contact.

2. *It's nice to have company.* Elders are becoming less marginal because there are so many of them (of us, actually). What was said earlier about the implications of a small peer group must now be reversed. The later adult years look a lot different in the eyes of people who are actually there. Fears and stereotypes will continue to weaken as they are replaced by the knowledge acquired by men and women who are experiencing "old age" in their diverse ways. The social and political potential of elderly people will not be fully realized just because of these differences in background, personalities, and situation. Nevertheless, elders will continue to command increasing respect as a fairly large set of people who can muster a good deal of power when required by the occasion. And perhaps—just perhaps—the prejudices that many elders hold against their own age group will also diminish in the years ahead as stereotypes of uselessness and helplessness continue to fade.

3. *Authentic social integration of the aged, the dying, and the grieving is not guaranteed, but there is reason for optimism.* The cult of youth has drawn much of its fervor from the fears of middle-aged people. I took Oscar Wilde's quote, "Is youth the only thing worth having?" for the subtitle of one my books (Kastenbaum, 1995) because it so clearly expresses the concern that all of life's treasures are stacked in one station along life's journey. People who are healthy and zestful in their middle years and who keep mentally and socially alive in their later adult years have much less occasion to worship or envy youth. Furthermore, the dying person at any age is less threatening, less marginalized when understood within a broad life-course perspective and given the benefit of expert palliative care and loving family support. What new stresses and horrors the new millennium

will bring is (perhaps fortunately) beyond our ken. However, there is now some real hope for integrating people within the human community throughout the total life's journey.

Symbolic Passage into the Millennium

Here is but a brief note on the millennium and its implications for attitudes toward aging and death. The passage from youth to age remains troubling for many people, the passage from health to terminal illness, likewise. The most readily available rituals for this whole sequence is the funeral/memorial process, and this does not do much good for the individual most chiefly involved. Anxieties tend to feast on uncertainty. Age and death anxieties are certainly salient here. Crossing the border not only to a new century but a new millennium provides still another opportunity to project one's fears and doubts ahead. As a society, for some time now we seem more inclined to project our private terrors rather than confident hopes when a new projection screen becomes available. Engross yourself in any dozen randomly selected science fiction movies and you will see mostly dangerous aliens who are dedicated to destroying our planet, and perhaps crawling inside our skins and drinking our blood while they are at it. (*E. T.* is a delightful exception: the bambino from outer space who represents our own innnocent inner child.) The most influential futuristic novels of the 20th century have imagined inhumanity on a grand scale (e.g., *1984*, *Brave New World*).

The millennium already comes with a pre-history of punitive violence. The internet swarms with messages about the price we sinners will pay. No matter that predictions of universal catastrophe made a thousand years ago mostly failed. Obviously, these horrific visions were really intended for us. There is a power to be wielded in crying, "The end of the world is at hand!" and those so disposed will no doubt continue to do so for a while. Fortunately, when humankind crosses the symbolic it is likely to find—well, let Ms. A. B. tell you what she told me many years ago. She was just about our best source of gossip within this large geriatric facility, a keen observer who seemed to be everywhere at once. I was surprised to receive a request to see her because she had become depressed. It was hard to imagine this bustling, spirited person having time for depression. But she was a little down. Why? Ms. A. B. took me by the arm and led me to the central "plaza" of the facility. "Look at him," she whispered. "I never want to be like him. He's ninety, you know!" She then revealed that she would be turning ninety herself next week and considered that to be a fate worse than death. I got to talking with her about how she felt when she reached eighty. She admitted that had not turned out so bad. So, I suggested, why don't we just wait a week and see what happens?" A day after her birthday party, I came by again. "So?" "Yes, it's all right, ninety. But look at Mr. Z! He's almost a hundred!" She smiled despite herself. "OK, I'll wait for that, too!"

There may be a few bumps as we cross into a new millennium, but far more interesting will be our continuing reconstructions of aging and death as we cope with both the predictabilities and astonishments of life.

Points to Remember

1. Aging, as transition to death, can be interpreted using concepts of border crossing, ritualistic passage, and liminality.
2. In the past, a scarcity of older people and "young aging" encouraged, with some notable exceptions, rather negative attitudes toward the aging and the aged. The rituals and markers accompanying the transition to old age were few and weak.
3. Death interpretations in the 20th century in the U.S. included several views of death: death as punishment, death as deliverance from misery, death as the beginning of a new life, death as the junkyard for the obsolete.
4. The 21st century may be expected to moderate the ritualized avoidance of the dying and the death.
5. New transition rituals that will help easing the transitions to older age will be accompanied by an increased fuzziness of the stereotyped lines of demarcation between generations.
6. Traditional ritual practices will coexist with the "objective" approach that deritualizes death
7. Death anxiety will be confined more to limbo situations, such as persistent vegetative states and being a victim of an accident or crime. People who live a long, fulfilling life will fear less death or damnation.
8. The aged and the dying are likely to become less marginal and to be better integrated in the society.

☐ References

Becker, E. (1973). *The denial of death.* New York: The Free Press.
Feifel, H. (Ed.). (1959). *The meaning of death.* New York: McGraw-Hill.
Foucault, M. (1984). *Language, counter-memory, practice.* Ithaca, NY: Cornell University Press.
Friedman, A. W. (1997). Modernist attitudes toward death. In S. Strack (Ed.), *Death and the quest for meaning* (pp. 109–134). New York: Jason Aronson.
Glaser, B. G., & Strauss, A. (1968). *Time for dying.* Chicago: Aldine.
Gould, S. J. (1997). *Questioning the millennium.* New York: Harmony Books.
Grimes. R. L. (1995). *Beginnings in ritual studies* (Rev. ed.). Columbia, SC: University of South Carolina Press.
Haney, C. A., Leimer, C., & Lowery, J. (1997). Spontaneous memorialization: Violent death and emerging mourning ritual. *Omega, 35,* 159–172.
Kastenbaum, R. (1994). Sages, saints, and sons of bitches. *Journal of Geriatric Psychiatry, 23,* 61–78.
Kastenbaum, R. (1995). *Dorian, Graying: Is youth the only thing worth having?* New York: Baywood.
Kastenbaum, R. (2000). *The psychology of death* (3rd ed.). New York: Springer.

Lorand, A. (1912). *Old age deferred.* Philadelphia: F A. Davis Co.

Rosenberg, C. E. (1987). *The care of strangers.* Baltimore: The Johns Hopkins University Press.

Sheets-Johnstone, M. (1990). *The roots of thinking.* Philadelphia: Temple University Press.

Taylor, J. (1615/1977). *Holy dying.* New York: Arno Press.

Turner, V. W. (1974). *Symbolic action in human society.* Ithaca, NY: Cornell University Press.

Van Gennep, A. V. (1909/1960). *The rites of passage.* (M. B. Vizedom & G. L. Caffee, Trans.). London: Routledge and Kegan Paul.

CHAPTER

Adrian Tomer

Death Attitudes and the Older Adult: Closing Thoughts and Open Questions

To practice death is to practice freedom. A man who has learned how to die has unlearned how to be a slave. Knowing how to die gives us freedom from subjection and constraint. Life has no evil for him who has thoroughly understood that loss of life is not an evil.

If any of us were plunged into old age all of a sudden I do not think that the change would be bearable. But, almost imperceptibly, Nature leads us by the hand down a gentle slope.

(both quotes, Montaigne, 1592/1993, The Complete Essays, p. 96)

The beginning of this project, as indicated in the introduction, was spurred by dissatisfaction with the lack of integration of death, and death-related concepts, into the mainstream life-span theorization. It seemed to me that this lack of integration amounted to a desire to maintain an idealistic concept of aging in which the end of life played no part. Two years later it seems that some progress has been made in filling this void. We see a relative abundance of articles, books, and conventions dealing with issues of meaning, spirituality, and old age. We see serious attempts at formulating new models and applying existent models to the understanding of old age as that age that faces death directly. Some of this effort is incorporated in the present volume. We are in a position to tentatively draw conclusions, pointing in those directions that require additional effort and work.

☐ Age Trends in Death Attitudes

The fact that older adults fear death less than younger people do was again documented in this volume. Thus, Thorson and Powell (Chapter 8) found age differences to be present not only at the macro level of the aggregative score for the Revised Death Anxiety Scale but, indeed, at the micro level of the items themselves. On only one out of the 25 items did the older adults in the study reported here score at a higher level than the young adults. This constitutes very convincing evidence, particularly if we remember that measurement at the level of items always contains a lot of "noise" that may mask the main effect when this effect is not large enough. Similar age differences are reported by Tomer and Eliason in Chapter 7. This type of finding should be combined with the conclusion reached by Fortner, Neimeyer, and Rybarczyk (see Chapter 6). Based on a comprehensive meta-analytical review of the existent literature they found no significant correlation with age in the older population. It is possible that there is a trend of decrease in death anxiety with increased age that levels off at some point. Alternatively, some cohort effects may be at work or perhaps, more intricately, we have a combination of both cohort and age effects. Longitudinal studies are needed to reach firm conclusions on this issue. Other results of the meta-analytical review are germane to the issue of a relationship between aging and death anxiety, for example the existence of a positive correlation between levels of death anxiety and physical problems and between death anxiety and institutionalization. With increased age, individuals are more at risk for developing chronic physical problems and are more at risk to be institutionalized. More studies of old-old adults and of institutionalized persons are needed, as indicated by the authors.

In addition to investigations dealing with levels or means, one would like to see more studies focusing on structures of death anxiety and/or death attitudes dimensions. Tomer and Eliason's Chapter 7 suggests the possibility that older people, perhaps as a result of rumination on the topic of death and dying, have a more complex structure of death anxiety. Should this result be replicated in further studies, the next question would be whether or not this increased complexity is a result of a developmental trend, a cohort effect or a combination of both. The question of complexity can be also extended from the domain of death anxiety to the domain of death attitude, in general.

☐ The Importance of Death Attitudes in Relation to Death Anxiety in Old Age

Wong, Reker, and Gesser (1994) have made important progress by articulating a model of death attitudes that involves different types of acceptance: avoidance, neutral acceptance and approach acceptance. In this volume (Chapter 2) Paul Wong emphasizes the importance of the latter two (and, particularly of death acceptance) as an optimal way to live and die. While Wong includes fear of death as an "attitude," Tomer and Eliason take a somewhat different approach when they construe death anxiety as a possible consequence of death attitudes. From the perspective of Chapter 9, death anxiety is mitigated by death acceptance. Interestingly, in the particular sample studied, it was neutral acceptance of death, rather than approach acceptance that was found to be related to decreases in death anxiety. Clearly this finding needs to be replicated, generalized in two other populations, and based on larger samples. The use of non-verbal indicators of death anxiety in future studies may serve to decrease the common variance that measures of death attitude and death anxiety have in common, as a result of being based on similar ways of measurement.

☐ Death Attitudes and Society's Values

While Wong addresses the topic of death attitudes at the level of the individual, several chapters consider the issue from a societal point of view. Thus, Thorson and Powell suggest that virtually everybody, including the older individual, internalizes the society's values that confer greater worth on a younger person's life who has "the whole life in front of him/her". From this perspective, lower levels of death anxiety represents less grief over a "lesser loss". Nancy Osgood in her treatment here of the elderly suicide (Chapter 10) takes a somewhat similar approach which is projected this time on the issues of assisted suicide and end-of-life decisions. The recent propensity to bestow on our elderly the right to be "assisted" in committing suicide, or the right to "renounce" life-prolonging technology, reflects, from the perspective of Chapter 11 the devaluation of old age and the low regard in which we hold our senior citizens.

☐ Death Attitudes and End-of-life Decisions

Nancy Osgood's chapter on elderly suicide in an ageist society (our own!) places also the issue of end-of-life decisions in the context of attitudes toward death and toward old age. Several other chapters in the book deal with the "hot" topic of end-of-life decisions from the perspective of the older adult (Chapter 11) and from the perspective of the professional—the nurse in this case (Chapters 12 and 13). Cicirelli's Chapter 11 shows how end-of-life decisions and preferences may be differentially connected to different dimensions of fear. One would hope that this type of work will generate the construction and the putting to test of causal models of end-of-life decisions and preferences. There is no doubt that such models need to incorporate ethnicity as one of the exogenous variables that may affect decisions and preferences, if not fear of death itself.

Chapter 12 on nurses' attitudes toward end-of-life issues in terminally ill persons provides interesting findings from the Israeli arena. Israeli nurses, similar to their Western counterparts, tend to have different attitudes and preferences vis-à-vis older adults and younger adults, for example to incline to prolong life of middle-aged patients (age 40) more than they incline to do so for an older patient (age 80). Consistent with this, the death of an old woman is likely to arouse less anxiety, frustration, and pain and more relief than the death of a young woman "their age". This result is consistent with the points made by Osgood and by Thorson and Powell regarding the relative "cheapness" of an older person's life and, indeed, are interpreted by the authors, Carmel and Ziedenberg, as deriving from the Western cultural emphasis on youth. The authors do not address directly in this chapter the problem of a connection between attitudes toward death and dying and attitudes about aging and old age. This issue is addressed by Steve DePaola in his treatment of death anxiety and attitudes toward older persons in nursing personnel. DePaola shows that personal anxiety toward one's own aging were predictive of death anxiety. His results make plausible a causal model in which negative views about older adults lead to anxiety toward one's own aging and to more fear of death. Such a model would be also consistent with the Comprehensive Model of Death Anxiety (Chapters 1 and 9) according to which causality flows primarily from attitudes to death anxiety. It is also possible that the causal direction is from death anxiety to anxiety about aging, and to negative attitudes about aging in general. Again, additional studies, preferably longitudinal, can be designed to test the direction of the causal relationship. Another issue, still in need of investigation, is how fear of death may affect end-of-life decisions. Cicirelli's findings suggest that the relationships between dimensions of death anxiety and end-of-life decisions are complex. For example, extrapolating Cicirelli's results obtained in a sample of older individuals to nursing personnel, we should expect more fear of being destroyed but less fear of the dying process to translate into more propensity to strive to maintain life. Obviously we need additional studies to answer this question.

Both chapters about the nursing personnel demonstrate again the importance of death education for nursing personnel, particularly for that personnel involved in end-of-life decisions. To quote from the Carmel–Ziedenberg chapter, this kind of education as well as the provision of emotional support "are essential for the benefit of both the nurses and their patients."

☐ Defending Against Death: Self-esteem and Beyond

According to the Terror Management theory (TMT), a main defense against death is identification with cultural values that increases self-esteem. Self-esteem acts as a buffer in this interpretation. This type of defense, as explained convincingly by McCoy, Pyszczynski, Solomon, and Greenberg in Chapter 3, is likely to become less efficient in older life. Two main roads seem to be open to the older adult that finds himself or herself closer to the end of life. One road is to try to attain self-esteem in ways that are less dependent on society's approval and validation. A more radical way of coping would be to need less defense by transcending the self. It seems to me that both ways are suggested as viable options by the TMT proponents. Older adults may be less in need of social validation for their self-esteem. On the other hand they express their self transcendence by becoming more involved with others and less concerned with themselves. While independence of social norms and generativity can be seen as fundamentally different strategies, they can be also perceived as step stones toward achieving a self-less self. Indeed this is what is being proposed in Chapter 3. There is no question, as the authors of this chapter will be probably the first to agree, that this proposal is both very interesting and largely speculative and, as such, in need of further empirical validation and perhaps of further theoretical development.

☐ Defending Against Death: Renouncing Meaning

If death is a threat to meaning, a logical way for the threatened individual would be to "renounce meaning" in order to defend oneself. Moreover, if this threat becomes more prominent in older age, we should see more of the tendency to renounce meaning and to see more withdrawal from basic life projects. Indeed this is Robert Firestone's major thesis in Chapter 4. This raises the question: Is there more microsuicidal behavior with increased age? We do have an increase in suicide ratio, particularly in white males, a finding that suggests an affirmative answer to this question. It is interesting to contrast Firestone's perspective in Chapter 4 with Wong's perspective in Chapter 2. In one case renouncing meaning serves as a defense mechanism in the face of the threat of death. In the second "realizing meaning" (perhaps a short definition for the meaning of "spirituality"), while not being a defense mechanism proper, is conducive to less death anxiety. Is there a real contradiction between these two approaches? I don't think so. It is certainly possible that different individuals will use different approaches or even that the same individual, at different points in time will use a meaning renouncing and a meaning enhancing approach. One would hope for the development of a model that will explain under what circumstances we should expect the one deployment of one strategy or the other

☐ The Meaning of Life and Death in Relation to Successful Aging

Rather than renouncing meaning to defend against death one can use death to infuse meaning in his or her life. As indicated in the introduction to this book and presented clearly by Wong in Chapter 2, life and death are interconnected in the sense that the meaning of one cannot be engaged without engaging the meaning of the other. It was remarked many times that death can enhance the perception of meaningfulness by making life more precious, precisely because of its limitation in time. The individual aware of his or her mortality will be driven by this perception to live more fully and/or to appreciate better life, to become more of a "spiritual being". Accordingly, Wong proposes a fundamental change in our approach to successful aging. The emphasis should be less on physical health, for example, (a goal that many cannot even approach) and more on spirituality. In Wong's own words successful aging is "80% attitude and 20% everything else". The literature surveyed by Wong elsewhere (Wong, 1998) suggests that, with increased age, there is an increase in religiosity as well as positive correlations between religiosity, personal meaning, and successful aging and/or life-satisfaction. Taking this together with the approach presented by McCoy and the other TMT proponents in Chapter 3, and together with our own proposals and findings (Tomer & Eliason, Chapters 1 and 9) it strongly suggests a developmental sequence. With increased age the adult individual becomes more and more aware of the limits of his or her existence, in terms of time and, eventually, in terms of what one can realistically hope to "achieve" in life (cf. Carstensen, Isaacowitz, & Charles, 1999).

The individual becomes also more aware of the futility of external ingredients of social recognition or, at least, becomes less dependent on those ingredients (position, status, etc.) for his or her self-esteem. In terms of chapter 3 the individual is relatively "independent from social validation". The result of this new awareness and independence is an increase in the intensity of the "will to meaning" (Frankl, 1963) and an increase in the search for "personal meaning" (Wong, 1998). The results of this intensified search can be (although do not **have** to be) a deeper spirituality and a renewed and strengthened sense of meaning and life satisfaction. Some empirical findings that we already mentioned are consistent with such a sequence. Other findings, for example Levinson's descriptions of the life cycle (Levinson, 1978, 1996) and its crises, also strongly suggest a continuous search for meaning throughout the adult life. While there are findings that makes such a sequence plausible, additional evidence based on longitudinal studies is needed to confirm that some individuals proceed on their way from adulthood to older age along the path described by this developmental sequence.

☐ Spirituality and Counseling

It is precisely because "success" in the realization of a sense of purpose and meaning in life is not guaranteed, that counseling of the older adult is important. Eliason (Chapter 15) proposes to use the Comprehensive Model of Death Anxiety (Chapter 1) for this purpose. In terms of this model, and as pointed by Eliason, the therapeutic relationship with the elderly person should focus on the two types of regret—past-related and future-related, and on issues of meaningfulness/meaninglessness. The technique of "reframing, as indicated by the author," may be very helpful in dealing with possible types of regret. At the same time there is no question that, given the shortness of life that lies ahead and the length of life that lies behind, the use of therapeutic techniques will always be difficult. No counseling can transform a meaningless existence into a meaningful existence. It would be difficult to expect even the transformation of an existence **perceived** to be meaningless into one perceived to be meaningful. It seems indeed appropriate, from a philosophical and methodological viewpoint as well as from a practical one, to consider meaningfulness a matter of degree. It would be also appropriate to try to infuse some modesty into our theoretical and practical discussions. While meaning is an important goal, one should also concede that we, human beings, can perhaps have access to only "partial meaningfulness". In other words, we should accept as a fact the existence of limits to our understanding and to our ability to see connections. A recognition of limits seems to be one of the main lessons of death and should be incorporated in a definition of "successful aging."

☐ Death attitudes in the 21st century

What would death and dying be 50 or 60 years from today? In the introduction to this book I raised the possibility that a period of decline in the second half of life, although not popular with anybody, may serve a positive function of introducing us gently to our own death. If gentle decline may serve from this point of view a positive role, more dramatic decline may increase our death anxiety. It seems indeed that the findings presented by Fortner, Neimeyer, and Rybarczyk relating physical problems to increased levels of death anxiety would be consistent with a view that expects significant decline in functioning to translate into an increased fear of death. So formulated the question is how medical and technological advances are going to impact the balance between no decline, gentle decline, abrupt decline and death and life with severe disability. There is no doubt, as indicated by Kastenbaum in his chapter on death attitudes and aging in the 21st century, that "being caught suspended between life and death" and the associated anxiety will become only more prevalent in the future. If Robert Kastenbaum is right and we'll see a letup of the cult of youth and an integration of the old and the dying, this may have a beneficial effect on the rationality of the present discussion regarding end-of-life decisions. In particular, such an integration may mitigate the fears (expressed by Nancy Osgood in her chapter) that assisting people to end their life, or otherwise not trying hard enough to maintain life, reflects biases of an ageist society and it leads to a "slippery slope" (for a discussion of the slippery slope argument see Prado, 1998). Such an integration should also be translated into a more flexible hospice system along the lines delineated by Stephen Connor in Chapter 14—in particular in the direction of a system that can accommodate a mixture of palliative and prolongative treatments for an increased number of terminally ill patients.

The influence of the changing technology and of the pace of change on the perception of time of the individual should also be considered. In a fast changing world individuals will perceive their lives as shorter (although perhaps also as richer). The perception that we are missing out on things will be possibly strengthened in such a world. In terms of the Comprehensive Model of Death Anxiety presented in Chapter 1, future-related regret may be intensified and with it death anxiety can be increased.

Thus, as described by Kastenbaum, there are reasons for optimism but also reasons for some concern regarding the development of death attitudes in the future. The future of death attitudes in relation to old age is inextricably connected to the future of what Wong calls "successful aging"—the realization of meaning throughout the lifespan and, in particular, in old age.

☐ References

Carstensen, L. I., Isaacowitz, D. M., & Charles, S. T. (1999). Taking time seriously—A theory of socioemotional selectivity, *American Psychologist, 54*(3), 165–181.
Frankl, V. E. (1962). *Man's search for meaning*. Boston: Beacon Press.
Levinson, D. J. (1978). *The seasons of a man's life*. New York: Knopf.
Levinson, D. J. (1996). *Seasons of a woman's life*. New York: Knopf.
Montaigne, M. (1993). *The complete essays* (M. A. Screech, Trans). London: Penguin Books. (Original work published 1592)

Prado, C. G. (1998). *The last choice: Preemptive suicide in advanced age* (2nd ed.). Westport, CT: Praeger.

Wong, P. T. P. (1998). Spirituality, meaning and successful aging. In P. T. P. Wong & P. S. Fry (Eds.), *The human quest for meaning* (pp. 359–394). Mahwah, NJ: Lawrence Erlbaum Assoc.

Wong, P. T. P, Reker, G. T., & Gesser, G. (1994). Death Attitudes Profile-Revised: A multidimensional measure of attitudes toward death. In R. A. Neimeyer (Ed.), *Death anxiety handbook: Research, instrumentation, and application* (pp. 121–148). Washington, DC: Taylor & Francis.

INDEX

Index note: page references in italics indicate a figure or table.

in ethnicity and fear of death study, 181–182, *182,* 183–184

in study of Revised Death Anxiety Scale (RDAS) structure, 112–121

generativity, 14–15, 92

gerotranscendence, 15, 91

Gesser, G., 3, 9, 10, 29, 100, 109, 248, 251

Global Belief in a Just World Scale, 140–143, *143,* 144–152

Goodman, L. M., 28–31

Greenberg, J., 11, 14, 37–58

H

Harmon-Jones, E., 41, 42

health status, impact on levels of death anxiety, 3–4

Heckhauser, J., 45–46, 49, 50

Heidegger, M., 28, 88–89

Hoelter, J. W., 215, 216

Hoge, D. R., 129

hospice care and the older person, 227–238, 287

I

institutionalization as death anxiety predictor, 97, 98–99, *99,* 101–102

integration and levels of death anxiety, 4

International Network on Personal Meaning, 32

Intrinsic Religious Motivation scale, 129–134

inward lifestyle in microsuicidal behavior, 71, 73

Israel, nurses' attitudes and patient age study, 193–207, 283

Israeli Medical Association and care of dying patients, 195

J

Jöreskorg, K. G., 17, 111, 115–116, *118,* 143–144

K

Kastenbaum, R., 96–97, 103, 124, 159, 176, 206, 257–279

L

Labouvie-Vief, G., 53, 57

Last Choice, The (Prado), 167–169

Leming Fear of Death Scale, 176

life planning, 5, *5,* 6, 13–14, 252

life review, 5, *5,* 6, 11–13, 105

in pastoral counseling, 250–252, 286

life sustaining treatment (LST), 201–204, *204,* 205–207

liminality, concept of, 258–260

LISREL, 17, 111

in study of a comprehensive Model of Death Anxiety, 143–144

Four Factors of the RDAS in Older Adults, 115, 116, *116,* 117

locus of control in ethnicity and fear of death study, 181–182, *182,* 183–184

Locus of Control Scale (Lumpkin's version), 140–142, *142,* 148–152

M

MacArthur Successful Aging Project, 23–24, 32, 33

marital status variable in ethnicity and fear of death study, 181–182, *182,* 183–184

Maximum Likelihood Method

in study of a comprehensive Model of Death Anxiety, 144

in study of Revised Death Anxiety Scale (RDAS) structure, 115, 117

McIntosh, J. L., 67, 70, 170

meaningfulness

in study of a comprehensive Model of Death Anxiety, 137–143, *143,* 147–152

of death, 5, *5,* 9–10

mental health

as death anxiety predictor, 97, 98–99, *99,* 102–103

and successful aging, 25–28

microsuicide and the elderly, 65–82, 285

fantasy bonds in, 74

inward lifestyle and physical health, 71, 73–74

negative thought patterns in, 70–71, *72,* 73

self/antiself system of, 69

societal influences of, 78–79

voice system in, 69–70

withholding and self-denial, 74–77

middle age, peaking of death anxiety, 3, 109

models

additive, 4

comprehensive, development of, 4–5, *5,* 6, 16–17, 294

mortality salience hypothesis in Terror Management Theory (TMT), 41–43

Multidimensional Fear of Death Scale (MFODS), 9

in ethnicity and fear of death study, 176, 179, *179,* 180, *180,* 181

factor structures of, 110, 111

in study of ethnicity and death anxiety, 215–223

Multidimensional Locus of Control, 181–182, *182,* 183–184